Adobe® InDesign® CS3

The Professional Portfolio

AGAINST THE CL CK

mastering graphic technology

Managing Editor: Ellenn Behoriam
Cover & Interior Design: Erika Kendra
Copy Editor: Laurel Nelson-Cucchiara
Proofreader: Angelina Kendra
Printing/Bindery: Prestige Printers

10   9   8   7   6   5   4   3   2

978-0-9764324-5-6 (spiral bound)

978-0-9815216-1-9 (perfect bound)

AGAINST THE CLOCK
mastering graphic technology

PO Box 260092, Tampa, Florida 33685
800-256-4ATC • www.againsttheclock.com

Acknowledgements

ABOUT AGAINST THE CLOCK

Against The Clock has been publishing graphic communications educational materials for more than 17 years, starting out as a Tampa, Florida-based systems integration firm whose primary focus was on skills development in high-volume, demanding commercial environments. Among the company's clients were LL Bean, The New England Journal of Medicine, the Smithsonian, and many others. Over the years, Against The Clock has developed a solid and widely-respected approach to teaching people how to effectively utilize graphics applications while maintaining a disciplined approach to real-world problems.

Against The Clock has been recognized as one of the nation's leaders in courseware development. Having developed the *Against The Clock* and the *Essentials for Design* series with Prentice Hall/Pearson Education, the firm works closely with all major software developers to ensure timely release of educational products aimed at new version releases.

ABOUT THE AUTHORS

Erika Kendra holds a BA in History and a BA in English Literature from the University of Pittsburgh. She began her career in the graphic communications industry as an editor at Graphic Arts Technical Foundation before moving to Los Angeles in 2000. Erika is the author or co-author of more than fifteen books about graphic design software, including QuarkXPress, Adobe Photoshop, Adobe InDesign, and Adobe PageMaker. She has also written several books about graphic design concepts such as color reproduction and preflighting, and dozens of articles for online and print journals in the graphics industry. Working with Against The Clock for more than seven years, Erika was a key partner in developing the new Portfolio Series of software training books.

Gary Poyssick, co-owner of Against The Clock, is a well-known and often controversial speaker, writer, and industry consultant who has been involved in professional graphics and communications for more than twenty years. He wrote the highly popular *Workflow Reengineering* (Adobe Press), *Teams and the Graphic Arts Service Provider* (Prentice Hall), *Creative Techniques: Adobe Illustrator*, and *Creative Techniques: Adobe Photoshop* (Hayden Books), and was the author or co-author of many application-specific training books from Against The Clock.

CONTRIBUTING AUTHORS, ARTISTS, AND EDITORS

A big thank you to the people whose comments and expertise contributed to the success of these books:

- **Sharon Neville**, Technical Communications Consultants
- **Debbie Davidson**, Sweet Dreams Designs
- **Carin L. Murphy**, Des Moines Area Community College
- **Craig Polanowski**, Fresno City College
- **Dean Bagley**, Against The Clock, Inc.

Thanks also to Laurel Nelson-Cucchiara, editor, and Angelina Kendra, proofreader, for their help in making sure that we all said what we meant to say.

PROJECT GOALS

Each project begins with a clear description of the overall concepts that are explained in the project; these goals closely match the different "stages" of the project workflow.

THE PROJECT MEETING

Each project includes the client's initial comments, which provide valuable information about the job. The Project Art Director, a vital part of any design workflow, also provides fundamental advice and production requirements.

PROJECT OBJECTIVES

Each Project Meeting includes a summary of the specific skills required to complete the project.

REAL-WORLD WORKFLOW

Projects are broken into logical lessons or "stages" of the workflow. Brief introductions at the beginning of each stage provide vital foundational material required to complete the task.

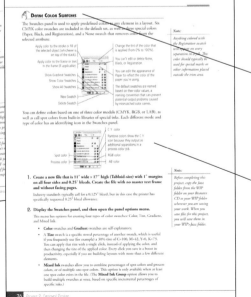

STEP-BY-STEP EXERCISES

Every stage of the workflow is broken into multiple hands-on, step-by-step exercises.

VISUAL EXPLANATIONS

Wherever possible, screen shots are annotated so students can quickly identify important information.

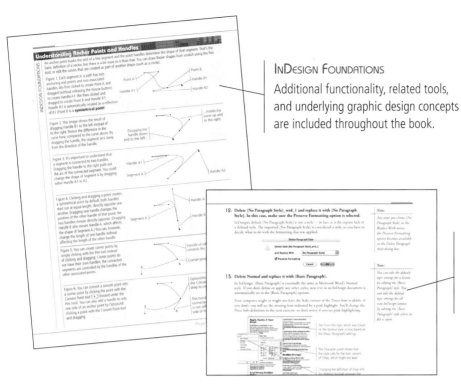

InDesign Foundations

Additional functionality, related tools, and underlying graphic design concepts are included throughout the book.

Advice and Warnings

Where appropriate, sidebars provide shortcuts, warnings, or tips about the topic at hand.

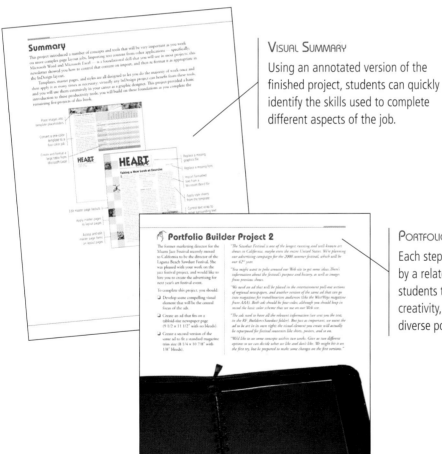

Visual Summary

Using an annotated version of the finished project, students can quickly identify the skills used to complete different aspects of the job.

Portfolio Builder Projects

Each step-by-step project is accompanied by a related freeform project, allowing students to practice their skills and exercise creativity, resulting in an extensive and diverse portfolio of work.

The Against The Clock *Portfolio Series* teaches graphic design software tools and techniques entirely within the framework of real-world projects; we introduce and explain skills where they would naturally fall into a real project workflow. For example, rather than an entire chapter about printing (which most students find boring), we teach printing where you naturally need to do so — when you complete a print-based project.

The project-based approach in the *Portfolio Series* allows you to get in depth with the software beginning in Project 1 — you don't have to read several chapters of introductory material before you can start creating finished artwork.

The project-based approach of the *Portfolio Series* also prevents "topic tedium" — in other words, we don't require you to read pages and pages of information about text (for example); instead, we explain text tools and options as part of larger projects (in this case, beginning with placing text on corporate identity pieces).

Clear, easy-to-read, step-by-step instructions walk you through every phase of each job, from creating a new file to saving the finished piece. Wherever logical, we also offer practical advice and tips about underlying concepts and graphic design practices that will benefit students as they enter the job market.

The projects in this book reflect a range of different types of InDesign jobs, from creating a corporate identity package to implementing a newsletter template to compiling a multi-chapter book. When you finish the eight projects in this book (and the accompanying Portfolio Builder exercises), you will have a substantial body of work that should impress any potential employer.

The eight InDesign CS3 projects are described briefly here; more detail is provided in the full table of contents (beginning on Page viii).

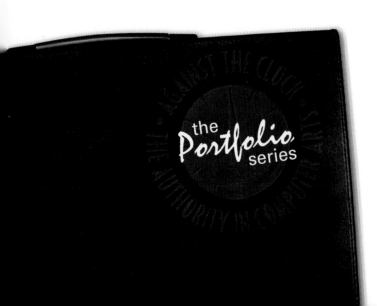

Project 1

Identity Package

- ❑ Setting up the Workspace
- ❑ Drawing in InDesign
- ❑ Formatting Basic Text
- ❑ Creating a Cohesive Layout
- ❑ Printing InDesign Files

Project 2

Festival Poster

- ❑ Building Graphic Interest
- ❑ Importing and Formatting Text
- ❑ Using Graphics as Text and Text as Graphics
- ❑ Outputting the File

Project 3

HeartSmart Newsletter

- ❑ Working with Templates
- ❑ Working with Style Sheets
- ❑ Working with Tables
- ❑ Preflighting and Packaging the Job

Project 4 — Letterfold Catering Menu

- Building a Folding Template
- Working with Imported Text
- Advanced Frame Options

Project 5 — Realty Collateral Booklet

- Working with Master Pages
- Controlling Text Flow
- Understanding Multi-Page Output

Project 6 — Versioned Product Brochure

- Controlling Color for Output
- Placing and Controlling Images
- Controlling and Checking Text
- Creating Multiple Layers

Project 7 — National Parks Info Pieces

- Experimenting with Layout Options
- Working with XML
- Working with Interactive Elements

Project 8 — Multi-Chapter Book Excerpts

- Combining Documents into Books
- Building a Table of Contents
- Building an Index
- Exporting Book Files
- Merging Data into an InDesign Layout

Some experts claim that most people use only a fraction — maybe 10% — of their software's capabilities; this is likely because many people don't know what is available. As you complete the projects in this book, our goal is to familiarize you with the entire tool set so you can be more productive and more marketable in your career as a graphic designer.

It is important to keep in mind that InDesign is an extremely versatile and powerful application. The sheer volume of available tools, panels, and features can seem intimidating when you first look at the software interface. Most of these tools, however, are fairly simple to use with a bit of background information and a little practice.

Wherever necessary, we explain the underlying concepts and terms that are required for understanding the software. We're confident that these projects provide the practice you need to create sophisticated artwork by the end of the very first project.

Contents

PREREQUISITES

The entire Portfolio Series is based on the assumption that you have a basic understanding of how to use your computer. You should know how to use your mouse to point and click, as well as to drag items around the screen. You should be able to resize and arrange windows on your desktop to maximize your available space. You should know how to access drop-down menus, and understand how check boxes and radio buttons work. It also doesn't hurt to have a good understanding of how your operating system organizes files and folders, and how to navigate your way around them. If you're familiar with these fundamental skills, then you know all that's necessary to use the Portfolio Series.

RESOURCE FILES

All of the files that you need to complete the projects in this book are on the provided Resource CD in the RF_InDesign folder. The main RF folder contains eight subfolders, one for each project in the book; you will be directed to the appropriate folder whenever you need to access a specific file. Files required to complete the related Portfolio Builder exercises are in the RF_Builders folder.

The Resource CD also includes a WIP folder, which also contains (mostly empty) subfolders for each project in the book. This is where you will save your work as you complete the various projects. In some cases, the location of a file will be extremely important for later steps in a project to work properly; that's why we've provided a specific set of folders with known file names.

Before you begin working on the projects in this book, you should copy the entire WIP folder to your hard drive or some other recordable media such as a flash drive; when we tell you to save a file, you should save it to the appropriate folder on the drive where you put that WIP folder.

ATC FONTS

You must install the ATC fonts from the Resource CD to ensure that your exercises and projects will work as described in the book; these fonts are provided on the Resource CD-ROM in the ATC Fonts folder. Specific instructions for installing fonts are provided in the documentation that came with your computer. You should replace older (pre-2004) ATC fonts with the ones on your Resource CD.

SYSTEM REQUIREMENTS

As software technology continues to mature, the differences in functionality from one platform to another continue to diminish. The Portfolio Series was designed to work on both Macintosh or Windows computers; where differences exist do from one platform to another, we include specific instructions relative to each platform.

One issue that remains different from Macintosh to Windows is the use of different modifier keys (Control, Shift, etc.) to accomplish the same task. When we present key commands, we always follow the same Macintosh/Windows format — Macintosh keys are listed first, then a slash, followed by the Windows key command.

System Requirements for Adobe InDesign CS3:

Windows®
- Intel® Pentium 4 or higher or equivalent
- Microsoft® Windows XP with Service Pack 2 or Windows Vista™ Home Premium, Business, Ultimate, or Enterprise
- 256MB of RAM (512MB recommended)
- 1.8 GB of available hard-disk space
- 1024×768 monitor resolution with 16-bit video card
- DVD-ROM drive
- QuickTime 7.1 required for multimedia features

Mac OS
- PowerPC® G4 or G5 or Intel-based Macintosh
- Mac OS X v.10.4.8
- 256MB of RAM (512MB recommended)
- 1.6 GB of available hard-disk space
- 1024×768 monitor resolution with 16-bit video card
- DVD-ROM drive
- QuickTime 7.1 required for multimedia features

When you first launch InDesign, you'll see the default user interface (or UI, as it's usually called) that Adobe defined as the basic toolset.

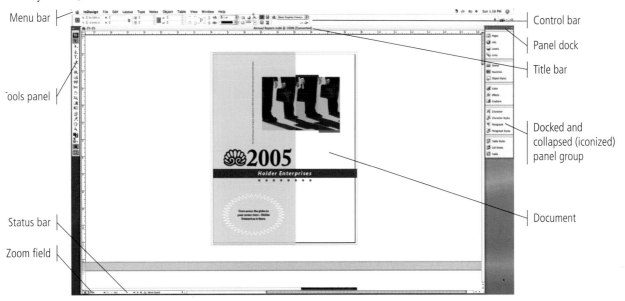

Menu bar · Tools panel · Status bar · Zoom field · Control bar · Panel dock · Title bar · Docked and collapsed (iconized) panel group · Document

MENUS

Similar to most other applications, InDesign has a menu bar across the top of the screen. If you've used a computer in the past, you're probably familiar with navigating menus. In InDesign, ten menus provide access to virtually all of the available options. (Macintosh users have two extra menus. The Apple menu provides access to system-specific commands. The InDesign menu follows the Macintosh system-standard format introduced in OS X for all applications; this menu controls basic application operations such as About, Hide, Preferences, and Quit InDesign.)

Some menu commands can be accessed using a keyboard shortcut. If a menu command has an associated shortcut, it's listed to the right of the specific command (such as the Zoom In and Show Frame Edges options in the image to the right).

Most of the commands in the View and Window menus are **toggles**, which means the same command is used to turn an option on and off. If a toggle command shows a checkmark, that option is active or visible; if there's no checkmark, that option is off or hidden.

> **Note:**
>
> *If a menu command isn't available for a specific image or selection, it appears grayed out.*

THE IMAGE WINDOW

Any file you open exists in its own document window. By default, the document window shows the page surrounded by a white **pasteboard** area (called Normal viewing mode); anything located entirely on the pasteboard is not included in the final output.

You can change the document window using the Screen Mode button at the bottom of the Tools panel. If you click and hold the button, you can choose a specific mode from the pop-up list.

In Normal mode, the page edge is marked by a solid black line; the page is surrounded by the pasteboard, and objects that extend past the page edge are entirely visible.

In Preview mode, the pasteboard is replaced by a gray area; anything that extends beyond the page edge (called a **bleed**) is truncated in the display.

In Bleed mode, the same gray area replaces the pasteboard; the page is surrounded by the user-defined bleed area (the safe distance that bleed objects need to extend).

In Slug mode, the page edge includes the bleed area, as well as the user-defined slug area. (A **slug** is information outside the page edge that is included in the output, such as file information or color bars.)

Note:

The same modes can be accessed in the View>Screen Mode submenu.

Note:

You'll learn more about bleeds and slugs as you complete the projects in this book.

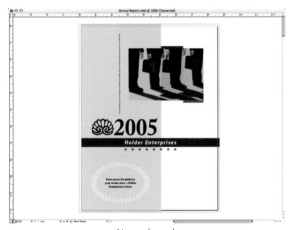

Normal mode

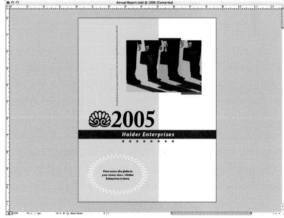

Preview mode

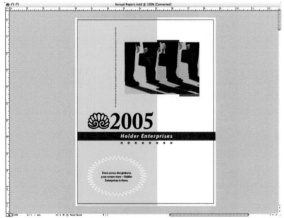

Bleed mode

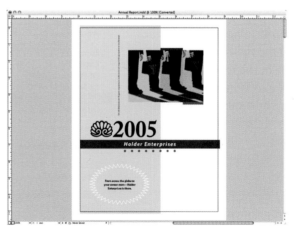

Slug mode

You can use the controls in the bottom-left corner of the document window to review the document structure for XML, change the view percentage, navigate through different pages and sections of the file, and monitor the file version status.

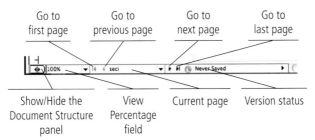
Go to first page
Go to previous page
Go to next page
Go to last page

Show/Hide the Document Structure panel
View Percentage field
Current page
Version status

Note:

File versions are important if you have the entire Creative Suite and are using Version Cue to manage a collaborative workflow.

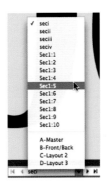

Clicking the arrow to the right of the View Percentage field opens a pop-up menu, where you can change the view to a specific magnification. You can also highlight the field manually and type any specific value between 5% and 4000%.

You can also navigate through pages using the buttons to the left and right of the Page field. Alternatively, you can open the Page pop-up menu and choose a specific page from the list.

Note:

You can also control the view percentage using options in the View menu.

The Control Bar

The Control bar (Window>Control) appears by default at the top of the screen, below the menu bar. The Control bar provides different options depending on what is selected in the layout.

When you select a frame, the Control panel displays options for resizing, repositioning, skewing, and rotating the frame, or applying an object style.

Note:

Roll the mouse cursor over a Control bar option to see the name of the option in a tool tip.

When you select text inside a frame, the Control panel displays either character or paragraph options. (Click the buttons on the left side of the Control panel to switch between the different sets of options.)

Key Command:

Option/Alt-click a Control bar option to open the related dialog box.

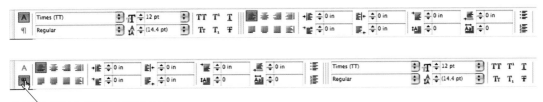

Use these buttons to toggle between the character and paragraph options.

If you have a large monitor, the Control bar displays additional options. For example, if a frame is selected, a 23″ monitor shows all the basic frame-related controls, as well as frame effects and transparency, text wrap, and object style options. For graphics frames, you'll also find content-fitting options; for text frames, you'll find column and vertical text alignment options.

Note:

You can change the options in the Control bar by opening the panel options menu and choosing Customize.

If text is selected, the extended Control bar shows all the character controls and all the paragraph controls at one time, as well as additional options related to text frames. (If you click the Paragraph button at the left side of the panel, you simply reverse the order of the visible options.)

Regardless of which tool is selected, three options always appear on the right side of the Control bar: Quick Apply, Go to Bridge, and Panel Options.

Quick Apply   Go to Bridge   Panel Options

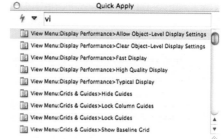

Clicking the Quick Apply button opens a special navigation dialog box. This feature lets you easily find and apply what you want — menu commands, user-defined styles, and so on — by typing a few characters in the text entry field, and then clicking the related item in the list.

The Go to Bridge button opens the separate Bridge application, which ships with and is installed with InDesign. The Panel Options button opens a pop-up menu where you can control the position of the panel (top, bottom, or floating) and customize the options that are available in the panel.

Using Adobe Bridge

INDESIGN FOUNDATIONS

Adobe Bridge, a stand-alone application that helps you browse and manage collections of files, is installed when you install InDesign.

Bridge includes a Favorites area where you can save quick links to specific locations on your system. The center displays thumbnail images of all files in the location you choose. File-specific information (such as a preview, metadata, and keywords) appears in different panes on the left and right sides of the window.

If you have the entire Adobe Creative Suite, Bridge can be accessed from any of the applications to improve integration between the different software packages.

Tools

InDesign CS3 includes no fewer than 32 different tools. The bottom of the Tools panel includes options for controlling the fill and stroke colors, as well as the screen mode you're using. You will learn how to use all of these tools as you complete the projects in this book. For now, you should simply take the opportunity to identify them.

Most of the default tools can be accessed with a single-key shortcut. If you hover your mouse over a tool, the pop-up **tool tip** shows the name of the tool, as well as a letter in parentheses. Pressing that letter on your keyboard switches to the associated tool (unless you're working with type).

If you don't see tool tips, check the Interface pane of the Preferences dialog box. The Tool Tips menu turns tool tips on (Normal), turns them off (None), or makes them appear as soon as the mouse cursor touches an object (Fast).

Because displaying 32 different tools individually would be unwieldy at best, the InDesign Tools panel groups related tools. Any tool with an arrow in the bottom-right corner includes related tools below it. If you click a tool and hold down the mouse button, these **nested** tools appear in a pop-up menu. If you choose one of the nested tools, that variation becomes the default choice in the Tools panel.

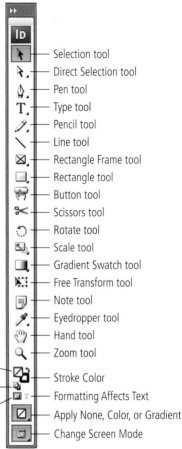

- Selection tool
- Direct Selection tool
- Pen tool
- Type tool
- Pencil tool
- Line tool
- Rectangle Frame tool
- Rectangle tool
- Button tool
- Scissors tool
- Rotate tool
- Scale tool
- Gradient Swatch tool
- Free Transform tool
- Note tool
- Eyedropper tool
- Hand tool
- Zoom tool
- Fill Color
- Restore Default Fill and Stroke
- Formatting Affects Container
- Stroke Color
- Formatting Affects Text
- Apply None, Color, or Gradient
- Change Screen Mode

In InDesign CS3, the default Tools panel is streamlined in a one-column format to take up less space on your screen. You can change to the standard two-column format of previous versions by clicking the dark grey area above the Tools panel (where the

Note:

Not all nested variations can be accessed with a keyboard shortcut. In the Frame tools, for example, the shortcut accesses only the main Rectangle Frame tool.

two arrows point to the right). If you want to switch back to one column, simply click the same area again (where the two arrows point to the left).

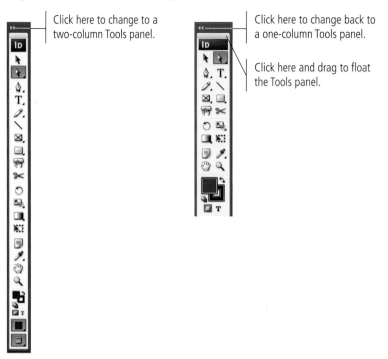

Click here to change to a two-column Tools panel.

Click here to change back to a one-column Tools panel.

Click here and drag to float the Tools panel.

You can also float the Tools panel independently on the document window by simply clicking the top of the Tools panel and dragging it away from the screen edge. When the Tools panel is floating, you can switch between the one- and two-column formats or display the Tools panel as a single horizontal row of tools.

Note:

You can also change the display of the floating Tools panel by choosing an option in the Floating Tools Panel menu in the Interface Preferences dialog box.

Click this button to toggle between a single-column, single-row, and two-column floating Tools panel.

INDESIGN FOUNDATIONS

You should explore which tools are available below the default tools. The following chart offers a quick reference.

↖ Selection tool	＼ Line tool	Scale tool *Shear tool*
↖ Direct Selection tool *Position tool*	⊠ Rectangle Frame tool ⊗ *Ellipse Frame tool* ⊗ *Polygon Frame tool*	Gradient Swatch tool *Gradient Feather tool*
✎ Pen tool *Add Anchor Point tool* *Delete Anchor Point tool* *Convert Direction Point tool*	▢ Rectangle tool ○ *Ellipse tool* ○ *Polygon tool*	Free Transform tool
		Note tool
T Type tool *Type on a Path tool*	Button tool	Eyedropper tool *Measure tool*
✎ Pencil tool *Smooth tool* *Erase tool*	✂ Scissors tool ↻ Rotate tool	Hand tool Zoom tool

PANELS

InDesign CS3 includes 41 panels (called palettes in previous versions of InDesign) that provide access to everything from the color in a box to special effects such as drop shadows and beveled edges. Virtually everything you do in InDesign requires interacting with at least one or two panels, although more often than not you'll use multiple panels to complete any given project.

The edges where the panels live are called the **dock**. A semi-transparent dark grey area marks the edge of the panel dock, which expands or contracts to fit whatever panels are in the dock. In the default workspace, the Tools panel is docked to the left edge of the screen; a number of additional panel groups are **iconized** (collapsed, showing only the icon) and docked to the right edge of the screen.

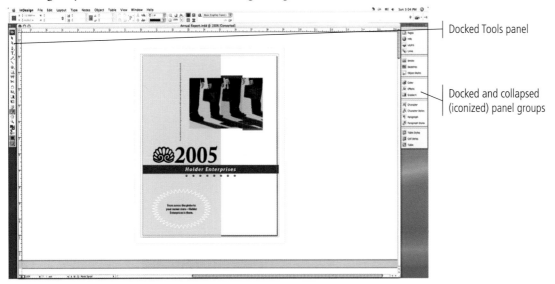

Docked Tools panel

Docked and collapsed (iconized) panel groups

Panels in the dock can be either collapsed or expanded. Clicking the top edge of the dock (the dark gray area) over an expanded column collapses the column to icons. Clicking over a collapsed column expands those panels.

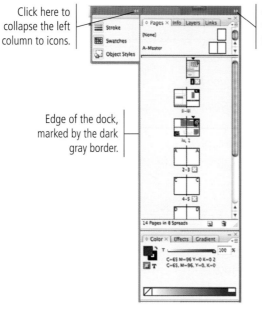

Click here to collapse the left column to icons.

Click here to expand the collapsed panels in the right column.

Edge of the dock, marked by the dark gray border.

Note:

You can shrink collapsed panels to only the icon by dragging the left edge of the docked panel group. You can also drag the edge to the left to reveal the panel names.

If you've collapsed panels to icons, you can access individual panels by clicking the associated buttons. A panel opens to the left of its button, directly on top of anything (including other panels) to the left.

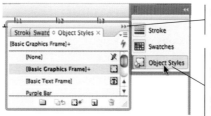

Click here to collapse the open panel.

Clicking the Object Styles panel icon opens the Object Styles panel on top of whatever exists to the left of the panel.

Control/right-clicking the dock header opens a contextual menu with the option to Auto-Collapse Icon Panels. If this option is active, icon panels automatically collapse when you click away from the panel. (This option is also available in the Interface pane of the Preferences dialog box, which you can open from the dock contextual menu.)

If the Auto-Collapse option is turned off, an expanded panel remains open until you close it by clicking the button in the panel's top-right corner. (Choosing the Auto-Collapse option in the contextual menu has the same effect as unchecking the related check box in the Interface pane of the Preferences dialog box.)

Note:

If you're on a Macintosh and don't have a two-button mouse, we highly recommend getting one. They're inexpensive, can be purchased in most retail stores, and save significant amounts of time when accessing contextual options.

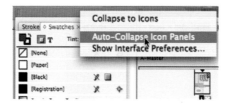

Panels can be toggled on and off using the Window menu. If you choose a panel in this menu that is already open in an expanded group, that panel is brought to the front of the group. If the panel is open in an iconized group, the panel pops out to the left of its icon. If you choose a panel that isn't currently open, it opens in the same position as it was when you last closed it (whether floating or in a group).

Any panel or panel group — including the Tools panel — can be floated by dragging the panel's tab or the group's title bar away from the dock.

You can close individual panels within a group (whether floating or docked) by clicking the "X" in the panel's tab, or you can close an entire panel group by clicking the "X" in the top-right corner of the group. Individual panels can also be dragged into different groups by dragging the panel's tab onto an existing group; the new group is highlighted with a blue edge.

Note:

If a panel (or panel group) is not docked, you can drag any edge to resize it.

You can change the size of a docked panel group by dragging the bottom or left edge of the group. If you drag the bottom edge of a docked group, other panels in the same column expand or contract to fit the available space. If you drag the left edge of a docked group, all other docked groups in the same column are also resized; any docked panels to the left of the resized column move but are not resized.

Panel groups can be moved within the dock by dragging the group title bar to a new position. Before you release the mouse button, a blue line indicates the new position of the panel or group.

Click here and drag to reposition the group within the dock, or drag out of the dock to convert the group to a floating group.

Click here to collapse the panel group.

Click here and drag out of the dock to create an independent floating panel, or drag the tab into a different panel group.

Click here to close the entire panel group.

Click here to close the Color panel.

Click here to access the panel options menu.

Click here and drag to make the panel group wider or narrower.

Click here and drag to make the panel group taller or shorter.

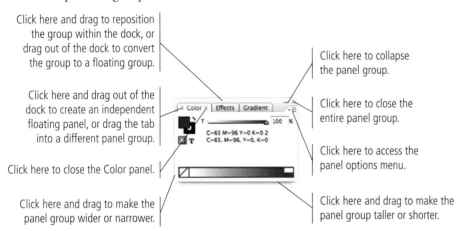

Customizing the Workspace

Different people use InDesign for different reasons, sometimes using only a very limited set of tools to complete very specific projects. InDesign has built in several sophisticated options for customizing the user interface, including the ability to define the menu options that are available and the keyboard shortcuts that are associated with menu commands, panel menus, and tools.

At the bottom of the Edit menu, two options (Keyboard Shortcuts and Menus) open different tabs of the same dialog box, where you can control these elements.

You can save sets of custom menus and keyboard shortcuts so you can access the same choices again without having to redo the work.

Note:

You can change InDesign to mimic the key commands of PageMaker 7 or QuarkXPress 4 by choosing those built-in options in the Set menu.

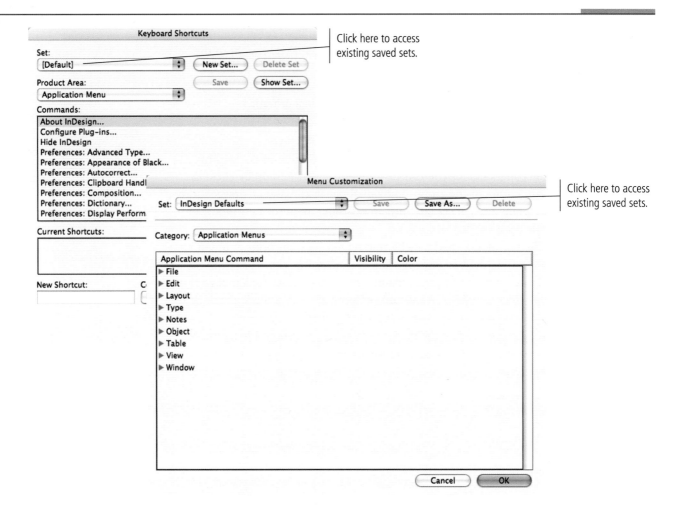

Click here to access existing saved sets.

Click here to access existing saved sets.

In addition to the menus and keyboard commands, you can also save entire work-spaces. For example, let's say that you primarily work on two different types of jobs — one that revolves around long documents and one that mostly involves working with layers and graphic effects. Each type of work requires specific panel sets. After months of work, you've even decided where you like those panels to be on your screen.

Choosing Window>Workspace>Save Workspace allows you to save any combination of the panel locations and custom menus. Custom workspaces are extremely useful in any environment where you are sharing a computer with other users. You can even copy the saved files from the Adobe InDesign CS3>Presets>Workspaces folder to access your saved settings on another computer.

Note:

If you modify the default sets, we highly recommend that you save the custom sets in addition to the defaults. In the Keyboard Shortcuts dialog box, you should use the New Set button; in the Menu Customization dialog box, you should use the Save As button.

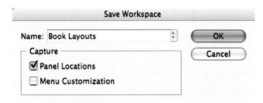

Once you've saved a workspace, you can call it again in the Window>Workspace menu. Whatever you saved in the custom workspace reappears on the screen, in the same position as when you saved the workspace (if you choose the Panel Locations check box when you save the workspace).

You can always return to the default InDesign workspace by choosing Default Workspace from the Window>Workspace menu.

Preferences

In addition to customizing the user interface, you can also customize the way many options work. The right side of the Preferences dialog box shows the options associated with the category selected in the left pane. As you work through the projects in this book, you learn how — and why — to adjust the various preferences. For now, it's enough to know where to find these options.

Note:

Preferences are accessed in the InDesign menu on Macintosh; on Windows, they are accessed in the Edit menu.

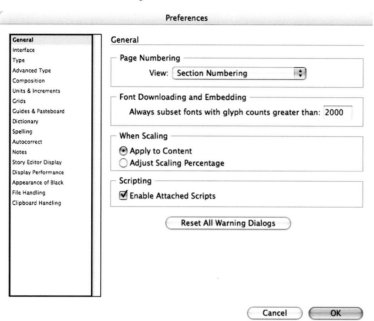

Identity Package

Your client, Tracey Dillon, is a local architect. She hired you to create a corporate identity package so she can begin marketing her services to local land development companies. She asked you first to develop a logo, and then to create the standard identity pieces (business card and letterhead) that she can use for business promotion and correspondence.

This project incorporates the following skills:

❑ Customizing the workspace to maximize your efficiency

❑ Creating new files in various sizes to meet the project needs

❑ Using the basic InDesign drawing tools to develop a logo

❑ Creating and formatting text

❑ Placing and manipulating external graphics files

❑ Incorporating color into the various design elements

❑ Exporting InDesign files as EPS and PDF to meet various end-use and output requirements

The Project Meeting

Client Comments

I've decided to open my own architectural services firm, and I need to start advertising. That means I need to brand my business so companies who need an architect will recognize and remember my name. I'm calling my business TD Associates.

I want a logo that really says "architect." Then I want you to use the logo on business cards, letterhead, and envelopes that I will have preprinted; I want a more professional feel than I can create using my laser printer. The printer I spoke with said I could do this for less money if I go "four-color" for the business card and letterhead, but "two-color" for the envelope; I really don't know what that means — I'm hoping that you do.

Art Director Comments

The logo is the first part of this project because you'll use it on the other three pieces. I have an idea that I think will meet the client's needs. Fortunately, Tracey is going to call her business "TD"; two important tools for an architect are a T-square and a measuring triangle. The T is obvious, and if you rotate the triangle — instant D!

Since logos are used on far more than just these three jobs in this one application, you'll save the final logo in a file format that can be used in different ways, and then place that file into the other three pieces. Tracey wants to print the card and letterhead in four-color and the envelope in two-color, so you'll have to create two different versions of the logo.

One of the colors will be black in this case, because most of the text on the letterhead and envelope should be black. We have to pick one other spot ink color; I think we should use some kind of blue since architects create blueprints.

Project Objectives

To complete this project, you will:

- ❏ Create a custom project workspace
- ❏ Create and save several different documents to meet different requirements for commercial printing
- ❏ Create a document preset for easy access to common job settings
- ❏ Draw basic shapes using native InDesign tools
- ❏ Work with Bezier paths to create complex shapes
- ❏ Edit shapes using the Pathfinder, Align, and Transform panels
- ❏ Apply color to fills and strokes
- ❏ Create and format basic text elements
- ❏ Import external text and graphics files
- ❏ Export an EPS file
- ❏ Print desktop proofs

Stage 1 Setting up the Workspace

The best way to start any new project is to prepare your workspace — just as any good chef sharpens the knives and locates all of the necessary ingredients before starting to cook. As you learned in the Interface chapter, InDesign allows you to save custom workspaces that can be called whenever you need them — a very useful function if you're working on a shared computer or if you move back and forth from one job to another on your own computer.

For this project, you'll start by defining a custom workspace with the tools you'll use throughout the project. This method establishes a baseline so your screen will match the screen shots shown throughout this project. It also allows you to recall the workspace if you need to quit and come back to a project later.

 CREATE THE PROJECT WORKSPACE

Since we created these projects, we know exactly which tools you'll use to complete each one. As you work on other projects, you might not know which tools you'll use, so you won't be able to create such clear workspaces at the beginning of the project. You can, however, start with a baseline (such as the default workspace) and add panels as you need them.

1. **Launch InDesign.**

2. **Choose Window>Workspace>Default Workspace.**

   This might or might not do anything, depending on what was done in InDesign before you started this project. The default workspace is what Adobe defined to appear when the application is first launched. If you change anything and quit InDesign, the program will remember your changes when you start it again.

   By calling the default workspace, you can start from the same place that you see in our screen shots. A number of panel groups are already placed in the iconized dock on the right side of the screen, the Tools panel is already docked in one-column format at the left side of the screen, and the Control bar appears immediately below the menu bar.

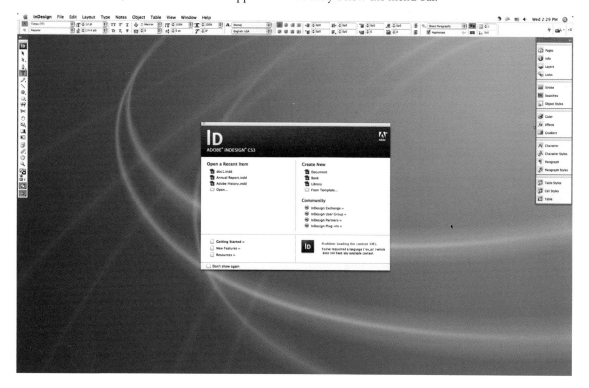

3. In the Welcome screen, check the Don't Show Again option and close the dialog box.

The Welcome screen includes a useful set of shortcuts for opening recently used documents, for creating new files, and for accessing helpful external resources. You can access all of these features from within the application, so you can simply dismiss the Welcome screen.

Note:

You can always redisplay the Welcome screen by choosing Help>Welcome Screen.

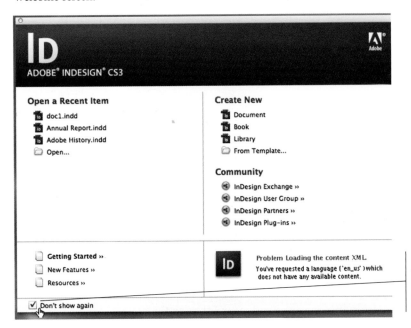

Click here to prevent the Welcome screen from reopening when you close all open InDesign files.

4. Control/right-click the dock above the top panel and choose Expand Dock.

For this project, you won't need many of the default panels. To maximize your efficiency, you're going to close the panels you don't need and add a couple that aren't in the default set. It's easier to do this when the entire panel set is expanded.

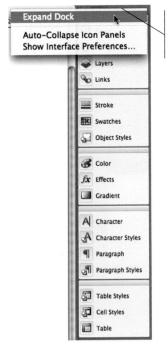

Control/right-click here to access options for the panel dock.

5. **In the bottom panel group (the one with the Table Styles panel showing), click the "X" (Close) button in the top-right corner to close the entire panel group.**

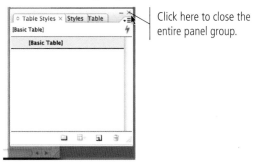

Click here to close the entire panel group.

6. **Use the same technique to close the top panel group (the one with the Links panel showing).**

7. **In the new bottom panel group, click the Character Styles tab to bring that panel to the top of the group.**

8. **Click the "X" in the Character Styles panel tab to close that panel.**

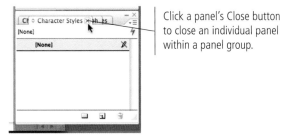

Click a panel's Close button to close an individual panel within an panel group.

9. **Using the same techniques, bring the Paragraph Styles panel to the front of the group, and then close it.**

10. **In the Color/Effects/Gradient panel group, click in the gray area behind the panel tabs, and then drag the group to the left and out of the dock.**

Click behind the panel tabs to drag the entire group.

Make sure you drag far enough so the group floats, instead of being dropped into a second column of the dock. If you see a light gray area pop up to the left of the dock, keep dragging; that "drawer" pops up to show that you are adding a panel (or group) to the dock, either below the existing column or in an adjacent column.

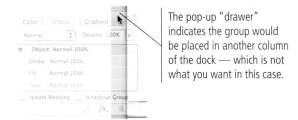

The pop-up "drawer" indicates the group would be placed in another column of the dock — which is not what you want in this case.

11. **Using the same techniques, close the Effects and Gradient panels from the now-floating group.**

12. **In the dock, close the Object Styles panel in the top group.**

13. **Click the Color panel tab and drag it onto the top panel group in the dock.**

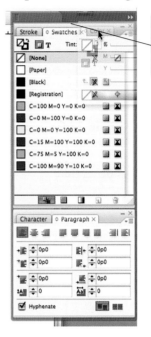

The blue border indicates that the panel you're dragging will be placed into the group with the Stroke and Swatches panels.

14. **Choose Window>Objects & Layout>Transform.**

    This opens a new floating panel group, with the Transform panel at the top of the stack.

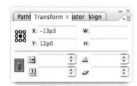

Note:

If you can't find a panel, almost every available panel (except Tabs) can be accessed in the Window menu.

15. **Close the Align and Navigator panels in this floating group.**

16. **In the floating group, click the gray area behind the two panel tabs and drag the group to the bottom of the panel dock.**

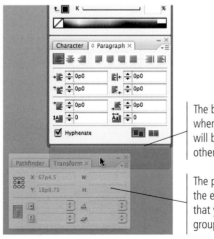

The blue line indicates where the panel or group will be placed in relation to other groups in the dock.

The pop-up "drawer" below the existing groups indicates that you can add panels or groups to the dock.

Note:

Panels in the default set open automatically in the dock, in the same group as they were originally placed. Other panels automatically open as floating panels in their last-used positions.

17. **Control/right-click the dock header and choose Collapse to Icons in the contextual menu.**

18. **Choose Window>Workspace>Save Workspace.**

19. **In the dialog box, type "Identity Workspace" in the Name field. Make sure the Panel Locations check box is selected, and then click OK.**

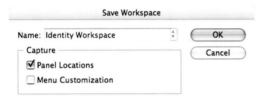

Your new workspace should now appear in the Window>Workspace menu. If you need to stop working and come back to this project at any time, you can recall the exact same set of tools (including the Tools panel and Control panel) with a single menu command.

Note:

If you want your panels to be "spring-loaded," you can choose the Auto-Collapse Icon Panels option in the dock contextual menu. We prefer our panels to stay open until we choose to close them, but this is a matter of individual preference.

Note:

You can delete a custom workspace by choosing Window> Workspace>Delete Workspace, and then choosing the workspace you want to remove in the Delete Workspace dialog box pop-up menu.

CREATE AND SAVE A BASIC InDESIGN FILE

This project ultimately requires four files: one for creating the logo, one for the business card, one for the letterhead, and one for the envelope. The logo file is basically freeform, since it's essentially an artboard on which to draw. The other three files have specific size and output requirements, which you can define when you create the files.

1. **Choose File>New>Document.**

    InDesign uses picas as the default unit of measurement when you first install the application. The measurements in this dialog box are all shown in picas, using the "ApB" notation (for A picas and B points).

    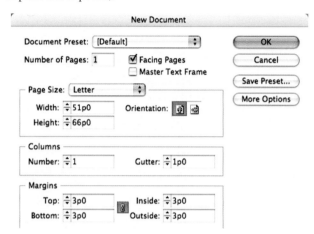

2. **Change the Width field to 3″ (make sure you type the inch mark).**

    When you enter a value in a unit other than the default, you have to include the alternate unit.

    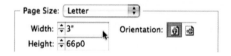

3. **Press Tab to move to the Height field.**

    If you work with units other than the default, InDesign makes the necessary conversion for you. This technique works in dialog boxes and panels — basically anywhere you can type a measurement.

    When you type a different value into the Width or Height field, the Page Size menu changes to Custom.

4. **Change the Height field to 3″.**

5. **Highlight the first Margins field (Top) and type "0".**

    You do not need to type the full 0p0 notation when you change measurements using the default units. Zero pica is still zero, so you don't need to worry about converting units.

Note:

Before completing this project, copy the Identity folder from the WIP folder on your Resource CD to your WIP folder wherever you are saving your work. When you save files for this project, you will save them in your WIP>Identity folder.

Key Command:

Create a new file by pressing Command/Control-N.

Note:

Picas are the measuring system traditionally used in typography; they are still used by many in the graphic communications industry.

1 pt. = 1/72 in.

12 pt. = 1 pica

1 pica = 1/6 in.

6 pica = 1 in.

Note:

InDesign recognizes measurements in points, picas, inches, inches decimal, millimeters, centimeters, ciceros, and agates.

6. Press Tab to move the highlight to the next field (Bottom).

You can use the chain button in the middle of the Margins area to easily define the same margin on all four sides of the document. If the chain button is active, all four margin fields will be the same.

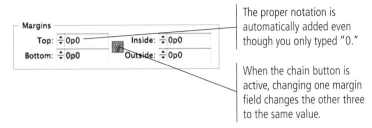

The proper notation is automatically added even though you only typed "0."

When the chain button is active, changing one margin field changes the other three to the same value.

Note:

The formal name of the chain button is Make All Settings the Same. When this option is active, the chain links are connected. When it is not active, the links appear to be broken.

Active ⊢— 🔒

Not active ⊢— 🔓

7. Click OK to create the new document.

The document window appears, with the file filling the available space. If you look in the bottom-left corner, you'll probably see that your file is displayed at more than than 100%.

8. If you don't see rulers at the top and left edges of the document window, choose View>Show Rulers.

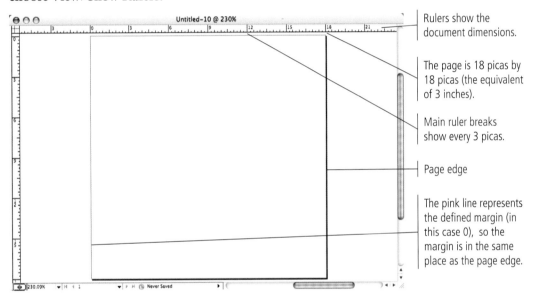

Rulers show the document dimensions.

The page is 18 picas by 18 picas (the equivalent of 3 inches).

Main ruler breaks show every 3 picas.

Page edge

The pink line represents the defined margin (in this case 0), so the margin is in the same place as the page edge.

9. Open the Preferences>Units & Increments dialog box (in the InDesign menu on Macintosh or in the Edit menu on Windows).

Since most people (in the United States, at least) think in terms of inches, we will use inches throughout the projects in this book.

10. In the Ruler Units area, choose Inches in the Horizontal and Vertical menus, and then click OK.

Key Command:

You can tab through the fields of most dialog boxes and panels in InDesign. Press Shift-Tab to move the highlight to the previous field in the tab order.

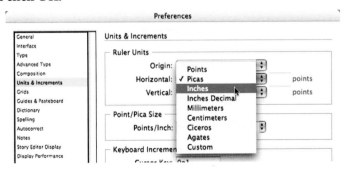

When you return to the document window, you'll see that the rulers now display in inches.

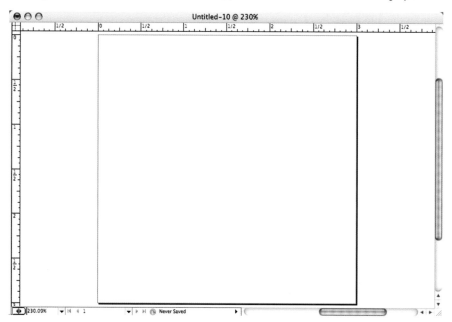

11. **Choose File>Save As.**

12. **Navigate to the WIP>Identity folder as the location where you will save this file.**

The extension ".indd" is automatically added on both Macintosh and Windows computers. You can use the Format menu to save a file as a document or as a template; you'll start working with templates in Project 3.

Note:

The first time you save a file, the Save command opens the same dialog box as the File>Save As command. After saving the file once, you can use Save to save changes to the existing file, or use Save As to create an additional file under a new file name.

13. **Change the file name (in the Save As field) to "logo.indd" and click Save.**

14. **Close the open document and continue to the next exercise.**

Using the Command Bar

A significant number of commonly used file-management features can be accessed in the Command bar, which is located in the Window>Object & Layout submenu. Since our goal is to teach you where the various options normally reside in the interface, we don't use the Command bar in these projects. It is, however, a useful panel to keep around. Use the following chart to identify the different features and shortcuts. You'll learn about the specific functionality throughout this book.

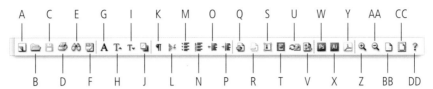

A. New document	K. Paragraphs panel	U. Update link
B. Open	L. Tabs	V. Place
C. Save	M. Bulleted list	W. Launch Photoshop
D. Print	N. Numbered list	X. Launch Illustrator
E. Find/Change	O. Decrease left indent	Y. Export Adobe PDF
F. Check spelling	P. Increase left indent	Z. Zoom in
G. Character panel	Q. Insert pages	AA. Zoom out
H. Increase font size	R. Remove pages	BB. Actual size
I. Decrease font size	S. Text frame options	CC. Fit spread in window
J. Swatches panel	T. Text wrap	DD. Help

 ## CREATE THE LETTERHEAD DOCUMENT

The most important aspect of a letterhead is to clearly and unobtrusively present the sender's contact information. The content on the letterhead — meaning the actual letter being sent — should be the main focus when someone receives a piece of your client's (or your) letterhead. This doesn't mean you can't be creative in the design, but it does mean that you shouldn't get carried away with huge, overbearing design elements that take away from the contents of the letter.

Some production-related concerns will dictate how you design your letterhead. In general, there are two ways to print a letterhead: commercially in large quantities, or one-offs on your desktop laser or inkjet printer. (The second method involves a letterhead template that you can create to write and print your letters from directly within InDesign, which is quite common among designers.)

If your letterhead is being printed commercially, it is probably being printed with multiple copies on a large press sheet, from which the individual sheets will be cut. (In fact, most commercial printing happens this way.) This type of printing typically means that design elements can run right off the edge of the sheet, called **bleeding**.

If you're designing for a printer that can only run letter-size paper, you have to allow enough of a margin area for your printer to hold the paper as it moves through the device (called the **gripper margin**); in this case, you can't design with bleeds. (Older desktop printers typically have a different minimum margin at the page edges; you're usually safe with 3/8″. Newer inkjet printers might have the capability to print 8.5 × 11″ with full bleed. In either case, consult your printer documentation to be sure.)

The letterhead for this project will be printed commercially. The printer said that the design can safely bleed on all four sides, and their equipment requires a 1/8″ bleed allowance.

Note:

These are only general rules. If you're using a commercial printer, always ask the output provider whether it's safe (and cost-effective) to design with bleeds, and find out how much allowance to include.

1. **With no file open in InDesign, open the Units & Increments Preferences dialog box (in the InDesign menu on Macintosh or the Edit menu on Windows).**

2. **Change both Ruler Units menus to Inches and click OK.**

   By changing the preferences with no file open, you're changing the application default preferences. Your changes will be applied to any new file you create, but not to already-existing files.

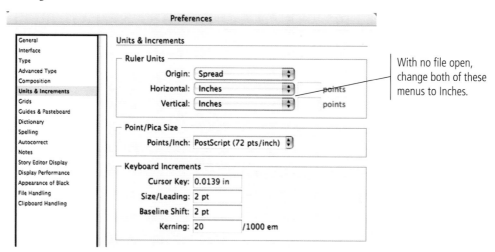

With no file open, change both of these menus to Inches.

3. **Choose File>New>Document.**

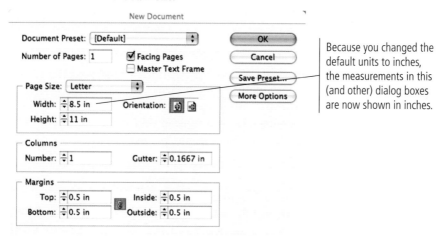

Because you changed the default units to inches, the measurements in this (and other) dialog boxes are now shown in inches.

4. **Make sure the Page Size menu is set to Letter.**

   You can use this menu to create a number of standard page sizes.

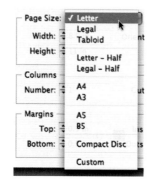

Note:

Choosing Custom in the Page Size menu has no real affect. This setting is automatically reflected as soon as you change the Width or Height fields from the standard measurements.

5. **With the chain button active in the Margins area, change the Top field to 0.75″. Press Tab so the value is applied to all four fields.**

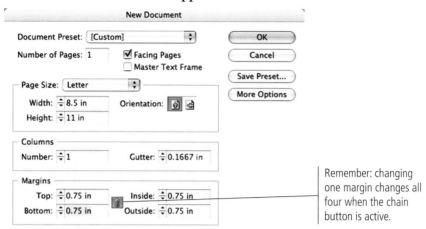

Remember: changing one margin changes all four when the chain button is active.

6. **At the top of the dialog box, uncheck the Facing Pages check box.**

   Facing pages are used when a printed job will be read left to right like a book — with Page 1 starting on the right, then Page 2 facing Page 3, and so on. Facing-page layouts are based on **spreads**, which are pairs of left-right pages as you flip through a book (e.g., Page 6 facing Page 7).

   When you work with non-facing pages, the Inside and Outside margin fields change to Left and Right respectively. Technically, non-facing pages do not have an inside (spine edge) or outside (face or trim edge), so there are only left and right sides.

Note:

You'll work extensively with facing pages starting in Project 4.

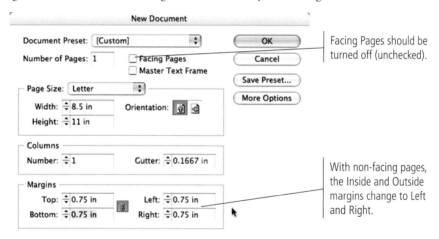

Facing Pages should be turned off (unchecked).

With non-facing pages, the Inside and Outside margins change to Left and Right.

7. **Click the More Options button.**

   The printer for this job says you need to include at least 1/8″ bleed allowance. In the Bleed and Slug area, you can specify that requirement so you'll see the appropriate marks later when you add design elements to the page.

8. To the right of the Bleed fields, make sure the chain button is active, and then change the first Bleed field to 0.125 (the decimal equivalent of 1/8″).

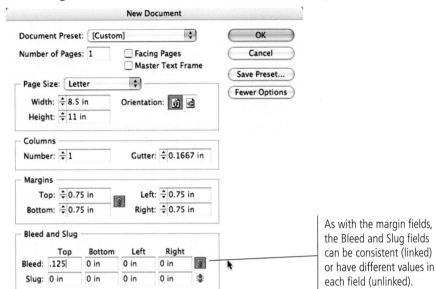

Note:

Your default units are now inches, so you don't have to type the units. You also don't have to type the leading "0" before the decimal point.

As with the margin fields, the Bleed and Slug fields can be consistent (linked) or have different values in each field (unlinked).

Note:

*A **slug** is an element entirely outside the page area, which will be included in the final output. The slug area can be used for file/plate information, special registration marks, color bars, or other elements.*

9. Click OK to create the new file.

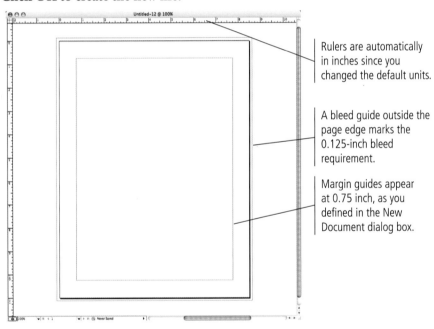

Rulers are automatically in inches since you changed the default units.

A bleed guide outside the page edge marks the 0.125-inch bleed requirement.

Margin guides appear at 0.75 inch, as you defined in the New Document dialog box.

10. Save the file as "TDletterhead.indd" in the WIP>Identity folder, and then close the file.

CREATE THE BUSINESS CARD DOCUMENT

When business cards are printed, they are almost always printed as multiple copies on a single sheet, and then trimmed from the sheet to the standard 3.5 × 2″ size. Not long ago, printers asked for business cards to be submitted already **imposed multiple-up** (the term for printing more than one copy of an item on the same page). This practice has largely fallen out of use, partly because software makes it easier for the printer to impose the cards, and partly because the small cards are often **ganged** on a press sheet with other jobs (printed on the sheet outside the main job margins, making efficient use of what would otherwise be wasted paper).

According to the printer, the TD business cards for this project will be printed on their own press sheets; the design can safely bleed on all four sides, and requires a 1/8″ bleed allowance. The printer also said you should allow a 1/8″ margin to avoid important elements being cut off when the cards are cut from the press sheet.

Note:

*The **live area** is the "safe" area inside the page edge, where important design elements should be kept. Because printing and trimming are mechanical processes, there will always be some variation — however slight. Elements that are too close to the page edge run the risk of being accidentally trimmed off.*

1. **Choose File>New>Document.**

   The New Document dialog box always defaults to the last-used Document Preset.

2. **In the Page Size area, change the Width to 2″ and the Height to 3.5″.**

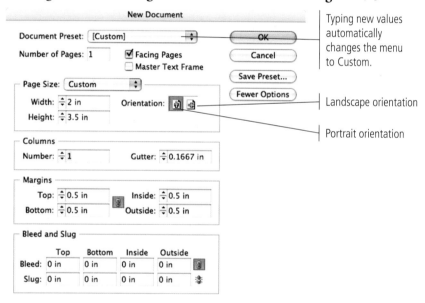

3. **Click the right (landscape) Orientation button.**

   The Orientation buttons automatically reflect the dimensions that you type (portrait orientation is taller than it is wide; landscape orientation is wider than it is tall). Clicking the opposite button reverses the values in the Width and Height fields.

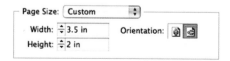

4. **Change the Margins and Bleed fields to 0.125″. Uncheck the Facing Pages option.**

5. **Click the Save Preset button.**

   A **preset** is a way to store groups of common settings so you can define them once and access the same set later with a single click. You'll apply this concept a number of times in InDesign, when you use style sheets, table styles, object styles, and output presets.

6. In the Save Preset dialog box, type "Bleed Business Card" in the Save Preset As field and click OK.

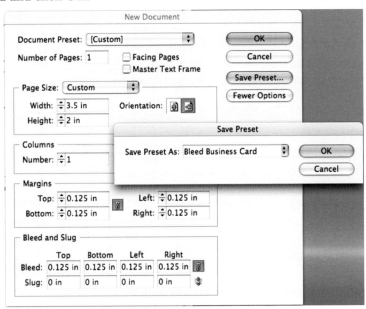

When you return to the New Document dialog box, your new preset appears as the selection in the Document Preset menu. Any time you need to create a business card with the same bleed and live areas, you can choose Bleed Business Card from this menu.

7. Click OK to create your new document.

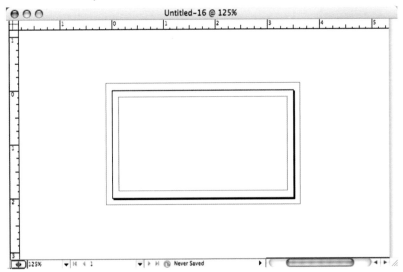

8. Save the file as "TDbusiness_card.indd" in your WIP>Identity folder, and then close the file.

Managing Document Presets

You can access and manage document presets in the File menu. If you choose one of the existing presets in the menu, the New Document dialog box opens, defaulting to the values in the preset you call (instead of defaulting to the application-default Letter-size page). All the settings you saved in the preset automatically reflect in the dialog box.

Document Presets	▶	Define...
Document Setup...	⌥⌘P	
User...		[Default]...
File Info...	⌥⇧⌘I	Bleed Business Card...

Document Presets

Presets:
[Default]
Bleed Business Card

OK
Cancel
New...
Edit...
Delete

Preset Settings:
Preset: [Default]
Page information
  Number of Pages: 1
  Facing Pages: Yes
  Master Text Frame: No
  Page Width: 8.5 in
  Page Height: 11 in

Load...
Save...

You can also create, edit, and manage presets by choosing Define in the Document Presets submenu. This command opens a dialog box that lists the existing presets.

- Select a preset and click Edit to change the associated options.

- Select a preset and click Delete to remove the preset from the application.

- Click New to open the New Document Preset dialog box, which is basically the same as the New Document dialog box, except the Preset menu is replaced with a field where you can type the preset name instead of clicking the Save Preset button.

- Click Save to save a preset (with the extension DCST) so it can be sent to and used on another computer.

- Click Load to import presets that were created on another computer.

CREATE THE ENVELOPE DOCUMENT

In general, printed envelopes can be created in two ways. You can create and print the design on a flat sheet, which will be specially **die cut** (stamped out of the press sheet), and then folded and glued into the shape of the finished envelope. Alternatively (and usually at less expense), you can print on pre-folded and -glued envelopes.

Both of these methods for envelope design have special printing requirements, such as not putting ink where glue will be applied (if you're printing on flat sheets), or not printing within a certain distance from the edge (if you're printing on pre-formed envelopes). Whenever you design an envelope, consult with the output provider who will print the job before you get too far into the project.

In this case, the design will be output on pre-folded #10 business-size envelopes (4 1/8 × 9 1/2"). The printer requires a quarter-inch gripper margin around the edge of the envelope where you cannot include any ink coverage.

Note:

You should become familiar with the common fraction-to-decimal equivalents:

1/8 = 0.125

1/4 = 0.25

3/8 = 0.375

1/2 = 0.5

5/8 = 0.625

3/4 = 0.75

7/8 = 0.875

1. **Choose File>New>Document.**

2. **Create a document preset named "Prefolded Envelope", using the following settings:**

Size (h × w):	**4.125" × 9.5" without facing pages**
Margins:	**0.25"**
Bleed:	**0"**

3. **Create a new file from the Prefolded Envelope preset.**

4. Save the new file as "TDenvelope.indd", and then close it.

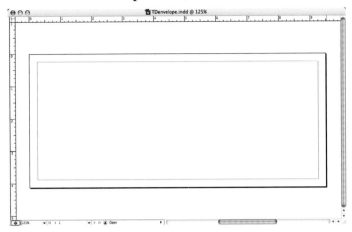

Standard Envelope Sizes

When designing envelopes, it is usually a good idea to stick with standard sizes. Non-standard sizes can result in extra printing and custom die-cut costs, as well as additional postage costs. (There are several thousand pages of rules about mailing in the United States; go to www.usps.gov for more information.)

The following tables include the most common sizes of two envelope styles, as well as the standard enclosure size that fits inside the envelope. (All measurements are shown in inches.)

A-Style Envelopes

Type	Size	Enclosure size
A-1	3.625 × 5.125	
A-2	4.375 × 5.75	4.25 × 5.5
A-6	4.75 × 6.5	4.5 × 6.25
A-7	5.25 × 7.25	5 × 6.875
A-8	5.5 × 8.125	5.25 × 7.75
A-Long	3.875 × 8.875	3.75 × 8.625
A-10	6 × 9.5	5.75 × 9.125

Standard Business & Correspondence Envelopes

Type	Size	Enclosure size
6 1/4	3.5 × 6	3.25 × 5.75
6 3/4	3.625 × 6.5	3.5 × 6.25
8 5/8	3.625 × 8.625	3.5 × 8.375
7	3.75 × 6.75	3.5 × 6.5
Monarch (7 3/4)	3.875 × 7.5	3.75 × 7.25
9	3.875 × 8.875	3.75 × 8.675
9 (policy)	4 × 9	3.75 × 8.5
10	4.125 × 9.5	4 × 9.25
DL	4.313 × 8.625	4.125 × 8.375
11	4.5 × 10.375	4.25 × 10.125
12	4.75 × 11	4.5 × 10.75
14	5 × 11.5	4.75 × 11.25
16	6 × 12	5.75 × 11.75

Standard Booklet Envelopes

Type	Size	Enclosure size
3	4.75 × 6.5	4.5 × 6
4 1/2	5.5 × 7.5	5.25 × 7
5	5.5 × 8.125	5.25 × 7.625
6	5.75 × 8.875	5.5 × 8.375
6 1/2	6 × 9	5.75 × 9
6 5/8	6 × 9.5	5.75 × 9
6 3/4	6.5 × 9.5	6.25 × 9
7 1/4	7 × 10	6.75 × 9.5
7 1/2	7.5 × 10.5	7.25 × 10
9	8.75 × 11.5	8.5 × 11
9 1/2	9 × 12	8.75 × 11.5
10	9.5 × 12.625	9.25 × 12.125
13	10 × 13	9.75 × 12.5

Stage 2 **Drawing in InDesign**

Now that you have the basic files you need, the next part of this project is to create the client's logo. There are several important points to keep in mind when you design a logo. First, logos should be representational; in other words, they are visual devices that suggest a concept without spelling out every detail. There are different schools of thought on the subject, but we believe that as a general rule logos should be relatively simplistic — suggesting the idea rather than being a photographic representation.

Second, logos need to be scalable. A company might place its logo on the head of a golf tee or on the side of a building. (This is a strong argument for the simpler line-art approach instead of photography.) Vector graphics — the kind you can create in InDesign — can be scaled as large or small as necessary without losing quality; photographs are raster images, and they can't be greatly enlarged or reduced without losing quality.

Third, you will almost certainly need more than one version of any given logo — and possibly in more than one file format. Different kinds of output require different formats (specifically, one set of files for print and one for the Web), and some types of jobs might require special options saved in the files (such as the four-color and two-color versions that you need to create the TD logo in this project).

CREATE AND TRANSFORM BASIC SHAPES

Although much drawing and illustration work — including creating logos — is done in a dedicated illustration program such as Adobe Illustrator, you can use the drawing tools in InDesign to create some types of artwork. InDesign and Illustrator are both Adobe products; the drawing tools in InDesign are actually a limited subset of the more comprehensive Illustrator toolset, which means you can create fairly sophisticated artwork entirely within the layout application.

1. **Choose File>Open.**

2. **Navigate to the WIP>Identity folder and select the logo.indd file that you created earlier. Click Open.**

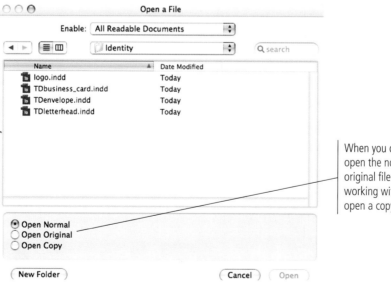

Key Command:

Access the Open dialog box by pressing Command/Control-O.

When you open a file, you can open the normal file, open the original file (relevant when working with templates), or open a copy of the existing file.

INDESIGN FOUNDATIONS

Vector graphics are composed of mathematical descriptions of a series of lines and geometric shapes. These files are commonly created in illustration ("drawing") applications such as Adobe Illustrator or in page-layout applications such as Adobe InDesign. Vector graphics are **resolution independent**; they can be freely scaled and are automatically output at the resolution of the output device.

Raster images are made up of a grid of individual pixels (rasters or bits) in rows and columns (called a **bitmap**). Raster files are **resolution dependent** — their resolution is determined when you scan, photograph, or otherwise create the file. (You can typically reduce raster images, but not enlarge them without losing image quality.) Raster image quality depends on the file's resolution; when you work with raster images, you need to understand the resolution requirements from the very beginning of the process:

- **Pixels per inch (ppi)** is the number of pixels in one horizontal or vertical inch of a digital raster file.

- **Lines per inch (lpi)** is the number of halftone dots produced in a horizontal or vertical linear inch by a high-resolution imagesetter in order to simulate the appearance of continuous-tone color.

- **Dots per inch (dpi)** or **spots per inch (spi)** is the number of dots produced by an output device in a single line of output. Dpi is sometimes used interchangeably (although incorrectly) with pixels per inch.

When reproducing a photograph on a printing press, the image must be converted into a set of different-sized dots that fool the eye into believing that it sees continuous tones. The result of this conversion process is a halftone image; the dots used to simulate continuous tone are called **halftone dots**. Light tones in a photograph are represented as small halftone dots; dark tones become large halftone dots. Prior to image-editing software, photos were converted to halftones with a large graphic-arts camera and screens. The picture was photographed through the screen to create halftone dots, and different screens produced different numbers of dots in an inch (hence the term dots per inch).

Screen Ruling

The screens used with old graphic-arts cameras had a finite number of available dots in a horizontal or vertical inch. That number was the **screen ruling**, or lines per inch of the halftone. A screen ruling of 133 lpi means that in a square inch there are 133 × 133 (17,689) possible locations for a halftone dot. If the screen ruling is decreased, there are fewer total halftone dots and a grainier image; if the screen ruling is increased, there are more halftone dots and a clearer image.

Line screen is a finite number based on a combination of the output device and paper. You can't randomly select a line screen. Ask your printer what line screen will be used before you begin creating images. If you can't find out ahead of time, or you are unsure, follow these general guidelines:

- Newspaper or newsprint: 85-100 lpi

- Magazine or general commercial printing: 133-150 lpi

- Premium-quality-paper jobs (such as art books or annual reports): 150–175 lpi (some specialty jobs might use 200 lpi or more)

Image Resolution

When a printer creates halftone dots, it calculates the average value of a group of pixels and generates a spot of appropriate size. An image's resolution controls the quantity of pixel data that the printer can read. Regardless of the source — camera, scanner, or files you create from scratch in a program such as Photoshop — images need to have sufficient resolution for the output device to generate enough halftone dots to create the appearance of continuous tone.

Ideally, the printer has four pixels for each halftone dot created. The relationship between pixels and halftone dots defines the rule of resolution for all raster-based images — the resolution of an image should be two times the screen ruling (lpi) that will be used for printing.

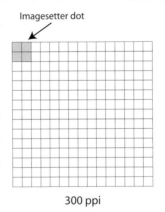
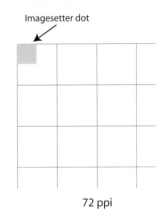

300 ppi   72 ppi

Each white square symbolizes a pixel in a digital image. The grey area shows the pixel information used to generate a halftone dot or spot. If an image only has 72 pixels per inch, the output device has to generate four halftone dots per pixel, resulting in poor printed quality.

The same raster image is reproduced here at 300 ppi (left) and 72 ppi (right). Notice the obvious degradation in quality when the resolution is set to 72 ppi.

When you open a file, the document window defaults to fill the available space on your screen. The document scales to fill the entire window. In this case, you're using the document as a drawing space, so a view percentage higher than 100% will be useful (remember, the actual document is only 3 × 3").

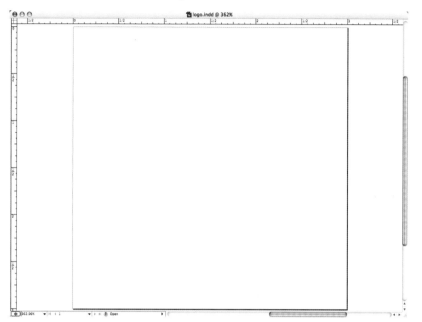

3. **In the Tools panel, click the Rectangle tool to select it.**

If you don't see the Rectangle tool, click and hold the default shape tool until the nested tools appear; slide over and down to select the Rectangle tool.

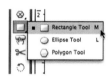

Note:

Tools with nested options default to show the last-used variation in the main Tools panel.

Understanding Line Art

INDESIGN FOUNDATIONS

Line art is a raster image made up entirely of 100% solid areas. The pixels in a line-art image have only two options: they can be all black or all white. Examples of line art are UPC bar codes or pen drawings.

The rule for line-art reproduction is to scan the image at the same resolution as the output device. Think about it like this: a 600 dpi printer can create a maximum of 600 × 600 (360,000) dots in one square inch. With line art, we want to give the printer the most information available, which in this case would be 600 pixels per inch. If the art is created and printed at only 300 ppi, then the printer would have to skip to every other possible space to place a dot. The result is known as "stair-stepping" or "bitmapping."

Most laser printers today image at 600 to 1200 dpi, but film on an image-setter is typically produced at a much higher resolution, possibly 2400 dpi or more. Fortunately, the human eye is not sensitive enough to discern bitmapping beyond 1200 dpi, so you can be fairly safe capturing line art at 1200 ppi.

A bitmap or line-art image has only two colors — black and white. There are no shades of gray or color.

4. Click near the left-center page edge and drag down and right to draw a rectangle.

The size of the rectangle isn't really important since you will change it to a specific size shortly.

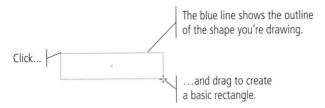

Click... The blue line shows the outline of the shape you're drawing.

...and drag to create a basic rectangle.

5. Release the mouse button to create the rectangle.

Every shape you create in an InDesign document has a **bounding box**, or a non-printing rectangle that marks the shape's outer dimensions. (Even a circle has a square bounding box, marking the largest height and width of the circle.) The bounding box has eight handles, which you can drag to change the size of the rectangle. If you can see an object's bounding box handles, that object is selected.

Bounding box handle

6. With the object selected, look at the bottom of the Tools panel.

Every object you create with the InDesign drawing tools has a stroke (border) and a fill (background) color — even if one or both of those is colored "None." The InDesign default values set the fill to None and the stroke to 1-pt. black for objects you create with the basic shape tools.

7. Click the Swap Fill and Stroke button.

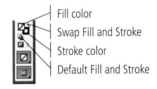

Fill color
Swap Fill and Stroke
Stroke color
Default Fill and Stroke

8. Click the Transform icon in the panel dock to expand the Transform panel.

The Transform panel shows the exact position and dimensions of the selected object(s). You can change any of these values by simply typing in the fields. The top-left area of the panel shows the **reference point** around which transformations will occur. (These points correspond to the object's bounding box handles, as well as to the object's exact center point.)

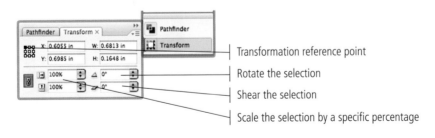

Transformation reference point
Rotate the selection
Shear the selection
Scale the selection by a specific percentage

9. **In the Transform panel, click the top-left reference point. Change the W (width) field to 0.25″ and the H (height) field to 2″, then press Return/ Enter to apply the change (or just click away from the object on the page.)**

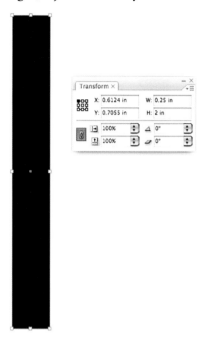

10. **Select the Rectangle tool again and click once near the top-center page edge.**

11. **In the Rectangle dialog box, set the Width to 1″ and the Height to 0.25″ and click OK.**

    Single-clicking with a shape tool lets you define specific measurements for the new shape.

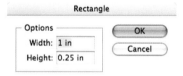

    The new shape appears with the default fill and stroke colors, even though you changed the first rectangle.

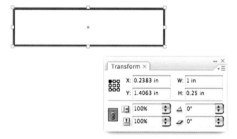

12. **Swap the fill and stroke colors in the second rectangle.**

13. **Choose the Selection tool (solid arrow) in the Tools panel.**

    The Selection tool is used to select entire objects; the Direct Selection tool (hollow arrow) is used to select parts of objects. This is an extremely important distinction, which will make more sense shortly.

14. Draw a marquee that touches any part of both rectangles.

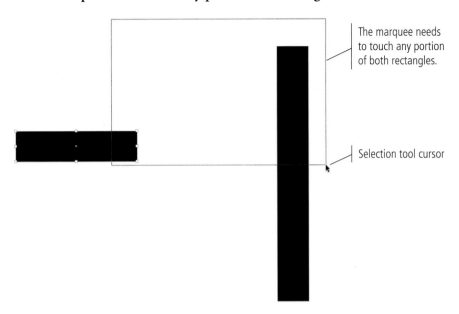

The marquee needs to touch any portion of both rectangles.

Selection tool cursor

15. With both objects selected, look at the Control bar above the document window.

Virtually any transformation that can be applied to the selected object(s) is available in the Control bar. You'll learn about most of these options in later projects; for now, however, you're going to use the alignment options to control the two selected objects.

These options are the same options you saw in the Transform panel.

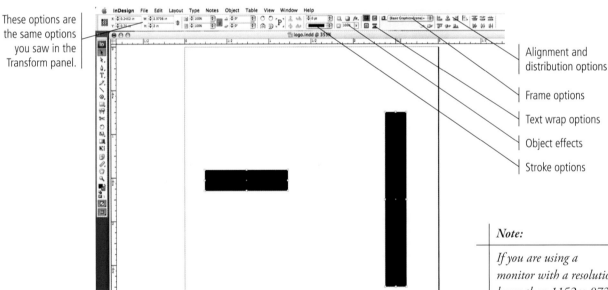

Alignment and distribution options

Frame options

Text wrap options

Object effects

Stroke options

16. In the alignment area, click the Align Horizontal Centers and Align Vertical Centers buttons.

You can use these options to align multiple selected objects to each other; align one or more objects to the page, spread, or margins; or distribute spacing between multiple objects.

Align Horizontal Centers

Align Vertical Centers

Note:

If you are using a monitor with a resolution lower than 1152 × 872 pixels, InDesign removes some options from the Control bar, including the Alignment and Distribution options. If you don't see the Align buttons in the Control bar, choose Window>Align and use the Align panel to complete these steps.

The center points of the two objects are now exactly on top of each other — and you can start to see the basic "T" shape.

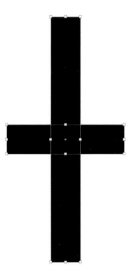

17. **Click anywhere away from the two objects to deselect them, and then click only the horizontal rectangle to select it.**

18. **Make sure the top-left reference point is selected. Click in the Y field of the Transform panel to place the insertion point at the end of the field, and then type "–0.5" (after the existing Y value).**

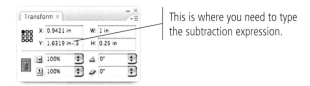

This is where you need to type the subtraction expression.

19. **Press Return/Enter to apply the change.**

If you want to move or change something by a specific value, InDesign can recognize mathematical transformations. In this case, you are subtracting 0.5″ from the Y (vertical) position — you're moving the object up by half an inch.

Note:

You can add, subtract, multiply, or divide values in an InDesign panel or dialog box. Use "+" to add, "–" to subtract, "" to multiply, or "/" to divide.*

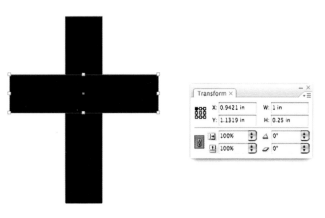

20. **Save the file and continue to the next exercise.**

The alignment and distribution options can combine to place objects in relation to each other, to the page, or both. The alignment options are fairly self explanatory; when multiple objects are selected, the objects will align based on the edge(s) or center(s) that you click.

Align Right Edges
Align Horizontal Centers
Align Left Edges
Align Top Edges
Align Vertical Centers
Align Bottom Edges

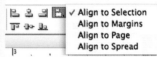

Distribute Top Edges
Distribute Vertical Centers
Distribute Bottom Edges
Distribute Right Edges
Distribute Horizontal Centers
Distribute Left Edges

The distribution options allow you to control the position of multiple objects relative to each other, or the position of a single object relative to the page. If you select multiple objects, you can use the distribution options to place equal amounts of space between the edge(s) or center(s) that you click.

If you click the button in the center, you can choose how one or more objects will align or distribute. You can use these options to align objects (for example) in the exact horizontal and vertical center of the page without making a single manual calculation.

✓ Align to Selection
Align to Margins
Align to Page
Align to Spread

Because you can align objects relative to the document, the align buttons are also available when only one object is selected, allowing you to align any single object to a precise location on the page.

CREATE AND EDIT ANCHOR POINTS AND CURVES

Vector objects are made up of line segments and anchor points, even if you don't create each point manually with the Pen tool. You can create many objects by starting with basic shapes, and then editing the points and segments to get the exact shape you want — in this case, the cross-piece of the T-square.

1. **With logo.indd open, use the Direct Selection tool to select only the horizontal rectangle.**

   Using the Direct Selection tool, you can access and edit the anchor points and curves that make up a shape.

   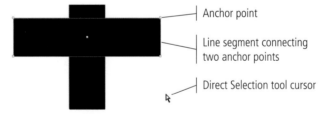

   Anchor point

   Line segment connecting two anchor points

   Direct Selection tool cursor

2. **In the Tools panel, click and hold the Pen tool and choose the Add Anchor Point tool from the pop-up menu.**

   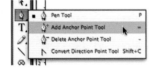

3. **Place the cursor over the top edge of the horizontal shape and click to add an anchor point to the line segment.**

   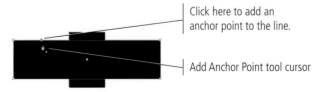

   Click here to add an anchor point to the line.

   Add Anchor Point tool cursor

4. **Repeat Step 3 to add two more points, using the following image as a guide.**

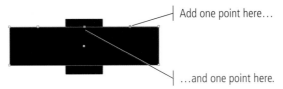

Add one point here…

…and one point here.

5. **Choose the Direct Selection tool and click the top-right anchor point of the rectangle.**

As we mentioned earlier, the Direct Selection tool is used to select parts of objects — in other words, you can use the tool to select individual anchor points that make up a shape.

6. **Press the Shift key, click the top-right anchor point, and drag down to make the right edge approximately one-fourth its original height.**

By pressing the Shift key, you constrain the point's movement to 45° angles — you can drag it straight up, down, across, or halfway between the two axes. (This technique works when moving any object or selection, using either selection tool.)

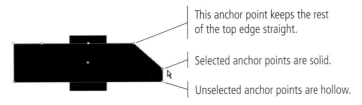

This anchor point keeps the rest of the top edge straight.

Selected anchor points are solid.

Unselected anchor points are hollow.

7. **Drag the remaining points on the top edge to match the shape in the following figure.**

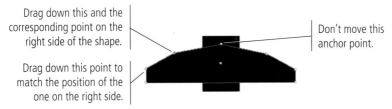

Drag down this and the corresponding point on the right side of the shape.

Drag down this point to match the position of the one on the right side.

Don't move this anchor point.

8. **Choose the Convert Direction Point tool (nested under the Add Anchor Point tool).**

Convert Direction Point tool

9. **Click the top-center anchor point of the shape and — without releasing the mouse button — drag to the left.**

The Convert Direction Point tool changes a corner point to a smooth point. **Smooth points** have handles that control the size and shape of the curves connected to the point. You can use the Direct Selection tool to drag individual handles for a selected anchor point.

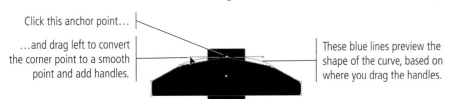

Click this anchor point…

…and drag left to convert the corner point to a smooth point and add handles.

These blue lines preview the shape of the curve, based on where you drag the handles.

Note:

The lines that connect anchor points based on the angle and length of the control handles are called Bezier curves.

10. Repeat Step 9 to add handles to the other two points on the top edge of the shape.

Convert and add handles to these two points.

11. Using the Direct Selection tool, drag the left-center point down and watch the effect on the curve handles.

The handles stay the same, but moving the point changes the shape of the connected curves because the other connected points have not changed.

Note:

Bezier curves can be difficult to master without a relatively deep understanding of geometry (at best) or trigonometry. The best training here is to practice until you can recognize and predict how moving a point or handle will affect the connected segments.

12. Select the point in the center-right side and drag it down to match the point on the left.

It doesn't have to be perfect; remember, this logo should suggest the idea of a T-square — it's not a photograph of a T-square.

13. Save the file and continue to the next exercise.

APPLY COLOR TO PAGE ELEMENTS

1. In the open logo.indd file, use the Selection tool to click the vertical rectangle to select it.

2. Choose Object>Arrange>Bring to Front.

You can use this menu to change the **stacking order** (the top-to-bottom order) of objects relative to each other. You can move the selected object(s) to the front or back of the stack using Bring to Front or Send to Back, or move objects one step up or back by choosing Bring Forward or Send Backward.

3. Collapse the Transform panel and click the Color icon in the panel dock to expand the Color panel.

4. In the Color panel, click the Fill swatch to bring it to the front (if it isn't already).

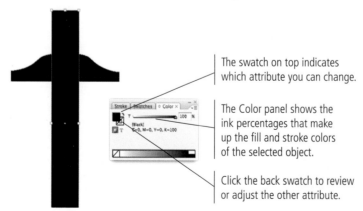

The swatch on top indicates which attribute you can change.

The Color panel shows the ink percentages that make up the fill and stroke colors of the selected object.

Click the back swatch to review or adjust the other attribute.

INDESIGN FOUNDATIONS

An anchor point marks the end of a line segment and the point handles determine the shape of that segment. That's the basic definition of a vector, but there is a bit more to it than that. You can draw Bezier shapes from scratch using the Pen tool, or edit the curves that are created as part of another shape (such as a circle).

Figure 1. Each segment in a path has two anchoring end points and two associated handles. We first clicked to create Point A and dragged (without releasing the mouse button) to create Handle A1. We then clicked and dragged to create Point B and Handle B1; Handle B2 is automatically created as a reflection of B1 (Point B is a **symmetrical point**).

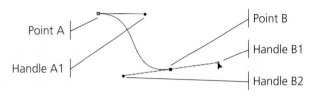

Point A
Handle A1
Point B
Handle B1
Handle B2

Figure 2. This image shows the result of dragging Handle B1 to the left instead of to the right. Notice the difference in the curve here, compared to the curve above. By dragging the handle, the segment arcs away from the direction of the handle.

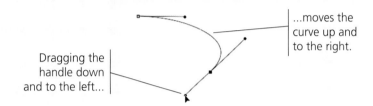

...moves the curve up and to the right.

Dragging the handle down and to the left...

Figure 3. It's important to understand that a segment is connected to two handles. Dragging the handle to the right pulls out the arc of the connected segment. You could change the shape of Segment A by dragging either Handle A1 or A2.

Handle A1
Segment A
Handle A2

Figure 4. Clicking and dragging a point creates a symmetrical point by default; both handles start out at equal length, directly opposite one another. Dragging one handle changes the position of the other handle of that point; the two handles remain directly opposite. (Dragging Handle B also moves Handle A, which affects the shape of Segment A.) You can, however, change the length of one handle without affecting the length of the other handle.

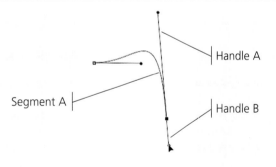

Handle A
Segment A
Handle B

Figure 5. You can create corner points by simply clicking with the Pen tool instead of clicking and dragging. Corner points do not have their own handles; the connected segments are controlled by the handles of the other associated points.

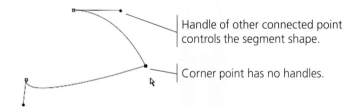

Handle of other connected point controls the segment shape.

Corner point has no handles.

Figure 6. You can convert a smooth point into a corner point by clicking the point with the Convert Point tool [ ] (nested under the Pen tool). You can also add a handle to only one side of an anchor point by Option/Alt clicking a point with the Convert Point tool and dragging.

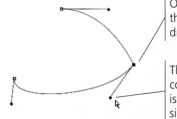

Option/Alt-click this point with the Convert Point tool and drag to create only one handle.

This handle controls the connected segment; the handle is not reflected on the other side of the point.

5. Click the Percentage field to the right of the slider and type "15". Press Return/Enter to apply the change.

You can change the color by typing a specific value or by dragging the slider below the color gradient.

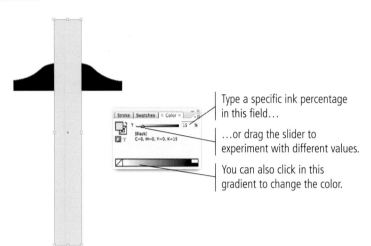

Type a specific ink percentage in this field...

...or drag the slider to experiment with different values.

You can also click in this gradient to change the color.

6. Click the Stroke swatch to bring it to the front, and then change the stroke value to 100% black.

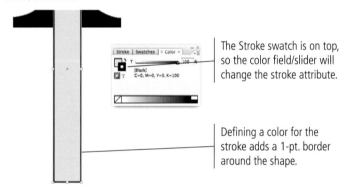

The Stroke swatch is on top, so the color field/slider will change the stroke attribute.

Defining a color for the stroke adds a 1-pt. border around the shape.

7. In the expanded panel group, click the Stroke tab to display the Stroke panel.

8. Click the arrow to the right of the Weight field and choose 0.25 pt.

You can type any specific value in the Weight field or choose one of the predefined weights from the menu.

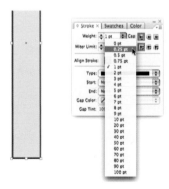

9. Using the same methods, select the horizontal cross-bar shape and change the fill to 85% black and the stroke to 0.25 pt. at 100% black.

10. Save the file and continue to the next exercise.

CREATE AND CONTROL LINES

InDesign includes two tools for creating lines: the Line tool for creating straight lines and the Pen tool for creating curved lines (although you can also create straight lines with the Pen tool). Working with straight lines is relatively straightforward, but don't dismiss them as inconsequential since straight lines are far more common than curved lines in a standard InDesign job.

1. **In the file logo.indd, click anywhere on the white space of the page to deselect both objects.**

2. **Select the Line tool in the Tools panel.**

    The vertical bar in the T-square is basically a ruler, which means it has marks indicating different measurements. You're going to use lines to add those marks. (The logo you're creating will be representational, so you don't have to be precise with these lines.)

3. **In the Stroke panel (with nothing selected on the page), change the Weight field to 0.25 pt.**

    The default value for new lines is 1-pt. black. For the marks on the ruler, 1-pt lines are too heavy, so you're going to create them at 0.25 pt.

4. **Near the top of the vertical "ruler", click about two-thirds of the way across, press the Shift key, and drag to the right edge of the rectangle.**

    Pressing Shift while drawing with the Line tool constrains the line to 45° increments.

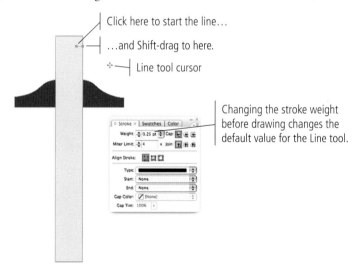

Click here to start the line…

…and Shift-drag to here.

Line tool cursor

Changing the stroke weight before drawing changes the default value for the Line tool.

Note:

You might want to zoom in to complete this stage of the drawing.

5. **Click away from the line to deselect it.**

6. **Using the Selection tool, click the line you just drew, press Option/Alt, and start dragging down. Before you release the mouse button, press Shift to constrain the movement to be perfectly vertical.**

    Pressing Option/Alt when you drag an object makes and moves a copy of the object (called **cloning**). By pressing Shift, you constrain the copy's movement to 45° increments so you can move the line exactly under the original.

This method only works if you precisely follow the directions in Step 6. If you Option/Alt-Shift-click-drag, you'll simply move the original. You must first Option/Alt-drag to make the copy, and then press Shift while you're dragging the copy. This technique also won't work unless you deselect the object before you Option/Alt-click-drag.

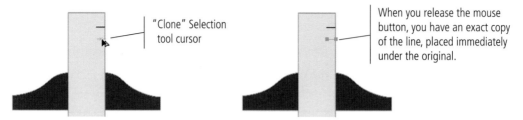

"Clone" Selection tool cursor

When you release the mouse button, you have an exact copy of the line, placed immediately under the original.

7. **Click away from the cloned line to deselect it, and then click it with the Direct Selection tool.**

8. **Click the left anchor point, and then Shift-drag that point to the right to make the second line shorter.**

   Rulers have both long and short marks, so your logo will as well.

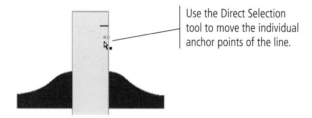

Use the Direct Selection tool to move the individual anchor points of the line.

9. **Using the cloning method you just learned, add more marks to the ruler, spaced randomly with no apparent pattern to the long-and-short line variations. Use the Selection tool to move the lines until you're satisfied with the result.**

10. **Choose View>Hide Frame Edges.**

    This command turns off the blue border that outlines the two shapes so you can see the actual stroke values. Frame edges can be very valuable when you're working with some objects, but they can be just as distracting in other cases (such as this one). Always remember that you can toggle the frame edges on and off in the View menu.

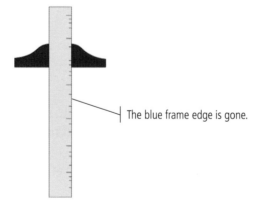

The blue frame edge is gone.

11. **Using the Selection tool, drag a marquee around the entire set of objects and choose Object>Group.**

By grouping the selected objects, those objects are now treated as a single cohesive unit — which is appropriate whenever more than one object makes up the entire design.

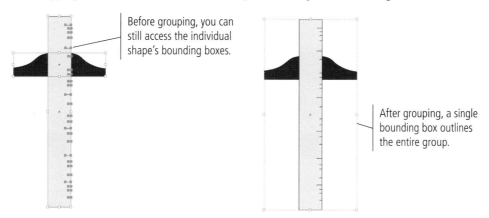

Before grouping, you can still access the individual shape's bounding boxes.

After grouping, a single bounding box outlines the entire group.

12. **Choose the Direct Selection tool in the Tools panel.**

Even when objects are grouped, you can still use the Direct Selection tool to access and modify the individual components of each grouped object.

Key Command:

Group objects by pressing Command/Control-G. Ungroup objects by pressing Command/Control-Shift-G.

13. **Switch back to the Selection tool and (with the group still selected) change the stroke weight to 0.5 pt.**

Changing a fill or stroke attribute when a group is selected affects all objects in the selected group.

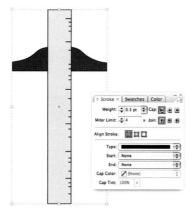

14. **Save the file and continue to the next exercise.**

CREATE IRREGULAR SHAPES WITH THE POLYGON TOOL

Many designs require shapes other than rectangles and ovals. The Pen tool can create complex objects of any shape, based on Bezier curves. The middle ground is creating straight-sided shapes with anything other than four sides — which is made easy using the Polygon tool.

1. **In the open logo.indd file, use the Selection tool to drag the existing group to the top-left corner of the page.**

2. **Choose the Polygon tool (nested under the Rectangle tool) in the Tools panel.**

INDESIGN FOUNDATIONS

The Stroke Panel in Depth

The Stroke panel includes considerably more options than the stroke weight. Most of these options are particularly relevant when working with thicker stroke weights; the thin blue line indicates the actual path, regardless of the specific stroke weight. The icons on the various buttons suggest what they do.

Toggle the Stroke panel options on and off in the panel options menu.

When the panel options are hidden, only the Stroke Weight field is visible.

The **Cap options** define the end treatment for a line segment; the end of a line can end exactly where the path ends, or it can extend beyond the end of the path with a rounded or flat cap. The Butt Cap option (left button) is the default setting.

Butt cap	Rounded cap	Projecting cap

The **Join options** determine the appearance of corner points. The default setting creates a mitered join, or you can choose rounded or beveled joins. The Miter Limit field specifies how long a corner point can be before it automatically converts to a beveled join; the miter limit is a factor of the stroke weight, so a setting of 2 means the corner point can be no more than 2 times the stroke weight.

Mitered join	Rounded join	Beveled join

The **Align Stroke options** determine where the stroke is placed in relation to the actual path. The default option aligns the center of the stroke to the path; you can also move the stroke entirely inside or entirely outside the path.

Align stroke to inside	Align stroke to outside	Align stroke to center

The lower half of the Stroke panel includes options for changing the stroke style or applying special end treatments such as arrowheads. If you choose a style that has a gap (a space between pieces of the style), you can also define a different color for the stroke gaps.

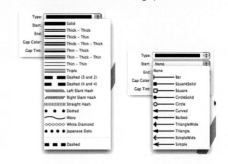

3. Click once on the right side of the page.

Clicking once opens the Polygon dialog box, where you can define the size of the new object, as well as the number of points and the inset percentage for every other point on the new shape.

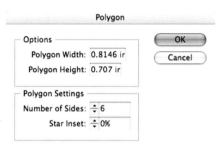

Note:

If you simply click and drag with the Polygon tool, you'll create a new shape with the tool's default settings.

4. Change the Width and Height fields to 1.5″. Change the Number of Sides field to 3, and make sure the Star Inset field is set to 0%.

5. Click OK to create the new shape.

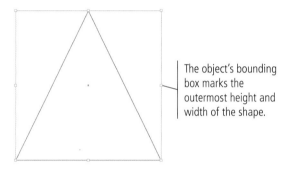

The object's bounding box marks the outermost height and width of the shape.

Note:

*To create a starburst, every other anchor point in the shape needs to be closer to the object's center. The **Star Inset** field determines how much closer those inside points will be to the center; an inset of 0% creates all points at the same distance from the object's center.*

6. Using the Direct Selection tool, click the top anchor point of the rectangle to select it.

7. Press Shift and drag the anchor point until the left side of the triangle is approximately vertical.

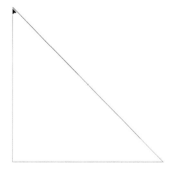

8. Switch to the Selection tool and choose Edit>Copy.

9. Choose Edit>Paste in Place to make an exact copy, exactly on top of the original.

10. **Choose the Scale tool in the Tools panel, and then click once near the center of the triangle (do not click the bounding box).**

    By default, the Scale tool treats the object's bounding box center as the reference point for the transformation; you can change the origin to any location by clicking once with the Scale tool.

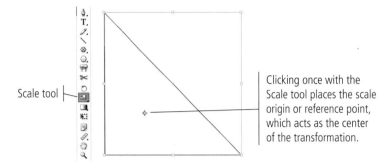

Scale tool

Clicking once with the Scale tool places the scale origin or reference point, which acts as the center of the transformation.

11. **Click the triangle's bottom-left bounding box handle, press Shift, and drag toward the center of the shape.**

    Pressing Shift constrains the object's proportions when you scale it.

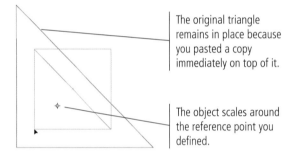

The original triangle remains in place because you pasted a copy immediately on top of it.

The object scales around the reference point you defined.

12. **Save the file and continue.**

 ## USE THE PATHFINDER TO CREATE COMPLEX OBJECTS

So far you've create basic shapes and lines and edited anchor points to create a non-standard shape. Some shapes require multiple paths (called **compound paths**) to create empty or void areas, such as the open space in the middle of the letter O or the middle of an architect's triangle. You use the Pathfinder to create this type of shape.

1. **In the open logo.indd file, use the Rectangle tool to create a rectangle that completely covers both triangles. Fill the rectangle with 50% black and send it to the back of the stacking order (Object>Arrange>Send to Back).**

    The two triangles have no fill color, so you can see the entire gray rectangle. You want the space between the two rectangles to be solid.

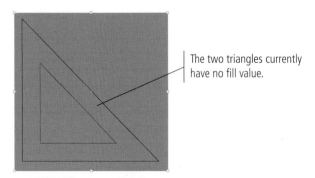

The two triangles currently have no fill value.

2. **Change the fill of the larger triangle to 0% black.**

There is a difference between no fill and 0% of a color. Using 0% of a color effectively creates a solid "white" fill. (In printing, solid white areas **knock out** or hide underlying shapes. A fill of None lets the underlying shape show through.)

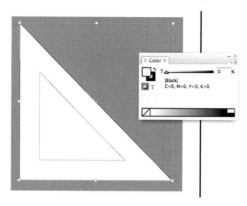

You now need to remove the inner triangle from the outer triangle so the gray background is visible in the center of the shape.

3. **Select both triangle shapes and expand the Pathfinder panel.**

4. **Click the Subtract button in the top half of the Pathfinder panel.**

The options in the Pathfinder panel can be used to combine multiple shapes or convert objects from one shape to another. The Subtract option removes the area of the front shape from the area of the back shape.

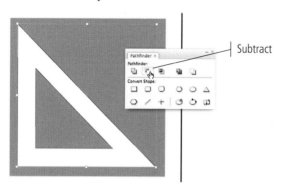

Note:

You can accomplish the same result by choosing Object>Paths>Make Compound Path.

5. **Delete the background rectangle, and then use the Line tool to add ruler marks around the outside edge of the triangle.**

6. **Select all the objects that make up the triangle and group them, and then change the stroke weight to 0.5 pt.**

Note:

You can return the two triangles to regular, individual objects by choosing Objects>Paths>Release Compound Paths.

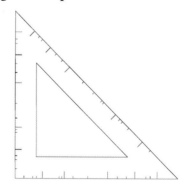

7. **Select the T-square group with the Selection tool.**

8. **In the Transform panel, open the panel options submenu and uncheck the Adjust Stroke Weight when Scaling option.**

   By default, scaling an object proportionally scales the stroke weight; for example, scaling a circle with a 2-pt. stroke by 50% results in a 1-pt. stroke. In this case, you want to maintain the 0.5-pt. stroke, so you are turning off this option.

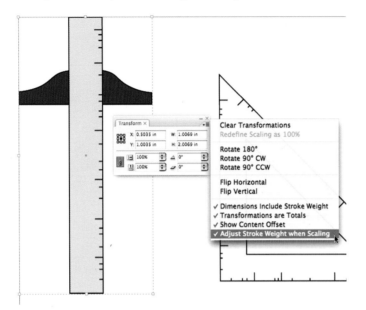

Note:

This option remembers the last-used setting. In many cases, you actually want the stroke weight to scale proportionally, so make sure you check this option if something looks wrong.

9. **Change the group width to 1″, the height to 2.5″, and rotate it by 15°.**

10. **Drag the triangle group to slightly overlap the ruler on the T-square group, leaving about 1/4″ space from the bottom of the triangle to the bottom of the T-square.**

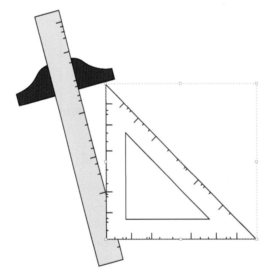

11. **Select both groups of objects and group them into a single group.**

12. **Using the Selection tool, make sure the drawing is inside the document page edges.**

13. **Save the file and continue.**

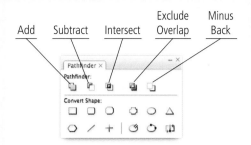

You can apply a significant number of transformations to objects using the Pathfinder panel. (The options in the Pathfinder panel are the same as those in the Object>Paths, Object>Pathfinder, and Object>Convert Shape submenus.)

The Pathfinder options allow you to create complex objects by combining multiple existing objects. When you use the Pathfinder options, all but the Subtract function applies the attributes of the front object to the resulting shape; the Subtract function maintains the attributes of the back object.

- **Add** results in the combined shapes of all selected objects.
- **Subtract** returns the shape of the back object minus any overlapping area of the front object.
- **Intersect** results in the shape of only the overlapping areas of selected objects.
- **Exclude Overlap** results in the shape of all selected objects minus any overlapping areas.
- **Minus Back** results in the shape of the front object minus any area where it overlaps other selected objects.

The Convert Shape options allow you to change the overall appearance of an object using one of the six defined, basic shapes or using the default polygon settings; you can also convert any existing shape to a basic line or an orthogonal (horizontal or vertical) line.

Finally, you can use the Path options to break (open) a closed path, connect (close) the endpoints of an open path, or reverse the path's direction (start becomes end and vice versa, which is relevant if you use stylized end treatments).

Stage 3 **Create and Format Basic Text**

Virtually every project you build in InDesign will involve text in one way or another. This logo project is no exception, even though you place and format only a single word.

InDesign is ultimately a page-layout application, not an illustration program. **Page layout** means combining text and graphic elements in a meaningful way to convey some kind of message. Text can be a single word (as in this logo), or thousands of pages of consecutive copy (as in a dictionary).

CREATE A SIMPLE TEXT FRAME

Digital page-layout software — especially InDesign — provides extremely precise control over virtually every aspect of every letter and word on the page. As you complete the projects in this book, you will learn how to control virtually every nuance of the text in your designs. For now, however, it's enough to learn how to place some text onto the page.

1. **In the open logo.indd file, select the Type tool in the Tools panel.**

2. **Click below the triangle and to the right of the T-square in the logo and drag down and right to create a text frame.**

   All text in InDesign (with the exception of type paths) must exist in a frame. To place text in a layout, you must first create the frame with the Type tool.

Note:

In an earlier exercise, you hid frame edges to see the thin strokes around shapes. If frame edges were visible, you would see a thin blue line marking the shape of the frame that you drew with the Type tool.

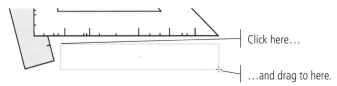

Click here...

...and drag to here.

When you release the mouse button, you see a flashing bar (called the **insertion point**) where you first clicked to create the text frame.

3. **Type "ASSOCIATES".**

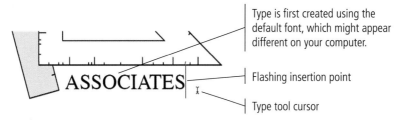

Type is first created using the default font, which might appear different on your computer.

Flashing insertion point

Type tool cursor

4. **Double-click the word you just typed to select it, and then expand the Character panel.**

   The Character panel presents a considerable number of options, most of which you will learn about later. For now, you need only to recognize the font and type size options.

5. **Click the arrow to the right of the Font field and scroll to find ATC Maple Ultra.**

Ultra is a variant of the ATC Maple font.

   The new font will be reflected in the document as soon as you choose it in the menu.

6. **Highlight the Type Size field and type "16", and then press Return/Enter to apply the change.**

   The Font menu shows every font available on your computer. If you choose a font variation from one of the submenus (such as Medium or Ultra, in this case), that variation automatically appears in the Font Variation menu of the Character panel.

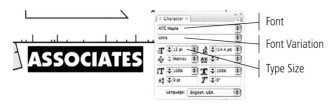

Font

Font Variation

Type Size

Note:

If any or all of your type disappears, you didn't make the text frame large enough. Use the Selection tool to enlarge the frame.

7. **With the text still selected, expand the Color panel.**

   Type is first set with a 100% black fill and no stroke. (You can apply a stroke to type, but you should be very, very careful when you do to avoid destroying the letter shapes.)

Selecting Text

You have a number of options for selecting type characters in a frame:

- Select specific characters by clicking with the Type tool and dragging.
- Place the insertion point and press Shift-Right Arrow or Left Arrow to select the character to the immediate right or left of the insertion point.
- Place the insertion point and press Shift-Up Arrow or Down Arrow to select all characters in the same position as the insertion point in the previous or next line.
- Place the insertion point and press Command/Control-Shift-Right Arrow or Left Arrow to select the entire word immediately to the right or left of the insertion point.
- Place the insertion point and press Command/Control-Shift-Up Arrow or Down Arrow to select the rest of paragraph immediately before or after the insertion point.
- Double-click a word to select the entire word.
- Triple-click a word to select the entire line that contains the word.
- Quadruple-click a word to select the entire paragraph that contains the word.

8. **Open the Color panel options menu and choose the CMYK color model.**

9. **In the Color panel, change the C (cyan) value to 100%, the M (magenta) value to 70%, and the K (black) value to 15%.**

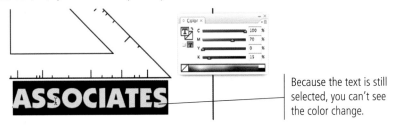

Because the text is still selected, you can't see the color change.

10. **Choose the Selection tool.**

Now that the text is no longer highlighted, you can see the change to the text color. (Remember, the Selection tool selects entire objects. In this case, the text frame is the object; you cannot select individual characters using the Selection tool.)

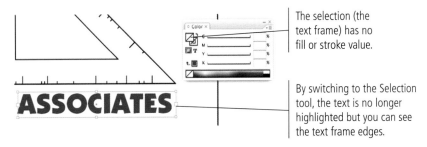

The selection (the text frame) has no fill or stroke value.

By switching to the Selection tool, the text is no longer highlighted but you can see the text frame edges.

11. **With the text frame selected, choose Type>Create Outlines.**

When a job is printed, any font used in the job must be available on the computer that sends the file to the output device. Logos need to be freely distributed to many different people on many types of systems, so it's best if you don't need fonts in a logo file. By converting the text to outlines, you eliminate the potential problem of a missing font file.

Note:

You can convert individual characters to inline objects by selecting specific characters before you choose Type>Create Outlines.

After converting the text to outlines, the text frame is gone; it is replaced by a bounding box for the group of letter shapes.

12. **Choose the Direct Selection tool in the Tools panel.**

Like any other drawing object, you can access the individual anchor points using the Direct Selection tool.

13. **Switch to the Selection tool, and then resize the group of letter shapes to completely fill the area below the triangle and to the right of the T-square.**

14. **Save the file and continue to the next exercise.**

EXPORT EPS FILES

Now that the logo is complete, you have to save it in the appropriate formats for the jobs you will create (the letterhead, business card, and envelope).

1. **With logo.indd open, choose File>Export and navigate to your WIP>Identity folder.**

2. **In the Format/Save As Type menu, choose EPS.**

   The EPS (Encapsulate PostScript) format is ideal for logo files since the format maintains vector data and supports transparency (the "holes" in a graphic where the paper color should show).

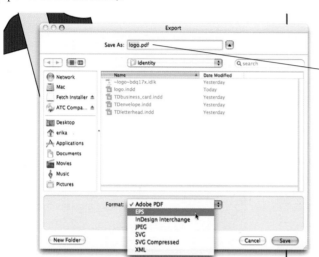

The file name defaults to the same name as the layout document you are exporting from. InDesign automatically adds the correct extension.

Why CMYK?

The CMYK color model, also called "process color," uses subtractive color theory to reproduce the range of printable colors by overlapping layers of cyan, magenta, yellow, and black inks in varying percentages from 0–100.

Using theoretically pure pigments, a mixture of equal parts of cyan, magenta, and yellow produces black. Real pigments, however, are not pure; the actual result of mixing these three colors usually appears as a muddy brown. The fourth color, black (K), is added to the three subtractive primaries to extend the range of printable colors and to allow much purer blacks to be printed than is possible with only the three primaries. Black is abbreviated as "K" because it is the "key" color to which others are aligned on the printing press. Using K for black also avoids confusion with blue in the RGB model.

In the following image, the left block is printed with 100% black ink. The right block is a combination of 100% cyan, 100% magenta, and 100% yellow inks.

In process color printing, the four process colors — cyan, magenta, yellow, and black (CMYK) — are imaged or separated onto individual printing plates. Each color separation is printed on a separate unit of a printing press. When printed on top of each other in varying percentages, the semi-transparent inks produce the range of colors in the CMYK gamut. Special (spot) colors are printed using specifically formulated inks as additional color separations.

3. In the Save As/File Name field, add "_cmyk" at the end of the file name and before the extension.

4. Click Save to see the Export EPS options, and then click Export.

5. In the layout, select the Associates group with the Selection tool.

6. **Expand the Swatches panel.**

   InDesign has a number of default options in the Swatches panel. There is one swatch for each primary color in the CMYK and RGB color models. There is also a special Registration color, which is used for trim and printer marks that need to appear on every separation of a job. [Paper] is basically white (a knock out), but the name used is more accurate because the paper for a particular job might not be white.

Note:

Clicking any of these swatches applies that color to the selected object in the document.

7. **Open the Swatches panel options menu and choose New Color Swatch.**

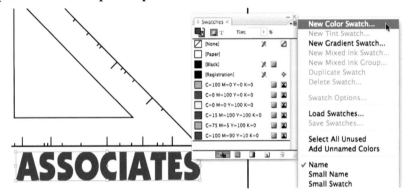

8. **In the New Color Swatch dialog box, choose Spot in the Color Type menu.**

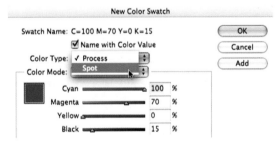

9. **Click the Color Mode menu and choose Pantone Solid Coated.**

   Spot colors are created with special premixed inks to produce a certain color with one ink layer. Spot colors are not built from the standard process inks used in CMYK printing. When you output a job with spot colors, each spot color appears on its own separation.

   These inks are used in two- and three-color documents, and they can be added to process-color documents when a special color, such as a corporate color, is needed. InDesign includes a number of built-in color libraries, including spot-color systems like Pantone, Toyo, and DIC.

   In the United States, the most popular collections of spot colors are the Pantone Matching System (PMS) libraries. TruMatch and Focoltone are also used in the United States. Toyo and DICColor (Dainippon Ink & Chemicals) are used primarily in Japan.

   Even though you can choose a color directly from the library on your screen, you should look at a swatch book to verify that you're using the color you intend. Special inks exist because many of the colors cannot be reproduced with process inks, nor can they be accurately represented on a computer monitor. If you specify special colors and then convert them to process colors later, your job probably won't look exactly as you expected.

Note:

When choosing special colors, ask your printer which ink system they support. If you designate TruMatch and they use Pantone inks, you won't get the colors you expected.

10. Place the insertion point in the Pantone field and type "2768".

You can also scroll through the list and simply click a color to select it.

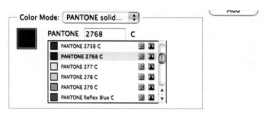

Note:

Spot colors are generally chosen from a swatch book — a book of colors printed with different inks, similar to the paint chip cards used in home decorating.

11. Click OK to return to the document window.

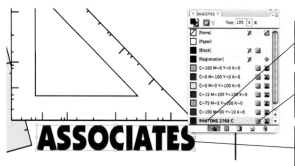

The new color swatch is added to the Swatches panel.

This icon indicates that the swatch is a spot color.

The selected object is automatically changed to the new spot color.

Export EPS Options

In the General tab, you can decide which page(s) you want to export, and whether to export single pages or entire spreads.

- **PostScript** defines compatibility with the different types of PostScript output devices (Level 2 or Level 3).

- **Color** specifies how color is represented in the exported file. Leave Unchanged leaves objects in their original color spaces. CMYK, Gray, and RGB convert all colors in the file to the respective color models.

- **Preview** controls the format of the embedded image preview for applications that can't display EPS files. TIFF can be viewed on Macintosh and Windows computers; PICT is a Macintosh-only file format.

- **Embed Fonts** specifies how to include fonts used in the pages you export. None does not embed the fonts; Complete embeds the entire font; Subset embeds only the necessary characters of fonts.

- **Data Format** determines how InDesign sends image data to a printer (ASCII or Binary).

- The **Bleed** fields determine how much of a bleed area will be included in the EPS file.

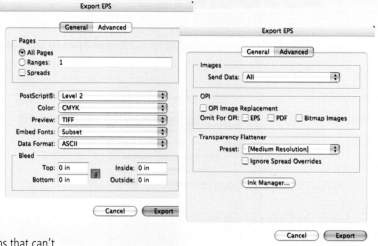

In the Advanced tab:

- **Images** determines how image data in bitmap images is included in the exported file. All embeds all high-resolution image data in the exported file; Proxy includes only low-resolution versions (72 dpi) of bitmap images.

- **OPI Image Replacement** is used if you are working in an Open Prepress Interface (OPI) server-based environment to replace low-resolution placement images with high-resolution graphics at output time. Omit For OPI selectively omits specific types of graphics.

- **Transparency Flattener** defines how transparent areas and effects are output; you'll learn about these options in Project 2.

12. **Choose File>Export, navigate to the Identity folder, name the file "logo_2c.eps", and click Save.**

Remember, the printer for this complete identity package wants to print the envelope as a two-color job. That's why you need both the four-color and two-color versions of the logo.

13. **In the Export EPS dialog box, make sure the Color menu is set to Leave Unchanged, and then click Export.**

You must use this option to maintain the spot color information in the EPS file instead of converting the color to CMYK.

14. **Close logo.indd.**

Stage 4 Creating a Cohesive Layout

Now that the logo is complete, it's time to put it together with the client's contact information. In other words, it's time to **lay out** the business card, letterhead, and envelope.

 PLACE EXTERNAL GRAPHICS FILES

1. **Open TDletterhead.indd from the WIP>Identity folder.**

2. **Click in the horizontal ruler and drag down to place a ruler guide at Y: 1.5".**

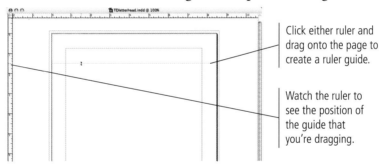

Click either ruler and drag onto the page to create a ruler guide.

Watch the ruler to see the position of the guide that you're dragging.

3. **Choose File>Place, navigate to the RF_InDesign>Identity folder and select blueprint_cmyk.tif.**

4. Click Open to load the cursor with the placed file.

You still have to place the loaded image in the document.

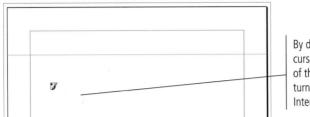

By default, the loaded Place cursor shows a small thumbnail of the file you're placing. You can turn off this feature in the Interface Preferences dialog box.

5. Click near the top-left corner of the page to place the image, and then use the Selection tool cursor to drag the image to the top-left bleed guides.

6. Click the bottom-center handle of the bounding box and drag up to the guide at 1.5".

Similar to text, every image in an InDesign layout exists in a frame; when you place an image, the containing frame is automatically created for you. When you edit the dimensions of a graphics frame, you do not affect the image contained within the frame.

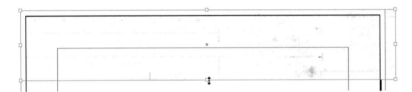

7. Drag a vertical guide from the left ruler to X: 1.5", and then drag the right-center bounding box handle of the graphics frame to the new vertical guide.

8. Show the Transform panel, and then click and drag around in the frame using the Direct Selection tool. Drag the picture until an area with detail shows in the frame.

If you want to affect the frame contents (the placed picture), you must use the Direct Selection tool.

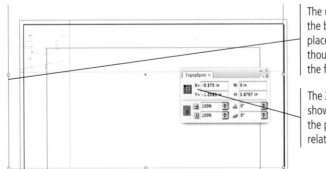

The red border shows the boundaries of the placed picture, even though they are beyond the frame edges.

The X and Y values show the position of the placed picture relative to its frame.

Note:

Even though you can't see the entire image, InDesign still has to process the hidden data when you output the file. Whenever possible, it's a better idea to crop the actual image in Photoshop and then place the cropped version into your InDesign layout.

9. **Using the Rectangle Frame tool, draw a frame directly over the blueprint image, using the page edge and the guides at 1.5″ as the frame boundaries.**

The Frame tools work exactly the same as the basic shape tools, except the result is a graphics frame instead of a simple shape.

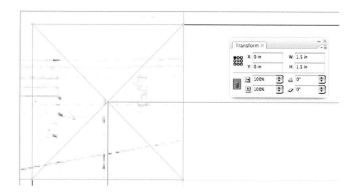

10. **With the empty frame selected, place the file logo_cmyk.eps from your WIP>Identity folder.**

If a frame is selected when you open the Place dialog box, the file is automatically placed into the frame instead of loaded into the cursor.

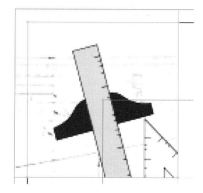

11. **Choose Object>Fitting>Fit Content Proportionally.**

You can use these menu options to resize the frame and its content relative to each other. Choosing Frame Fitting Options opens a dialog box where you can define how much to clip each edge of the image, the alignment reference point, and how content will be scaled when placed into an empty frame.

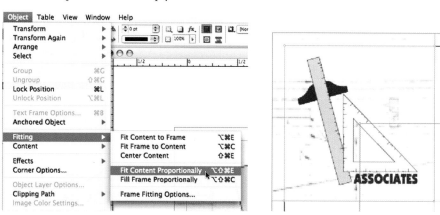

12. **Save the file and continue to the next exercise.**

PLACE AN EXTERNAL TEXT FILE

You already know how to create a text frame and type text. You can also import text that was created in an external text editor or word-processing application, which is a common situation when creating page layout jobs.

1. **With TDletterhead.indd open, make sure nothing is selected in the layout and choose File>Place.**

   If you leave the graphics frame selected from the end of the previous exercise, the text might be placed into the graphics frame — which isn't what you want.

2. **Navigate to contact.txt in the RF_InDesign>Identity folder and click Open.**

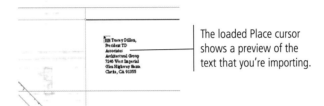

The loaded Place cursor shows a preview of the text that you're importing.

3. **Click the loaded Place cursor near the top page edge, directly to the right of the placed graphics.**

Placing text from a file automatically creates a text frame to contain the text.

4. **Using the Selection tool, drag the top and right edges of the text frame until they snap to the margin guides. Drag the bottom edge to snap to the ruler guide at Y: 1.5".**

5. **Choose Type>Show Hidden Characters.**

   Each line in this text is separated by a paragraph return character. When you reduce the height of the text frame, the seven paragraphs no longer fit within the available space.

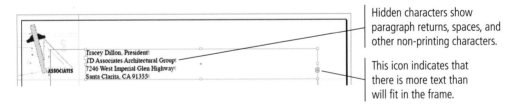

Hidden characters show paragraph returns, spaces, and other non-printing characters.

This icon indicates that there is more text than will fit in the frame.

6. **Choose the Type tool and click in the text frame to place the insertion point.**

7. **Choose Edit>Select All to highlight all the text in the frame (including the text you can't see).**

8. **Using the Character panel, change the selected text to 8-pt. ATC Pine Italic.**

9. **Select only the first line and change the text to 18-pt. ATC Maple Ultra.**

10. **Select only the second line and change the text to 13-pt. ATC Maple Medium.**

11. **Click at the end of the first address line to place the insertion point, and then press Shift-Right Arrow to select the paragraph return character.**

12. **Press the Spacebar twice, type the pipe character (Shift-Backslash), and then add two more spaces.**

    When you type with text highlighted, whatever you type replaces the highlighted text.

13. **Repeat Steps 11 and 12 to move all the contact information into the same paragraph.**

    Extra paragraph returns exist after the Web address, so InDesign thinks there is still more text than will fit. You should remove the extra paragraph returns to get rid of the overset text icon on the text frame edge. This problem is extremely common when working with imported text.

    Tracey Dillon, President
    TD Associates Architectural Group
    7246 West Imperial Glen Highway | Santa Clarita, CA 91355 | Phone: 661-555-0743 | Fax: 661-555-0744 | www.tdaag.com

    The extra paragraph returns cause the overset text icon to show.

14. **Place the insertion point at the end of the line and press the Forward Delete key to remove the extra paragraph returns.**

    You can't delete the end-of-story character.

    Tracey Dillon, President
    TD Associates Architectural Group
    7246 West Imperial Glen Highway | Santa Clarita, CA 91355 | Phone: 661-555-0743 | Fax: 661-555-0744 | www.tdaag.com

    The overset text icon is gone.

    Key Command:

    The Forward Delete key is below the Help key on Macintosh or the Insert key on Windows.

15. **Using the Color panel, change the color of the first line to C=100, M=70, Y=0, K=15.**

    If you only see a black slider in the Color panel, choose CMYK from the panel options menu.

16. **Save the file and continue.**

CONTROL PARAGRAPH FORMATTING

Character formatting includes any option that affects the appearance of selected characters, such as font, size, horizontal scale, and a host of others. Paragraph formatting options, on the other hand, affect an entire paragraph (everything between two paragraph return characters). Paragraph formatting can control everything from indents to the space between paragraphs to lines above and below paragraphs.

Note:

If you want to apply the same formatting to more than one consecutive paragraph, you can drag to select any part of the target paragraphs. Any paragraph that's even partially selected will be affected.

1. **With TDletterhead.indd open, drag a horizontal guide to line up with the bottom of the word Associates in the placed logo.**

2. **Place the text insertion point in the contact information paragraph and expand the Paragraph panel.**

3. **Adjust the Space Before Paragraph value until the contact information lines up with the guide you created in Step 1.**

   Changes to paragraph formatting apply to the entire paragraph; you only have to place the insertion point instead of manually selecting the paragraph.

4. **Using the Line tool, draw a 4-pt. horizontal line at Y: 1.5″ that bleeds past both page edges. Change the stroke color to C=100, M=70, Y=0, K=15 using the Color panel.**

   You can press Shift to constrain the line to horizontal while you draw it.

5. **Choose Preview in the Screen Mode menu at the bottom of the Tools panel.**

   Preview mode shows you the page without guides or frame edges. The pasteboard is gone, replaced by a gray background that runs up to the page edge.

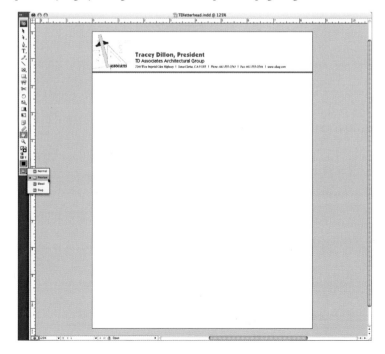

6. **Choose Bleed in the Screen Mode menu.**

The Bleed mode extends the Preview mode, showing the bleed area you defined in the New Document dialog box. You can use this mode to make sure all bleed objects extend far enough to meet the defined printer requirements. If any bleed object doesn't extend to the bleed edge, you should fix it before you output the file.

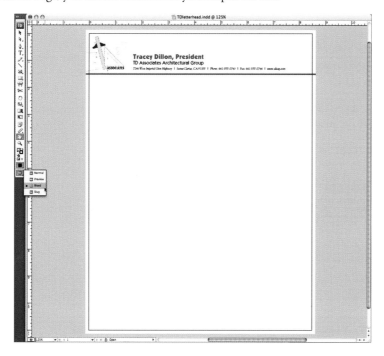

7. **Return to Normal screen mode, save the file, and continue to the next exercise.**

COPY OBJECTS AND IMPORT SPOT COLORS

By this point, you've learned how to create different types of objects, how to import external graphics and text files, and how to control various objects and frames on the page. You're now going to create the 2-color envelope, which uses many of the same skills you already know and expands on those skills in ways that are specific to designing with spot colors.

1. **Open the TDenvelope.indd file from your WIP>Identity folder.**

2. **Activate the letterhead layout and drag a marquee that selects all the objects at the top of the page except the horizontal line.**

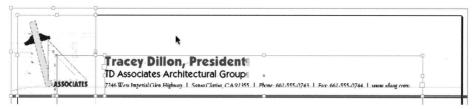

3. **Choose Edit>Copy, and then close the letterhead layout.**

4. **With the envelope layout window active, choose Edit>Paste.**

5. **Drag the pasted elements so the blueprint image extends 1/8″ past the top and left page edges.**

   You can copy elements from one layout to another by simply copying and pasting. This is a useful technique, but there are several problems in this case.

   First, the printer said the envelope layout can't bleed. You'll need to adjust the graphic elements to stay within the 1/4″ margin guides.

   Second, the envelope is going to be printed 2-color. The logo and blueprint image are both CMYK, as is the color used for your client's name. You need to replace these elements with the two-color versions.

   Third, the contact information is far too long for a business envelope. You'll need to reformat the text to be appropriate for an envelope.

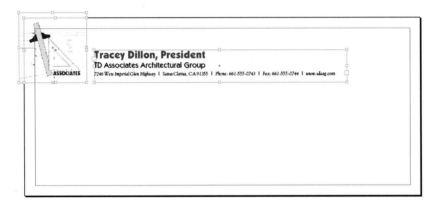

6. **Select the blueprint image with the Selection tool and choose File>Place. Navigate to the blueprint_grey.tif file and click the Replace Selected Item check box before clicking Open.**

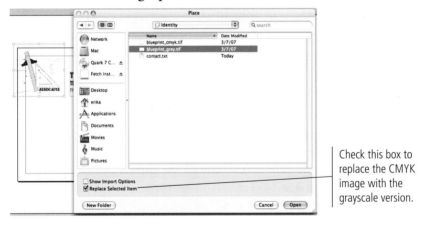

   Check this box to replace the CMYK image with the grayscale version.

7. **Drag the top-left corner of the graphics frame to the top-left margin guide.**

8. Using the same technique, replace the CMYK version of the logo with the 2-color version you created earlier (logo_2c.eps).

9. Drag the top-left corner of the graphics frame to the top-left margin guide, and then fit the content to its frame (Object>Fitting>Fit Content Proportionally).

10. With the logo frame selected, choose Object>Select>Next Object Below to select the blueprint image.

It can be difficult to select underlying objects, especially if they are completely covered by another object. The options in this menu allow you to easily navigate through the stacking order.

11. Expand the Swatches panel.

12. With the blueprint image selected, activate the Fill swatch in the Swatches panel, click the Pantone 2768 C swatch, and then change the Tint field to 10%.

This step illustrates two things: first, when you place an EPS file that was saved with a spot color, the spot color swatch is automatically imported into the InDesign Swatches panel.

Second, this technique of applying a color to grayscale images is a fairly common method for adding visual interest to 2-color print jobs.

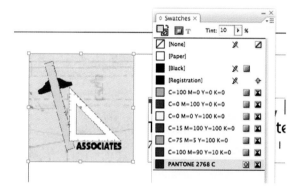

13. Drag a marquee to select both graphics frames, and then group them. Click the bottom-right handle of the group bounding box, and then press Command-Option-Shift/Control-Alt-Shift and drag up and to the left to resize the frames to about 1″ square.

Using all three modifier keys, you can dynamically resize both frames and their contained graphics.

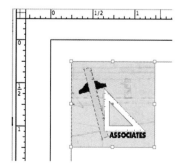

14. Drag the top edge of the text frame to the top margin guide, and the left edge of the text frame to be 1/8″ to the right of the graphics.

15. Make the following changes to the text:

- In the address line, delete all the text after the zip code (envelope return addresses typically don't include phone numbers or Web addresses).

- Change the first line of text to 12 pt. using the Pantone 2768 C color.

- Change the second line of text to 10 pt.

- Change the Space Before Paragraph value for the first address line to 0.02″.

- Add a paragraph return to move the city, state, and zip code to their own paragraph, and then delete the pipe character from the end of the address line.

- Change the Space Before Paragraph value for the city line to 0.

Note:

When you add a paragraph return, the 0.5″ Space Before Paragraph value is also applied to the new paragraph.

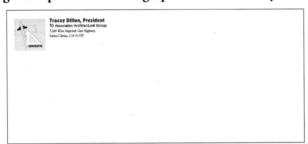

16. Save the file and continue.

 ## DESIGN THE BUSINESS CARD

Using all of the skills you've learned so far, complete the business card layout. Keep the following points in mind as you complete the layout:

- The most important point of a business card is to clearly present the contact information.

- The business card can bleed on all four sides.

- The business card will be printed as a four-color job. Use the CMYK versions of the blueprint and logo.

- You are building a complete identity package, so the different pieces should have a consistent look. Use whatever fonts you prefer, but if you use different fonts on the business card, you should also change the fonts on the letterhead and envelope.

Our solution is shown here; yours will probably be different in one or more ways.

Stage 5   Printing InDesign Files

For a printer to output pages at high resolution, some method of defining the page and its elements is required. These definitions are provided by specialized computer programs called Page Description Languages (PDLs). The most widely used PDL is Adobe PostScript; the current version is PostScript 3.

The PostScript PDL uses mathematics to define the shape and position of elements on a page. When a file is output to a PostScript-controlled device, the raster image processor (RIP) creates a PostScript print file that includes a mathematical description detailing the construction and placement of the various page elements. The print file precisely maps the address of each pixel on the page.

In the printer, the RIP then interprets the description of each element into a matrix of ones (black) and zeros (white). The output device uses this matrix to reconstruct the element as a series of individual dots or spots that form a high-resolution bitmap image on film or paper. PostScript makes computer files device independent — files can be printed at any resolution on a wide variety of PostScript output devices, from a 300-dpi laser printer to a 3,000-dpi imagesetter, with predictable results.

Not every printer on the market is capable of interpreting PostScript information. Low-cost, consumer-level inkjet printers, common in the modern graphic design market, are generally not PostScript compatible. Some desktop laser printers can handle PostScript, at least with an additional purchase. You should consult the technical documentation that came with your printer to make certain that you can print PostScript information.

The commercial printing industry operates almost entirely based on the PostScript page-description language. For this reason, the information presented in this chapter assumes you are using a PostScript-based printer. If your printer is non-PostScript compatible, some (possibly many) features in the Print dialog box will be unavailable.

Print Desktop Proofs

There are two important points to remember about using inkjet and laser proofs. First, inkjet printers are usually not PostScript driven. Because the commercial output process revolves around the PostScript language, proofs should always be created using a PostScript-compatible printer. If not, they will not accurately represent what will be output in final production. Second, inkjet and laser printers do not accurately represent color.

Having said that, every job leaving your workstation should be accompanied by a desktop proof. At its most basic, the desktop proof is an example of a file's contents at a given time. You'll generate several different versions of proofs as your job advances through the production process — from word-processed copy all the way to a full-size mockup of the finished layout. The final proofs you create and send to your service provider will serve as their bible when they produce your job. These proofs can't be close — they must be exact. Whether your job is a single-color business card or a multiple-color brochure, if you deliver a perfect set of proofs to your service provider, they have no excuse but to deliver a perfect job to you.

Additionally, you should confirm that the supplied proof shows the most recent version of a job file. Many designers create a laser proof, and then make just one more change to the file before submitting it to a service provider. When the service provider can't produce a proof that matches the one you supplied, the workflow stops until you verify that the disk file is the most current, and that the supplied proof is "mostly correct except for…"

Note:

You can purchase a software RIP (such as the one we use from Birmy Graphics) that will allow you to print PostScript information to some inkjet printers. Consult your printer documentation to see if this option is available.

1. **Open TDletterhead.indd from your WIP>Identity folder.**

2. **Chose File>Print.**

    The Print dialog box includes dozens of options in eight different categories.

    The most important options you'll select are the Printer and PPD (PostScript printer description) at the top of the dialog box. InDesign reads the information in the PPD to determine which of the specific print options are available for the current output.

3. **Choose the printer you want to use in the Printer menu, and choose the PPD for that printer in the PPD menu (if possible).**

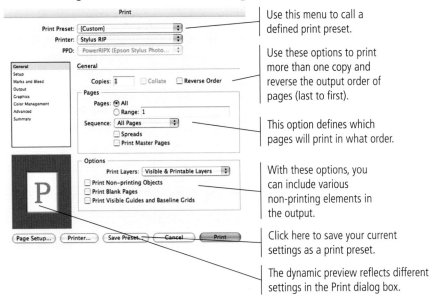

Use this menu to call a defined print preset.

Use these options to print more than one copy and reverse the output order of pages (last to first).

This option defines which pages will print in what order.

With these options, you can include various non-printing elements in the output.

Click here to save your current settings as a print preset.

The dynamic preview reflects different settings in the Print dialog box.

Note:

A print preset is a way to store many different settings in a single menu choice. You can save print presets just as you save document presets for creating new documents.

4. **Click the Setup option in the list of categories in the left pane.**

    These options determine the paper size that will be used for the output (not to be confused with the page size), the paper orientation, and page scaling and positioning options relative to the paper size.

5a. **If your printer can print to tabloid-size paper, choose Tabloid in the Paper Size menu, and then choose Centered from the Page Position menu.**

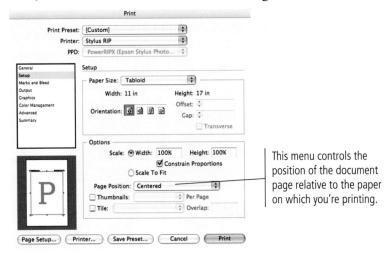

This menu controls the position of the document page relative to the paper on which you're printing.

5b. If you can only print to letter-size paper, choose the landscape paper orientation option, and then activate the Tile check box.

To output a letter-size page at 100% on letter-size paper, you have to tile to multiple sheets of paper; using the landscape paper orientation allows you to tile to 2 sheets instead of 4 (as shown in the preview area).

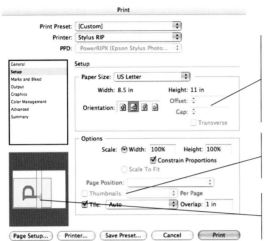

Offset and Gap fields should only be used when a job is output to an imagesetter or high-end proofing device. They define page placement on a piece of oversized film or on a printing plate.

Use this menu to print multiple-page thumbnails on a single piece of paper.

The overlap area is reflected in the preview; this area will print on both pieces of paper.

6. Click the Marks and Bleed option in the list of categories in the left pane. Activate the All Printer's Marks option and change the Offset field to 0.125″ (1/8″). Make sure the Use Document Bleed Settings option is checked.

You can specify individual printer's marks, or simply print them all. For proofing purposes, the crop and bleed marks are the most important ones to include.

Note:

Some printers require printer's marks to stay outside the bleed area, which means the offset should be at least the same as or greater than the defined bleed area.

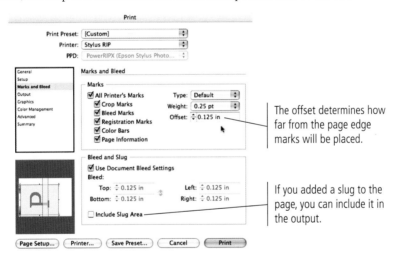

The offset determines how far from the page edge marks will be placed.

If you added a slug to the page, you can include it in the output.

Composite and Separation Proofs

INDESIGN FOUNDATIONS

Composite proofs print all colors on the same sheet, which allows you to judge page geometry and the overall positioning of all elements. You probably do this constantly as you work on the file, but it's important to supply the service provider with a final set as well. They need to know the overall look of the page as much as you do. Composite proofs should include **registration marks** (special printer's marks that are used to check the alignment of individual inks when the job is printed) and page information, and they should always be output at 100% size.

After you have verified page geometry and elements, you should print a set of **color-separated proofs**. This is your chance to make certain that everything will print in the exact color that you specified. When you print separated proofs, make certain that you print all of the colors in the layout.

You should review each page and confirm that each element is matched to the correct color. If you mistakenly left a spot color as process (or vice versa), nothing will alert you faster than separated laser proofs.

7. **Click the Output option in the list of categories in the left pane. If you can print color, choose Composite CMYK in the Color menu; otherwise, choose Composite Gray.**

In the Color menu, you can choose the color model you want to use. (If you have a black-and-white printer, this menu will default to Composite Gray.) If you chose either Separations option in the menu, the Inks list shows which inks (separations) will be included in the output.

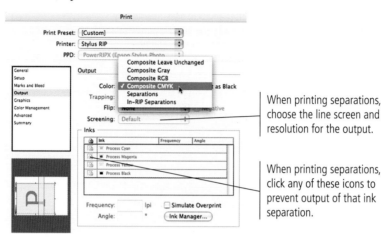

When printing separations, choose the line screen and resolution for the output.

When printing separations, click any of these icons to prevent output of that ink separation.

Note:

The other options (Trapping, Flip, Frequency, Angle, and Ink Manager) in this dialog box are reserved for high-end commercial output to a filmsetter or imagesetter.

8. **Click the Graphics option in the list of categories in the left pane.**

These are the same options you used when you saved the logo as an EPS file.

9. **Click the Advanced option in the list of categories in the left pane.**

These options are the same as those in the Advanced tab of the Export EPS dialog box.

Note:

We're intentionally skipping the Color Management options for now. Those options will be explained in depth in Project 6.

10. **Click the Summary option in the list of categories in the left pane.**

This dialog box presents a textual summary of the options you've chosen in the other categories. We rarely use this pane, but it's there if you need it.

11. **Click Print to output the page.**

12. **When the document comes back into focus, save and close it.**

13. **Using what you just learned about the Print dialog box options, print full-size proofs (with printer's marks) of the envelope and business card layouts. If necessary, tile the envelope layout to multiple sheets.**

14. **Close the layout files when you're finished.**

Summary

Although logos are more commonly created in Adobe Illustrator, InDesign has many of the tools you need to create sophisticated vector graphics like the logo you created in this project. You used the basic shape tools and the Pen tool, as well as the Pathfinder panel, to create the final logo to your client's specifications.

Once you completed the logo, you used one of the most basic — and most important — features available in InDesign: creating new documents to meet specific project needs. You learned how to define page sizes and margins, and how to define bleed settings to meet the printer's stated requirements. You also learned about document presets, which can save common page settings so you can later apply the same choices in a single click. To create the three different pieces, you learned about the difference between "four-color" and "two-color" and generated different versions of the logo for each type of job.

You also learned the very basics of working with text and graphics frames — creating the frames and adding content, then applying basic formatting to the text you created. You will build on these basic skills as you complete the rest of the projects in this book.

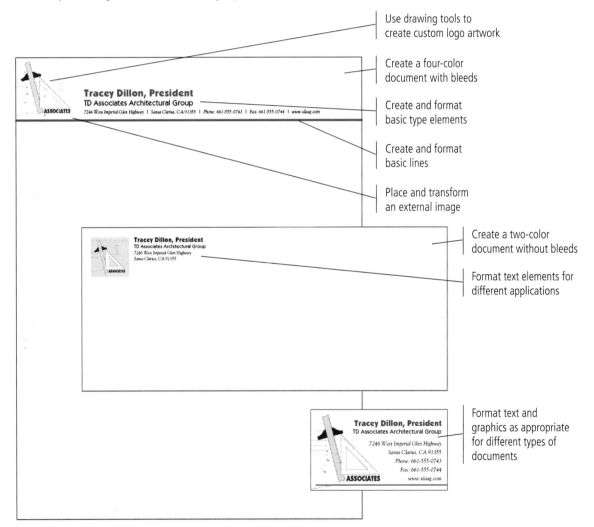

Use drawing tools to create custom logo artwork

Create a four-color document with bleeds

Create and format basic type elements

Create and format basic lines

Place and transform an external image

Create a two-color document without bleeds

Format text elements for different applications

Format text and graphics as appropriate for different types of documents

Portfolio Builder Project 1

The owner of your agency is pleased with your work on behalf of Tracey Dillon's new company. She has decided to create more formal branding for the design agency, and wants you to create a new logo and the accompanying collateral pieces with the new logo.

To complete this project, you should:

❏ Develop a compelling logo that suggests the agency's purpose (graphic design).

❏ Incorporate the agency's name (Creative Concepts) in the logo.

❏ Build the letterhead, envelope, and business cards with the same technical specs that you used to design the TD Associates pieces.

"We've been so busy since opening that we never really took the time to brand our own business. But if we want to continue growing and winning new clients, I think it's time we corrected that oversight.

"We've always focused on packaging design until now, but I want to diversify and offer a full range of graphic design solutions (corporate identity, direct mail, product marketing, etc.).

"For the logo, I want something that really says 'graphic design' — how can we convince clients that we can design their logos if we don't have a good design for our own? Find some kind of imagery that people will immediately recognize as graphics or art related.

"Use your own contact information as placeholder text for the collateral pieces. The business card needs to have space for a name, title, and email address. The letterhead should have the physical address, phone number, and Web site. The envelope should include only the physical address and Web site.

"Our agency's second anniversary is coming up in about a month, and I want to have a reception for clients and potential clients to celebrate. I'd like to unveil our new identity at the event, so you should finish this project within a week."

Festival Poster

Your client is the promoter for the Miami Beach Jazz Festival, which is held annually at several locations throughout the South Beach area. The client wants to create posters that will be plastered all over the city, from local restaurants and clubs to bus stops to construction sites that don't say "Post No Bills." This type of poster needs very little text, and it needs to be eye-catching from a distance — the graphics should be large and vivid, and the poster should have only a little bit of text set in a large, easy-to-read font.

This project incorporates the following skills:

❑ Creating a file with the appropriate settings for a four-color, commercially printed poster

❑ Using gradients, graphics, and image effects to attract the viewer's attention

❑ Adding text elements and applying formatting appropriate for a poster

❑ Threading a single text story across multiple text frames

❑ Understanding the different options for formatting characters and paragraphs

❑ Using inline graphics to highlight important text elements

❑ Creating a PDF file that meets the printer's requirements

The Project Meeting

The poster is basically the "play bill" for the festival, and it will be plastered all over the city. We want it to be really attractive and vivid so the main focus — and most of the poster real estate — is on the graphics. But the text also has to be readable; I emailed the text for the bottom of the poster this morning.

I found a great illustration of a saxophone player that we'd like to use as the main image. We were wondering if you can put text coming out of the end of the sax? If you can, this year's festival tag line is "Move Your Feet to the Beat." I also found some nice beach images that might be good backgrounds, so those are included as well. Our posters in the past have always been 11 × 17″, and we want to stick with that size.

We have all the pieces you need, based on what the client provided, so you can get started composing the layout. Most of this job is going to be compositing multiple images and formatting text. But I want you to go beyond basic image placement. InDesign includes a lot of tools for manipulating images; use some of those to make sure this poster consists of more than just plain pictures.

You already know the page size, and according to the printer the poster needs a 1/4″ bleed allowance just to be safe. The final poster should be saved as a PDF using the printer's specs, which I'll email to you.

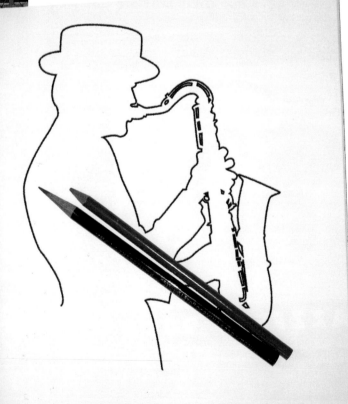

To complete this project, you will:

❏ Create a print layout using a master text frame

❏ Convert the content type of frames

❏ Create a custom gradient to add visual impact

❏ Create a custom frame using an image clipping path

❏ Apply visual effects to unify various graphic elements

❏ Thread the flow of text through multiple text frames

❏ Format text characters and paragraphs to effectively convey a message

❏ Place inline graphics to highlight important textual elements

❏ Create a PDF file for commercial output

Stage 1 Building Graphic Interest

In Project 1, you learned the basics of placing graphics into a layout and drawing shapes using built-in tools. You know that graphics and text are contained in frames, and that objects (including graphics frames) can have stroke and fill attributes. You can use those foundational skills to build virtually any InDesign layout.

InDesign also includes a number of options for extending your artistic options beyond simply compositing text and graphics that were finalized in other applications. The first stage of this project incorporates a number of these creative tools to accomplish your client's stated goal of grabbing the viewer's attention with vivid, attractive graphics.

Navigating InDesign Pages

INDESIGN FOUNDATIONS

Most InDesign projects — especially oversize ones like this poster — require some amount of zooming in and out to various view percentages, as well as navigating around the layout within its window. As we show you how to complete different stages of the workflow, we usually won't tell you when to change your view percentage because that's largely a matter of personal preference. But you should understand the different options for navigating around an InDesign file so you can easily and efficiently get where you want to go, when you want to go there.

Whatever your view percentage, you can use the Hand tool to drag the file around in the document window. This tool only changes what is visible in the window; it has no effect on the elements in the layout.

You can click with the Zoom tool to increase the view percentage in specific, predefined intervals from a minimum of 5% up to 4000%. When the Zoom tool is active, you can press Option/Alt to zoom out through the same predefined percentages. If you drag a marquee with the Zoom tool, you can zoom into a specific location; the area surrounded by the marquee will fill the available space in the document window. You can also type a specific view percentage in the field at the bottom left of the document window.

Alternatively, you can zoom in and out using the options in the View menu or their associated keyboard shortcuts. The zoom in/out options in the View menu step through the same predefined view percentages as clicking with the Zoom tool.

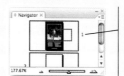

- Zoom In   Command/Control-Equal (=)
- Zoom Out   Command/Control-Hyphen (-)
- Fit Page in Window   Command/Control-Zero (0)
- Fit Spread in Window   Command/Control-Shift-Zero (0)
- Actual Size (100%)   Command/Control-1
- Entire Pasteboard   Command-Option-Shift-Zero/Control-Alt-Shift-Zero

One additional option — and perhaps the most versatile when navigating individual pages at close views — is the Navigator panel, which combines all of these navigation options in a small interface. (Another option, the Pages panel, is useful for navigating layouts with multiple pages. You'll learn about that panel in Project 3.)

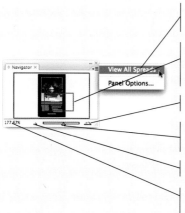

View the entire sequence of layout pages instead of only the current page.

Drag the red rectangle to change which part of the image is visible in the document window.

Click to zoom in in predefined steps.

Drag this slider to dynamically change the view percentage.

Click to zoom out in predefined steps.

Type in this field to see a specific view percentage.

When all spreads are showing, the page numbers appear to the left and right of each thumbnail.

DEFINE COLOR SWATCHES

The Swatches panel is used to apply predefined colors to any element in a layout. Six CMYK color swatches are included in the default set, as well as three special colors (Paper, Black, and Registration), and a None swatch that removes color from the selected attribute.

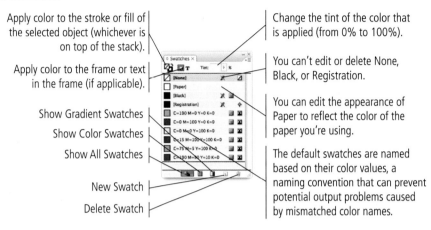

Apply color to the stroke or fill of the selected object (whichever is on top of the stack).

Apply color to the frame or text in the frame (if applicable).

Show Gradient Swatches

Show Color Swatches

Show All Swatches

New Swatch

Delete Swatch

Change the tint of the color that is applied (from 0% to 100%).

You can't edit or delete None, Black, or Registration.

You can edit the appearance of Paper to reflect the color of the paper you're using.

The default swatches are named based on their color values, a naming convention that can prevent potential output problems caused by mismatched color names.

Note:

Anything colored with the Registration swatch will appear on every separation in a job. This color should typically be used for special marks or other information placed outside the trim area.

You can define colors based on one of three color models (CMYK, RGB, or LAB), as well as call spot colors from built-in libraries of special inks. Each different mode and type of color has an identifying icon in the Swatches panel.

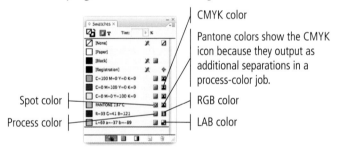

Spot color

Process color

CMYK color

Pantone colors show the CMYK icon because they output as additional separations in a process-color job.

RGB color

LAB color

Note:

Before completing this project, copy the Jazz folder from the WIP folder on your Resource CD to your WIP folder wherever you are saving your work. When you save files for this project, you will save them in your WIP>Jazz folder.

1. **Create a new file that is 11″ wide × 17″ high (Tabloid-size) with 1″ margins on all four sides and 0.25″ bleeds. Create the file with no master text frame and without facing pages.**

   Industry standards typically call for a 0.125″ bleed, but in this case the printer has specifically requested 0.25″ bleed allowance.

2. **Display the Swatches panel, and then open the panel options menu.**

   This menu has options for creating four types of color swatches: Color, Tint, Gradient, and Mixed Ink.

   - **Color** swatches and **Gradient** swatches are self-explanatory.

   - A **Tint** swatch is a specific stored percentage of another swatch, which is useful if you frequently use (for example) a 30% tint of C=100, M=42, Y=0, K=73. You can apply that tint with a single click, instead of applying the color, and then changing the tint of the applied color. Every click you save is a boost in productivity, especially if you are building layouts with more than a few different elements.

   - **Mixed Ink** swatches allow you to combine percentages of spot colors and process colors, or of multiple one-spot colors. This option is only available when at least one spot color exists in the file. (The **Mixed Ink Group** option allows you to build multiple swatches at once, based on specific incremental percentages of specific inks.)

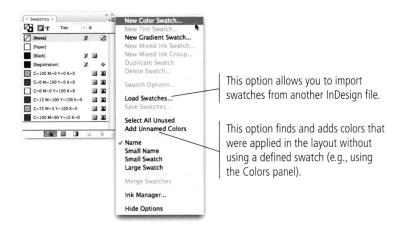

This option allows you to import swatches from another InDesign file.

This option finds and adds colors that were applied in the layout without using a defined swatch (e.g., using the Colors panel).

3. **Choose New Color Swatch in the panel options menu.**

4. **Leave the Name with Color Value option checked. Make sure the Color Type is set to Process and the Color Mode is set to CMYK.**

There is no industry standard for naming colors, but InDesign comes close with the Name with Color Value option. This type of naming convention — basing names on the color components — serves several purposes:

- You know exactly what components the color contains, so you can easily see if you are duplicating colors.
- You can immediately tell that the color should be a process build rather than a special ink or spot color.
- You avoid mismatched color names and duplicate spot colors, which are potential disasters in the commercial printing process.

Mismatched color names occur when a defined color name has two different values — one defined in the page layout and one in an image file that you place into your layout. When the files are output, the output device might be confused by different definitions for the same color name; the imported value might replace the project's value for that particular color name (or vice versa). The change could be subtle, or it could be drastic.

A similar problem occurs when the same spot color is assigned different names in different applications. For example, you might define a spot color in InDesign as "Border Color"; another designer might define the same spot color in Illustrator as "Spec Blue." When the illustration is placed in the InDesign layout, two different spot-color separations exist, even though the different color names have the same values.

5. **Define the color with 0% Cyan, 70% Magenta, 95% Yellow, and 0% Black, and then click OK.**

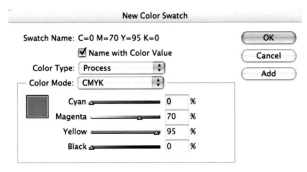

6. **Create two more process-color swatches using the following ink values:**

    Color 1: C=0, M=10, Y=75, K=0

    Color 2: C=0, M=40, Y=0, K=100

The third color, 100% black with 40% magenta, is called a **rich black** or **super black**. By itself, plain black ink often lacks density. Rich blacks are commonly used to add density or "temperature" to flat black; adding magenta results in "warmer" blacks and adding cyan results in "cooler" blacks.

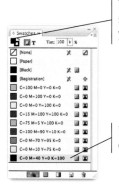

The top icon in the stack (fill or stroke) determines which attribute you will change.

Your three colors are all process colors using the CMYK model.

Note:

Using the Fill and Stroke swatches at the top of the Swatches panel, you can apply different colors to the fill and stroke of selected text.

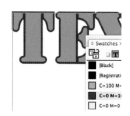

7. **Using the Rectangle tool, create a rectangle that covers the entire page and extends to the defined bleed guides. Fill the rectangle with the rich black color and apply no stroke color.**

8. **Save the file as "poster.indd" in your WIP>Jazz folder and continue to the next exercise.**

Color by Numbers

If you base color choices solely on what you see on your monitor, it would be safe to assume that your perfect blue sky might not look quite right when it's printed with process-color inks. Even if you have calibrated your monitor, no monitor is 100% effective at simulating printed color. As long as monitors display color in RGB, there will always be some discrepancies.

You should have some sort of process color chart, available from commercial publishers (some printers might even provide charts produced by the exact press on which your job will be printed). These charts contain small squares of process ink builds so you can see, for example, what a process build of C=10, M=70, Y=30, K=20 will look like when printed. These guides usually show samples in steps of 5% or 10%, printed on both coated and uncoated paper (because the type of paper or substrate can dramatically affect the final result).

When you define process colors in an InDesign project, you should enter specific numbers in the CMYK fields to designate your color choices, rather than relying on your screen preview. As you gain experience defining colors, you will become better able to predict the outcome for a given process-ink build. Rely on what you know to be true rather than what you hope will be true.

The same concept is also true when using special ink libraries. You should have — and use — swatch books with samples of the special inks. You can't rely on the monitor preview to choose a special ink color. Instead, find the color in a printed swatch book, and then enter the number in the Pantone field (for example) below the color swatches.

Total Area Coverage

When defining the ink values of a process-color build, you must usually limit your **total area coverage** (TAC, also called **total ink density**), or the amount of ink used in a given color. This might sound complex, but it can be easily calculated by adding the percentages of each ink in the color. If a color is defined as C=45, M=60, Y=90, K=0, the total area coverage is 195% (45 + 60 + 90 + 0). Maximum TAC limits are between 240% and 320% for offset lithography, depending on the paper being used. If you exceed the TAC limits for a given paper-ink-press combination, your printed job might end up with excess ink bleed, smearing, smudging, show-through, or a number of other printing errors because the paper cannot absorb all of the ink.

DEFINE AND APPLY A GRADIENT

A gradient, also called a blend, can be used to create a smooth transition from one color to another. You can apply a gradient to any object using the Gradient panel, or you can save a gradient swatch if you plan to use it more than once.

The Gradient panel controls the type and position of applied gradients. You can apply either linear or radial gradients, change the angle of linear gradients, and change the color and location for individual stops along the gradient ramp.

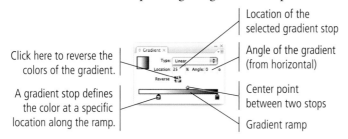

Click here to reverse the colors of the gradient.

A gradient stop defines the color at a specific location along the ramp.

Location of the selected gradient stop

Angle of the gradient (from horizontal)

Center point between two stops

Gradient ramp

1. **Make sure nothing is selected in the layout, then choose New Gradient Swatch from the Swatches panel options menu.**

2. **Click the gradient stop on the left end of the gradient ramp to select it.**

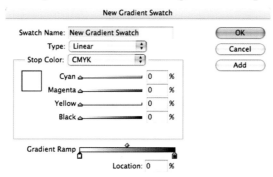

3. **Make sure Linear is selected in the Type menu, and then choose Swatches in the Stop Color menu.**

   You can define gradients using LAB values, CMYK percentages, RGB values, or existing color swatches.

4. **With the first stop selected, click the gold swatch that you defined in the previous exercise.**

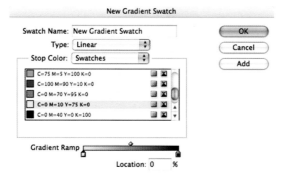

5. **Select the second gradient stop (on the right end of the ramp), and then click the orange swatch that you created earlier.**

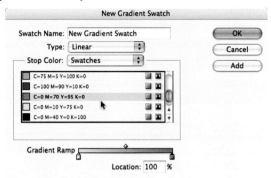

6. **Name the gradient "Gold to Orange" and click OK.**

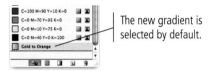

The new gradient is selected by default.

7. **Using the basic Rectangle tool, create a rectangle that fills the area within the margin guides.**

    The rectangle should be filled with the new gradient by default since that swatch was selected in the Swatches panel when you created this rectangle.

8. **Using either the Control bar or the Transform panel, activate the top-left proxy point and change the rectangle height to 10″.**

9. **In the Gradient panel (Window>Gradient), change the Angle field to 90° to rotate the gradient.**

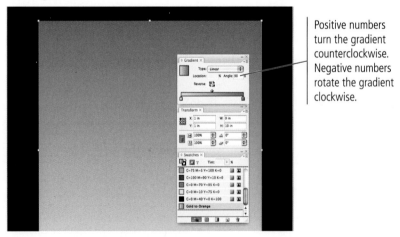

Positive numbers turn the gradient counterclockwise. Negative numbers rotate the gradient clockwise.

10. **Apply a 6-pt. stroke to the rectangle.**

11. **Click the Stroke swatch at the top of the Swatches panel to bring that attribute to the front, and then click the Gold to Orange gradient swatch to apply it to the stroke.**

    Remember, the attribute on top of the stack is the one you are currently changing. It is easy to forget this and accidentally change the fill instead of the stroke (or vice versa).

The Gradient Tools

Clicking a gradient swatch adds a gradient to the selected object, beginning at the left edge and ending at the right edge (for linear gradients), or beginning at the object's center and ending at the object's outermost edge (for radial gradients). When you drag with the Gradient tool, you define the length of the gradient without regard to the object you're filling. Using the Gradient tool, you can draw the gradient at any angle or length.

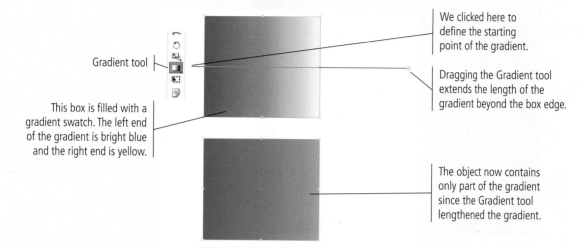

Gradient tool

We clicked here to define the starting point of the gradient.

Dragging the Gradient tool extends the length of the gradient beyond the box edge.

This box is filled with a gradient swatch. The left end of the gradient is bright blue and the right end is yellow.

The object now contains only part of the gradient since the Gradient tool lengthened the gradient.

The Gradient Feather tool, nested under the Gradient tool, has a similar function but produces different results. Rather than creating a specific-colored gradient, the Gradient Feather tool creates a gradient mask that blends an object from solid to transparent.

Gradient Feather tool

Clicking here defines the starting point of the gradient mask (the area that will be entirely solid).

Dragging here defines the end point of the gradient mask (the area that will be entirely transparent).

The gradient mask blends the object from solid to transparent, allowing background objects to show through.

12. In the Gradient panel, change the gradient angle to –90° so the stroke goes from gold at the top to orange at the bottom (the reverse of the fill).

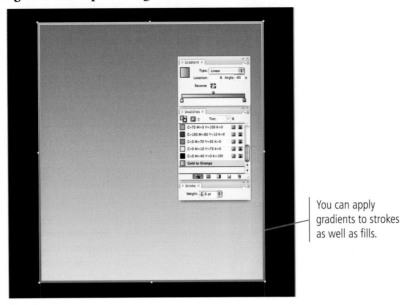

You can apply gradients to strokes as well as fills.

13. Save the file and continue.

 ## CREATE VISUAL IMPACT WITH TRANSPARENCY

The image effects and transparency controls in InDesign provide options for adding dimension and depth, allowing nearly unprecedented creative control directly in the page layout. You can change the transparency of any object (or individual object attributes), apply different blending modes so objects blend smoothly into underlying objects, and apply creative effects such as drop shadows and beveling.

Transparency and effects are controlled in the Effects panel. You can change these options for an entire object (fill and stroke), only the stroke, only the fill, the text (if you're working with a text frame), the graphic (if you're working with a graphics frame), or all objects in a group.

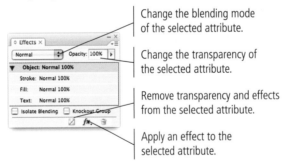

Change the blending mode of the selected attribute.

Change the transparency of the selected attribute.

Remove transparency and effects from the selected attribute.

Apply an effect to the selected attribute.

Note:

The Graphic option in the Effects panel is only available when a placed graphic is selected with the Direct Selection tool. Group replaces Object in the list only when a group is selected with the Selection tool.

Note:

Effects applied to text apply to all text in the frame; you can't apply effects to individual characters.

Technical Issues of Transparency

Because all of these features and options have some relation to transparency, you should understand what transparency is and how it affects your output. **Transparency** is the degree to which light passes through an object so objects in the background are visible. In terms of page layout, transparency means being able to "see through" objects at the top of the stacking order to objects at the bottom of the stacking order.

Because of the way printing works, applying transparency in print graphic design is a bit of a contradiction. Commercial printing is, by definition, accomplished by overlapping a mixture of (usually) four semi-transparent inks in different percentages to reproduce a range of colors (the printable gamut). In that sense, all print graphic design requires transparency.

But *design* transparency refers to the objects on the page. The trouble is, when a halftone dot is printed, it's either there or it's not. There is no "50% opaque" setting on a printing press. This means that a transformation needs to take place behind the scenes, translating what we create into what a printing press produces.

When transparent objects are output, overlapping areas of transparent elements are actually broken into individual elements (where necessary) to produce the best possible results. Ink values in the overlap areas are calculated by the application, based on the capabilities of the mechanical printing process; the software converts what we create into the elements that are necessary to print.

When you get to the final stage of this project, you'll learn how to preview and control the output process for transparent objects.

1. **In the file poster.indd, use the Selection tool to select the gradient-filled rectangle.**

2. **Choose Object>Content>Graphic.**

Note:

You can also Control/ right-click an object and change its content type in the contextual menu.

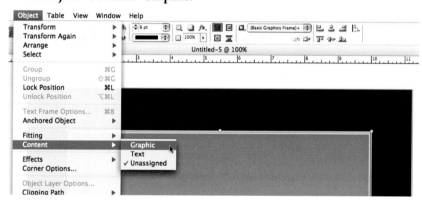

When you create a frame with one of the basic shape tools, it is considered "unassigned" because it is neither a text frame nor a graphics frame. You can convert any type of frame (graphics, text, or unassigned) to a different type using this menu.

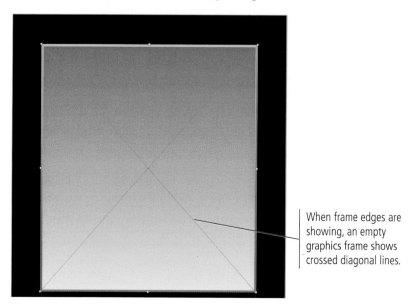

When frame edges are showing, an empty graphics frame shows crossed diagonal lines.

3. **Open the Interface Preferences dialog box, and make sure the Show Thumbnails on Place option is checked.**

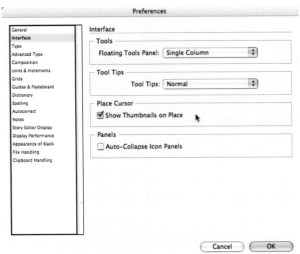

4. **Click OK to close the Preferences dialog box.**

5. **Choose File>Place. Navigate to the RF_InDesign>Jazz folder, choose sunset.jpg, and click Open.**

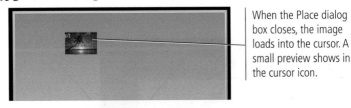

When the Place dialog box closes, the image loads into the cursor. A small preview shows in the cursor icon.

6. **Click the loaded cursor anywhere inside the gradient-filled graphics frame.**

By clicking the loaded cursor inside an existing frame, the image is placed inside the frame.

Note:

If Replaced Selected Item was checked in the Place dialog box, the image will be automatically placed into the selected frame.

Note:

If you click in an empty area when the cursor is loaded, the image will be placed where you click; a new graphics frame will be created using the image's dimensions.

7. **Open the Effects panel (Window>Effects).**

When you select an object with the Selection tool, you can apply different effects to the entire object, the object fill, the object stroke, or text within the object.

8. **Using the Direct Selection tool, click the sunset image to select only the image (not the frame).**

When you select only the placed image, you can apply effects to the image itself, independent of the frame.

Blending Modes

Blending modes control how colors in an object (blend colors) interact with colors in underlying objects (base colors). Objects are set to Normal by default, which simply overlays the top object's color onto underlying objects. (If the top object is entirely opaque, there will be no effect on underlying objects.)

- **Multiply** multiplies (hence the name) the base color by the blend color, resulting in a darker color. Multiplying any color with black produces black; multiplying any color with white leaves the color unchanged.

- **Screen** is basically the inverse of Multiply, always returning a lighter color. Screening with black has no effect; screening with white produces white.

- **Overlay** multiplies or screens the blend color to preserve the lightness or darkness of the base color.

- **Soft Light** darkens or lightens base colors depending on the blend color. Blend colors lighter than 50% lighten the base color (as if dodged); blend colors darker than 50% darken the base color (as if burned).

- **Hard Light** combines the Multiply and Screen modes. Blend colors darker than 50% are multiplied, and blend colors lighter than 50% are screened.

- **Color Dodge** brightens the base color. Blend colors lighter than 50% significantly increase brightness; blending with black has no effect.

- **Color Burn** darkens the base color by increasing the contrast. Blend colors darker than 50% significantly darken the base color by increasing saturation and reducing brightness; blending with white has no effect.

- **Darken** returns the darker of the blend or base color. Base pixels that are lighter than the blend color are replaced; base pixels that are darker than the blend color do not change.

- **Lighten** returns whichever is the lighter color (base or blend). Base pixels that are darker than the blend color are replaced; base pixels that are lighter than the blend color do not change.

- **Difference** inverts base color values according to the brightness value in the blend layer. Lower brightness values in the blend layer have less of an effect on the result; blending with black has no effect.

- **Exclusion** is similar to difference, except that mid-tone values in the base color are completely desaturated.

- **Hue** results in a color with the luminance and saturation of the base color and the hue of the blend color.

- **Saturation** results in a color with the luminance and hue of the base color and saturation of the blend color.

- **Color** results in a color with the luminance of the base color and the hue and saturation of the blend color.

- **Luminosity** results in a color with the hue and saturation of the base color and the luminance of the blend color (basically the opposite of the Color mode).

INDESIGN FOUNDATIONS

9. **With the Graphic item selected in the Effects panel, choose the Screen option in the Blending Mode menu.**

The image now blends into the gradient background, but there is still a hard line marking the bottom edge of the placed image.

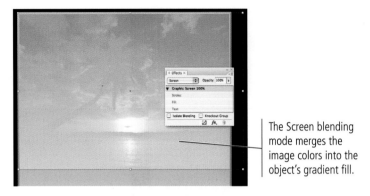

The Screen blending mode merges the image colors into the object's gradient fill.

10. **Click the FX button at the bottom of the Effects panel and choose Gradient Feather.**

This opens the Effects dialog box to the Gradient Feather options.

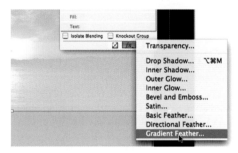

11. **In the Effects dialog box, click the Preview check box so you can preview your results before accepting/applying them.**

The Gradient Feather effect creates a gradient mask so an object can blend into underlying objects instead of leaving a hard edge. The mask is created using a black-to-white gradient. Anything under the black area of the gradient will be entirely visible and anything under the transparent area of the gradient will be hidden; areas in the middle of the gradient will be partially visible.

12. **Click in the Angle circle and drag until the field shows −90° (the line should point straight down).**

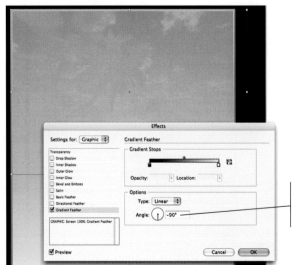

The angle changes the direction of the Gradient Feather effect.

Note:

When you create a mask with the Gradient Feather tool, the Gradient Feather effect is automatically applied.

13. Drag the left gradient stop until the Location field shows 75%.

By extending the solid black part of the gradient to the 75% location, the top three-quarters of the masked image will be entirely visible; only the bottom fourth of the image will blend into the background.

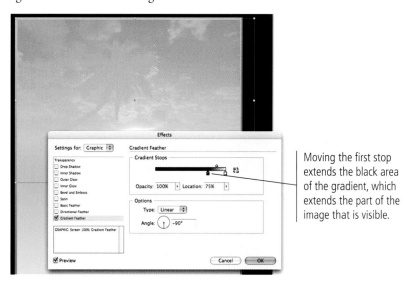

Moving the first stop extends the black area of the gradient, which extends the part of the image that is visible.

14. Click OK to close the Effects dialog box and apply your choices.

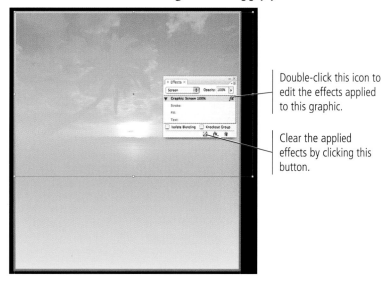

Double-click this icon to edit the effects applied to this graphic.

Clear the applied effects by clicking this button.

Note:

Effects in InDesign are non-destructive, which means that you aren't affecting the physical file data.

15. Save the file and continue to the next exercise.

InDesign offers nine different effects options, which you can apply individually or in combinations to create unique flat and dimensional effects for any object. The effects can be applied by clicking the FX button at the bottom of the Effects panel, by clicking the FX button in the Control bar, or by choosing from the Object>Effects menu.

Drop Shadow and Inner Shadow

Drop Shadow adds a shadow behind the object. **Inner Shadow** adds a shadow inside the edges of the object. For both types, you can define the blending mode, color, opacity, angle, distance, offset, and size of the shadow.

- **Distance** is the overall offset of the shadow, or how far away the shadow will be from the original object. The Offset fields allow you to define different horizontal and vertical distances.

- **Size** is the blur amount applied to the shadow.

- **Spread** (for Drop Shadows) is the percentage that the shadow expands beyond the original object.

- **Choke** (for Inner Shadows) is the percentage that the shadow shrinks into the original object.

- **Noise** controls the amount of random pixels that are added to the effect.

The **Object Knocks Out Shadow** option for drop shadows allows you to knock out (remove) or maintain the shadow underneath the object area. This option is particularly important if the original object is semi-transparent above its shadow.

The **Use Global Light** check box is available for the Drop Shadow, Inner Shadow, and Bevel and Emboss effects. When this option is checked, the style is linked to the "master" light source angle for the entire file. Changing the global light setting affects any linked shadow or bevel effect applied to any object in the entire file. (If Use Global Light is checked for an effect, changing the angle for that effect also changes the Global Light angle. You can also change the Global Light settings by choosing Object>Effects>Global Light.)

Outer Glow and Inner Glow

Outer Glow and **Inner Glow** add glow effects to the outside and inside edges (respectively) of the original object. For either kind of glow, you can define the blending mode, opacity, noise, and size values.

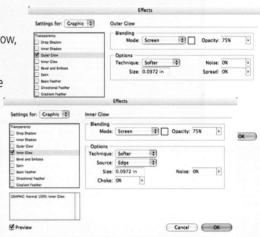

- For either kind of glow, you can define the **Technique** as Precise or Softer. **Precise** creates a glow at a specific distance; **Softer** creates a blurred glow and does not preserve detail as well as Precise.

- For Inner Glows, you can also define the **Source** of the glow (Center or Edge). **Center** applies a glow starting from the center of the object; **Edge** applies the glow starting from the inside edges of the object.

- The **Spread** and **Choke** sliders affect the percentages of the glow effects.

Bevel and Emboss

This effect has five variations or styles:

- **Inner Bevel** creates a bevel on the inside edges of the object.
- **Outer Bevel** creates a bevel on the outside edges of the object.
- **Emboss** creates the effect of embossing the object against the underlying layers.
- **Pillow Emboss** creates the effect of stamping the edges of the object into the underlying layers.

Any of these styles can be applied as **Smooth** (blurs the edges of the effect), **Chisel Hard** (creates a distinct edge to the effect), or **Chisel Soft** (creates a distinct, but slightly blurred edge to the effect).

You can change the **Direction** of the bevel effect. **Up** creates the appearance of the layer coming out of the image; **Down** creates the appearance of something stamped into the image. The **Size** field makes the effect smaller or larger, and the **Soften** option blurs the edges of the effect. **Depth** increases or decreases the three-dimensional effect of the bevel.

In the Shading area, you can control the light source's **Angle** and **Altitude** (think of how shadows differ as the sun moves across the sky). Finally, you can change the blending mode, opacity, and color of both highlight and shadows created with the Bevel or Emboss effect.

Satin

Satin applies interior shading to create a satiny appearance. You can change the blending mode, color, and opacity of the effect, as well as the angle, distance, and size.

Basic Feather, Directional Feather, and Gradient Feather

These three effects soften the edges of an object:

- **Basic Feather** equally fades all edges of the selected object (or attribute) by a specific width. The **Choke** option determines how much of the softened edge is opaque (high settings increase opacity and low settings decrease opacity). **Corners** can be Sharp (following the outer edge of the shape), Rounded (corners are rounded according to the Feather Width), or Diffused (fades from opaque to transparent). Noise adds random pixels to the softened area.

- **Directional Feather** allows you to apply different feather widths to individual edges of an object. The **Shape** option defines the object's original shape (First Edge Only, Leading Edges, or All Edges). The **Angle** field allows you to rotate the feathering effect; if you use any angle other than a 90° increment (i.e., 90, 180, 270, 360), the feathering will be skewed.

- **Gradient Feather** creates a gradient mask that blends from solid (black) to transparent. This effect underlies the Gradient Feather tool. You can move the start and end stops to different locations along the ramp, or add stops to define specific transparencies at specific locations. You can also choose from a Linear or Radial Gradient Feather effect, and change the angle of a Linear Gradient Feather effect.

CREATE AN IRREGULAR GRAPHICS FRAME

You can create basic graphics frames using the Rectangle, Ellipse, and Polygon Frame tools. You can also create a Bezier shape with the Pen tool, and then convert the shape to a graphics frame — which means you can create a frame in virtually any shape. However, it requires a lot of work to trace complex graphics with the Pen tool; fortunately, you can use other options to create complex frames from objects in placed graphics.

1. **Choose File>Place and navigate to the JazzManOutline.ai file in the RF_InDesign>Jazz folder.**

2. **Make sure the Replace Selected Item option is not selected, and then click Open.**

   If you had the gradient rectangle selected, and you did not uncheck the Replace Selected Item option, the jazz man image would be placed in the gradient-filled frame instead of being loaded into the cursor.

3. **Click anywhere in the white space around the page edge to place the graphic.**

4. **Using the Control bar or the Transform panel, position the top-left corner of the graphic at X: 1″, Y: 3.3″.**

5. **Click the placed graphic with the Direct Selection tool, and then choose Object>Clipping Path>Options.**

   A clipping path is a hard-edged outline that masks an image. Areas inside the path are visible; areas outside the path are hidden.

6. **Choose Detect Edges in the Type menu.**

   InDesign can access Alpha channels and clipping paths that are saved in an image, or you can create a clipping path based on the image content.

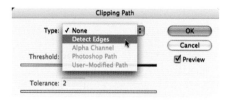

Note:

The User-Modified Path option is selected by default if you use the Direct Selection tool to edit the path in the layout.

Because this graphic is a vector graphic filled with a solid color with well-defined edges, InDesign can create a very precise clipping path based on the information in the file.

7. **Check the Include Inside Edges option.**

When this option is not checked, InDesign generates a clipping path based only on the outside edges of the image. As you can see, the Include Inside Edges option generates a compound clipping path that removes holes in the middle of the outside path. (This is the same principle you used in Project 1 to remove the interior of the architect's triangle.)

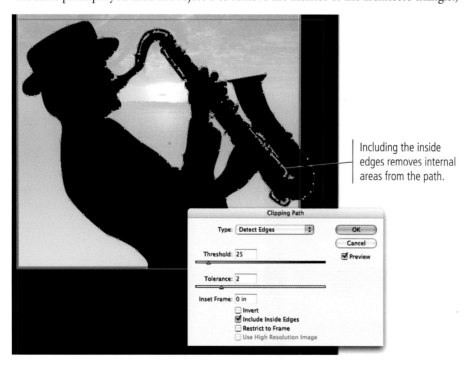

Including the inside edges removes internal areas from the path.

When you generate a clipping path in InDesign, you can refine the path using several different options.

Threshold specifies the darkest pixel value that will define the resulting clipping path. In this exercise, the placed image is filled with solid black, so you can set a very high Tolerance value to refine the clipping path. In images with greater tone variation (such as a photograph), increasing the Tolerance value removes lighter areas from the clipped area.

Tolerance specifies how similar a pixel can be to the Threshold value before it is hidden by the clipping path. Increasing the Tolerance value results in fewer points along the clipping path, generating a smoother path. Lowering the Tolerance value results in more anchor points and a potentially rougher path.

Inset Frame shrinks the clipping path by a specific number of pixels. You can also enter a negative value to enlarge the clipping path.

Invert reverses the clipping path, making hidden areas visible and vice versa.

Include Inside Edges creates a compound clipping path, removing inner areas of the object if they are within the Threshold and Tolerance ranges.

Restrict to Frame creates a clipping path that stops at the visible edge of the graphic. You can include the entire object — including areas beyond the frame edges — by unchecking this option.

Use High Resolution Image generates the clipping path based on the actual file data instead of the preview image.

8. **Click OK to close the dialog box and create the clipping path.**

9. **Choose Object>Clipping Path>Convert Clipping Path to Frame.**

10. **Using the Direct Selection tool, click inside the clipping path to select the JazzManOutline.ai file.**

11. **Press Delete/Backspace to delete the placed file but leave the frame you just created.**

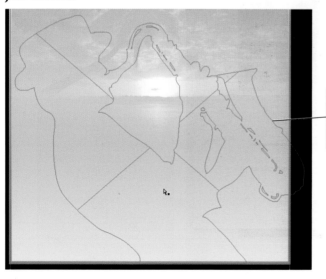

Deleting the original image leaves the frame that you created based on the InDesign-generated clipping path.

12. **Choose File>Place, navigate to palms.jpg in the RF_InDesign>Jazz folder, and click Open.**

13. **Click inside the empty frame with the loaded cursor to place the image inside the frame.**

14. **Using the Direct Selection tool, click the palms image to select it.**

15. **In either the Control bar or the Transform panel, change the image's position to X: –0.25″, Y: –0.25″.**

When you select an image with the Direct Selection tool, the Control bar fields define the position of the graphic *relative to* its containing frame. Negative numbers move the graphic up and to the left from the frame edge; positive numbers move the graphic down and to the right.

16. **Click the irregular frame with the Selection tool to select the frame (not the placed graphic).**

17. **In the Control bar, click the Drop Shadow button.**

This button applies a drop shadow using the default options; the Effects dialog box does not open.

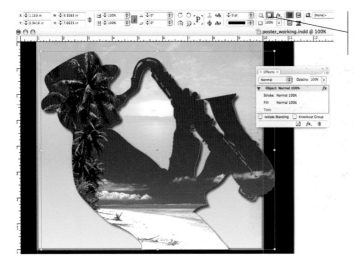

Click here to apply a drop shadow using the default settings.

18. **Save the file and continue to the next stage.**

Stage 2 Importing and Formatting Text

Placing text is one of the most important aspects of page-layout software, whether you create the text directly within InDesign or import it from an external file. InDesign provides all the tools you need to format text, from choosing a font to automatically creating hanging punctuation.

CONTROL TEXT THREADING

Some layouts require only a few bits of text, while others include numerous pages of text. Depending on how much text you have to work with, you might place all the layout text in a single frame, or you might cut and paste different pieces of a single story into individual text frames. In other cases, you might thread text across multiple frames — maintaining the text as a single story but allowing flexibility in frame size and position.

1. Using the Type tool, create a text frame that is 1″ high and 9″ wide (it fills the width between the margin guides). Using either the Control bar or the Transform panel, make sure the top-left corner of the text frame is positioned at X: 1″, Y: 11.25″.

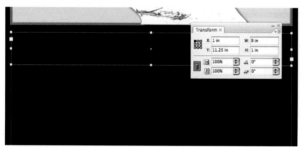

2. Create three more text frames using the following parameters:

Frame 2	X: 1″	W: 3.2″
	Y: 12.45″	H: 3.55″
Frame 3	X: 5″	W: 5″
	Y: 12.45″	H: 3.55″
Frame 4	X: 1″	W: 9″
	Y: 16″	H: 0.5″

Text Frame 1

Text Frame 2

Text Frame 3

Text Frame 4

3. Using the Selection tool, click in the white pasteboard area to deselect all the frames.

4. **Choose File>Place. Navigate to the file named jazzfest.doc in the RF_InDesign>Jazz folder and click Open.**

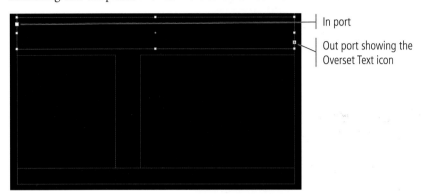

The cursor is loaded with the text file you selected.

Note:

If a frame were selected and the Replace Selected Item option checked, the text file would be placed directly into the selected frame.

5. **Click the loaded cursor in the first text frame.**

Whenever a text frame is selected, you can see the In and Out ports that allow you to link one text frame to another. In this case, the Out port shows the overset text icon, indicating that the placed file has more text than can fit within the frame.

In port

Out port showing the Overset Text icon

Note:

At this point, you can't see the text because text defaults to black, and your poster has a black background.

6. **Using the Type tool, click anywhere in the first text frame.**

When you click in a text frame with the Type tool, you see a flashing insertion point wherever you click (or in the top-left corner if there is no text in the frame). This insertion point marks the location where text will appear when you type or paste it into the document.

7. **Choose Edit>Select All to select all text in the frame (including the text that doesn't fit in the frame).**

The Select All command selects all text in the story, whether that story exists in a single frame or is threaded across multiple frames. This command also selects overset text that doesn't fit into the current frame (or thread of frames).

Note:

If you see the Overset Text icon (the red plus sign), the story does not fit in the current frame (or series of frames). You should always correct overset text.

8. **In the Swatches panel, make sure the Text icon is selected at the top of the panel, and then click the Paper swatch.**

In four-color (process) printing, there is no white ink. To achieve white, you have to remove the colors underneath the white areas, which is called a **knockout**. By removing or knocking out underlying colors, the paper shows through — whether white or some other color. (For example, if you print on yellow paper, knockout areas will show the yellow paper.) This is why InDesign refers to this swatch as "Paper" instead of "White."

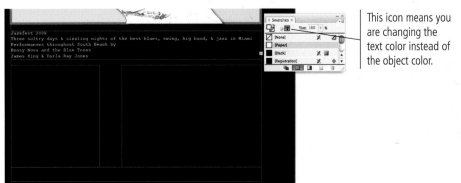

This icon means you are changing the text color instead of the object color.

9. **Using either Selection tool, click the Out port of the first text frame.**

   Clicking the Out port loads the cursor with the rest of the text in the story.

10. **Immediately click the second frame to link it to the first frame.**

11. **Repeat this process to link from the second frame to the third, and then from the third frame to the fourth.**

    You can define the thread of text frames even when there is no text to fill those frames. Simply use the Direct Selection tool to click the Out port of one frame, and then click the frame you want to add next in the thread.

12. **Choose View>Show Text Threads.**

    As long as this option is toggled on, you see the thread arrows whenever one of the text frames in the thread is selected.

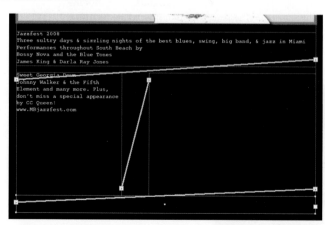

13. **Save the file and continue to the next exercise.**

Key Command:

You can also press Command/Control while the Type tool is active to click a text-frame Out port and thread the frames.

DEFINE MANUAL FRAME BREAKS

When you thread text from one frame to another (or to multiple columns in the same frame), you often need to control exactly where a story breaks from frame to frame. InDesign includes a number of commands for breaking text in a precise location.

1. **Using the Type tool, click at the end of the first line to place the insertion point.**

2. **Choose Type>Insert Break Character>Frame Break.**

   InDesign provides several special break characters that allow you to control the flow of text, from line to line, from column to column, and from frame to frame. The Frame Break character forces all following text into the next frame in the thread.

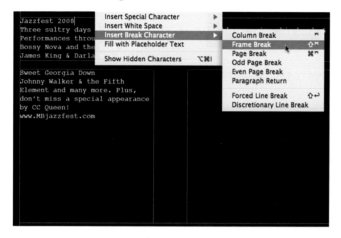

3. **Choose Type>Show Hidden Characters.**

   When you placed the Frame Break character at the end of the first line, everything following was pushed to the next frame — including the paragraph return character that had been the end of the first line.

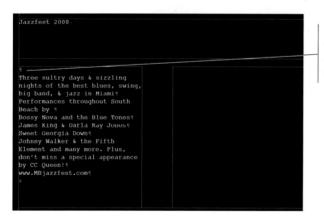

Hidden characters include the paragraph return character, spaces, and even the frame-break character.

4. **With the insertion point flashing at the beginning of the second frame, press Forward Delete to remove the extra paragraph return.**

5. **With hidden characters visible, highlight the paragraph return character at the end of the first sentence in this second frame.**

   To highlight the character, place the insertion point before the ¶ and press Shift-Right Arrow.

Note:

The Forward Delete key is the one directly below the Help/Insert key on most standard keyboards. If you are using a laptop, place the insertion point at the beginning of the first sentence in the second frame ("Three sultry days…") and press Delete/Backspace.

6. **Add another Frame Break character.**

When text is highlighted — including hidden formatting characters — anything you type, paste, or enter using a menu command replaces the highlighted text.

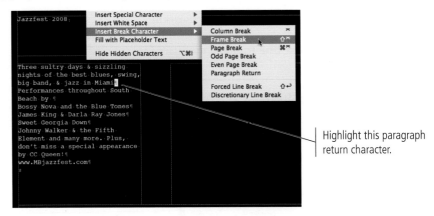

Highlight this paragraph return character.

7. **Use the same technique to move only the last paragraph (the Web address) into the fourth text frame.**

8. **Save the file and continue to the next exercise.**

Key Command:

Press Enter (on the numeric keypad) to add a Column Break.

Press Shift-Enter (numeric keypad) to add a Frame Break.

Press Command/Control-Enter (numeric keypad) to add a Page Break, which pushes all text to the first threaded frame on the next page.

Press Shift-Return/Enter to add a Line Break, which starts a new line without starting a new paragraph.

APPLY CHARACTER FORMATTING

Once text is in a frame, you need to define how it will look. Character formatting attributes determine the appearance of individual letters, such as the font and type size. These attributes can be controlled in the Character panel or the Control bar.

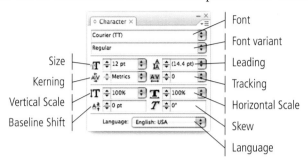

- A **font** contains all the characters (or **glyphs**) that make up the typeface, including upper- and lowercase letters, numbers, special characters, etc. (Fonts must be installed and activated on your computer to be accessible in InDesign.)

- **Size** is the height of a typeface measured in points.

- **Leading** is the distance from one baseline to the next. InDesign treats leading as a character attribute, even though leading controls the space between lines of an individual paragraph. (Space between paragraphs is controlled using the Space Before option in the Paragraph panel.) To change leading for an entire paragraph, you have to first select the entire paragraph. This approach means that you can change the leading for a single line of a paragraph by selecting any character(s) in that line; however, changing the leading for any character in a line applies the same change to the entire line that contains those characters.

- **Vertical Scale** and **Horizontal Scale** artificially stretch or contract the selected characters. This scaling is a quick way of achieving condensed or expanded type if those variations of a font don't exist.

- **Kerning** increases or decreases the space between pairs of letters. Kerning is used in cases where particular letters in specific fonts need to be brought together manually to eliminate a too-tight or too-spread-out appearance. Manual kerning is usually necessary in headlines or other large type. Many commercial fonts have built-in kerning pairs, so you won't need much hands-on intervention with kerning. InDesign defaults to use the kerning values stored in the **font metrics**.

- **Tracking**, also known as "range kerning," refers to the overall tightness or looseness across a range of characters.

- **Baseline Shift** moves the selected type above or below the baseline by a specific number of points. Positive numbers move the characters up; negative values move the text down.

- **Skew** artificially slants the selected text, creating a false italic appearance. This option badly distorts the look of the type and should be used sparingly (if ever).

Note:

You can change the default leading behavior by checking the Apply Leading to Entire Paragraph option in the Type Preferences dialog box.

Note:

Type that has been artificially condensed or expanded with the Scale options looks bad — the scaling destroys the type's metrics. You should use a condensed or expanded version of a typeface before resorting to horizontal or vertical scaling.

Note:

*Tracking and kerning are applied in thousandths of an **em** (or the amount of space occupied by an uppercase "M," which is usually the widest character in a typeface).*

In addition to the options in the basic Character panel, several type styling options are also available in the panel options menu or in the Control bar.

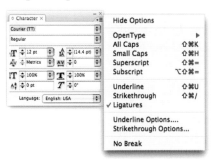 

- **All Caps** changes all the characters to capital letters. This only changes the appearance of the characters; they are not permanently converted to capital letters. To change the case of selected characters to all capital letters — the same as typing with Caps Lock turned on — use the Type>Change Case menu options.

- **Small Caps** makes lower-case letters look like small versions of capitals by artificially reducing the point size of a regular capital letter to a set percentage of that point size.

- **Superscript** and **Subscript** artificially reduce the selected character to a specific percentage of the point size; they raise (for superscript) or lower (for subscript) the character from the baseline to a position that is a certain percentage of the leading.

- **Underline** places a line below the selected characters.

- **Strikethrough** places a line through the middle of selected characters.

- **Ligatures** are substitutes for certain pairs of letters, most commonly fi, fl, ff, ffi, and ffl. (Other pairs such as ct and st are common for historical typesetting, and ae and oe are used in some non-English-language typesetting.)

1. **Triple-click the first line of text in the story to select it.**

2. **In the Character panel, change the highlighted text to 72-pt. ATC Maple Ultra.**

   There are three primary types of fonts: PostScript (Type 1), TrueType, and OpenType. InDesign identifies the font types with different icons in the Font menus.

   - **PostScript fonts** have two file components (outline and printer) that must both be available for successful output.
   - **TrueType fonts** have a single file, but (until recently) were primarily used on the Windows platform.
   - **OpenType fonts** are contained in a single file that can include more than 60,000 glyphs (characters) in a single font. OpenType fonts are also cross-platform, which means the same font file can be used on both Macintosh and Windows.

Note:

Many typefaces have an "expert" variation with "cut" small caps, meaning they were designed from the start to be used as small caps. OpenType fonts also often have Small Caps sets of extended characters.

Note:

The size and position options for Superscript and Subscript, as well as the size option for Small Caps, are controlled in the Advanced Type Preferences dialog box.

Note:

Choosing Underline Options or Strikethrough Options in the Character panel options menu allows you to change the weight, offset, style, and color of the line for those styles.

Note:

There are other types of fonts, including PostScript Type 3 and Multiple Master, but these should generally be avoided.

---

3. **Open the Character panel options menu and choose the All Caps option.**

4. **Change the Tracking field to 200.**

5. **Click four times on the paragraph in the second frame to select the entire paragraph.**

   Clicking twice selects an entire *word*, clicking three times selects an entire *line*, and clicking four times selects the entire *paragraph*.

6. **Change the selected text to 34-pt. ATC Pine Bold Italic.**

   Using these settings, the paragraph doesn't entirely fit in its available space (or at least, not yet). Because the frame is threaded, the paragraph flows into the third frame, and the rest of the text reflows accordingly.

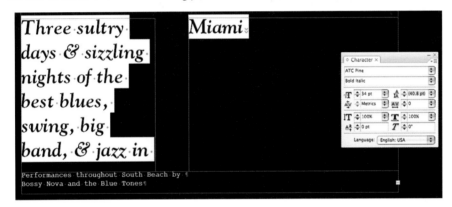

Note:

Leave the Leading at the automatic setting. By default, InDesign automatically applies leading as 120% of the type size.

7. **With the same text selected, change the Horizontal Scale field to 90%.**

   Horizontal and vertical scaling are useful for artificially stretching or contracting fonts that do not have condensed or extended versions. Be careful using these options, though, since the artificial scaling alters the character shapes and can make some fonts very difficult to read (especially at smaller sizes).

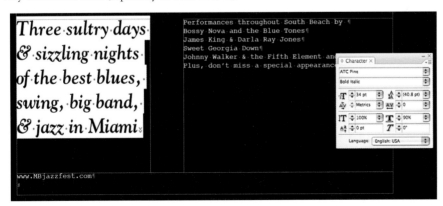

8. **Click four times to select the first paragraph in the third frame, and then drag down to select the other paragraphs in the same frame.**

   When you triple-click to select an entire line, dragging up or down selects the entire lines above or below the one you first clicked.

9. **With all the text in the third frame selected, apply 22-pt. ATC Pine Bold Italic with 90% horizontal scaling.**

10. **Change the Web address in the fourth text frame to 26-pt. ATC Maple Medium.**

11. **Save the file and continue to the next exercise.**

 ### APPLY PARAGRAPH FORMATTING

Paragraph formatting affects how your page looks and reads. Attributes that affect the entire paragraph — such as alignment, indents, and space before and after paragraphs — can be controlled in the Paragraph panel or the Control bar.

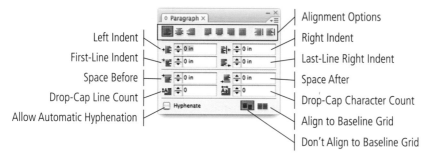

To apply paragraph formatting, you simply place the insertion point anywhere in a paragraph. Since paragraph formatting affects the entire paragraph, you don't have to select all of the text manually.

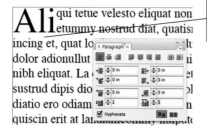

The paragraph doesn't have to be selected to apply paragraph formatting.

Understanding the Baseline Grid

The baseline grid is a type of non-printing guide used for controlling and aligning type. You can show the baseline grid by choosing View>Grids & Guides>Show Baseline Grid. You'll see a series of light blue lines that extend down the entire page in specific intervals.

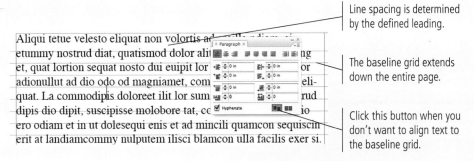

Line spacing is determined by the defined leading.

The baseline grid extends down the entire page.

Click this button when you don't want to align text to the baseline grid.

You can force paragraphs to align to the baseline grid, which overrides the defined leading.

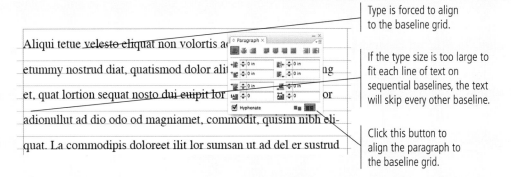

Type is forced to align to the baseline grid.

If the type size is too large to fit each line of text on sequential baselines, the text will skip every other baseline.

Click this button to align the paragraph to the baseline grid.

You can change the baseline grid in the Grids pane of the Preferences dialog box. The Start position can be relative to the top of the page (default) or to the top margin. You can also change the increment between lines (the default is approximately 1 pica). The View Threshold value determines the smallest view percentage at which the baseline grid will be visible.

1. **Place the cursor anywhere in the paragraph in the second frame.**

2. **In the Paragraph panel, click the Align Right button.**

   Paragraph formatting applies to the entire paragraph where the insertion point is placed, or to any paragraph that is entirely or partially selected. (A paragraph does not have to be entirely selected to change its paragraph formatting attributes.)

   The insertion point is placed in this paragraph.

Note:

In InDesign, a paragraph is defined as all text between two paragraph return characters (¶), even if the paragraph exists on a single line.

3. Place the insertion point anywhere in the fourth frame (with the Web address) and apply centered paragraph alignment.

4. Place the insertion point in the last paragraph of the third frame and apply right paragraph alignment.

5. Select any part of the first through fifth lines in the third frame.

6. In the Paragraph panel, change the Space Before Paragraph field to 0.09".

These settings apply to any paragraph that is entirely or partially selected.

7. Select any part of the second through fifth lines in the same frame and change the Left Indent field to 0.5".

8. Highlight the space character at the end of the fifth line (after the word "Element") and press Return/Enter.

When you break an existing paragraph into a new paragraph, the paragraph attributes of the original are applied to the new paragraph as well.

9. Place the insertion point at the beginning of the fifth paragraph (before "Johnny") and press Delete/Backspace.

10. Press Return/Enter to separate the two paragraphs again.

This is an easy way to copy paragraph formatting from one paragraph to the next. When you re-separate the two paragraphs, the "Johnny" paragraph adopts the paragraph formatting attributes of the "Sweet Georgia Down" paragraph.

11. Save the file and continue to the next exercise.

INDESIGN FOUNDATIONS

You can use the Eyedropper tool to copy character and paragraph attributes (including color), then apply those attributes to other type.

To copy formatting from one piece of text to another, simply click with the Eyedropper tool on the formatting you want to copy. If any text is currently selected when you click the Eyedropper tool, the selected text is automatically re-formatted. If nothing is selected, the Eyedropper tool "loads" with the formatting attributes — the tool icon reverses directions and shows a small I-beam icon in the cursor.

The Eyedropper tool cursor when it is "loaded" with formatting attributes.

You can click the loaded Eyedropper tool on any text to change its formatting, or click and drag to format multiple paragraphs at once. As long as the Eyedropper tool remains selected, you can continue to select text to apply the same formatting. You can also change the formatting in the Eyedropper tool by pressing Option/Alt and clicking text with the new formatting attributes that you want to copy.

By default, the Eyedropper tool copies all formatting attributes. You can change that behavior by double-clicking the tool in the Tools panel to access the Eyedropper Options dialog box. Simply uncheck the options you don't want to copy (including individual options in each category), and then click OK.

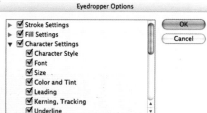

USE OPTICAL MARGIN ALIGNMENT

At times, specific arrangements of text can cause a paragraph to appear out of alignment, even though it's technically aligned properly. Punctuation at the beginning or end of a line — such as quotation marks at the beginning of a line or the commas in lines four and five of the second text frame — often cause this kind of optical problem. InDesign includes a feature called Optical Margin Alignment to correct this apparent problem.

1. **Hide the text threads and frame edges.**

   Although the paragraph is correctly right-aligned, the text in the second frame might appear off because of the commas at the ends of lines three and four.

   > Three sultry days
   > & sizzling nights
   > of the best blues,
   > swing, big band,
   > & jazz in Miami

   Note:

   You might want to toggle the visibility of frame edges (View>Show Frame Edges) as you work on this exercise.

2. **Open the Story panel (Window>Type & Tables>Story) and make sure the Optical Margin Alignment option is checked.**

   When Optical Margin Alignment is turned on, punctuation marks move outside the text margins (either to the left for left-aligned text or right for right-aligned text). Moving punctuation outside the margins is often referred to as **hanging punctuation**.

3. **Place the insertion point in the first paragraph (the one that now infringes on the second frame).**

4. **Choose Ignore Optical Margin in the Paragraph panel options menu.**

   The Optical Margin Alignment option applies to an entire story (including all text frames in the same thread), not just the selected paragraph. If necessary, you have to manually turn it off for individual paragraphs.

The insertion point is in the first paragraph, which was thrown off by turning on the Optical Margin Alignment option.

5. **In the Story panel, change the Size field to 34 pt.**

   The field in the Story panel tells InDesign what size type needs to be adjusted. The best effect is usually created by defining the size of the type that needs adjusting.

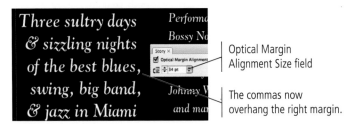

Optical Margin Alignment Size field

The commas now overhang the right margin.

6. **Save the file and continue to the next stage of the project.**

Stage 3 Graphics as Text and Text as Graphics

Now that you are familiar with the basic options for formatting characters and paragraphs, you can begin to add style to a layout using two different techniques — flowing text along a path, and placing graphics inline with text. (There is, of course, a lot more to learn about working with text than what you're doing in this project. You'll learn all the different options as you complete the rest of the projects in this book.)

PLACE INLINE GRAPHICS

The graphics frames you create on a page float over the other elements in the layout. You can position graphics frames over other objects to hide underlying elements, or you can apply a runaround so text wraps around a picture box.

You can also place images as inline graphics, which means they are anchored to the text in the position you place them. If the text reflows in the text box, inline objects reflow with the text and maintain the correct position. This feature can be very useful for placing custom bullets (which you will do in this exercise), or for a variety of other purposes where sidebar text needs to remain in proximity to the main body copy.

There are two methods for creating inline objects. For simple applications, such as a graphic bullet, you can simply place the graphic and format it as a text character. (An inline graphic is treated as a single text character in the story; it is affected by many of the paragraph-formatting commands, such as space before and after, tab settings, leading, and baseline position.) For more complex applications, you can use the options in the Object>Anchored Object menu.

1. **Place the insertion point at the beginning of the second line in the third frame (before the word "Bossy").**

2. **Choose File>Place and navigate to note.ai in the RF_InDesign>Jazz folder.**

3. **Make sure the Replace Selected Item option is checked, and then click Open.**

   If the insertion point is flashing in a story when you place a graphic using the Replace Selected Item option, the graphic is automatically placed as an inline object.

The line spacing automatically adjusts to accommodate the placed image.

Note:

You can also select an existing object, cut or copy it, place the insertion point, and then paste the object inline where the insertion point flashes.

4. **Select the inline graphic with the Selection tool, and then scale the graphic and frame to 50% horizontally and vertically.**

   Although inline graphics are anchored to the text, they are still graphics contained in graphics frames. You can apply the same transformations that you would to any other placed graphic.

Note:

When you select the frame with the Selection tool, resizing the frame also resizes the frame content.

5. **Choose Object>Anchored Object>Options.**

6. **Make sure the Inline option is checked, and change the Y Offset field to –0.07".**

   A negative number moves the anchored object down; a positive number moves the anchored object up.

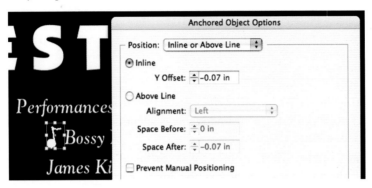

7. **Click OK, and then place the insertion point between the anchored object and the letter "B."**

8. **Press Shift-Left Arrow to select the anchored object, and then copy the highlighted object/character.**

9. **Place the insertion point at the beginning of the next paragraph and paste the copied object.**

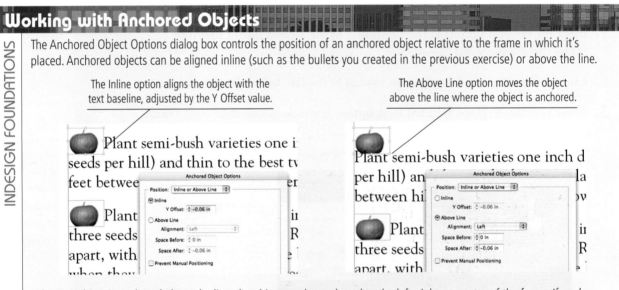

The Anchored Object Options dialog box controls the position of an anchored object relative to the frame in which it's placed. Anchored objects can be aligned inline (such as the bullets you created in the previous exercise) or above the line.

The Inline option aligns the object with the text baseline, adjusted by the Y Offset value.

The Above Line option moves the object above the line where the object is anchored.

When an object is anchored above the line, the object can be anchored to the left, right, or center of the frame. If you're using facing pages, you can also choose **Toward Spine** or **Away from Spine** so the anchored object will be placed in the appropriate position relative to the spread center (for example, all sidebars have to be on the inside edge near the spine). Finally, you can choose **Text Alignment**, which is the alignment applied to the paragraph (including indent values).

When you use the Above Line option, you can also define the space before and after the anchored object. The Space Before option defines the position of the object relative to the bottom of the previous line of text. A positive value moves the object (and the following text) down; a negative value moves the object (and the following text) up toward the previous line. The Space After option defines the position of the object relative to the first character in the line below the object. A positive value moves the following text down, and a negative value moves the following text up.

When you work with anchored objects, you can use the Selection tool to drag the object up or down (in other words, change its position relative to the text where it's anchored). If the Prevent Manual Positioning option is checked, you can't drag the anchored object in the layout.

10. Paste the anchored graphic again at the beginning of the next two paragraphs.

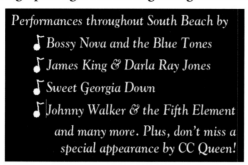

Performances throughout South Beach by
♪ Bossy Nova and the Blue Tones
♪ James King & Darla Ray Jones
♪ Sweet Georgia Down
♪ Johnny Walker & the Fifth Element
and many more. Plus, don't miss a
special appearance by CC Queen!

11. Save the file and continue to the next exercise.

Custom Anchor Options

For more complex applications — such as when you need to move the anchored object outside the text frame — you can choose Custom in the Anchored Object Options Position menu.

The **Relative to Spine** option, which aligns objects based on the center spread line, is only available if your layout has facing pages. When selected, objects on one side of a spread (such as a sidebar in the outside margin) remain on the outside margin even if the text reflows to a facing page.

The **Anchored Object Reference Point** defines the location on the object that you want to align to the location on the page.

The **Anchored Position Reference Point** defines the location on the page to which you want to anchor an object.

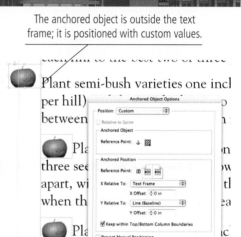

The anchored object is outside the text frame; it is positioned with custom values.

The **X Relative To** field defines what you want to use as the basis for horizontal alignment — Anchor Marker, Column Edge, Text Frame, Page Margin, or Page Edge. The **X Offset** setting moves the object left or right.

The **Y Relative To** field specifies what the object aligns with vertically — Line (Baseline), Line (Cap Height), Line (Top of Leading), Column Edge, Text Frame, Page Margin, Page Edge. The **Y Offset** setting moves the object up or down.

If **Keep Within Top/Bottom Column Boundaries** is checked, the anchored object will stay inside the text column if reflowing text would otherwise cause it to move outside the boundaries (for example, outside the top edge of the frame if the anchoring text is the first line in a column). This option is only available when you select a line option, such as Line (Baseline) for Y Relative To.

You can manually reposition a custom-anchored object by simply dragging the anchored object with the Selection tool. You can also review the anchored position by choosing View>Show Text Threads.

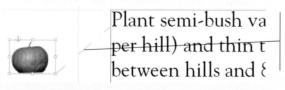

Plant semi-bush va
per hill) and thin t
between hills and &

When text threads are showing, a dashed blue line indicates the position of anchored objects.

Creating Anchored Placeholders

If you want to create an anchored object but don't yet have the content, you can use the Object>Anchored Object>Insert option to define the placeholder object.

This dialog box allows you to create a frame (unassigned, graphics, or text) of a specific size, and even apply object and paragraph styles if those exist. The Position options are the same as those in the Anchored Object Options dialog box. (You can always resize and reposition the anchored object later.)

CREATE TYPE ON A PATH

Instead of simply flowing text into a frame, you can also create unique typographic effects by flowing text onto a path. A text path can be any shape that you can create in InDesign, whether it's a simple shape created with one of the basic shape tools, a complex graphic you drew with the Pen tool, or a path created by converting a clipping path to a frame.

1. **Place the file text_path.tif in the layout, positioned at X: 0″, Y: 0″.**

   This image is simply a guide that you will use to create the text path shape.

2. **Choose the Pen tool. Change the stroke value to 1-pt. Magenta (C=0, M=100, Y=0, K=0) and the fill value to None.**

   Because the line in the placed image is black, you're using magenta so you can differentiate your line from the one in the image.

3. **Using the Pen tool, click once on the left end of the line in the placed image.**

   This first click anchors the first point of the path you're drawing.

4. **Click about half way between the point you just set and the topmost arc of the curve, and then drag right to create handles for the second anchor point.**

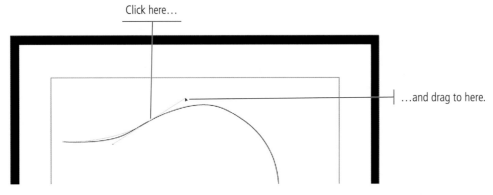

5. **Click again near the middle of the arc on the right, and then drag to create handles for the point.**

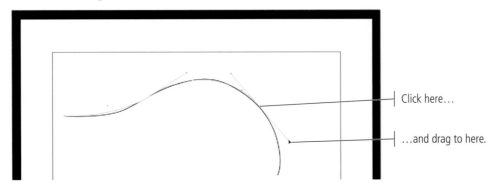

6. **Click one final time on the right end of the line.**

   Don't worry if your path isn't perfect the first time; you can always edit the anchor points and handles with the Direct Selection tool.

7. **Using the Direct Selection tool, drag the handles of the two middle anchor points until your line is close to the one in the placed image.**

8. **Choose the Type on a Path tool. Move the cursor near the path until the cursor shows a small plus sign in the icon, and then click the path.**

   This action converts the line from a regular path to a type path.

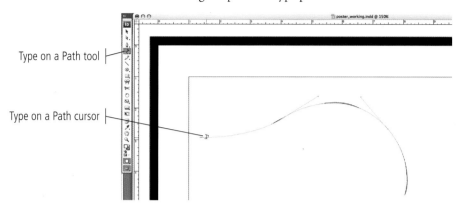

9. **Type the following: Move your feet to the beat!**

10. **Format the path type as 49-pt. ATC Maple Ultra.**

11. **Delete the text_path.tif image you used as a guide.**

12. **Click the text path line with the Selection tool to select it.**

13. **In the Swatches panel, change the object's fill and stroke values to None.**

    A text path can have a fill and stroke value just like any other path.

14. **Click the Text Color button at the top of the Swatches panel, and then click the Black swatch to change the text color.**

    You don't have to select the actual text on a path to change its color. You can use the buttons at the top of the Swatches panel to change the color attributes of either the path or the text.

Note:

When a text path has no stroke color, you can still view the path by choosing View>Show Frame Edges.

15. **Click the bar at the left edge of the text path and drag slightly to the right.**

As you drag, the left edge of the text moves as well. This marks the orientation point of the text on the path.

Drag this line to move the starting point of the text along the path.

16. **Press Command/Control-Z to return the orientation point to the left end of the line.**

17. **Place the insertion point in the text path and apply right paragraph alignment.**

You can control paragraph formatting on a path just as you can format paragraphs in a frame.

18. **Save the file and continue to the final stage of the project.**

Text Path Options

You can control the appearance of type on a path by choosing Type>Type on a Path>Options. You can apply one of five effects, change the alignment of the text to the path, flip the text to the other side of the path, and adjust the character spacing around curves (higher Spacing values remove more space around sharp curves).

- The **Rainbow** (default) effect keeps each character's baseline parallel to the path.

- The **Skew** effect maintains the vertical edges of type while skewing the horizontal edges around the path.

- The **3D Ribbon** effect maintains the horizontal edges of type while rotating the vertical edges to be perpendicular to the path.

- The **Stair Step** effect aligns the left edge of each character's baseline to the path without rotating any characters.

- The **Gravity** effect aligns the center of each character's baseline to the path, keeping vertical edges in line with the path's center.

The **Align options** determine which part of the text (Baseline, Ascender, Descender, or Center) aligns to which part of the path (Top, Bottom, or Center).

Stage 4 Outputting the File

If your layout contains transparency or effects, those transparent areas will typically need to be flattened for output. **Flattening** divides transparent artwork into the necessary vector and raster objects. Transparent objects are flattened according to the settings in the selected flattener preset, which you choose in the Advanced options of the Print dialog box (or in the dialog box that appears when you export as PDF, EPS, or another format).

When you work with transparency, InDesign converts affected objects to a common color space (either CMYK or RGB) so transparent objects of different color spaces can blend properly. To avoid color mismatches between different areas of the objects on screen and in print, the blending space is applied both on screen and in the flattener. You can define which space to use in the Edit>Transparency Blend Space menu; for print jobs, make sure the CMYK option is selected.

Flattener Presets

INDESIGN FOUNDATIONS

InDesign includes three default flattener presets:

- **[Low Resolution]** works for desktop proofs that will be printed on low-end black-and-white printers, and for documents that will be published on the Web.
- **[Medium Resolution]** works for desktop proofs and print-on-demand documents that will be printed on PostScript-compatible color printers.
- **[High Resolution]** works for commercial output on a printing press and for high-quality color proofs.

You can also create your own flattener presets by choosing Edit>Transparency Flattener Presets, and clicking New in the dialog box. You can also use the Transparency Flattener Presets dialog box to load flattener presets created on another machine — such as one your service provider created for their specific output device and/or workflow.

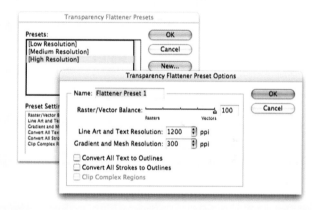

- The preset **Name** will be listed in the related output menus. You should use names that suggest the preset's use, such as "PDF for XL Printing Company." (Using meaningful names is a good idea for any asset that can have a name, from color swatches to output presets. "My Preset 12" is meaningless — possibly even to you after a few days — but "Preset for HP Indigo" tells you exactly when to use those settings.)
- **Raster/Vector Balance** determines how much vector information will be preserved when artwork is flattened. This slider ranges from 0 (all information will be flattened as rasters) to 100 (maintains all vector information).
- **Line Art and Text Resolution** defines the resulting resolution of vector elements that will be rasterized, up to 9600 ppi. For good results in commercial printing applications, this option should be at least 600–1200 ppi (ask your output provider what settings they prefer you to use).
- **Gradient and Mesh Resolution** defines the resolution for gradients that will be rasterized, up to 1200 ppi. This option should typically be set to 300 ppi for most commercial printing applications.
- **Convert All Text to Outlines** converts all type to outline shapes; the text will not be editable in a PDF file.
- **Convert All Strokes to Outlines** converts all strokes to filled paths.
- **Clip Complex Regions** forces boundaries between vector objects and rasterized artwork to fall along object paths, reducing potential problems that can result when only part of an object is rasterized.

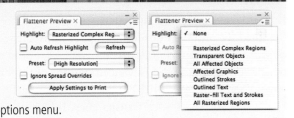

Because of the potential problems that can arise when transparent elements are flattened, you can use the Flattener Preview panel (Window>Output>Flattener Preview) to highlight areas that will be affected by flattening. If you are working on a layout with multiple pages or spreads, you can apply different flattener settings to individual spreads by displaying a specific spread, and then choosing Spread Flattening in the Pages panel options menu.

You can highlight different kinds of areas and determine which flattener preset to use. Clicking Refresh displays a new preview version based on your settings. You can also choose Auto Refresh Highlight.

- **None** displays the normal layout.
- **Rasterized Complex Regions** highlights areas that will be rasterized based on the Raster/Vector Balance defined in the applied preset.
- **Transparent Objects** highlights objects with opacity of less than 100%, objects with blending modes, objects with transparent effects (such as drop shadows), and objects with feathering.
- **All Affected Objects** highlights all objects affected by transparency, including the transparent objects and the objects overlapped by transparent objects. All of these objects will be affected by flattening.
- **Affected Graphics** highlights all placed image files affected by transparency.
- **Outlined Strokes** highlights all strokes that will be converted to filled objects when flattened.
- **Outlined Text** highlights all text that will be converted to outlines when flattened.
- **Raster-Fill Text and Strokes** highlights text and strokes that will have rasterized fills as a result of flattening.
- **All Rasterized Regions** highlights objects (and parts of objects) that will be rasterized when flattened.

EXPORT A PDF FILE FOR PRINT

1. **Choose File>Export.**

2. **Navigate to your WIP>Jazz folder as the destination and choose Adobe PDF in the Format/Save As Type menu.**

3. **Click Save.**

   Before the PDF is saved, you have to define the settings that will be used to generate the PDF file.

4. **Choose High Quality Print in the Adobe PDF Preset menu.**

   The Adobe PDF Preset menu includes six PDF presets that meet common industry output requirements.

   Because there are so many ways to create a PDF — and not all of those ways are optimized for the needs of commercial printing — the potential benefits of the file format are often undermined. The PDF/X specification was created to help solve some of the problems associated with bad PDF files entering the prepress workflow. PDF/X is a subset of PDF that is specifically designed to ensure files have the information necessary for and available to the digital prepress output process. Ask your output provider whether you should apply a PDF/X standard to your files, and if so, which version to use.

Note:

You can manage PDF Presets by choosing File>Adobe PDF Preset>Define. The dialog box that appears lists the built-in presets, as well as any that you have created. You can also import presets from other users or export presets to send to other users.

The Compatibility menu determines which version of the PDF format you will create. This is particularly important if your layout uses transparency. PDF 1.3 does not support transparency, so the file will require flattening. If you save the file to be compatible with PDF 1.4 or later, the transparency information will be maintained in the PDF file; it will have to be flattened later in the process.

5. **Review the options in the General pane.**

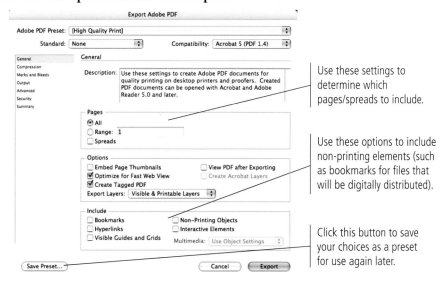

Use these settings to determine which pages/spreads to include.

Use these options to include non-printing elements (such as bookmarks for files that will be digitally distributed).

Click this button to save your choices as a preset for use again later.

- **Embed Page Thumbnails** creates a thumbnail preview for each page being exported, or one thumbnail for each spread if the Spreads option is selected.

- **Optimize for Fast Web View** optimizes the PDF file for faster viewing in a Web browser by allowing the file to download one page at a time.

- **Create Tagged PDF** automatically tags elements based on a subset of Acrobat tags (including basic formatting, lists, and more).

- **View PDF after Exporting** opens the PDF file after it has been created.

- **Create Acrobat Layers** saves each InDesign layer as an Acrobat layer within the PDF. Printer's marks are exported to a separate marks and bleeds layer. Create Acrobat Layers is only available only when Compatibility is set to Acrobat 6 (PDF 1.5) or later.

- **Export Layers** determines whether you are outputting All Layers (including hidden and non-printing layers), Visible Layers (including non-printing layers), or Visible & Printable Layers.

6. Review the Compression options.

The compression options determine what — and how much — data will be included in the PDF file. This set of options is one of the most important when creating PDFs, since too-low resolution results in bad-quality printing and too-high resolution results in extremely long download times.

Before you choose compression settings, you need to consider your final goal. If you're creating a file for commercial printing, resolution is more important than file size. If your goal is a PDF that will be posted on the Web for general consumption, file size is equally (if not more) important than pristine image quality.

You can define a specific compression scheme for color, grayscale, and monochrome images. Different options are available depending on the image type:

- JPEG compression options are lossy, which means data is thrown away to create a smaller file. When you use one of the JPEG options, you can also define an Image Quality option (from Low to Maximum).

- ZIP compression is lossless, which means all file data is maintained in the compressed file.

- CCITT compression was initially developed for fax transmission. Group 3 supports two specific resolution settings (203 × 98 dpi and 203 × 196 dpi). Group 4 supports resolution up to 400 dpi.

- Run Length Encoding (RLE) is a lossless compression scheme that abbreviates sequences of adjacent pixels. If four pixels in a row are black, RLE saves that segment as "four black" instead of "black-black-black-black."

If you don't compress the images in a layout, your PDF file may be extremely large. For a commercial printing workflow, large file size is preferable to poor image quality. If you don't have to submit the PDF file via modem transmission, large file size is not an issue. If you do have to compress the files, ask your service provider what settings they prefer you to use.

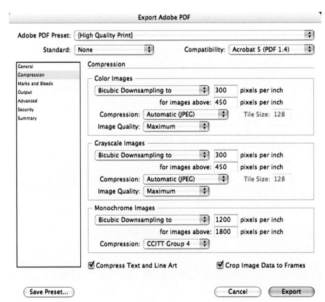

Note:

Since you chose the High Quality Print preset, these options default to settings that will produce the best results for most commercial printing applications.

When you resize an image in the layout, you are changing its effective resolution. The **effective resolution** of an image is the resolution calculated after any scaling has been taken into account. This number is equally — and sometimes more — important than the original image resolution. The effective resolution can be calculated with a fairly simple equation:

Original resolution ÷ (% magnification ÷ 100) = Effective resolution

If a 300-ppi image is magnified 150%, the effective resolution is:

300 ppi ÷ 1.5 = 200 ppi

If you reduce the same 300-ppi image to 50%, the effective resolution is:

300 ppi ÷ 0.5 = 600 ppi

In other words, the more you enlarge a raster image, the lower its effective resolution becomes. Reducing an image results in higher effective resolution, which is often unnecessary and can result in unnecessarily large PDF files.

When you create a PDF file, you also specify the resolution that will be maintained (for each of the three image types) in the resulting PDF file. The Resolution option is useful if you want to throw away excess resolution for print files, or if you want to create low-resolution files for proofing or Web distribution.

- **Do Not Downsample** maintains all the image data from the linked files in the PDF file.
- **Average Downsampling To** reduces the number of pixels in an area by averaging areas of adjacent pixels. Apply this method to achieve user-defined resolution (typically 72 or 96 dpi for Web-based files or 300 dpi for print files).
- **Subsampling To** applies the center pixel value to surrounding pixels. If you think of a 3 × 3-block grid, subsampling enlarges the center block (pixel) — and thus, its value — in place of the surrounding eight blocks.
- **Bicubic Downsampling To** creates the most accurate pixel information for continuous-tone images. This option also takes the longest to process, and it produces a softer image. To understand how this option works, think of a 2 × 2-block grid — bicubic resampling averages the value of all four of those blocks (pixels) to interpolate the new information.

7. **In the Marks and Bleeds options, check the Crop Marks option and change the Offset field to 0.125″ (1/8″). Check the Use Document Bleed Settings option.**

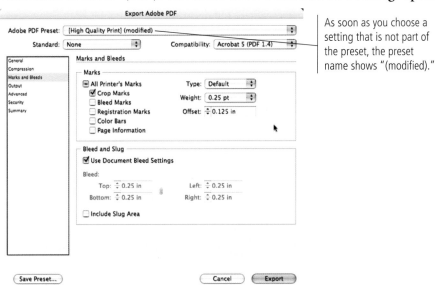

As soon as you choose a setting that is not part of the preset, the preset name shows "(modified)."

8. **In the Compatibility menu, choose Acrobat 4 (PDF 1.3).**

9. **In the Advanced options, choose High Resolution in the Transparency Flattener Preset menu.**

10. **Click the Save Preset button in the bottom-left corner of the dialog box. Name the new preset "High Quality Print – Flattened".**

11. **Click OK to close the Save Preset dialog box, and then click Export to create your PDF file.**

12. **If you see a warning message, click OK.**

   Your PDF file will be flattened, so some features are unavailable. You didn't use those features (hyperlinks, bookmarks, etc.) in this project, however, so you don't have to worry about this warning for now.

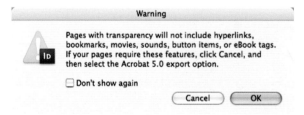

13. **When the spooling window (Generating PDF) closes, your file is complete. Close the InDesign file.**

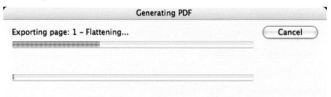

Note:

The Output options relate to color management, which you will use in Project 6. The Security options allow you to add password protection to a PDF file.

Summary

This project combined form and function — presenting the client's information in a clear, easy-to-read manner, while using large graphic elements to grab the viewer's attention and reinforce the message of the piece. As the client requested, the main focus is on the graphics in the top two-thirds of the piece while the relevant text is large enough to be visible but isn't the primary graphic element.

Completing this poster required a number of different text formatting options, including more sophisticated paragraph controls and controlling the flow of text across multiple frames. You should now understand the difference between character and paragraph formatting, and know where to find the different options when you need them.

The graphics options in InDesign give you significant creative control over virtually every element of your layouts. Custom colors and gradients add visual interest to any piece, while more sophisticated tools like non-destructive transparency and other effects allow you to experiment entirely within your page layout until you find exactly the look you want to communicate your intended message.

Create and format text on a path

Create custom swatches and gradients for frame fills and strokes

Use blending modes to blend an image into the frame background fill

Use a gradient feather to add soft edges to a placed image

Create a custom graphics frame from an InDesign-generated clipping path

Place graphics as anchored inline objects

Use optical margin alignment to align punctuation outside the text frame

Control text flow across multiple text frames

Portfolio Builder Project 2

The former marketing director for the Miami Jazz Festival recently moved to California to be the director of the Laguna Beach Sawdust Festival. She was pleased with your work on the jazz festival project, and would like to hire you to create the advertising for next year's art festival event.

To complete this project, you should:

❏ Develop some compelling visual element that will be the central focus of the ads.

❏ Create an ad that fits on a tabloid-size newspaper page (9 1/2 × 11 1/2″ with no bleeds).

❏ Create a second version of the same ad to fit a standard magazine trim size (8 1/4 × 10 7/8″ with 1/8″ bleeds).

"The Sawdust Festival is one of the longest running and well-known art shows in California, maybe even the entire United States. We're planning our advertising campaign for the 2008 summer festival, which will be our 42nd year.

"You might want to poke around our Web site to get some ideas. There's information about the festival's purpose and history, as well as images from previous shows.

"We need an ad that will be placed in the entertainment pull-out sections of regional newspapers, and another version of the same ad that can go into magazines for travel/tourism audiences (like the WestWays magazine from AAA). Both ads should be four-color, although you should keep in mind the basic color scheme that we use on our Web site.

"The ads need to have all the relevant information (we sent you the text, in the RF_Builders>Sawdust folder). But just as important, we want the ad to be art in its own right; the visual element you create will actually be repurposed for festival souvenirs like shirts, posters, and so on.

"We'd like to see some concepts within two weeks. Give us two different options so we can decide what we like and don't like. We might hit it on the first try, but be prepared to make some changes on the first versions."

HeartSmart Newsletter

Your client is a non-profit foundation that focuses on health education and public awareness. The client publishes a monthly newsletter to people on various mailing lists they purchase from a list-management vendor. They want to make a few changes to their existing newsletter template, and they want you to take over the production layout once the template has been revised.

This project incorporates the following skills:

- Opening and modifying an existing layout template
- Managing missing font and link requests
- Replacing graphics files to meet specific color output needs
- Formatting text with template style sheets
- Controlling text-frame inset, alignment, and wrap attributes
- Creating a table with data from a Microsoft Excel worksheet
- Preflighting the final layout and creating a job package

The Project Meeting

Client Comments

In the past our newsletter was printed black-only, since we ran it off a digital copier. We recently won a grant that will allow us to broaden our reach; the printer said because we're going to print so many newsletters now, we can actually go to four-color printing and still pay less per piece than we used to pay for the black-only copies. The printer also recommended going to a self-mailer format, which will save us money on both envelopes and postage (no envelope means less weight).

We need a couple of other changes too. First, we want to go from four columns to three on the front, and from three columns to two on the back. The checkerboard area on the front usually has four pictures, and the bar at the top of the back has a single image; those all used to be gray, but now you can add color to the whole layout.

We'd like you to make the necessary modifications to the template, and then implement the template for the current issue. We sent you the pictures we want to use for this issue, as well as the three text pieces (the main article, a sidebar for the front, and the story for the back). There's also a table in Microsoft Excel format that we want to include on the back.

Art Director Comments

Whenever you work with a file that someone else created, there is a potential for problems. When you first open the template, you'll have to check the fonts and images and make whatever adjustments are necessary. Make sure you save the file as a template again before you build the new issue.

Moving from grayscale to color isn't too big a deal — it's actually easier than going from color to grayscale since color adds possibilities instead of limiting them. You have the opportunity to add color to design elements (including style sheets), and you should also use the color version of the masthead instead of the grayscale one.

The printer said they prefer to work with native application files instead of PDF, so when you're finished implementing the layout, you'll need to check the different elements and then create a final job package.

Project Objectives

To complete this project, you will:

- ❏ Handle requests for missing fonts and images
- ❏ Edit master-page elements to meet new requirements
- ❏ Save a layout file as a template
- ❏ Access master-page elements on the layout pages
- ❏ Format imported text using template style sheets
- ❏ Build and format a table using data from a Microsoft Excel spreadsheet
- ❏ Create a final job package for the output provider

Stage 1 Working with Templates

Templates are commonly used whenever you have a basic layout that will be implemented more than once — for example, the structure of a newsletter remains the same but the content for each monthly issue changes. InDesign templates are special types of files that store the basic structure of a project. Well-planned templates can store layout elements such as nonprinting guides that mark different areas of the job; placeholder frames that will contain different stories or images in each revision; elements that remain the same in every revision, such as masthead text and images; and even formatting information that will be applied to different elements so the elements can be consistent from one issue to the next.

When you work with a template file (with the extension ".indt"), you open and build onto a copy of the original template. Instead of simply saving your changes to the existing layout file, working from a template file means the first time you save you must use the Save As command and save the file under a new name. Opening a template is similar to creating a new Untitled file from scratch, except the new file from the template has all the bits and pieces that are part of the template layout.

MANAGE MISSING FONTS AND IMAGES

Templates can store a wealth of information, including a number of options for formatting text. Placeholder text frames and style sheets include font information. When you work with digital layout files, it's important to understand that fonts are external files of data that describe the font for on-screen display and for the output device. The fonts you use in a layout need to be available on any computer that will be used to open and work with the file. InDesign stores a reference to the fonts you use, but it does not store the actual font data.

1. **Open the file HeartSmart.indt from the RF_InDesign>HeartSmart folder.**

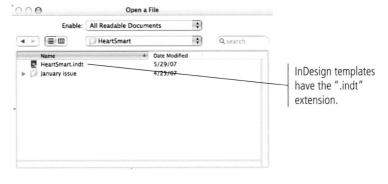

InDesign templates have the ".indt" extension.

2. **Review the information in the Missing Fonts dialog box, and then click OK.**

   Any time you open a file that calls for fonts you don't have, you see this warning. You could blindly fix the problem now (without knowing what will be affected), but we prefer to review problem areas before making changes.

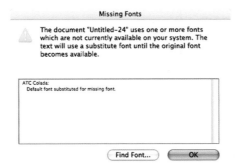

Note:

Before completing this project, copy the HeartSmart folder from the WIP folder on your Resource CD to your WIP folder wherever you are saving your work. When you save files for this project, you will save them in your WIP>HeartSmart folder.

Note:

Missing fonts are one of the most common problems in the digital graphics output process. This is one of the primary advantages of using PDF files for output — PDF can store actual font data so you don't need to include separate font files in your job package. However, PDF can't solve the problem of fonts used in a layout template.

3. Review the information in the second warning message.

As it does with fonts, InDesign stores links to any images placed in a layout; the actual placed-file data is not stored in the InDesign file. If placed files are not available in the same location as when they were originally placed, you'll see a warning message when you open the file.

4. Click Don't Fix.

Again, you could correct the problems now, but it's always a good idea to review problem images before you make changes.

Note:

If you click Fix Links Automatically, you'll see a navigation dialog box that asks you to locate missing links. Modified links will automatically update to the most current data in the linked file — which could cause serious problems if the file has been significantly changed.

5. Open the Pages panel.

The Pages panel is the easiest way to navigate through different pages in a layout, including the master page(s). You can navigate to any page in the layout by simply double-clicking the page's icon.

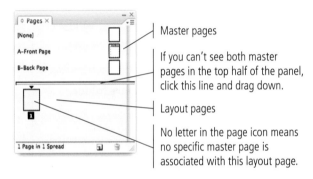

Master pages

If you can't see both master pages in the top half of the panel, click this line and drag down.

Layout pages

No letter in the page icon means no specific master page is associated with this layout page.

Think of master pages as templates for different pages within the layout; this file, for example, has two master pages: Front Page and Back Page (the letters preceding each master page name are automatically added and used to identify which layout pages are associated with which master page. (This will make more sense shortly.)

6. Double-click the A-Front Page icon to display that layout in the document window.

The top area of the newsletter (the **masthead** area) includes the newsletter logotype, as well as the "Published by…" line and the issue date. A pink highlight around the type shows that the font used in this area is not available.

Note:

If the masthead information is not highlighted, open the Composition pane of the Preferences dialog box and make sure the Highlight Substituted Fonts option is checked.

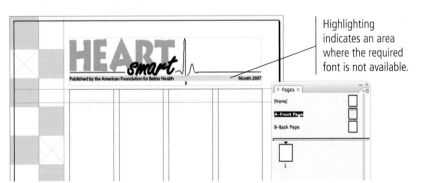

Highlighting indicates an area where the required font is not available.

7. **Using the Type tool, click the frame with the missing font to place the insertion point.**

The Control bar (and Character panel, if it's open) shows the missing font name in brackets. Any time you see a font name in brackets, you know you have a potential problem.

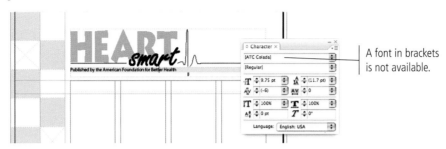

A font in brackets is not available.

8. **Choose Type>Find Font.**

The Find Font dialog box lists every font used in the layout — including missing ones (with a warning icon). You can use this dialog box to replace any font — including missing ones — with another font that is available on your system.

9. **Highlight ATC Colada in the Fonts in Document list and click the More Info button.**

The bottom section of the dialog box shows information about the selected font, including the places where it is used (in this case, 66 characters on the A-Front Page).

10. **In the Replace With area, choose ATC Oak Normal in the Font Family menu.**

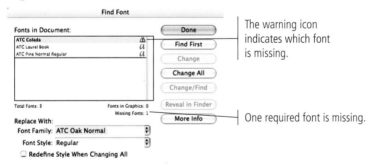

The warning icon indicates which font is missing.

One required font is missing.

Note:

If a font is used in style sheets, you can apply your font replacement choices to style sheet definitions by checking the Redefine Style When Changing All option.

11. **Click Change All to replace all instances of ATC Colada with ATC Oak Normal.**

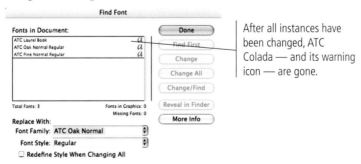

After all instances have been changed, ATC Colada — and its warning icon — are gone.

Note:

You can click the Find Next button to review individual instances of a missing font, click the Change button to change the identified instance, or click the Change/Find button to replace the current instance and find the next one.

12. **Click Done to close the Find Font dialog box.**

Once you've replaced the missing font, the pink highlighting disappears.

13. **Save the file as "template_working.indd" in your WIP>HeartSmart folder and continue to the next exercise.**

REPLACE MISSING GRAPHICS

Placed graphics can cause problems if those files aren't where they're supposed to be (or at least where InDesign thinks they should be). Placed graphics files can be either **missing** (they were moved from their original location after they were placed in the layout, or the name of the file was changed) or **modified** (they were resaved after being placed into the layout, changing the linked file's "time stamp" but not its location or file name). In either case, you need to correct these problems before the file can be successfully output.

1. **With template_working.indd open, display the Links panel (Window>Links).**

   The Links panel lists every file that is placed in your layout. Missing images show a red stop-sign icon; modified images show a yellow yield sign.

2. **Click masthead_gray.ai in the list and click the Go to Link button.**

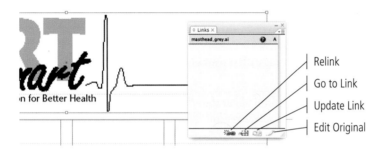

   - The **Relink** button opens a navigation dialog box so you can identify a file's new location or place a different file.

   - The **Go to Link** button selects the relevant graphics frame in the document and changes the document view to show that file.

   - The **Update Link** button updates modified graphics links or opens a navigation dialog box so you can locate missing links.

   - The **Edit Original** button opens the selected link in its native application so you can make changes. When you save the file in its native application and return to InDesign, the changes are automatically updated in your layout.

3. **With the file still selected in the panel, click the Relink button.**

4. **Navigate to masthead_color.ai in the RF_InDesign>HeartSmart>January issue folder and click Open.**

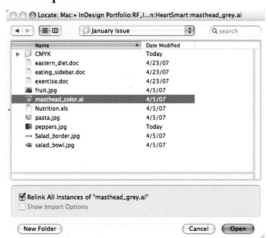

Note:

The Relink All Instances option is a tremendous timesaver if, for example, a logo is placed dozens of times throughout a layout. You need to relink the file only once and all placed instances of the file will be relinked.

5. **Click Yes in the warning message.**

   Because you are linking to a different file name than the originally placed file, InDesign asks you to verify that you want to use the new file. This is simply a verification failsafe that can help you avoid accidentally relinking a placed object to the wrong file.

6. **Save the file and continue to the next exercise.**

 ## EDIT MARGIN AND COLUMN GUIDES

Your client wants to make several changes to the layout, including fewer columns and incorporating color into various elements. These changes will recur from one issue to the next, so you should change the template instead of simply changing the elements in each individual issue.

Note:

You can change the default margins and columns for a layout by choosing File>Document Setup.

1. **With the A-Front Page master layout visible in the document window, choose Layout>Margins and Columns.**

   Every layout has a default setup, which you define when you create the file. Master pages have their own margin and column settings that might or might not be different than the default document settings.

2. **In the Margins and Columns dialog box, change the Columns field to 3 and the Gutter field to 0.2″, and then click OK.**

   Changing the column guides doesn't affect the text frame; you have to change the text frame independently.

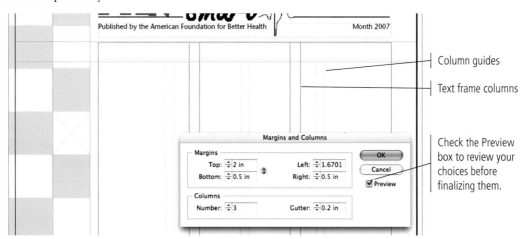

3. **Select the 4-column text frame on the page with the Selection tool.**

4. **Choose Object>Text Frame Options.**

5. **Change the Number of Columns field to 3 and the Gutter field to 0.2" to match the changed column guides. Click OK to close the dialog box.**

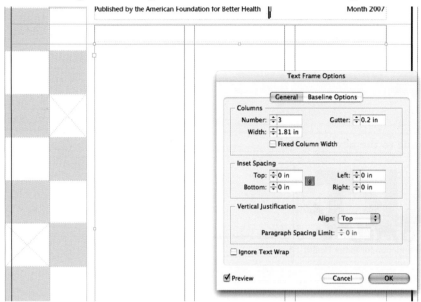

6. **In the Pages panel, double-click the B-Back Page icon to display that layout in the document window.**

7. **Click the horizontal page ruler at the top of the window and drag a page guide to the vertical center of the page (5").**

8. **Choose Layout>Margins and Columns.**

9. **Change the Bottom margin to 5.25", change the Columns field to 2, and then click OK.**

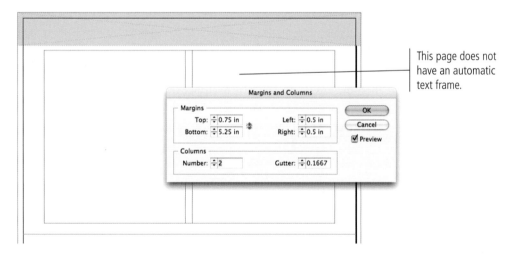

This page does not have an automatic text frame.

10. **Save the file and continue to the next exercise.**

INDESIGN FOUNDATIONS

There are two kinds of pages in an InDesign layout:

- **Layout pages** are the pages on which you place text and images.

- **Master pages** are the pages on which you place recurring information, such as running heads (information at the top of the page) and footers (information at the bottom of the page).

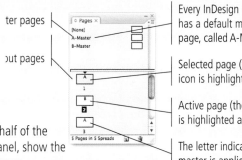

Every InDesign layout has a default master page, called A-Master.

Selected page (the icon is highlighted)

Active page (the page number is highlighted and bold)

The letter indicates which master is applied to the page.

Master pages are accessed and controlled in the top half of the Pages panel. Layout pages, in the lower half of the panel, show the letter that corresponds to the master applied to that page.

Master pages are one of the most powerful features in professional page layout software. Think of a master page as a template for individual pages; anything on the master appears on the related layout page(s). Changing something on a master layout applies the same changes to the related layout pages (unless you already changed that same attribute, such as the fill color, on the layout pages).

The Pages panel options menu (shown right) has a number of indispensable options for working with master pages:

- **New Master** opens a dialog box where you can assign a custom prefix, a name, whether the master will be based on another master page, and the number of pages (from 1 to 10) to include in the master layout.

- **Select Unused Masters** highlights all master pages that are not associated with at least one layout page (and not used as the basis of another master page). This option can be useful if you want to clean up your layout and remove extraneous elements.

- **Master Options** opens a dialog box with the same options that you define when you create a new master.

- **Apply Master to Pages** allows you to apply a specific master to selected pages. You can also apply a specific master to a layout by dragging the master icon onto the layout page icon in the lower half of the panel.

- **Save as Master** is useful if you've built a layout on a layout page and want to convert that layout to a master. Instead of copying and pasting the objects, you can activate the page and choose Save as Master.

- **Load Master Pages** lets you import entire master pages from one InDesign file to another. Assets such as colors and style sheets used on the imported masters will also be imported into the current InDesign file.

Insert Pages...
Move Pages...
New Master...
Duplicate Spread
Delete Spread
Select Unused Masters

Master Options...
Apply Master to Pages...
Save as Master
Load Master Pages...

Hide Master Items
Override All Master Page Items   ⌥⇧⌘L
Remove All Local Overrides
Detach All Objects from Master

Allow Master Item Overrides on Selection

✓ Allow Document Pages to Shuffle
✓ Allow Selected Spread to Shuffle

Numbering & Section Options...
Spread Flattening   ▶

Panel Options...

- **Hide/Show Master Items** toggles the visibility of master items on layout pages.

- **Override All Master Page Items** allows you to access and change master items on a specific layout page. (This command functions on a page-by-page basis.) You can also override individual objects by pressing Command/Control-Shift and clicking the object you want to override.

- **Remove All Local Overrides** reapplies the settings from the master items to related items on the layout page. (This option toggles to Remove Selected Local Overrides if you have a specific object selected on the layout page.)

- **Detach All Objects from Master** breaks the link between objects on a layout page and objects on the related master; in this case, changing items on the master has no effect on related layout page items. (This selection toggles to Detach Selection From Master if you have a specific object selected on the layout page.)

- **Allow Master Overrides on Selection**, active by default, allows objects to be overridden on layout pages. You can protect specific objects by selecting them on the master layout and toggling this option off.

One of the advantages to using a template is eliminating repetitive tasks. So you don't have to redo the same work for future issues of the newsletter, you're going to add the mailing information and color on the master page of the template file.

1. **With B-Back Page visible in the document window, place the file masthead_color.ai.**

2. **Using the Control bar, scale the placed file to 55% proportionally and position it (using the top-left reference point) at X: 0.5″, Y: 5.25″.**

   You can scale a placed picture (and its frame) by selecting it with the Selection tool. You can scale the placed picture within its frame (without affecting the frame) by selecting it with the Direct Selection tool.

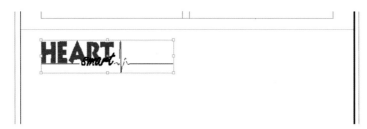

3. **Create a new text frame with the following dimensions:**

X: 0.5″	W: 2.25″
Y: 5.9″	H: 0.5″

4. **In the new text frame, type:**

   American Foundation for Better Health
   P.O. Box 76936
   Houston, TX 77020

   The text won't all fit into the frame yet; you have to change the formatting to fit it into the frame.

5. **Select all the text (Edit>Select All) and format it as 8-pt ATC Oak Normal.**

6. **Select the gray box at the top of the page. In the Swatches panel, select the Fill options and then click Pantone 1945 C to change the color of the frame.**

   The gray rectangle was actually filled with 20% black; changing the color does not affect the tint, so the rectangle is now filled with 20% of the Pantone color.

7. **Using the Type tool, create a text frame that fills the margins on the Back Page layout.**

8. **Choose Object>Text Frame Options. Change the frame to 2 columns with a 0.2″ gutter.**

   Since every issue of the newsletter has a story in this area of the back, it makes sense to create the text frame as part of the master page (and template).

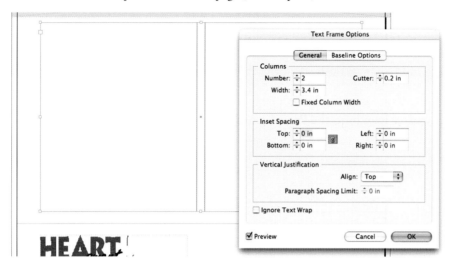

9. **Double-click the A-Front Page icon in the Pages panel.**

10. **Click the gray square in the top-left corner of the page, and then change the fill to Pantone 1945 C.**

    Because all the gray squares were created by overlaying white ("Paper") frames on top of a single gray rectangle, you have to change the color only once.

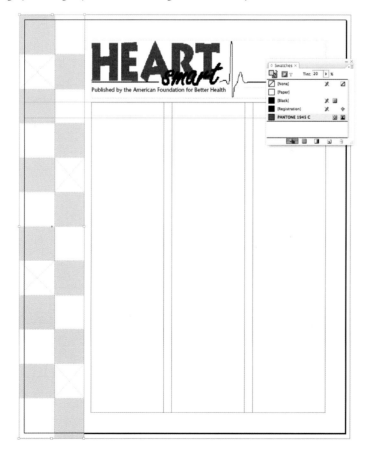

11. **Save your work and continue to the next exercise.**

SAVE A NEW TEMPLATE

Every issue has the same page structure — one front page and one back page. These layouts are already prepared as master pages, but you have to apply those master pages to the layout pages for individual issues. Since this will occur for every issue, it will remove two more clicks from the process if you set up the layout pages as part of the template.

1. **With template_working.indd open, double-click the Page 1 icon in the Pages panel.**

2. **Drag the A-Front Page master icon onto the Page 1 icon in the lower half of the Pages panel.**

When a master page is applied to a layout page, everything on the master page is placed on the layout page.

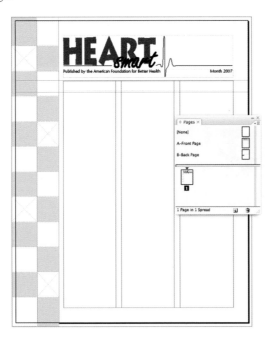

3. **Click the B-Back Page icon and drag it into the bottom half of the Pages panel (below the Page 1 icon).**

You can add new pages to your layout by dragging any of the master page icons into the lower half of the panel.

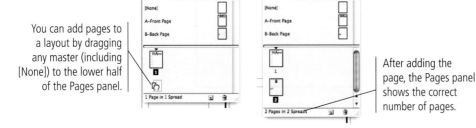

You can add pages to a layout by dragging any master (including [None]) to the lower half of the Pages panel.

After adding the page, the Pages panel shows the correct number of pages.

4. Choose File>Save As.

5. Navigate to your WIP>HeartSmart folder as the location for saving the template.

6. Change the file name to "HeartSmart_New.indd".

7. In the Format/Save As Type menu, choose InDesign CS3 Template.

   The extension automatically changes to ".indt", the correct extension for InDesign template files.

8. Click Save to save the template file.

9. When the save is complete, close the InDesign file.

 ## CREATE A NEW FILE BASED ON THE TEMPLATE

Now that you've made the client's requested changes and saved a new template, you can easily begin each new issue by simply opening the template. Only a few things need to be addressed before you are ready to go.

1. Choose File>Open and navigate to your WIP>HeartSmart folder.

2. Click the HeartSmart_New.indt file and click Open.

   When creating a new file from a template, you have to open the template file. Opening a template file actually opens a new untitled document with all the same elements that are saved in the template.

3. **Double-click the Page 1 icon in the Pages panel to show it in the document window.**

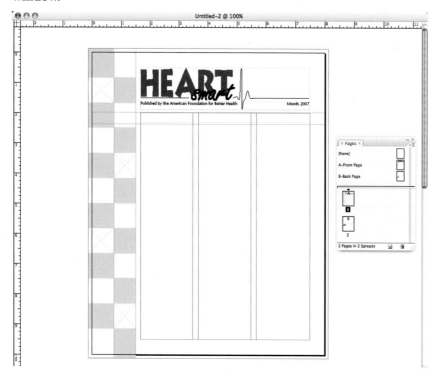

4. **Click the empty area near the top margin guide to select the empty text frame.**

This step will have no effect, and nothing will be selected. By default, you can't select master page items on a layout page; changes have to be made on the master page.

When you change an object on a master page, the same changes reflect on associated layout pages. For example, if you change the red box to blue on A-Front Page, the red box will turn blue on Page 1 as well.

In many cases, however, you might need to change a master page item for only a single page in the layout — a common occurrence when you use placeholder text or graphics frames on a master page. In this case, you have to override the master page layout for the specific layout page, which allows you to select and change master page items on individual layout pages.

5. **Control/right-click the Page 1 icon and choose Override All Master Page Items.**

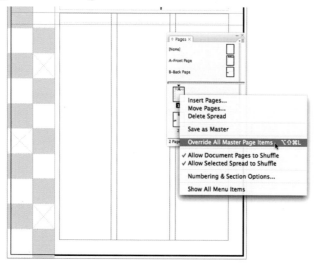

6. **Now click near the top margin guide to select the empty text frame.**

   By overriding the master page layout for this page, you can now select and change master page items — including the text frame — on the layout page.

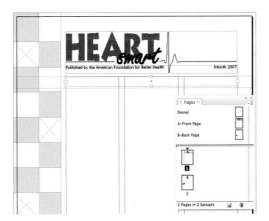

7. **Double-click the Page 2 icon to show that page in the document window.**

8. **Control/right-click the Page 2 icon and choose Override All Master Page Items.**

   You can now select and change the text frame on Page 2, as well as the other objects from the B-Back Page master.

   These eight steps need to be completed for every new issue of the newsletter, so you can save yourself time by resaving the template with these new changes.

9. **Choose File>Save As and navigate to the WIP>HeartSmart folder.**

10. **Change the file name to "HeartSmart_New.indd", and then choose InDesign CS3 Template in the Format/Save As Type menu.**

    When you choose the Template option in the Format menu, the extension automatically changes to ".indt".

11. **Click Save. When you see a warning message asking if you want to overwrite the existing template, click Replace/Yes.**

Templates sometimes require changes, as is the case in this project. You can overwrite the original template by choosing File>Save As, navigating to the original template location, and saving the revised template with the exact same file name.

12. **Close the template file.**

 ## Implement the Newsletter Template

By saving your work as a template, you've eliminated a significant amount of repetitive work that would otherwise need to be redone for every issue. There are still some tasks that will need to be done for each issue, such as changing the issue date and adding images to the front and back pages. These elements will change in each issue, so they can't be entirely "templated." But if you review the layout as it is now, you'll see that the template does include placeholders for these elements — so completing these elements is greatly simplified.

1. **Open the file HeartSmart_New.indt.**

2. **Immediately save the file as "HeartSmart_January.indd" in your WIP>HeartSmart folder.**

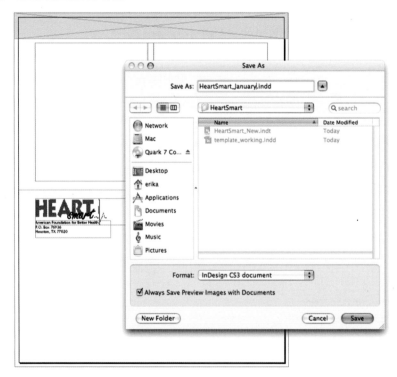

3. Using the Type tool, highlight "Month 2007" in the masthead area of Page 1 and type "January 2008".

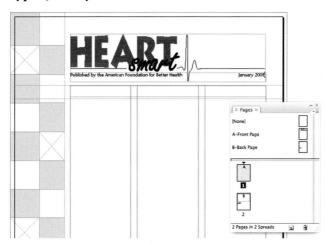

4. Select the first empty graphics frame in the checkerboard pattern on the left side of the page.

5. Choose File>Place. Navigate to the file fruit.tif in the RF_InDesign> HeartSmart>January issue folder. Make sure the Replace Selected Item box is checked, and then click Open.

Note:

By checking the Replace Selected Item option, the image will be placed into the selected graphics frame.

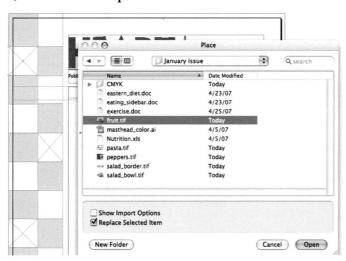

6. Click the placed graphic with the Direct Selection tool to select only the graphic (not the containing frame).

7. Scale the placed graphic (not the frame) to 60% proportionally, and drag the picture inside the frame so the peach is roughly centered in the space.

Note:

To scale the picture and not the frame, select the picture with the Direct Selection tool and use either the Transform panel or Control bar.

8. Using the same technique, place the following images in the remaining three graphics frames in the checkerboard pattern:

Second frame: pasta.tif, scaled to 50%

Third frame: peppers.tif, scaled to 50%

Fourth frame: salad_bowl.tif, scaled to 75%

9. **Drag each image within its frame until you are satisfied with the visible area of the pictures.**

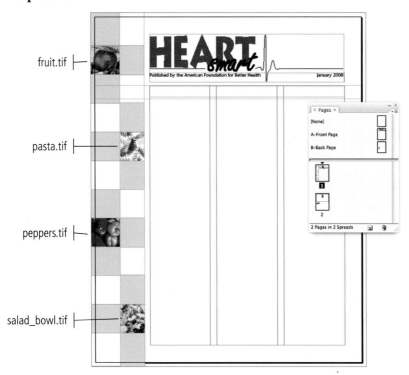

10. **On Page 2, place the file salad_border.tif into the graphics frame at the top of the page.**

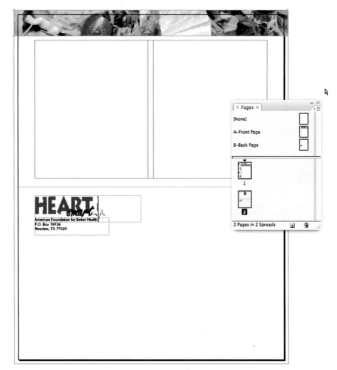

11. **Save the file and continue to the next stage of the project.**

Stage 2 Working with Style Sheets

The principles of good design state that headings, subheadings, body copy, and other editorial elements should generally look the same throughout a single job — in other words, editorial elements should be consistent from one page to another, whether the job is two pages or two hundred.

In Project 2 you learned about the different text-formatting options that can be applied in an InDesign layout. For any bit of text, there are dozens of character- and paragraph-formatting options, from the font and type size to the space above and below paragraphs. Whenever you work with longer blocks of copy, you'll apply the same group of formatting options to multiple pieces of text.

If you were to change each editorial element manually, you would have to make hundreds of clicks to create a two-page newsletter. Fortunately, InDesign includes the ability to easily store groups of text-formatting options as **styles**, which can be applied to any text with a single click.

The major advantages of using styles are ease of use and enhanced efficiency. Changes can be made instantly to all text defined as a particular style. For example, you might easily modify leading in the Body Copy style or change the font in the Subhead style from Helvetica to ATC Oak Bold. When a style definition changes, any text that uses that style automatically changes, too.

InDesign supports both character styles and paragraph styles. **Character styles** apply only to selected words; this type of style is useful for setting off a few words in a paragraph without affecting the entire paragraph. **Paragraph styles** apply to the entire body of text between two ¶ symbols; this type of style defines the appearance of the paragraph, combining the character style used in the paragraph with the line spacing, indents, tabs, and other paragraph attributes.

Styles are most advantageous when working with text-intensive documents that have recurring editorial elements, such as headlines, subheads, and captions; when working with several people concurrently on the same projects; and when creating projects with specific style requirements, such as catalogs or magazines.

In this project, the client's original template included a number of styles for formatting the text in each issue. Because the text frames already exist in the template layout, you only need to import the client's text and apply the existing styles. (In Project 4, you'll import styles from a Microsoft Word file and another InDesign file, as well as define your own new styles.)

Note:

Styles ensure consistency in text and paragraph formatting throughout a publication. Rather than trying to remember how you formatted a sidebar 45 pages ago, you can simply apply a predefined Sidebar style.

Note:

Paragraph style sheets define character attributes and paragraph attributes; character style sheets define only the character attributes. In other words, a paragraph style sheet can be used to format text entirely — including font information, line spacing, tabs, and so on.

Apply Template Style Sheets

Most InDesign jobs will incorporate some amount of client-supplied text, which might be sent to you in the body of an email or saved in any number of different text file formats. Many text files will be supplied from Microsoft Word, the most popular word-processing application in the United States market.

Microsoft Word includes fairly extensive options for formatting text (although its not quite as robust or sophisticated as what you can do with InDesign). Many Microsoft Word users apply **local formatting** (selecting specific text and applying character and/or paragraph attributes); more sophisticated Microsoft Word users build text formatting styles similar to what you will use in InDesign.

1. **With Page 1 of HeartSmart_January.indd open, choose File>Place and navigate to the file exercise.doc in the RF_InDesign>HeartSmart> January issue folder.**

Note:

All the text files for this project are in the RF_InDesign> HeartSmart>January issue folder.

2. **Make sure the Show Import Options box is checked and click Open.**

3. **In the resulting dialog box, review the options in the Formatting section.**

   When you import a Microsoft Word file into InDesign, you can either preserve or remove formatting that is saved in the Microsoft Word file (including styles defined in Microsoft Word).

4. **Make sure the Preserve Styles and Formatting option is selected; make sure the Import Styles Automatically radio button is selected and choose Auto Rename in both conflict menus. Click OK.**

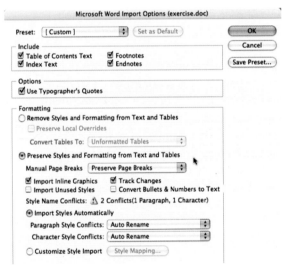

5. **If you see a Missing Font warning, click OK.**

   You're going to replace the Microsoft Word formatting with InDesign styles, which should correct this problem.

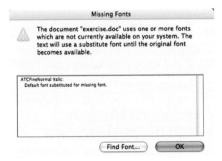

6. **Click the loaded cursor in the empty text frame at the top (the one that touches the top margin guide).**

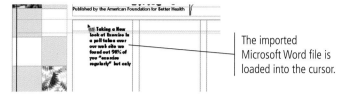

The imported Microsoft Word file is loaded into the cursor.

Remember, clicking with the loaded cursor places the loaded text into the text frame.

7. **Click the Out port on the text frame to load the rest of the story into the cursor, and then click the loaded cursor in the empty three-column frame below the heading.**

Overflow text from the first frame is loaded into the cursor.

Note:

When you load the cursor with overset text, the loaded cursor shows the text from the beginning of the story — even though the beginning is already placed. This is a quirk of the software; when you click with the loaded cursor, the text will flow into the new frame at the proper place in the story.

8. **Open the Paragraph Styles panel (Window>Type & Tables>Paragraph Styles).**

You should be able to guess the purpose of these styles from their names. It's always a good idea to use indicative names whenever you create styles or other user-defined assets.

9. **Place the insertion point in the first paragraph of the imported story (the main heading) and look at the Paragraph Styles panel.**

When you imported the Microsoft Word file, you preserved the formatting in the file; this is usually a good idea so you can see what the writer intended. However, now that the text is imported into your layout, you want to apply the template styles so the text in this issue will be consistent with other issues.

When you import text into InDesign, any number of new styles might appear in the Styles panels; the most common imported style is Normal. Text in a Microsoft Word file is typically formatted with the Normal style — even if you don't realize it; user-applied formatting is commonly local (meaning it is applied to selected text instead of using a defined style).

The imported text appears to be preformatted, but the Paragraph Styles panel tells a different story. This paragraph is formatted as "Normal+." Whenever you see a plus sign next to a style name, the selected text includes some formatting other than what is defined in the style.

Note:

You can reapply the basic style definition to selected text by clicking the Clear Overrides button at the bottom of the Paragraph Styles panel.

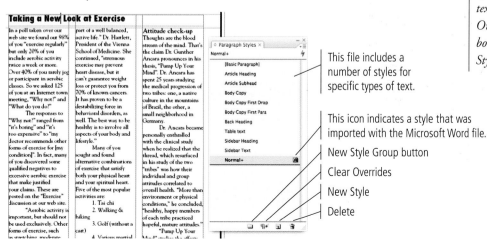

This file includes a number of styles for specific types of text.

This icon indicates a style that was imported with the Microsoft Word file.

New Style Group button

Clear Overrides

New Style

Delete

10. **With the insertion point still in place, click the Article Heading style in the Paragraph Styles panel.**

Using styles, you can change all formatting attributes of selected text with a single click.

Note:

Paragraph styles can include character attributes as well as paragraph attributes; character styles can only define character-formatting attributes.

11. **Place the insertion point anywhere in the first paragraph of body copy, and then drag to select the rest of the visible text in the three-column frame.**

12. **Click the Body Copy style in the Paragraph Styles panel.**

Paragraph styles apply to any paragraph that is partially or entirely selected. You don't have to select an entire paragraph before applying a paragraph style.

13. Format the first paragraph using the Body Copy First Drop style.

14. Half-way down the second column, format the subheading ("Attitude Checkup", after the numbered list) with the Article Subhead style.

15. Format the next paragraph (after the subhead) with the Body Copy First Para style.

16. On Page 2 of the layout, place the story eastern_diet.doc into the two-column text frame and apply the following styles:

- Format the first paragraph with the Back Heading style.
- Format the second paragraph with the Body Copy First Para style.
- Format the rest of the story with the Body Copy style.

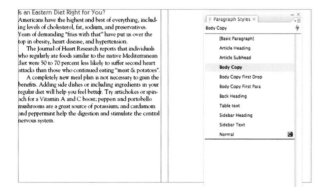

17. Save the file and continue to the next exercise.

Microsoft Word files can include a fairly sophisticated level of formatting attributes, from basic text formatting to defined paragraph and character styles to automatically generated tables of contents. When you import a Word file into InDesign, you can determine whether to include these elements, as well as how to handle conflicts between imported elements and elements that already exist in your InDesign layout.

If these elements exist in the Microsoft Word file, checking the associated boxes imports those elements into your InDesign file.

Choose this option to convert straight quote marks to typographer's or "curly" quotes.

Choose this option to strip out all formatting applied in the file and import the file as plain text.

Choose this option to import the Microsoft Word file, including formatting.

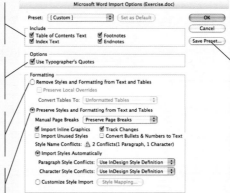

Click this button to save your choices as a preset, which you can call again in the Preset menu when importing other Word files.

Manual Page Breaks determines how page breaks in Word translate to InDesign; you can preserve manual breaks, convert them to column breaks, or ignore them. Word users tend to force breaks where appropriate in the text file — which rarely translates to a properly formatted InDesign layout. More often than not, you'll end up removing Word-defined page breaks, but it might be a good idea to include them in the import and remove them after you've reviewed the text.

If graphics have been placed into a Word file, the **Import Inline Graphics** option allows you to include those graphics as anchored objects in the InDesign story. If you choose to include graphics, it is important to understand that the graphics might be embedded in the story instead of linked to the original file; this depends on how the graphic was placed into the Word file.

When you include inline graphics with a Microsoft Word file, placed graphics might be embedded into the file instead of linked to the original graphics file.

If you choose **Import Unused Styles**, all styles in the Word file will be imported into InDesign. These styles might require fonts you don't have; if an unused style calls for a missing font, you might spend a lot of time fixing unnecessary problems.

Word includes a powerful collaboration tool called Track Changes, which allows one person to review another person's changes to a file. (As publishers, we use this feature every day so editors and authors can review each other's changes.) If you check the **Track Changes** option, any tracked changes from the Word file will be included in your InDesign layout. This might cause a lot of items to show up in your text that aren't supposed to be there (typos, errors, or, for example, something the general counsel office removed from the original text for a specific legal reason).

Convert Bullets & Numbering to Text allows you to convert automatically generated numbering and bullet characters into actual text characters. This option is extremely useful if the text includes lists; if you don't check this option, you'll have to manually re-enter the bullets or line numbers into the imported text.

The **Style Name Conflicts** area warns you if styles in the Word file conflict with styles in the InDesign file (in other words, if they have the same style names but different definitions in the two locations). If you are importing styles from the Word file, you have to determine how to resolve these conflicts.

Import Styles Automatically allows you to choose how to handle conflicts in paragraph and character styles. **Use InDesign Style Definition** preserves the style as you defined it; text in the Word file that uses that style will be reformatted with the InDesign definition of the style. **Redefine InDesign Style** replaces the layout definition with the definition from the Word file. **Auto Rename** adds the Word file to the InDesign file with "_wrd_1" at the end of the style name.

If you choose **Customize Style Import**, the Style Mapping button opens a dialog box where you can review and control specific style conflicts.

Click a style in the left column...

...and then choose which InDesign style to use in place of the Microsoft Word style.

CREATE A SIDEBAR BOX

Many page layouts have a primary story (which might flow across multiple pages) as well as related-but-not-connected stories called **sidebars**. These elements are usually not linked to the main story, and they are often placed in their own boxes with some unique formatting to draw attention to the box. Amateur designers often create three separate elements to achieve this effect — an unnecessary degree of complexity when you can change multiple text frame options to create the effect with a single object.

1. **On Page 1 of HeartSmart_January.indd, create a text frame with the following dimensions (based on the top-left reference point):**

    X: 3.67″   W: 3.95″
    Y: 6.6″   H: 3″

2. **Fill the text frame with a 20% tint of Pantone 1945 C.**

Text Frame Options

INDESIGN FOUNDATIONS

You can change any number of text frame attributes using the Text Frame Options (Object>Text Frame Options) dialog box.

If a text frame has more than one column, the **gutter** value defines the space between columns. If **Fixed Column Width** is selected, changing the number of columns changes the width of the frame to accommodate the defined number of columns. (For example, 3 columns at 2″ each with a 0.25″ gutter would require the frame to be 6.5″ wide.) If Fixed Column Width is not checked, the number of columns is evenly divided in the existing frame width.

Inset Spacing is the distance at which text is moved in from the frame edges. You can define different values for each edge or link all four edges to a consistent value.

Clicking any of the arrow buttons changes the field value by 0.0625 inch.

When this button is highlighted, all four inset values are the same.

Text can be aligned to the top, center, or bottom of a frame, or justified (stretched) to fill the frame height.

Click this check box to immediately see the results of your choices.

If you check the **Ignore Text Wrap** option, the selected text frame is not affected by the wrap attributes of overlying objects.

In addition, you can control fill and stroke attributes of a text frame, as you would any other object, using the Swatches and Stroke panels.

The frame is selected, so you can change the fill and stroke attributes of the frame.

Some of these options are also available in the right side of the Control bar when a frame is selected with one of the selection tools. It is important to note that some changes to text frames also affect the text inside the frame; scaling, flipping, rotating, or skewing a frame also scales, flips, rotates, or skews the text inside that frame.

Change frame content type

Apply effects to frame

Number of columns

Frame position and dimensions

Frame angle

Rotate frame

Apply drop shadow

Frame style

Fit frame to content

Frame (and content) scaling

Flip frame

Frame transparency

Vertical alignment

Frame skew

Frame stroke weight and style

Text wrap options

Align options

3. **Place the file eating_sidebar.doc (from the RF_InDesign>HeartSmart>January issue folder) into the new frame, preserving the formatting in the imported file.**

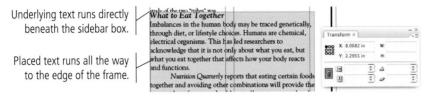

Underlying text runs directly beneath the sidebar box.

Placed text runs all the way to the edge of the frame.

4. **Format the first line of the sidebar with the Sidebar Heading style.**

5. **Format the rest of the text in this frame using the Sidebar Text style.**

   If a paragraph includes local formatting, simply clicking a new style name might not work perfectly. As you can see in this example, the first two words are italicized; in the Paragraph Styles panel, the Sidebar Text style shows a plus sign — indicating that some formatting other than the style definition has been applied.

6. **Place the insertion point in the second sidebar paragraph.**

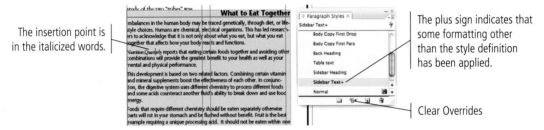

The insertion point is in the italicized words.

The plus sign indicates that some formatting other than the style definition has been applied.

Clear Overrides

7. **Click the Clear Overrides button at the bottom of the Paragraph Styles panel.**

8. **Select the first two words of the second sidebar paragraph and change the font to the Italic variant of the ATC Oak font.**

9. **With the same text frame selected, choose Object>Text Frame Options.**

10. **Make sure the Preview option is checked, and then change the Top Inset field to 0.1″.**

    Text inset is the distance text is moved away from the inside edge of its containing frame.

11. **Make sure the chain button is active so all four inset values are the same and press Tab to move the highlight and apply the new Inset Spacing values.**

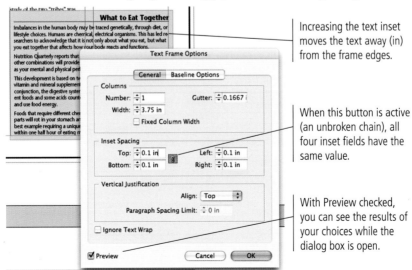

Increasing the text inset moves the text away (in) from the frame edges.

When this button is active (an unbroken chain), all four inset fields have the same value.

With Preview checked, you can see the results of your choices while the dialog box is open.

12. In the Vertical Justification Align menu, choose Justify.

Text can be vertically aligned to the top, bottom, or center of its containing frame, or it can be justified — stretched to extend the entire height of the containing frame.

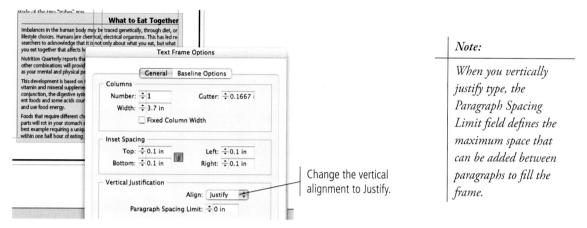

Change the vertical alignment to Justify.

Note:

When you vertically justify type, the Paragraph Spacing Limit field defines the maximum space that can be added between paragraphs to fill the frame.

13. Click OK to close the dialog box and apply your choices.

Text Wrap Options

You can wrap text around any object, including text and graphics frames and other objects that you draw in InDesign. Text wraps are largely controlled in the Text Wrap panel (Window>Text Wrap), although you can change the basic wrap attributes in the Control bar.

InDesign allows five different options for wrapping text around an object:

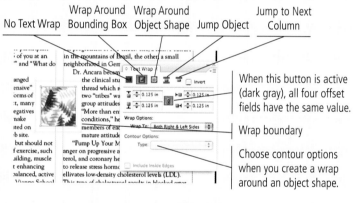

No Text Wrap — Wrap Around Bounding Box — Wrap Around Object Shape — Jump Object — Jump to Next Column

When this button is active (dark gray), all four offset fields have the same value.

Wrap boundary

Choose contour options when you create a wrap around an object shape.

- **No Text Wrap** allows text to run directly under the object.

- **Wrap Around Bounding Box** creates a straight-edged wrap around all four sides of the object's bounding box.

- **Wrap Around Object Shape** creates a wrap in the same shape as the selected object. When you use this option, you can also determine which contour option to use:

  - **Bounding Box** creates the wrap boundary based on the object's bounding box dimensions.
  - **Detect Edges** creates the boundary with the same detection options you used in Project 2 to create a clipping path.
  - **Alpha Channel** creates the boundary from an Alpha channel saved in the placed image.
  - **Photoshop Path** creates the boundary from a path saved in the placed image.
  - **Graphic Frame** creates the boundary from the containing frame.
  - **Same as Clipping** creates the boundary from a clipping path saved in the placed image.
  - **User-Modified Path** appears by default if you drag the anchor points of the text wrap boundary.

- **Jump Object** keeps text from appearing to the right or left of the frame.
- **Jump to Next Column** forces surrounding text to the top of the next column or frame.

Regardless of which wrap you apply, you can define the Offset value, or the distance that surrounding text will remain from the object. (If you use the Object Shape wrap option, you can define only a single Offset value; for the other three wrap types, you can define a different offset value for each edge.)

If you use the Bounding Box or Object Shape wrap option, you can also define the Wrap To options — whether the wrap is applied to a specific side (right, left, right and left, or the largest side), or toward or away from the spine.

14. **Open the Text Wrap panel (Window>Text Wrap).**

    Text wrap is the distance underlying text flows around the edge of a frame or other object.

15. **Click the sidebar frame with the Selection tool, and then click the second button from the left in the Text Wrap panel.**

16. **Change the Top Wrap field to 0.1″ and make sure the chain button is active so all four wrap values are the same.**

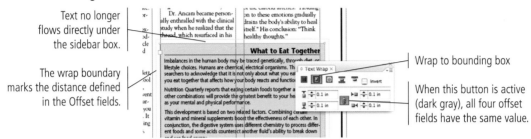

Text no longer flows directly under the sidebar box.

The wrap boundary marks the distance defined in the Offset fields.

Wrap to bounding box

When this button is active (dark gray), all four offset fields have the same value.

17. **Select the three-column text box and open the Text Frame Options dialog box. Choose Justify in the Vertical Justification Align menu and click OK.**

    This command exactly aligns the bottom lines in the two right columns.

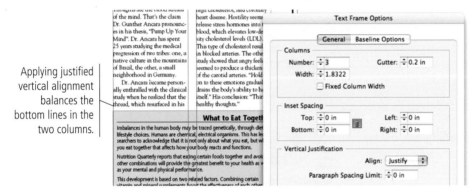

Applying justified vertical alignment balances the bottom lines in the two columns.

18. **Save the file and continue to the next stage of the project.**

Stage 3 Working with Tables

Many page layouts incorporate tables of information, from basic tables with a few rows and columns to multi-page catalog spreadsheets with thousands of product numbers and prices. InDesign includes a number of options for building tables, each having advantages and disadvantages depending on what you need to accomplish. Regardless of which method you use to create a table, the same options are available for formatting the table, the cells in the table, and the content in the cells.

When you place an insertion point in an existing text frame, you can create a new table from scratch by choosing Table>Insert Table. This method allows you to define your own table parameters, including the number of rows and columns, the number of header and footer rows (top and bottom rows that appear in every instance of the table if the table breaks across multiple columns or frames), and even a defined style for the new table (table styles store formatting options such as gridline weight and color, cell inset, and other attributes that you will learn about in this stage of the project).

You can also create a table by selecting a series of **tab-delimited text** in the layout and choosing Table>Convert Text to Table. (Tab-delimited means that the content of each column is separated by a tab character.) Using this method, the new table becomes an inline object in the same text frame that contained the original tabbed text.

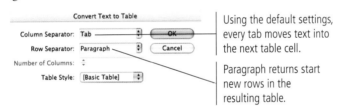

Using the default settings, every tab moves text into the next table cell.

Paragraph returns start new rows in the resulting table.

Key Command:

Pressing Tab moves the insertion point from one table cell to the next (left to right, top to bottom).

Finally, you can create a new table in InDesign by placing a Microsoft Excel file (Microsoft Excel is probably the most common application for creating spreadsheets). You'll use this method to complete this stage of the HeartSmart newsletter project.

PLACE A MICROSOFT EXCEL TABLE

Microsoft Excel spreadsheets can be short tables of text or complex, multi-page spreadsheets of data. In either case, Microsoft Excel users tend to spend hours formatting their spreadsheets for business applications. Those formatting options are typically not appropriate for commercial printing applications, but they give you a better starting point in your InDesign file than working from plain tabbed text.

1. **Display Page 2 of the file HeartSmart_January.indd.**

2. **Choose File>Place and navigate to the file nutrition.xls in the RF_InDesign>HeartSmart>January issue folder.**

3. **Uncheck the Replace Selected Item option, make sure Show Import Options is checked, and click Open.**

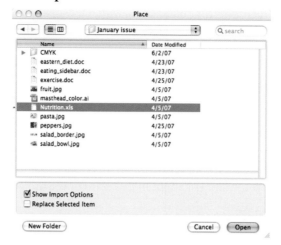

4. **Review the options in the resulting dialog box. Make sure your options match what is shown in the following image and then click OK.**

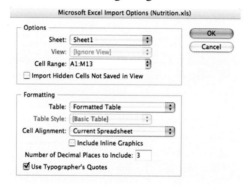

If you get a warning about missing fonts, click OK; you're going to reformat the table text in the next exercise so missing fonts won't be a problem.

5. **With the table loaded into the cursor, click in the empty area in the lower half of the page.**

The new table is placed into the layout; a text frame is automatically created to contain the table. (The table currently extends beyond the right edge of the text frame, and the overset text icon in the frame's Out port indicates that the frame is not high enough to fit all the rows of the table).

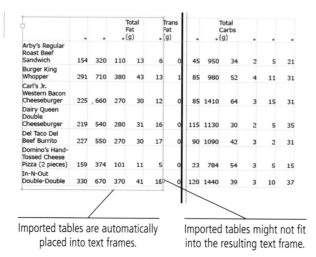

Imported tables are automatically placed into text frames.

Imported tables might not fit into the resulting text frame.

			Total Fat (g)	Trans Fat (g)			Total Carbs (g)				
Arby's Regular Roast Beef Sandwich	154	320	110	13	6	0	45	950	34	2	5	21
Burger King Whopper	291	710	380	43	13	1	85	980	52	4	11	31
Carl's Jr. Western Bacon Cheeseburger	225	660	270	30	12	0	85	1410	64	3	15	31
Dairy Queen Double Cheeseburger	219	540	280	31	16	0	115	1130	30	2	5	35
Del Taco Del Beef Burrito	227	550	270	30	17	0	90	1090	42	3	2	31
Domino's Hand-Tossed Cheese Pizza (2 pieces)	159	374	101	11	5	0	23	784	54	3	5	15
In-N-Out Double-Double	330	670	370	41	18	0	120	1440	39	3	10	37

Note:

Obviously this table still needs some significant modification to make it a cohesive part of the newsletter layout. Some placed tables require more work than others, but be prepared to do at least some clean-up work whenever you place a spreadsheet or table.

6. **Click the table with the Selection tool and choose Object>Fitting> Fit Frame to Content.**

   This is the same command you can use to resize a graphics frame; in this case, you're making the text frame big enough to show the entire table. Because the new frame size extends beyond the bottom edge of the pasteboard, you might not be able to scroll down far enough to see the new bottom edge (and the bottom rows of the table).

Note:

You can also Control/ right-click the table and choose Fitting>Fit Frame to Content from the contextual menu.

7. **Drag the text frame with the table up into the right column of the top half of the page.**

   You should now be able to see the bottom row of the table.

			Total Fat (g)		Trans Fat (g)			Total Carbs (g)				
Arby's Regular Roast Beef Sandwich	154	320	110	13	6	0	45	950	34	2	5	21
Burger King Whopper	291	710	380	43	13	1	85	980	52	4	11	31
Carl's Jr. Western Bacon Cheeseburger	225	660	270	30	12	0	85	1410	64	3	15	31
Dairy Queen Double Cheeseburger	219	540	280	31	16	0	115	1130	30	2	5	35
Del Taco Del Beef Burrito	227	550	270	30	17	0	90	1090	42	3	2	31
Domino's Hand-Tossed Cheese Pizza (2 pieces)	159	374	101	11	5	0	23	784	54	3	5	15
In-N-Out Double-Double	330	670	370	41	18	0	120	1440	39	3	10	37
KFC Original Recipe Drumstick & Thigh	185	500	290	33	9	0	240	1500	16	0	0	36
McDonald's Big Mac	216	590	310	34	11	0	85	1070	47	3	8	24
Taco Bell Beef Burrito Supreme	247	440	160	18	7	0	35	1220	52	8	5	17
Wendy's Big Bacon Classic	282	570	260	29	12	0	100	1460	46	3	11	34
RDA (based on...				65	20		300	2400	300	25		

8. **Save the file and continue to the next exercise.**

FORMAT CELL CONTENTS

When you work with tables in InDesign, think of the cells as a series of text frames. Text in a table cell is no different than text in any other text frame; it can be formatted using any of the options you've already learned about, including defined paragraph and character styles.

1. **In the open file, select the Type tool and click in the top-left cell of the table.**

2. **Drag to the bottom-right table cell to highlight all cells in the table.**

3. **Click Table Text in the Paragraph Styles panel to format all the text in the selected table cells.**

4. **Click the Clear Overrides button at the bottom of the Paragraph Styles panel to apply only the base style definition to the text.**

Similar to files from Microsoft Word, some options in Microsoft Excel spreadsheets might require this two-step process to apply your style definitions to the selected text.

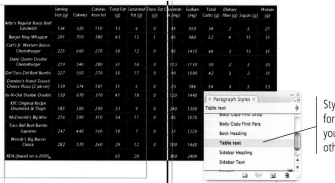

Styles can be used to format table text just as you would format any other text in the layout.

5. **Place the cursor over the first column. When you see a down-pointing arrow, click to select the entire column.**

You can also select rows by placing the cursor immediately left of a row and clicking when the cursor changes to a right-facing arrow.

The down-pointing arrow means you can click to select the entire column.

	Serving Size (g)	Calories	Calories from fat	Total Fat (g)	Saturated Fat (g)	Trans Fat (g)	Cholester- ol (mg)	Sodium (mg)	Total Carbs (g)	Dietary Fiber (g)	Sugars (g
Arby's Regular Roast Beef Sandwich	154	320	110	13	6	0	45	950	34	2	5
Burger King Whopper	291	710	380	43	13	1	85	980	52	4	11
Carl's Jr. Western Bacon Cheeseburger	225	660	270	30	12	0	85	1410	64	3	15
Dairy Queen Double Cheeseburger	219	540	280	31	16	0	115	1130	30	2	5
Del Taco Del Beef Burrito	227	550	270	30	17	0	90	1090	42	3	2
Domino's Hand-Tossed Cheese Pizza (2 pieces)	159	374	101	11	5	0	23	784	54	3	5
In-N-Out Double-Double	330	670	370	41	18	0	120	1440	39	3	10
KFC Original Recipe Drumstick & Thigh	185	500	290	33	9	0	240	1500	16	0	0
McDonald's Big Mac	216	590	310	34	11	0	85	1070	47	3	8
Taco Bell Beef Burrito Supreme	247	440	160	18	7	0	35	1220	52	8	5
Wendy's Big Bacon Classic	282	570	260	29	12	0	100	1460	46	3	11
RDA (based on a 2000..				65	20		300	2400	300	25	

Note:

You have to use the Type tool to select table cells, either individually, in a specific area, or as entire rows/columns.

6. **Using the Control bar or Paragraph panel, change the selected row to left paragraph alignment.**

Text is still text, even though it is placed inside a table cell. You can apply all the same text formatting options to table text that you can apply to text in a regular text frame.

7. **Save the file and continue to the next exercise.**

FORMAT CELL ATTRIBUTES

As we mentioned in the previous exercise, table cells are very similar to regular text frames. Individual cells can have different attributes such as height and width, text inset, vertical positioning, and text orientation. These options can be controlled in the Table panel, the Control bar, and the Cell Options dialog box.

1. **Continue working in the open file. Click in the second cell of the first row, and then drag to select all cells in the row except the first cell.**

2. **In the Table panel (Window>Type & Tables>Table), choose Exactly in the Row Height menu, and then change the associated field to 0.875".**

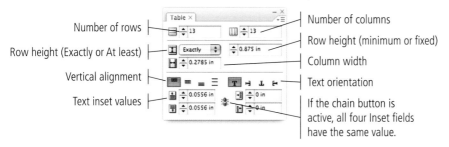

- Number of rows
- Row height (Exactly or At least)
- Vertical alignment
- Text inset values
- Number of columns
- Row height (minimum or fixed)
- Column width
- Text orientation
- If the chain button is active, all four Inset fields have the same value.

3. **Change the Column Width field to 0.2785".**

4. **Click the Rotate Text 270° button so the left edge of the text aligns to the bottom edge of the cell.**

5. **Click the Align Center button so the text in each cell is centered top to bottom.**

   Because the text is rotated, this button actually aligns the text between the left and right cell edges. It's important to remember that the vertical align options are based on the orientation of the text.

6. **Using either the Control bar or the Paragraph panel, apply left paragraph alignment to the selected text.**

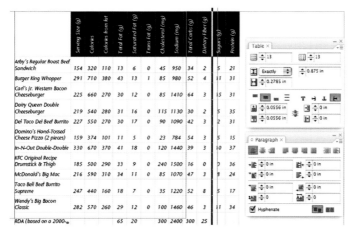

7. **Click the second cell in the second row and drag to select all the cells that contain numeric data.**

8. **Using the Table panel, apply centered vertical alignment to the selected cells.**

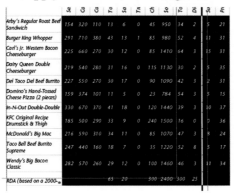

9. **Select the first four cells in the last row and choose Table>Merge Cells.**

   This function extends the contents of a single cell across multiple cells.

10. **Select the entire first column of the table and change the Left Inset value to 0.0625".**

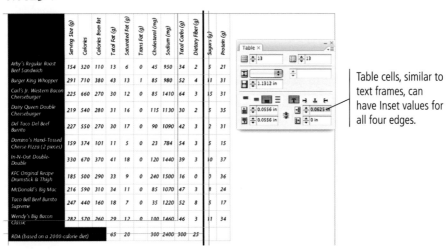

Table cells, similar to text frames, can have Inset values for all four edges.

11. **Place the cursor over the edge of the first column until the cursor becomes a two-headed arrow.**

   When you see this cursor, you can drag the gridline to resize a column or row.

12. **Drag right until the column is wide enough to allow the Wendy's product name to fit on one line.**

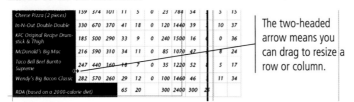

The two-headed arrow means you can drag to resize a row or column.

Note:

Resizing the width of a cell resizes the entire column; resizing the height of a cell resizes the entire row.

13. Place the insertion point in the cell with the Wendy's product.

When you make the column wide enough to fit the text, the row automatically shrinks to one row. In the Table panel, you can see that the Row Height menu is set to At Least; this option allows cells to shrink to fit the height of cell contents, down to the defined minimum height.

When At Least is selected, table rows resize to fit the content.

14. Save the file and continue to the next exercise.

Controlling Cell Attributes

INDESIGN FOUNDATIONS

Basic attributes of individual table cells can be defined in the Text tab of the Cell Options dialog box (Table>Cell Options). The Cell Inset, Vertical Justification, First Baseline, and Text Rotation options are exactly the same as for regular text frames.

The only choice unique to tables is **Clip Contents to Cell**. If you set a fixed row height that is too small for the cell content, an overset text icon appears in the lower-right corner of the cell. (You can't flow text from one cell to another. You have to edit the cell content or resize the cell to be large enough for the content.) If you check the Clip Contents to Cell option, any content that doesn't fit in the cell will be clipped.

Similar to any text frame, a table cell can have its own fill and stroke attributes. These attributes can be defined in the Strokes and Fills tab of the Cell Options dialog box, or using the Swatches and Stroke panels.

The Rows and Columns tab controls the row height and column width. If **At Least** is selected in the Row Height menu, you can define the minimum and maximum possible row height; rows will automatically expand and shrink if you add or remove text, or if you change the text formatting in a way that requires more or less space. If **Exactly** is selected in the Row Height menu, you can define the exact height of the cell.

If you're working with an extremely long table, you can break the table across multiple frames by threading (as you would for any long block of text). The **Keep Options** can be used to keep specific (selected) rows together after a break, and they determine where those rows will go based on your choice in the Start Row menu.

Finally, you can add diagonal lines to specific cells using the Diagonal Lines tab. You can apply the lines in either direction (or both) and choose a specific stroke weight, color, style, and tint. The Draw menu determines whether the line is created in front of or behind the cell's contents.

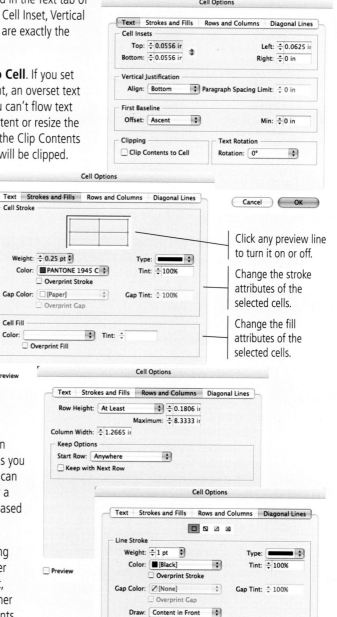

Click any preview line to turn it on or off.

Change the stroke attributes of the selected cells.

Change the fill attributes of the selected cells.

DEFINE TABLE FILLS AND STROKES

Table cells — similar to text frames — can also have fill and stroke attributes. InDesign includes a number of options for adding color to tables, from changing the stroke and fill of an individual cell to defining patterns that repeat every certain number of rows and/or columns.

1. **Continue working in the open file. With the insertion point anywhere in the table, choose Table>Table Options>Table Setup.**

2. **In the Table Setup tab, apply a 0.5-pt. solid border of 100% Pantone 1945 C.**

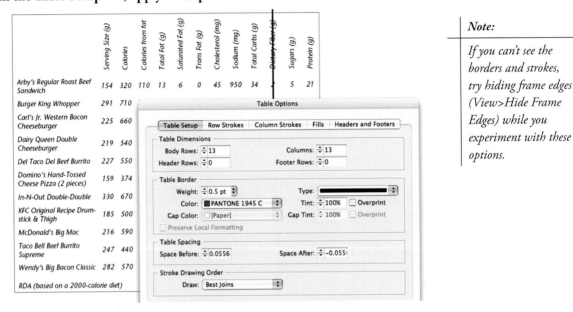

Note:

If you can't see the borders and strokes, try hiding frame edges (View>Hide Frame Edges) while you experiment with these options.

3. **In the Fills tab, choose Every Other Row in the Alternating Pattern menu.**

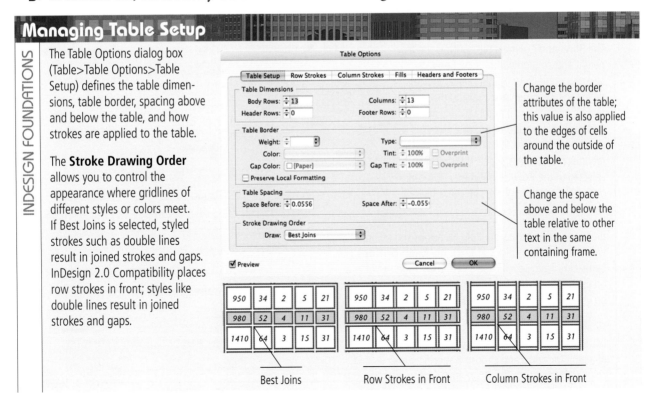

Managing Table Setup

INDESIGN FOUNDATIONS

The Table Options dialog box (Table>Table Options>Table Setup) defines the table dimensions, table border, spacing above and below the table, and how strokes are applied to the table.

The **Stroke Drawing Order** allows you to control the appearance where gridlines of different styles or colors meet. If Best Joins is selected, styled strokes such as double lines result in joined strokes and gaps. InDesign 2.0 Compatibility places row strokes in front; styles like double lines result in joined strokes and gaps.

Change the border attributes of the table; this value is also applied to the edges of cells around the outside of the table.

Change the space above and below the table relative to other text in the same containing frame.

Best Joins   Row Strokes in Front   Column Strokes in Front

4. **Set the First field to 1 row and apply 20% Pantone 1945 C.**

5. **Set the Next field to 1 row and apply None as the color.**

6. **Click OK to apply your choices.**

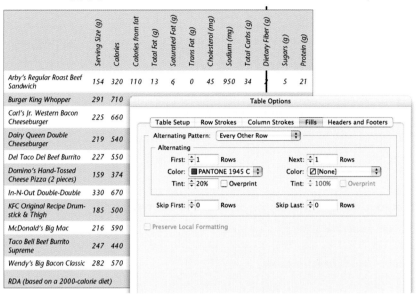

	Serving Size (g)	Calories	Calories from fat	Total Fat (g)	Saturated Fat (g)	Trans Fat (g)	Cholesterol (mg)	Sodium (mg)	Total Carbs (g)	Dietary Fiber (g)	Sugars (g)	Protein (g)
Arby's Regular Roast Beef Sandwich	154	320	110	13	6	0	45	950	34		5	21
Burger King Whopper	291	710										
Carl's Jr. Western Bacon Cheeseburger	225	660										
Dairy Queen Double Cheeseburger	219	540										
Del Taco Del Beef Burrito	227	550										
Domino's Hand-Tossed Cheese Pizza (2 pieces)	159	374										
In-N-Out Double-Double	330	670										
KFC Original Recipe Drumstick & Thigh	185	500										
McDonald's Big Mac	216	590										
Taco Bell Beef Burrito Supreme	247	440										
Wendy's Big Bacon Classic	282	570										
RDA (based on a 2000-calorie diet)												

7. **Select the last row in the table. Using the Swatches panel, change the cell fill tint to 50%.**

   Remember, table cells are very similar to individual text frames. You can change the color of cell fills and strokes using the Swatches panel, and you can change the cell stroke attributes using the Stroke panel.

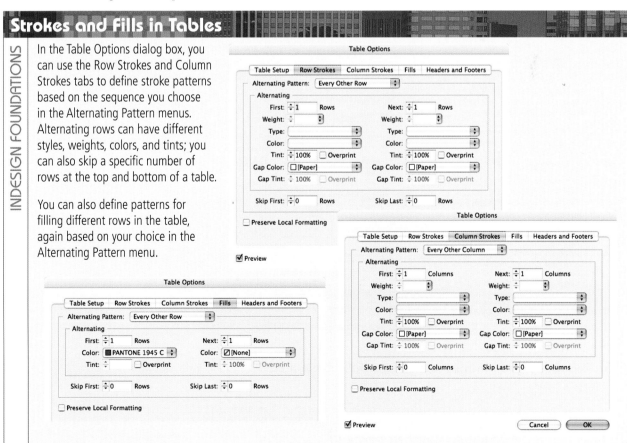

8. **Select all cells in the table and choose Table>Cell Options>Strokes and Fills.**

9. **In the preview area of the dialog box, click all three horizontal lines to remove the strokes from the tops and bottoms of the cells.**

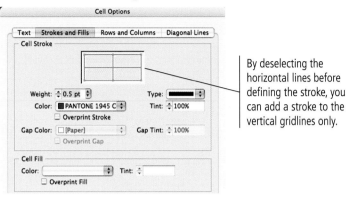

By deselecting the horizontal lines before defining the stroke, you can add a stroke to the vertical gridlines only.

Note:

If you place the cursor at the top-left corner of the table, it changes to a diagonal arrow icon. Clicking with this cursor selects all cells in the table.

10. **Apply a 0.5-pt, 100% Pantone 1945 C stroke using the Solid stroke type.**

    This changes the attributes for the vertical gridlines for all selected cells.

11. **Click OK to apply the stroke values to your table.**

12. **Click the table with the Selection tool, and then fit the frame to the table (Object>Fitting>Fit Frame to Content).**

13. **Drag the table until the top-right corner of the frame snaps to the top-right margin guide on Page 2.**

14. **With the frame still selected, click the second button in the Text Wrap panel so the Eastern Diet story wraps around the frame that contains the table. Change the Left Wrap field to 0.125".**

    A table is always contained inside a text frame. To control the wrap around a table, you have to actually apply the wrap attributes to the frame that contains the table.

Note:

You can apply different stroke values to every cell in a table (although you probably wouldn't want to).

Note:

Remember, you can turn off the Link button in the Text Wrap panel to apply different wrap values to each side of the frame.

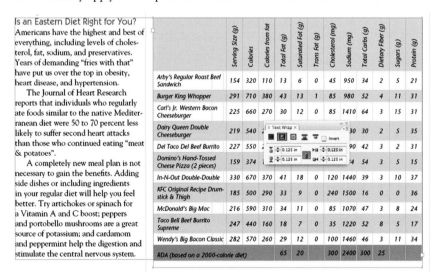

15. **Save the file and continue to the next stage of the project.**

INDESIGN FOUNDATIONS

Long tables of data might require more than one text frame (or column, depending on the table). In this case, you can break a table across multiple frames and use repeating headers and footers for information that needs to be part of each instance of the table (for example, column headings). Repeating headers and footers eliminate the need to manually insert the repeating information in each instance of the table.

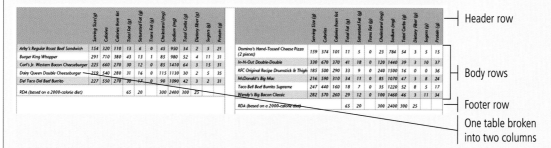

— Header row

— Body rows

— Footer row

— One table broken into two columns

Repeating header and footer rows are dynamically linked; this means that changing one instance of a header or footer changes all instances of the same header or footer.

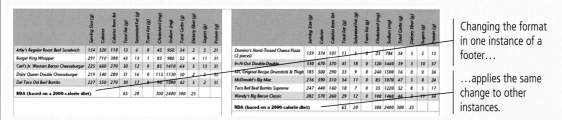

Changing the format in one instance of a footer...

...applies the same change to other instances.

Finally, this capability also means the headers and footers remain at the top and bottom of each instance even if other body rows move to a different instance.

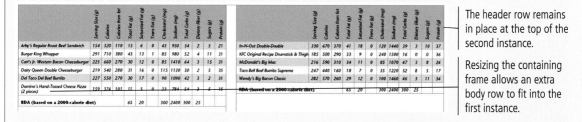

The header row remains in place at the top of the second instance.

Resizing the containing frame allows an extra body row to fit into the first instance.

You can add new header and footer rows to a table when you create the table, or by changing the options in the Headers and Footers tab of the Table Options dialog box. You can also convert existing rows to headers or footers by selecting one or more rows and choosing Table>Convert Rows>To Header or To Footer. You can also control these elements in the Headers and Footers dialog box.

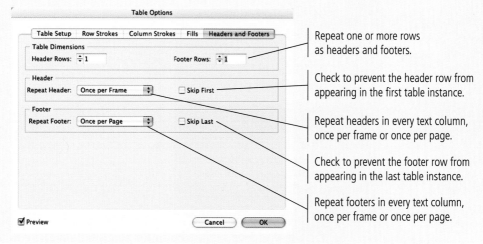

Repeat one or more rows as headers and footers.

Check to prevent the header row from appearing in the first table instance.

Repeat headers in every text column, once per frame or once per page.

Check to prevent the footer row from appearing in the last table instance.

Repeat footers in every text column, once per frame or once per page.

If you've spent any amount of time refining the appearance of a table, and you think you might want to use the same format again, you can save your formatting choices as styles. InDesign supports both table styles and cell styles, which are controlled in the Table Styles panel and Cell Styles panel.

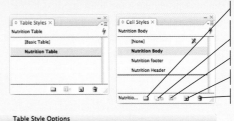

New style group

Clear attributes not defined by style

Clear Overrides

New style

Delete

Table and cell styles use the same concepts as text-formatting styles. You can apply a cell style by selecting the cells and clicking the style name in the Cell Styles panel. Clicking a style in the Table Styles panel applies the style to the entire selected table.

The Clear Overrides button clears text-formatting options; the Clear Attributes button clears cell attributes.

Table styles store all the options that can be defined in the Table Setup dialog box (except for header and footer rows). You can also define cell styles (called **nesting styles**) for specific types of rows, as well as the left and right columns in the table.

Cell styles store all the options that can be defined in the Cell Options dialog box. You can also define the paragraph style applied to cells using that style.

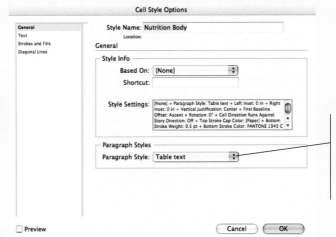

Nest cell styles for specific types of table rows and the left and right columns.

Nest a paragraph style into a cell style to format the cell contents as well as the cell itself.

Stage 4 Preflighting and Packaging the Job

When you submit an InDesign layout to a commercial output provider, you need to send all the necessary pieces of the job — the layout file, any placed (linked) graphics, and the fonts used in the layout. Before you copy everything to a disk and send it out, however, you should check your work to make sure the file is ready for commercial printing.

When you opened the original template at the beginning of this project, you saw the warnings associated with missing fonts and graphics. You should also check that everything is in the correct color space (typically CMYK for printing). You can check fonts, images, and colors manually using the Find Font dialog box, Links panel, and Swatches panel; but InDesign includes a packaging utility that makes it relatively easy to check for common errors (called **preflighting**) and package the necessary bits for the printer.

 EVALUATE THE LAYOUT

1. **With Page 1 of HeartSmart_January.indd showing, choose File>Preflight.**

   This process evaluates the basic contents of the layout for common problems (missing fonts, missing or modified graphics, and so on).

   The Summary pane shows an overview of the results; potential problems are flagged with a yellow warning icon.

Note:

   This is certainly not an extensive preflight check, but it does verify the most common errors introduced during the design process.

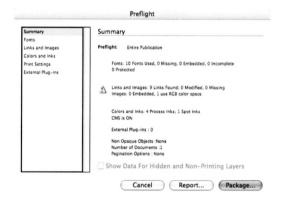

2. **Click Fonts in the list on the left.**

   This view shows every font used in the layout. If you have a very long list of fonts, you might want to choose the Show Problems Only option.

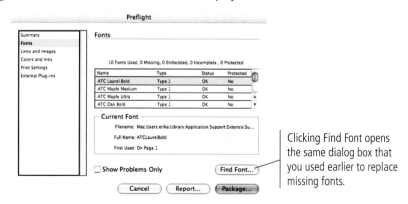

   Clicking Find Font opens the same dialog box that you used earlier to replace missing fonts.

3. **Click Links and Images in the list.**

   This view shows all graphics placed in the layout, including the type and color mode of each image and the status of each link. Because this layout will be output in CMYK color mode, you should replace RGB images with CMYK versions (which you will do shortly).

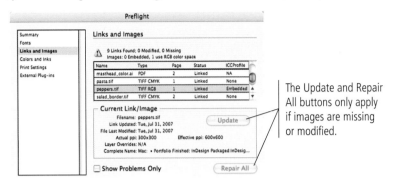

The Update and Repair All buttons only apply if images are missing or modified.

Note:

Some output processes can convert RGB images to CMYK on the fly. Ask your printer whether images need to be converted before output.

4. **Click Colors and Inks in the list of categories on the left.**

   This layout includes a Pantone ink. This job will be printed four-color (using only CMYK inks), so the Pantone separation needs to be corrected.

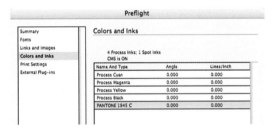

5. **Click Cancel to return to the document.**

6. **In the Swatches panel, Control/right-click the Pantone 1945 C swatch and choose Swatch Options.**

Note:

You can also simply double-click a swatch in the Swatches panel to open the Swatch Options dialog box.

7. **In the Color Type menu, choose Process instead of Spot, and then click OK.**

   Keep in mind that many spot colors are outside the CMYK gamut, which means they can't be accurately reproduced using the CMYK model. When these colors are converted to CMYK, there will be some **color shift** when the ink is converted to the nearest possible CMYK equivalent. Depending on the color being converted, the shift can be subtle or dramatic.

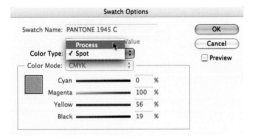

8. **In the Links panel, select peppers.tif and click the Go to Link button.**

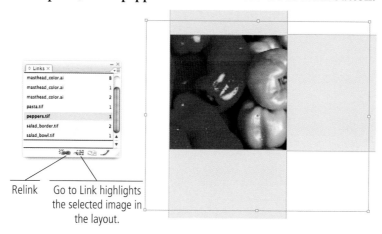

Relink   Go to Link highlights the selected image in the layout.

9. **Click the Relink button. Navigate to the peppers_cmyk.tif file in the RF_InDesign>HeartSmart>January issue>CMYK folder and click Open.**

If you see the Image Import Options dialog box, just click OK.

When you relink the selected image, the scaling and positioning of the placed graphic are maintained for the new image.

Note:

When you relink a placed image, you have the option to Relink All Instances in the bottom of the navigation dialog box. If this option is selected, all instances of the same placed file will be replaced with the new file.

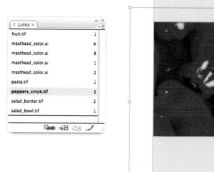

10. **Choose File>Preflight again.**

The errors have been fixed, so it's safe to create the job package.

Note:

You can also choose File>Package to create a job package without preflighting the job.

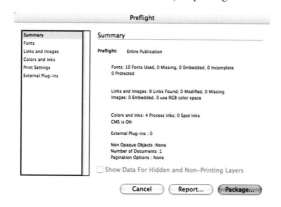

11. **Click Package in the Preflight dialog box.**

12. **If you see a message asking you to save, click Save.**

13. **In the Printing Instructions dialog box, fill in your contact information, and then click Continue.**

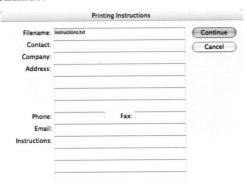

14. **Navigate to your WIP>HeartSmart folder as the target location and click Save/Package.**

Note:

When you create a job package, InDesign automatically creates a new folder for the job using the file name and the word "Folder" as the package name.

15. **Read the resulting warning and click OK.**

Similar to any software, you purchase a license to use a font — you do not own the actual font. It is illegal to distribute fonts freely, as it is illegal to distribute copies of your software. Most (but not all) font licenses allow you to send your copy of a font to a service provider, as long as the service provider also owns a copy of the font. Always verify that you are not violating font copyright before sending out a job.

When the process is complete, the necessary job elements appear in the job folder.

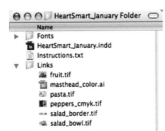

16. **Close the InDesign file.**

Summary

This project introduced a number of concepts and tools that will be very important as you work on more complex page layout jobs. Importing text content from other applications — specifically, Microsoft Word and Microsoft Excel — is a foundational skill that you will use in most projects; this newsletter showed you how to control that content on import, and then re-format it as appropriate in the InDesign layout.

Templates, master pages, and styles are all designed to let you do the majority of work once and then apply it as many times as necessary; virtually any InDesign project can benefit from these tools, and you will use them extensively in your career as a graphic designer. This project provided a basic introduction to these productivity tools; you will build on these foundations as you complete the remaining five projects of this book.

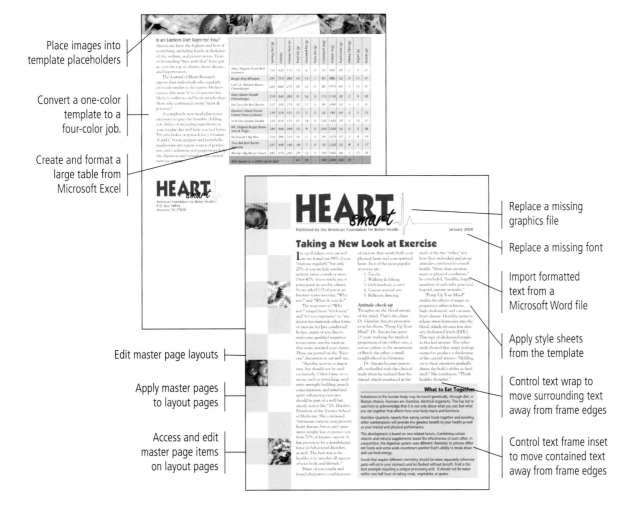

Place images into template placeholders

Convert a one-color template to a four-color job.

Create and format a large table from Microsoft Excel

Edit master page layouts

Apply master pages to layout pages

Access and edit master page items on layout pages

Replace a missing graphics file

Replace a missing font

Import formatted text from a Microsoft Word file

Apply style sheets from the template

Control text wrap to move surrounding text away from frame edges

Control text frame inset to move contained text away from frame edges

Portfolio Builder Project 3

The Humane Society wants to create a wall calendar to give away as a part of its annual fundraising drive. Each month will be on one sheet, which can be flipped over when the month is over.

To complete this project, you should:

❏ Design a layout that incorporates the month grid, as well as space for an image and four coupons.

❏ Use whatever page size you think is most appropriate for the job.

❏ Use the master page to build the basic structure of each page (month) in the calendar.

❏ Find images or illustrations for each month that don't require a licensing fee.

"We're a not-for-profit organization; we try to dedicate most of our finances to caring for our furry (and feathery, and leathery) friends. The printer has donated the resources to print the job, and your agency has donated your time as well — for which we're extremely grateful.

"In the past, we've sent out preprinted address labels, note pads, and even little beanie animals as incentives for donations. This year we want to offer a wall calendar as an incentive.

"We want each month to have a different picture of an animal — cute, cuddly, happy pictures of people with their pets to encourage adoption. Make sure you include different kinds of animals though; the Humane Society isn't just for dogs and cats. Can you find images that won't cost anything to use?

"Each month will also include a set of three coupons for local pet-related businesses. When you build the layout, plan space for those; when the layout's done, we'll let our donor companies know how much space they have for the coupons.

"One final thing: we thought it might be fun to include a monthly 'fun fact' about animals. Can you find some little text snippets on the Internet or in a book to include each month?"

Letterfold Catering Menu

Your client is a local patisserie that offers corporate catering services in addition to its in-store breakfast, brunch, and bakery products. To promote their business, the client wants to create a letterfold brochure that highlights their breakfast catering menu. They also want to include a basic form that people can fill out and enter to win a free office breakfast — a common technique for gathering potential clients' contact information.

This project incorporates the following skills:

❑ Building a template for specific folding requirements

❑ Importing text from a Microsoft Word file

❑ Editing imported style sheets

❑ Controlling tabs to format columns of text

❑ Using object styles to reduce repetitive tasks

❑ Working with embedded clipping paths and Alpha channels

❑ Controlling irregular text wraps

❑ Using a library to access frequently used objects

Our business has been doing well, but we're hoping to expand our catering services. We want you to create a simple brochure featuring our breakfast catering menu, with lots of pictures to go with the text. We also want to include a little form that we can use to gather prospective clients' contact information, and maybe a quote from one of our happy customers. (We put one at the end of the text. If you can use it, great; if not, just delete it.)

A lot of people design folding documents incorrectly. Some people use a six-page layout with each page the size of the final folded job; other people use two pages, each one divided into three equal "columns." In both cases, all the panels on the job are the exact same width — which is wrong.

Paper has inherent thickness; any panel that folds "in" to the other panels needs to be smaller than the other panels. In the case of a letterfold brochure such as the one you're designing here, the inside panel needs to be 1/16″ smaller than the other panels.

Different types of folding documents also have different facing- or non-facing page requirements. For a letterfold, the job needs to be set up as facing pages because the front and back need to mirror each other. The right-facing page has the front panel, back panel, and the outside of the folding flap; the left-facing page has the three inside panels.

The last item to remember is that the brochure will be a self-mailer; the back panel needs to be left blank, with only the return address in the corner.

To complete this project, you will:

- ❑ Create a template that meets requirements for common folding documents
- ❑ Create a folding grid on a master page
- ❑ Use the slug area to mark folding panels
- ❑ Import and edit style sheets from a Microsoft Word file
- ❑ Create new styles based on existing formatting in the layout
- ❑ Create a basic form using tabs, fill characters, and box inset values
- ❑ Use object styles to apply consistent formatting to multiple frames
- ❑ Call an embedded clipping path
- ❑ Apply a feathered Alpha channel that is embedded in a Photoshop file
- ❑ Control text wraps around basic frames and irregular shapes
- ❑ Create an InDesign library file to store frequently used objects and groups

Stage 1   **Building a Folding Template**

When working with folding (multi-panel) documents, many people mistakenly assume that the trim size of the job is the size it appears after folding. In fact, the trim size of a folded document is actually the size of the sheet before it's folded. This section describes how to properly set up multi-panel documents that fold in a variety of ways.

There are two basic principles to remember when dealing with documents that fold:

- Paper has thickness. The thicker the paper, the more allowance you need to plan for the fold.

- Folding machines are mechanical devices. They process large amounts of material and are accurate to about 0.0125″. Paper sometimes shifts as it flows through the machine's paper path, just as it can in a laser printer or photocopier.

Facing vs. Non-Facing Pages

As a general rule, you should use facing pages any time the design will be read like a book — left to right, Page 2 printed on the back of Page 1 and facing Page 3, and so on. For facing-page layouts, the left page mirrors the right page of each spread. The side margins are referred to as "Inside" (near the spine or binding) and "Outside" (away from the binding) instead of "Left" and "Right."

When you plan a nonstandard folding document, it is also important to decide whether it should be created with or without facing pages. The fold marks on the front and back of a sheet should line up. This means that if one panel of a document is a different size than the others, the back side of the sheet has to mirror the front.

In the following illustration, a document has one fold — a smaller panel that folds over to cover half of the inside of the brochure. Fold marks on the outside layout have to mirror the inside of the brochure so that, when folded, the two sides line up properly.

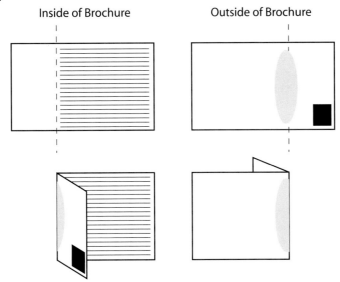

Inside of Brochure   Outside of Brochure

Note:

Layout pages can be viewed as individual pages, or they can be viewed as two or more pages at a time, which is called a **spread**.

Note:

Depending on the job you're designing — including some jobs that are printed on two sides of the same page — you might need to create facing pages or non-facing pages.

Note:

Some service providers give their clients folding templates to use for building a layout. You should ask your service provider if these templates are available before you waste time and effort reinventing the wheel.

Basic Types of Folds

There are several standard types of folded documents, each with specific formulas for setting up the layout.

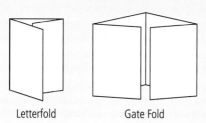

Letterfold   Gate Fold

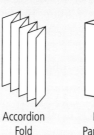

Accordion   Double
Fold   Parallel Fold

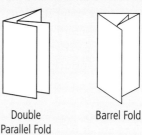

Barrel Fold

Letterfold (often incorrectly called "trifold" because it results in three panels) brochures can be printed at any size. There are three panels to a side and two folds; letterfold brochures should be created with facing pages because the two sides of the sheet need to mirror each other.

The formula for creating a letterfold brochure typically requires the panel that folds in to be 1/16" narrower than the two outside panels. (Ask your service provider if 1/16" allowance is enough based on the type of paper you're using.) Half of the area removed from the inside panel (1/32") is added to each of the outside two panels.

> Trim size ÷ 3 = Starting panel size
>
> Fold-in panel = Starting panel size − 1/16"
>
> Outside panels = Starting panel size + 1/32"

Gate folds result in a four-panel document. The paper is folded in half, and then each half is folded in half toward the center so the two ends of the paper meet at the center fold. The formula for creating a gate fold is similar to the formula for the letterfold brochure; the panels that fold in are 1/16" narrower than the two outside panels. Gate-fold brochures can be created with non-facing pages.

> Trim size ÷ 4 = Starting panel size
>
> Fold-in panels = Starting panel size − 1/32"
>
> Outside panels = Starting panel size + 1/32"

Accordion folds — a comparatively unusual format — can have as many panels as you prefer. When it has six panels (three on each side), it's often referred to as a "Z-fold" because it looks like the letter Z. Because the panels don't fold into one another, an accordion-fold document has panels of consistent width. Accordion-fold brochures can be created with non-facing pages.

> Paper Size ÷ Number of Panels = Panel Size

Double-parallel folds are commonly used for eight-panel rack brochures (such as those you often find in a hotel or travel agency). Again, the panels on the inside are 1/16" narrower than the outside panels. This type of fold uses facing pages because the margins need to line up on the front and back sides of the sheet. Double parallel-fold brochures should be created with facing pages.

> Trim size ÷ 4 = Starting panel size
>
> Outside panels = Starting panel size + 1/32"
>
> Fold-in panels = Starting panel size − 1/32"

Barrel folds (also called **roll folds**) are perhaps the most common fold for 14 × 8.5" brochures. The two outside panels are full size, and each successive panel is 1/16" narrower than the previous one. Barrel-fold brochures should be created with facing pages.

> Trim size ÷ 4 = Starting panel size
>
> Outside panels = Starting panel size + 1/16"
>
> Fold-in panel 1 = Starting panel size − 1/32"
>
> Fold-in panel 2 = Starting panel size − 3/32"

SET UP FOLDING GUIDES

It is important to consider the output process when planning a job with documents that are not just a single sheet of standard-size paper — documents with multiple pages folded one or more times, or other non-standard page sizes. The mechanics of commercial printing require specific allowances for cutting, folding, and other finishing processes.

You should note that the issues presented here have little to do with the subjective elements of design. Layout and page geometry are governed by physical realities, including mechanical limitations in the production process. These principles are rules, not suggestions. If you don't leave adequate margins, for example, elements of your design will be cut off or won't align properly from one page to the next. It won't matter how good a design looks on your monitor if it's cut off the edge of a printed page.

1. **Create a new document with a page size of 11 × 8.5″, (landscape orientation) with 0.25″ margins on all four sides and one column.**

2. **Select the Facing Pages option and deselect the Master Text Frame option.**

3. **Define a 0.125″ bleed and 0.5″ slug on all four sides of the layout.**

Note:

Before completing this project, copy the Cafe folder from the WIP folder on your Resource CD to your WIP folder wherever you are saving your work. Save the files for this project in your WIP>Cafe folder.

4. **Click OK to create your new file.**

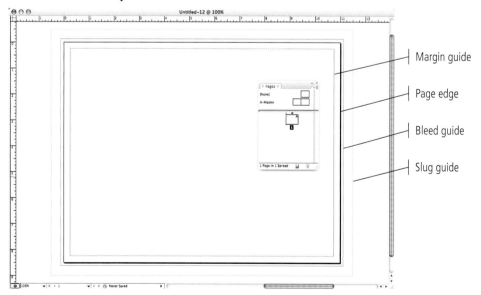

Margin guide

Page edge

Bleed guide

Slug guide

5. In the Pages panel, double-click the A-Master icon to access the master page layout.

It's a good idea to create folding grids on a master page layout so you can easily apply the same set of guides to any page in the layout. This is far quicker than manually placing the guides on individual pages.

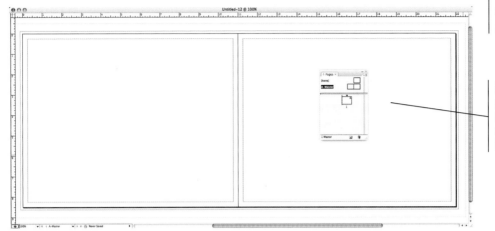

Note:

It doesn't matter if you double-click the master page name or icon; both display the master page in the document window.

Layouts with facing pages have two opposing pages in each master-page layout.

6. On the left page of the master page layout, drag vertical guides for the folds to the following X positions: 3.687″ and 7.375″.

You can place very precise guides by dragging a guide onto the page, and then changing the guide position in the Control bar. (The Control bar also shows the dynamic location of guides as you drag them.)

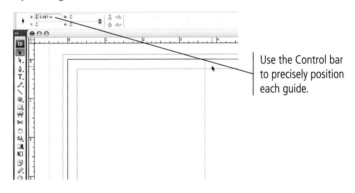

Use the Control bar to precisely position each guide.

Note:

The left-facing page will be the inside panels of the brochure.

The right-facing page will be the outside panels.

7. Show the right page of the spread in the layout and look at the ruler above the spread line.

By default, InDesign rulers are based on the top-left corner of the entire spread. The ruler above the spread line (the black line between the two pages of the spread) continues at 11″ instead of starting again at 0 for the right page.

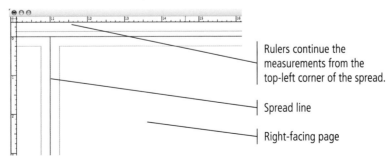

Rulers continue the measurements from the top-left corner of the spread.

Spread line

Right-facing page

8. In the Units & Increments pane of the Preferences dialog box, choose Page in the Ruler Units Origin menu and click OK.

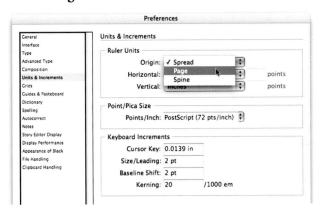

Above the spread line, the ruler now starts over at 0 for the right-facing page.

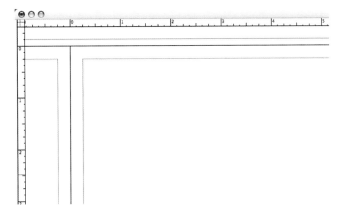

9. On the right-facing page, place vertical guides at X: 3.625″ and 7.312″.

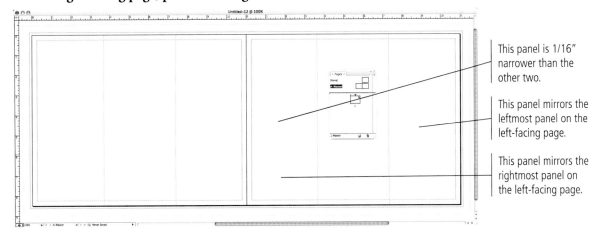

This panel is 1/16″ narrower than the other two.

This panel mirrors the leftmost panel on the left-facing page.

This panel mirrors the rightmost panel on the left-facing page.

10. **Drag the zero point crosshairs (in the top-left corner of the project window) to the first vertical guide on the left master page.**

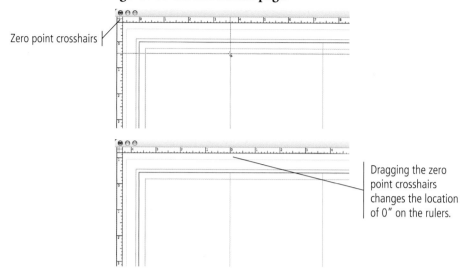

Zero point crosshairs

Dragging the zero point crosshairs changes the location of 0" on the rulers.

11. **Drag vertical guides 0.25" from both sides of the fold guide to create margin areas around the fold.**

Once the zero point is placed over the folding guide, margins can easily be set at 0.25" on either side of the folding guide.

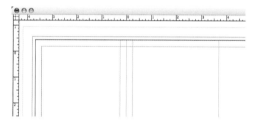

12. **Repeat this process to place guides at 0.25" on both sides of each of the fold guides on the master layout (left- and right-facing pages).**

13. **Double-click the zero point crosshairs (in the top-left corner of the project window) to reset the zero point to the top-left corner of the layout page.**

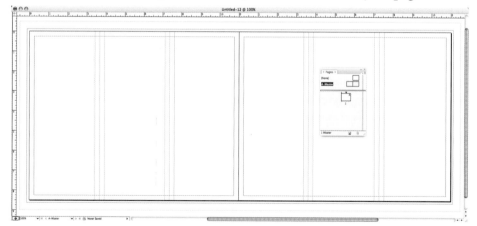

14. **Choose View>Grids & Guides>Lock Guides to prevent the guides from being accidentally moved.**

15. **Save the file in your WIP>Cafe folder as "letterfold.indd".**

ADD SLUG INFORMATION AND PLACEHOLDERS

When you work with folding grids, it's easy to forget which panel goes where. You can use the layout slug area to add nonprinting elements as self-reminders, as well as place folding marks that the output provider can use as a reference. These elements, similar to the guides, should be placed on the master-page layout.

1. **With letterfold.indd open, make sure the A-Master layout is showing in the document window.**

2. **Select the Type tool and create a text frame above the left panel of the left-facing page, between the bleed and slug guides.**

3. **Type "INSIDE LEFT PANEL" in the frame and apply centered paragraph alignment using either the Paragrah panel or the Control bar.**

4. **Open the Text Frame Options dialog box and apply centered vertical frame alignment.**

Note:

Open the Text Frame Options dialog box in the Object menu, or using the contextual menu for a specific object.

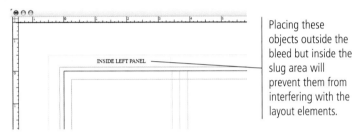

Placing these objects outside the bleed but inside the slug area will prevent them from interfering with the layout elements.

5. **Choose Window>Attributes to open the Attributes panel.**

6. **Make sure the text frame is selected and check the Nonprinting box.**

   These objects are only for your information; they don't need to be included in the output.

Note:

If you want to print these frames, you can override this setting using the Print Nonprinting Objects option in the General print settings.

7. **Control/right-click the text frame and choose Allow Master Item Overrides to deactivate the toggle option and protect this object on associated layout pages.**

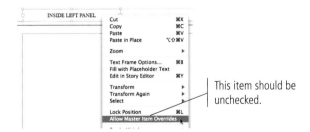

This item should be unchecked.

8. **Using the Selection tool, press Option/Alt-Shift and then drag the text frame to the right.**

   By pressing Option/Alt while dragging, you are creating an exact copy or **clone** of the original object. This technique will be invaluable for many types of jobs.

Key Command:

Pressing Shift while cloning constrains the clone movement to 45° angles from the original object.

The cursor changes when you press Option/Alt to clone an object.

9. Change the text in the clone to "INSIDE CENTER PANEL".

10. Repeat this process to place a text frame over each panel on both sides of the spread, using the following text:

Right column, left page	INSIDE RIGHT PANEL
Left column, right page	FOLD-IN FLAP
Center column, right page	BACK PANEL (MAILING AREA)
Right column, right page	FRONT PANEL

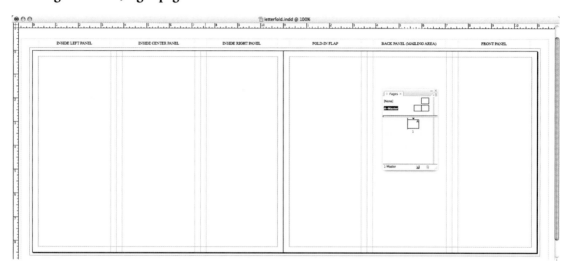

11. Using the Line tool, click in the slug area (near the guide that marks the slug edge) above the first fold guide on the left page.

12. Press Shift and drag down to the bleed guide.

Pressing Shift constrains the line to 45° angles; the line you're drawing now should be exactly vertical.

Note:

This line (and the others you will clone from it) are marks to indicate the location for folds in the printed document.

Because the line is entirely outside the trim area, it will be included if the slug area is output, but will not interfere with the artwork inside the trim area.

13. In the Stroke panel, change the line to a 0.5-pt dashed stroke with a 3-pt dash and gap.

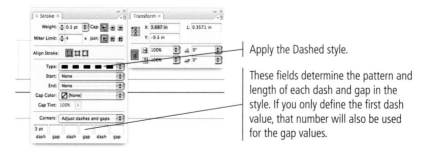

Apply the Dashed style.

These fields determine the pattern and length of each dash and gap in the style. If you only define the first dash value, that number will also be used for the gap values.

14. Using either the Transform panel or the Control bar, change the line's position to X: 3.687″ (the same as the first folding guide).

15. **Control/right-click the dashed line and toggle off the Allow Master Item Overrides option.**

16. **Clone (Option/Alt-click and drag) the line and place copies above and below each folding guide on both pages of the spread.**

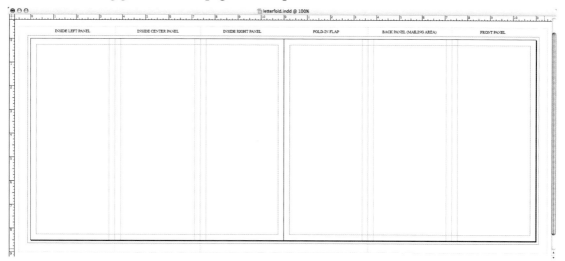

17. **Save the file and continue to the next exercise.**

 ## SAVE A TEMPLATE

As the previous exercises demonstrated, setting up a brochure properly can be time-consuming. Once you create a folding grid, it's a good idea to save the layout as a template so the same guides can be applied to any similar type of layout. Every time you want to create a letterfold brochure, you can open the template and begin with an empty file that contains only the correct guides and marks.

1. **With A-Master of letterfold.indd open, create a text frame in each panel of the layout.**

   These placeholders will be available whenever you implement the layout. Remember, every click you can save by adding template elements will save that much time later — every time you re-use the same template.

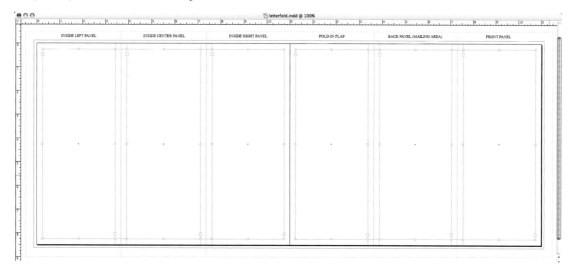

2. **Choose File>Save As and navigate to your WIP>Cafe folder.**

3. **Choose InDesign CS3 Template in the Format/Save As Type menu and click Save.**

Remember, choosing the template option in the Format/Save As Type menu automatically changes the extension to "indt."

4. **Close the file and continue to the next stage of the project.**

Stage 2 Working with Imported Text

In Project 3 you used styles in an InDesign template to format the text imported from a Microsoft Word file. By applying styles, you can apply multiple formatting attributes — both character and paragraph — with a single click. InDesign is not the only software that supports text-formatting styles; Microsoft Word also incorporates this functionality.

Many of your clients will submit text with local formatting — they highlight some text and change the font, size, spacing, etc. — that you will strip out and replace with the proper InDesign translations. More sophisticated users, however, will send files that are extensively formatted with Microsoft Word styles. In this case, you can import the styles from Microsoft Word directly into your InDesign layout to use as the basis for your work.

 ## IMPORT AND THREAD TEXT ACROSS FRAMES

1. **Create a new file from the letterfold.indt template that is in your WIP>Cafe folder.**

   Remember, to create a new file from a template, you have to open the template file.

2. **Double-click the Page 1 icon to make it active in the document window.**

   Page 1 of a new document — whether created from scratch or based on an existing template — is always associated with the default master page (A-Master).

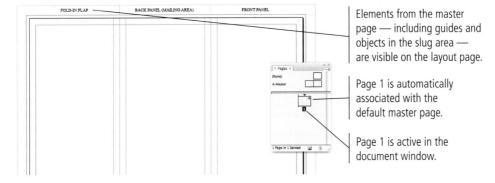

Elements from the master page — including guides and objects in the slug area — are visible on the layout page.

Page 1 is automatically associated with the default master page.

Page 1 is active in the document window.

3. Open the Pages panel options menu and choose Insert Pages.

Note:

You can disassociate Page 1 from the default master by dragging the [None] master page icon onto the Page 1 icon.

4. In the Insert Pages dialog box, make sure you are adding 1 page, after Page 1, using the A-Master layout.

This dialog box allows you to add a specific number of pages, in a specific location, using any existing master page layout as the master.

Note:

You can also add new pages into the layout by dragging a master page icon into the lower half of the Pages panel.

5. Click OK to add the second page to the layout.

In a layout with facing pages, new pages are added sequentially as left- or right-facing pages. Following convention, right-facing pages have odd numbers and left-facing pages have even numbers. (You can override this option using section numbering, which you will do in Project 8.)

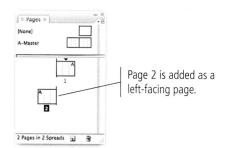

Page 2 is added as a left-facing page.

6. Control/right-click the Page 1 icon in the Pages panel and choose Override All Master Page Items.

Unlike the Allow Master Item Override option in the master page layout, the Override All Master Page Items command is not a toggle switch; once you override the master page items for a specific layout page, you can't reverse the command by choosing the option again.

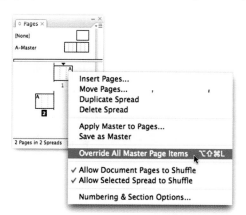

Note:

The Override All Master Page Items command would be better named "Detach All Master Page Items" because you are detaching items from the related master page so they now exist on the main layout page.

The Override All Master Page Items command allows you to access the text frames you created on the master layout. You won't be able to access the guides, which are locked, or the nonprinting slug items, which you protected by toggling off the Allow Master Item Overrides option.

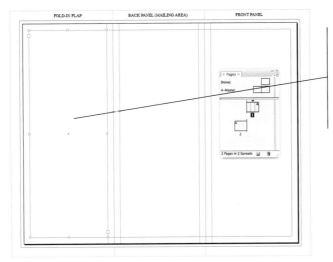

After overriding master page items on Page 1, you can select and modify — and add text to — the text frames from the master layout.

7. **Repeat Step 6 for Page 2.**

8. **Save the file as "cafe.indd" in your WIP>Cafe folder and continue to the next exercise.**

Note:

You can Shift-click to select multiple pages in the Pages panel and override master page items for all selected pages at one time.

 IMPORT STYLES FROM MICROSOFT WORD

In the previous project you learned the basics of importing the Normal style from a Microsoft Word file. When your clients use more sophisticated styles in their layouts, you need to understand what to do with those styles when you import the files into your layout.

1. **With cafe.indd open, display Page 2 in the document window and make sure nothing is selected in the file.**

2. **Choose File>Place. Navigate to your RF_InDesign>Cafe folder and choose menu.doc.**

3. **Make sure the Show Import Options box is checked and click Open.**

    The Formatting section of the Import Options dialog box shows that there is one conflict between the styles in the Microsoft Word file and the styles in the InDesign file.

The Microsoft Word file has one paragraph style that conflicts with a style in the InDesign layout.

Note:

Since you haven't created any styles in the InDesign file yet, you could simply use the imported style. But we generally prefer to import everything the client did so we can see important issues, and then make whatever changes are necessary in the InDesign file.

4. **Under Preserve Styles and Formatting from Text and Tables, make sure the Import Styles Automatically option is selected and choose Auto Rename in the Paragraph Style Conflicts menu. Click OK.**

This option allows you to maintain the same-named styles from both the Microsoft Word file and the InDesign layout.

5. **If you see a Missing Fonts warning, review the information and then click OK.**

When you import Microsoft Word files with their formatting, you see this warning more often than not.

Many actions in Microsoft Word — such as using the B or I buttons to apply **faux bold** or **faux italic** type styles — can cause problems in InDesign because InDesign tries to translate those faux formatting options to the best-possible "real" font variant required for commercial printing applications.

The good news is that in many cases, you can replace the fonts used in the Microsoft Word file with something that is more appropriate for your overall design. It would be a waste of time to correct these font problems until you know whether you need to do so. In this case, you're eventually going to replace the style that calls for the missing fonts, so there's no point in spending time resolving the missing-font problem.

6. **In the document window, press Option/Alt and move the cursor over the text frame on the left side of Page 2 (the inside of the brochure).**

Normally, clicking with the loaded text cursor fills the current frame and leaves overset text as overset text. By pressing Option/Alt before clicking, however, you can keep overset text loaded in the cursor so you can choose the next frame where the story will thread (called **semi-automatic text flow**).

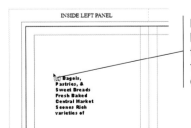

Pressing Option/Alt converts the loaded text cursor to the semi-auto flow cursor so you can direct the flow of the story into more than one text frame.

Note:

Semi-automatic text flow works on one frame at a time, so you have to Option/Alt-click each frame to keep overset text loaded in the cursor. You can automatically flow an entire story by Shift-clicking with the loaded cursor. In this case, pages are added as necessary to accommodate the entire story.

7. **While holding the Option/Alt key, click in the text frame on the left side of the page.**

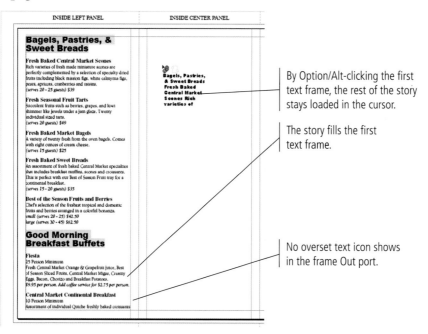

By Option/Alt-clicking the first text frame, the rest of the story stays loaded in the cursor.

The story fills the first text frame.

No overset text icon shows in the frame Out port.

8. **Option/Alt-click the second text frame on the page to place more of the story.**

9. **Click the third frame to place the rest of the story.**

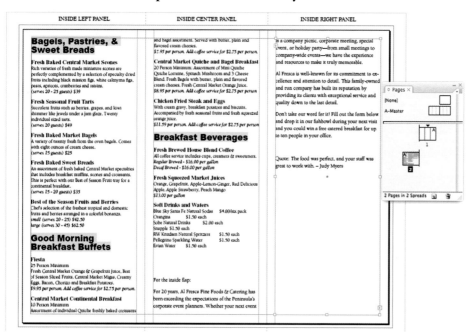

10. **Place the insertion point in the first paragraph of the story and look at the Paragraph Styles panel.**

The Paragraph Styles panel shows what style is applied to the current paragraph — in this case, Heading 1. (The pink highlight also shows the location of missing fonts.)

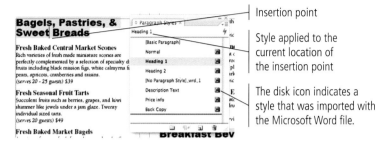

Insertion point

Style applied to the current location of the insertion point

The disk icon indicates a style that was imported with the Microsoft Word file.

11. **Click in different areas of different formatting throughout the story and review which styles are applied to which paragraphs.**

12. **Save the file and continue to the next exercise.**

 ## IMPORT AND REPLACE INDESIGN STYLES

In many instances, the styles you need for a particular job have already been created for another job. For example, a particular client likes to use 12-pt. Garamond with 14-pt. leading for the main body copy in every job. If you've already spent the time to create styles once, you can simply import them into your current file instead of recreating the same styles over and over again.

1. **With cafe.indd open, choose Load All Text Styles from the Paragraph Styles panel options menu.**

You could also choose Load Paragraph Styles, but the Load All Text Styles allows you to access both character and paragraph styles in a single pass, instead of requiring two steps to import the two different types of styles.

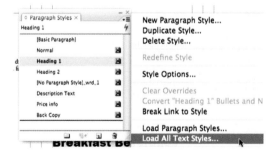

2. **Navigate to the file cafe_styles.indd in the RF_InDesign>Cafe folder and click Open.**

This file contains several styles that were used when the restaurant owner created the in-store menus. The client would like to use some of the same styles in the mailing brochure for consistency.

3. **The Load Styles dialog box shows all the styles available in the cafe_styles.indd file.**

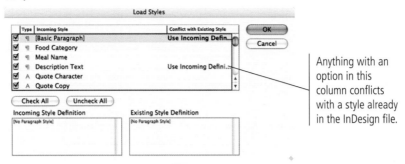

Anything with an option in this column conflicts with a style already in the InDesign file.

4. **Click the box to the left of [Basic Paragraph] to uncheck that style.**

   Anything checked will be imported; anything unchecked will not be imported.

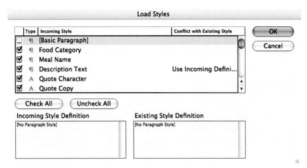

5. **Click Description Text, and then choose Auto-Rename in the conflict-resolution menu.**

   As for conflicts with styles in Microsoft Word files, it's a good idea to maintain the imported information until you determine exactly what you need.

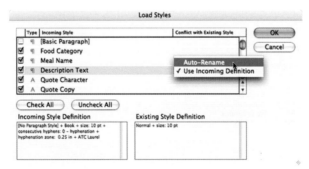

6. **Click OK to import the selected styles (three paragraph and three character).**

The imported InDesign styles do not show the disk icon.

7. **Using the Selection tool, click anywhere in the pasteboard to deselect the text frames in the layout.**

8. **In the Paragraph Styles panel, drag Heading 1 to the trash icon at the bottom of the panel.**

Deleting a style is as simple as dragging the style to the trash icon.

9. **In the resulting dialog box, choose Food Category in the Replace With menu and click OK.**

   If you delete a style sheet that's being used, you have to determine what to do with text that uses the style you want to delete. If you want to maintain the formatting of that text without applying a different style, you can choose [No Paragraph Style].

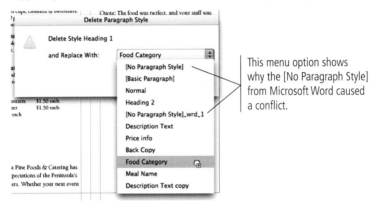

This menu option shows why the [No Paragraph Style] from Microsoft Word caused a conflict.

   After the Heading 1 style is replaced with the Food Category style, the associated headings in the layout change their appearance to match the new style definition.

Food Category does not call for Arial Black Bold Italic, so the pink highlighting is gone.

10. **Delete Heading 2 and replace it with Meal Name.**

11. **Delete Description Text and replace it with Description Text copy.**

12. Delete [No Paragraph Style]_wrd_1 and replace it with [No Paragraph Style]. In this case, make sure the Preserve Formatting option is selected.

InDesign's default [No Paragraph Style] is not a style — in fact, it is the express lack of a defined style. The imported [No Paragraph Style] is considered a style, so you have to decide what to do with the formatting that was applied.

Note:

Any time you choose [No Paragraph Style] in the Replace With menu, the Preserve Formatting option becomes available in the Delete Paragraph Style dialog box.

13. Delete Normal and replace it with [Basic Paragraph].

In InDesign, [Basic Paragraph] is essentially the same as Microsoft Word's Normal style. If you don't define or apply any other styles, new text in an InDesign document is automatically set in the [Basic Paragraph] options.

Your computer might or might not have the Italic variant of the Times font available; if you don't, you will see the missing font indicated by a pink highlight. You'll change the Price Info definition in the next exercise, so don't worry if you see pink highlighting.

Note:

You can edit the default type settings for a layout by editing the [Basic Paragraph] style. You can edit the default type settings for all new InDesign layouts by editing the [Basic Paragraph] style when no file is open.

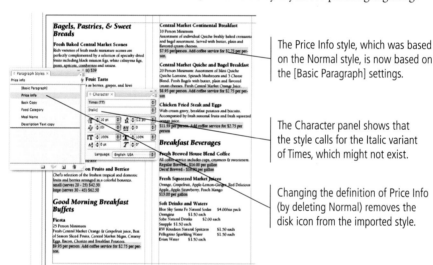

The Price Info style, which was based on the Normal style, is now based on the [Basic Paragraph] settings.

The Character panel shows that the style calls for the Italic variant of Times, which might not exist.

Changing the definition of Price Info (by deleting Normal) removes the disk icon from the imported style.

14. Save the file and continue to the next exercise.

INDESIGN FOUNDATIONS

By completing the first three projects, you've already learned about a considerable number of options for formatting text — both character and paragraph attributes — but there's still more to learn. The important point here is that styles can store a very large number of settings, which you'll see when you complete the next exercise.

Use the following chart as a reminder of exactly what can be stored in a paragraph style definition, as well as where to find the equivalent in the application interface for selected text. (Character styles include a subset of these same options: General, Basic Character Formats, Advanced Character Formats, Character Color, OpenType Features, Underline Options, and Strikethrough Options.)

Category	Options			Application Equivalent
General	Based On Style Settings	Next Style Reset to Base	Shortcut Apply Style to Selection	N/A
Basic Character Formats	Font Family Leading	Style Kerning	Size Tracking	Character panel
	Case	Position	Styles	Character panel options menu
Advanced Character Formats	Horizontal Scale Skew	Vertical Scale Language	Baseline Shift	Character panel
Indents and Spacing	Alignment Left & Right Indent Space Before	Balance Ragged Lines First Line Indent Space After	Ignore Optical Margin Last Line Indent Align to Grid	Paragraph panel
Tabs	X position	Leader	Align On	Tabs panel (Type menu)
Paragraph Rules	Rule Above On Width Rule attributes (Weight, Type, Color, etc.)	Rule Below On Offset	Left & Right Indents Gap attributes	Paragraph panel options menu
Keep Options	Keep with Next [N] Lines Start Paragraph		Keep Lines Together	Paragraph panel options menu
Hyphenation	Hyphenate On/Off (and all related options)			Paragraph panel options menu
Justification	Word Spacing Auto Leading	Letter Spacing Single Word Justification	Glyph Scaling Composer	Paragraph panel options menu
Drop Caps and Nested Styles	Number of Lines	Number of Characters		Paragraph panel
	Character Style for Drop Characters Align Left Edge Nested Styles	Scale for Descenders		Paragraph panel options menu
Bullets and Numbering	List Type Text After Bullet	List Style Character Style	Bullet Character Bullet/Number Position	Paragraph panel options menu
Character Color	Fill Color, Tint, Overprint attributes Stroke Color, Tint, Weight, Overprint attributes			Swatches panel
OpenType Features	Titling, Contextual, & Swash Alternates Ordinals, Fractions, Discretionary Ligatures, Slashed Zero, Figure Style, Positional Form Stylistic Sets			Character panel options menu
Underline Options	Underline On	Stroke attributes	Gap attributes	Character panel options menu
Strikethrough Options	Strikethrough On	Stroke attributes	Gap attributes	Character panel options menu

EDIT STYLE DEFINITIONS

In most cases, the styles that you import with a text file will need at least some modification — if for no other reason than InDesign has more sophisticated options that are relevant to commercial printing. (Of course, your clients are probably not designers either — that's why they hired you. Their formatting choices are probably not up to par with professional-quality graphic design, so you'll need to make at least some changes.)

1. **With cafe.indd open, place the insertion point in any of the paragraphs with meal price information (if you don't have the Italic variant of Times, these paragraphs are highlighted in pink).**

   The Paragraph Styles panel shows that this text is formatted with the Price Info style and calls for the Italic variant of Times (which might not be available).

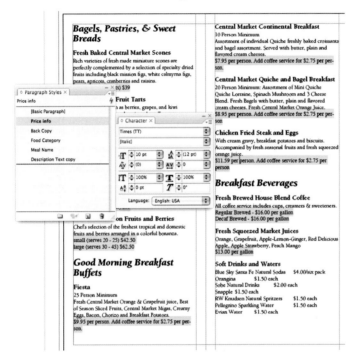

2. **Control/right-click Price Info in the Paragraph Styles panel and choose Edit "Price Info" in the contextual menu.**

Editing styles is both easy and efficient — when you change the options in a style definition, any text formatted with that style is reformatted with the changed definition.

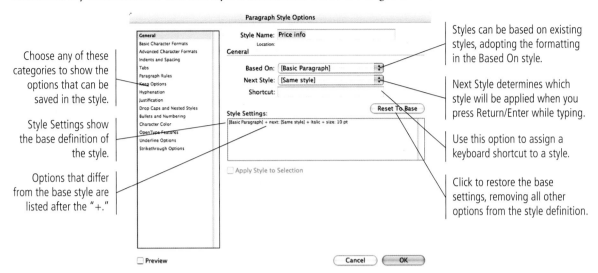

Choose any of these categories to show the options that can be saved in the style.

Style Settings show the base definition of the style.

Options that differ from the base style are listed after the "+."

Styles can be based on existing styles, adopting the formatting in the Based On style.

Next Style determines which style will be applied when you press Return/Enter while typing.

Use this option to assign a keyboard shortcut to a style.

Click to restore the base settings, removing all other options from the style definition.

3. **Click Basic Character Formats in the list of categories and choose ATC Laurel in the Font Family menu.**

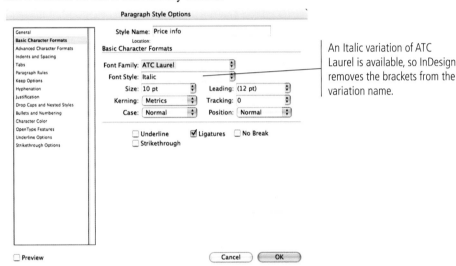

An Italic variation of ATC Laurel is available, so InDesign removes the brackets from the variation name.

Note:

*When one style refers to or calls another in some way (called **nesting styles**), the style on which another style is based is called the **parent** in the parent/child relationship. If a paragraph style calls a character style as part of its formatting definition, the paragraph style is considered the parent in the nesting relationship. See the accompanying discussion on Understanding Nested Styles.*

4. **Click OK to return to the document.**

The new font is applied to text formatted with the Price Info style.

5. **Control/right-click the Food Category style in the Paragraph Styles panel and choose Edit "Food Category".**

6. **Click Paragraph Rules in the list of formatting categories and make sure the Preview option is checked.**

   Paragraph rules are simply lines that are attached to a specific paragraph. Rules can be placed above or below any paragraph (or above *and* below a paragraph) to add visual interest and importance to specific text elements.

7. **With Rule Below showing in the first menu, check the Rule On box.**

8. **Change the rule weight to 6 pt. Change the rule color to C=100, M=25, Y=50, K=25 with a 20% tint.**

   This swatch is used by one of the styles that you imported from another InDesign file in the previous exercise. When you import a style from one InDesign file to another, any other required assets — such as color swatches — are also imported into the current file.

Choose Rule Above or Rule Below to change the settings for each rule.

Check this box to add a rule above or below paragraphs formatted with this style.

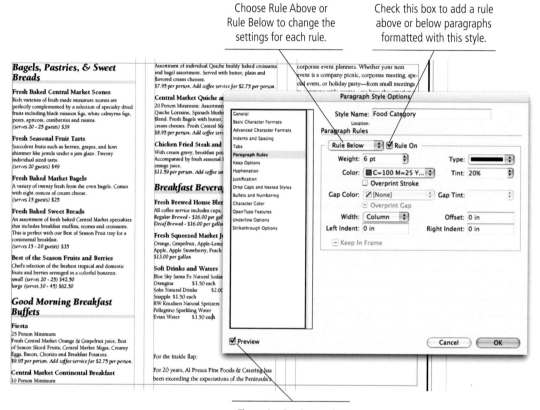

The active Preview option shows the result of adding the rule below the style.

9. **Change the Offset field to –0.03".**

   By default, paragraph rules align to the baseline of the text (the top edge of the rule touches the text baseline). The Offset value moves the position of the rule relative to the baseline; negative numbers move the rule up, and positive numbers move the rule down.

   Breakfast Be Before changing the Offset value

   Breakfast Be After changing the Offset value

   The Width option defines whether the rule extends the length of the text in the paragraph or across the entire width of the column (or frame, if it's a one-column frame). You can also use the Left Indent and Right Indent fields to move the rule in from the column (or frame) edge by a specific distance.

10. Click OK to close the dialog box and return to the layout.

By editing the style definition, you automatically changed the appearance of all three paragraphs formatted with the Food Category style.

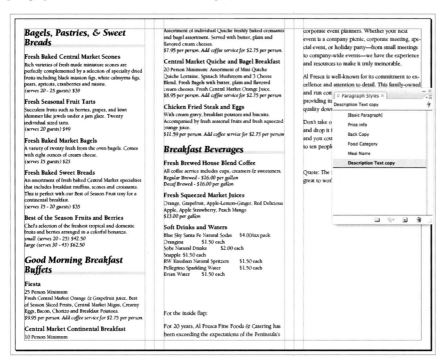

11. Save the file and continue to the next exercise.

Cut and Delete Text

In some cases, you may want to thread text across multiple frames (as you did for the three text frames on the inside of this brochure). In other cases, you may want to break a single story into multiple stories to prevent text from accidentally flowing into the wrong place.

In this brochure, you need to move the inside flap copy to the text frame on the inside flap (on Page 1). Rather than creating a thread from Page 2 to Page 1, you are going to cut the text from Page 2 and move it to Page 1.

1. With Page 2 of cafe.indd showing, highlight the text beginning with "For the Inside Flap" (at the bottom of the middle panel) to the end of the story.

This kind of text notation is common in imported client text.

2. Cut the text from the frame (Edit>Cut or Command/Control-X).

When you cut text from a story, the text is stored in the clipboard so you can paste it somewhere else.

3. Using the Type tool, click the empty text frame on the left side of Page 1 and paste the text you cut from Page 2 (Edit>Paste or Command/Control-V).

4. Highlight the entire first paragraph in the frame ("For the inside flap:") and press Delete/Backspace.

Pressing Delete/Backspace removes the selected text from the story; the deleted text is not stored in the clipboard.

InDesign supports two kinds of nested styles. The first is the basic parent/child relationship, in which one style is based on another. When you base one style on another, you change all related styles by changing the parent style. For example, the Body Copy style calls for 10-pt. Jansen Text with a 0.3" first-line indent. Body Copy No Indent applies the same settings, but as the name suggests, has a first-line indent of 0" (appropriate for the first paragraph after headings, for example).

The Body Copy No Indent style is based on the Body Copy style, and the first-line indent value was changed in the child style. If you later change the definition of Body Copy to use Optima instead of Jansen Text, the same change will trickle down to Body Copy No Indent as well.

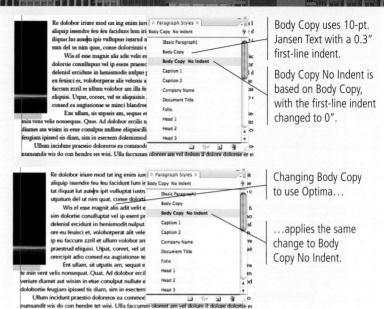

Body Copy uses 10-pt. Jansen Text with a 0.3" first-line indent.

Body Copy No Indent is based on Body Copy, with the first-line indent changed to 0".

Changing Body Copy to use Optima…

…applies the same change to Body Copy No Indent.

The second type of nested style incorporates different character styles for specific parts of a paragraph. You can use nested character styles for drop caps, bulleted lists, and numbered lists.

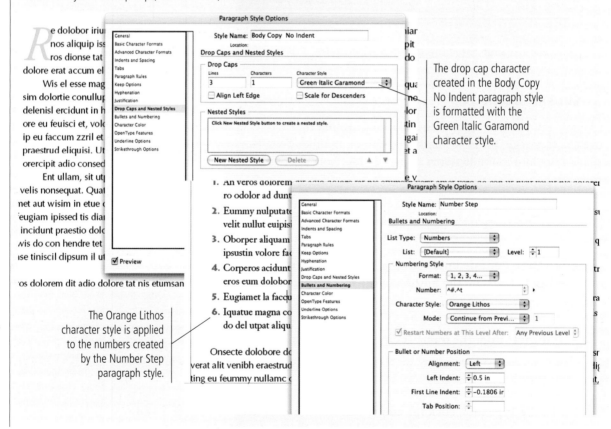

The drop cap character created in the Body Copy No Indent paragraph style is formatted with the Green Italic Garamond character style.

The Orange Lithos character style is applied to the numbers created by the Number Step paragraph style.

5. **Highlight the last paragraph in the frame (the one that begins with the word "Quote") and cut it.**

6. **Create a new text frame with the following parameters:**

   X: 1.875″   W: 1.5″

   Y: 2.9″   H: 1.5″

7. **Apply a text wrap to the frame based on the frame's bounding box.**

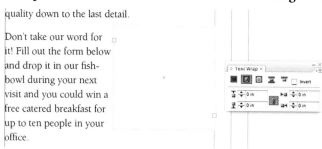

8. **Place the insertion point in the empty text frame and paste the text that you cut in Step 5.**

9. **Delete the word "Quote" (and the following colon and space) from the pasted text.**

10. **Save the file and continue to the next exercise.**

Note:

If you click inside an existing text frame, you simply place the insertion point in that frame.

To create this text frame, you have to start by drawing the frame somewhere outside the bounds of the existing text frames, then use the Transform panel or Control bar to position the frame at the specified location.

Building Complex Nested Styles

INDESIGN FOUNDATIONS

You can also set up complex arrangements of nested styles to apply specific character formatting to certain ranges of text within a paragraph. To automatically format a bold run-in paragraph, for example, you can define one character style for the first sentence of a paragraph, and then switch to another character style for the rest of the paragraph. For a sequence of paragraphs with the same formatting structure (such as a glossary), you can even loop back to the first style in the sequence.

In the following example, the TOC 2 paragraph style includes a sequence of nested character styles to format the different parts of each listing:

- The first two words of each paragraph ("Stage N") are formatted with the Stage Number character style.
- The paragraph switches to the Stage Name character style up to the first tab character it finds.
- The paragraph switches to the Page Number character style through the next four characters (to accommodate the tab character and up to three-digit page numbers).

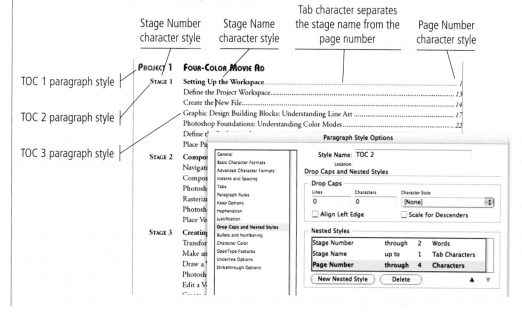

CREATE A STYLE FOR PULL QUOTES

Your client asked you to include a **pull quote**, which is a special visual treatment for text that is either pulled from the story (hence the name) or somehow supports the surrounding text. The pull quote for this layout will use the following structure:

- The first character in the pull quote will be a quotation mark formatted using the Quote Character character style.

- The text of the quote will be formatted with the Quote Copy character style. All quotes will have one or more paragraphs.

- The author's name (preceded by an en dash) will be formatted with the Quote Author character style.

You could simply format these elements in the layout, but nested styles allow you to create the structure once and apply it anywhere.

1. **On Page 1 of the open cafe.indd file, place the insertion point anywhere in the pull quote text frame.**

2. **Apply right paragraph alignment to the paragraph, and then change the frame's vertical alignment to bottom.**

3. **Highlight the en dash before the author's name and copy it to the clipboard.**

4. **With the insertion point in the quote paragraph, click the Create New Style button in the Paragraph Styles panel.**

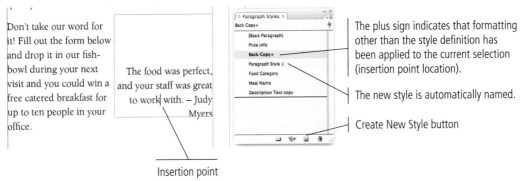

Insertion point

5. **Without moving the insertion point, click Paragraph Style 1 in the panel.**

When you create a new style, the style has the same formatting as the currently selected text (or location of the insertion point). When you click the new style to apply it, nothing changes in the layout because the style already has the same formatting as the selected paragraph.

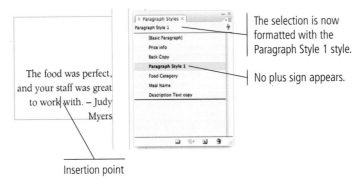

Insertion point

6. **Control/right-click Paragraph Style 1 in the panel and choose Edit "Paragraph Style 1".**

7. **Change the style name to "Pull Quote" and make sure the Preview check box is active.**

8. **Click Drop Caps and Nested Styles in the list of categories to display those options.**

9. **Click the New Nested Style button.**

Note:

Double-click a paragraph style name in the panel to open the Paragraph Style Options dialog box.

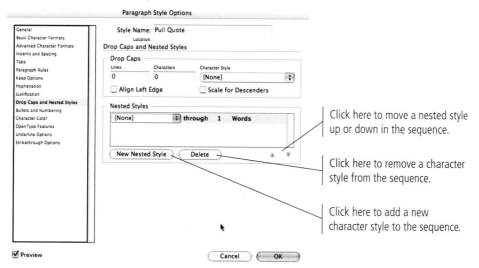

Click here to move a nested style up or down in the sequence.

Click here to remove a character style from the sequence.

Click here to add a new character style to the sequence.

10. **Click the first menu (the one that says "[None]") and choose Quote Character in the list of available character styles.**

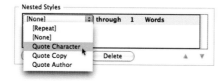

Note:

These same options can be applied to a paragraph in the layout by choosing Drop Caps and Nested Styles from the Paragraph panel options menu.

11. **Click the Words menu and choose Characters from the list.**

Nested styles can be applied up to or through a specific character sequence; if you choose the Through option, the character(s) you define will be formatted with the character style you define.

The first character in any pull quote will be formatted with the Quote Character character style; in this case, you can leave the default Through option.

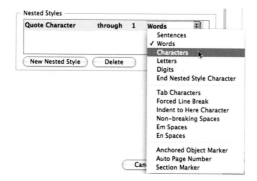

Because the Preview option is checked, the layout shows the result of your choices.

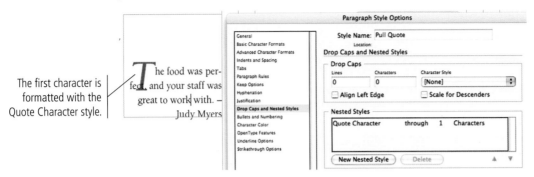

The first character is formatted with the Quote Character style.

12. **Add another nested style to the list, applying the Quote Copy character style and using the Up To option instead of the Through option. Choose Characters in the fourth menu.**

13. **Click the word Characters in the menu and press Command/Control-V to paste the en dash that you copied at the beginning of this exercise.**

   You can define a specific character by selecting the menu and typing the character you want to use. In this case, you're formatting all text up to the en dash that precedes the author's name.

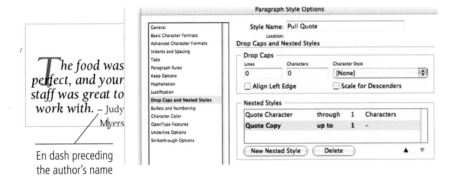

En dash preceding the author's name

14. **Add a third nested style to the list, applying the Quote Author character style through six words.**

   In this case, you want the style to go through the end of the paragraph. The Words option looks at space characters to determine where a "word" starts and ends. Using six words should cover most names (including titles, initials, etc.). If you found a name with more than six words, you could edit the style to include more words.

15. **Display the Basic Character Formats category of options and change the Leading value to 18 pt, then click OK to return to the document.**

Key Command:

*Option/Alt-Hyphen is the key command for inserting an **en dash**, which is a special character typically used to separate ranges (as in 2–5 hours or January 13–15) in place of the word "through."*

Macintosh users can actually type the en dash in the dialog box field; this doesn't work for Windows users, who have to copy the character from the layout and paste it into the dialog box field.

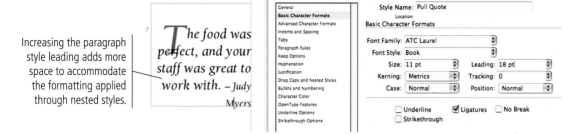

Increasing the paragraph style leading adds more space to accommodate the formatting applied through nested styles.

16. Place the insertion point at the beginning of the pull quote and add a quotation mark.

The nested styles apply the Quote Character style to the first character in the paragraph. When you type a new first character (the quotation mark), the style is applied to the new character instead of the T.

17. Place the insertion point before the en dash and press Shift-Return/Enter.

Remember, this is the key command for a forced line break or "soft return," which starts a new line without starting a new formal paragraph.

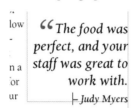

Note:

The formatting choices for this document intentionally omit the closing quotation mark.

18. Save your work and continue to the next exercise.

Nested Style Character Options

- **Sentences** applies the style up to or through the defined number of sentences. InDesign recognizes the end of a sentence based on periods, question marks, or exclamation marks. (Quotation marks following the punctuation are included as part of the sentence.)

- **Words** applies the style up to or through the defined number of words. InDesign recognizes the division of individual words by space characters.

- **Characters** applies the style up to or through the defined number of characters. Nonprinting characters such as tabs and spaces are included in the count.

- **Letters** applies the style up to or through the defined number of letters.

- **Digits** applies the style up to or through the defined number of Arabic numerals (0–9).

- **End Nested Style Character** applies the style up to or through a manually added End Nested Style character (Type>Insert Special Character>Other>End Nested Style Here).

- **Tab Characters** applies the style up to or through a nonprinting tab character. (Choose Type>Show Hidden Characters to see tab characters in the text.)

- **Forced Line Break** applies the style up to or through a nonprinting forced line break character.

- **Indent to Here Character** applies the style up to or through a nonprinting Indent to Here character.

- **Spaces** (Non-Breaking, Em, and En) apply the style up to or through the different space characters.

- **Anchored Object Marker** applies the style up to or through an inline graphic (which exists by default wherever you have an inline object in the text).

- **Auto Page Number** and **Section Marker** apply the style up to or through a page number or section name marker.

CONTROL TAB FORMATTING

Some people incorrectly rely on the spacebar for aligning columns of text, or they rely on the default tab stops (usually every half-inch in InDesign and Microsoft Word) and add as many tab characters as they need to line up text. Both methods can be time consuming, and both are unnecessary to properly format tabbed text.

1. **With Page 2 of the open cafe.indd file visible, make sure hidden characters are showing (Type>Show Hidden Characters).**

2. **Select the seven paragraphs after the Soft Drinks heading and choose Type>Tabs.**

   This is the only panel that cannot be accessed in the Window menu. Depending on your document window, the Tabs panel might appear randomly on your screen. If the top edge of the active text frame is visible, the Tabs panel will automatically appear at the top of the frame.

Note:

Many client files will have multiple tab characters separating one bit of text from another. You should almost always remove extra tab characters and use tab-formatting options to create the appropriate columns.

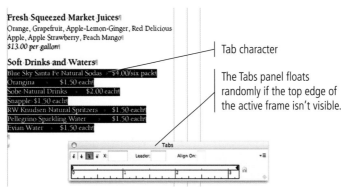

Tab character

The Tabs panel floats randomly if the top edge of the active frame isn't visible.

3. **Make sure the top of the text frame is visible and click the Snap Above Frame button to position the Tabs panel above the text frame.**

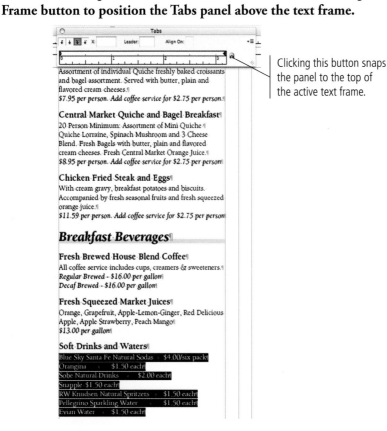

Clicking this button snaps the panel to the top of the active text frame.

4. **Click the right-justified tab marker in the Tabs panel, and then click the ruler to add a tab stop.**

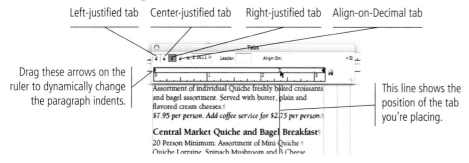

Left-justified tab   Center-justified tab   Right-justified tab   Align-on-Decimal tab

Drag these arrows on the ruler to dynamically change the paragraph indents.

This line shows the position of the tab you're placing.

5. **With the stop you just added selected on the ruler, change the X field to 3.1″ and the Leader field to period-space.**

You can either drag markers on the ruler to place tab stops, or define a precise location.

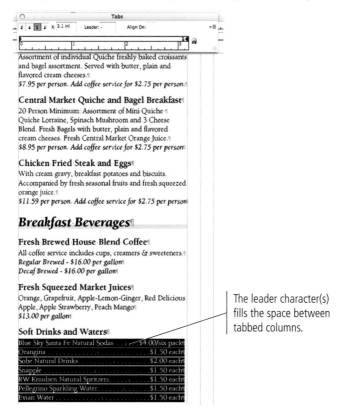

The leader character(s) fills the space between tabbed columns.

Note:

If you use the Align-on-Decimal tab, you can define a different alignment character in the Align On field.

6. **With the same lines selected, create a new paragraph style, change its name to "Price Line", and then apply that style to the selected text.**

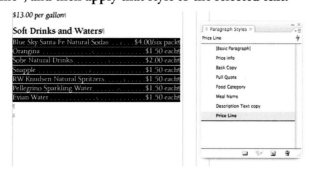

7. **Save the file and continue to the next stage of the project.**

Stage 3 Advanced Frame Options

You've already learned how to place graphics and control them within their frames. There are, of course, many more options available for working with graphics. Some of these (such as object styles and InDesign libraries) will improve your productivity by automating repetitive tasks. Other options (such as accessing elements stored in image files) enhance your creative capabilities when designing a page layout.

DEFINE AN OBJECT STYLE

Similar to paragraph and character styles, an object style stores multiple formatting options in a single unit so you can apply all the settings with one click. Also similar to text-formatting styles, object styles are dynamic — which means that changing an object style automatically changes the appearance of any object that uses that style. Object styles can include virtually any attribute that you can apply to a frame in the layout.

Object styles are accessed and managed in the Object Styles panel (Window>Object Styles). Every layout includes a default [Basic Graphics Frame] and a default [Basic Text Frame], which will be applied to all frames you create in the layout.

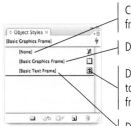

Click None to separate a specific (selected) frame from the Basic default style.

Default settings for new graphics frames

Drag one of these icons to another style to change the default graphics and text frame settings to a different existing style.

Default settings for new text frames

Note:

If you want to change the default attributes of new frames, you should edit the [Basic Graphics Frame] or [Basic Text Frame] object styles.

If you change these options when no file is open, the changes will apply in all new files.

1. **With cafe.indd open, create a rectangle graphics frame in the right panel of Page 1 using the following dimensions:**

   X: 6.5″   **W: 2.8″**

   Y: 2″   **H: 1.7″**

2. **Apply a 2-pt. frame using C=100, M=25, Y=50, K=25 at 100%.**

3. **In the Object Styles panel, click the Create New Style button.**

   Object styles follow the same basic principles as text-formatting styles. When you create the new style, it is added with the default name "Object Style [N]" and has the same settings as the currently selected object ("N" is just a sequential number).

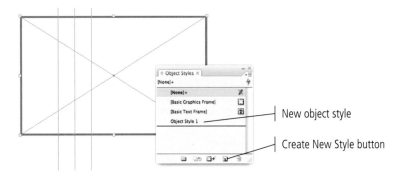

New object style

Create New Style button

4. **Control/right-click Object Style 1 in the panel and choose Edit Object Style 1 in the contextual menu.**

5. **In the Object Style Options dialog box, change the style name to "Green Stroke Frame".**

Note:

Double-click an object style in the panel to open the Object Style Options dialog box for that style.

6. **In the Style Settings panel, expand the Stroke options to review the settings.**

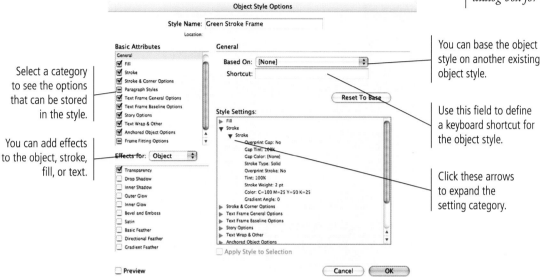

Select a category to see the options that can be stored in the style.

You can add effects to the object, stroke, fill, or text.

You can base the object style on another existing object style.

Use this field to define a keyboard shortcut for the object style.

Click these arrows to expand the setting category.

7. **Click OK to rename the style and return to the document.**

8. **With the original graphics frame still selected, click Green Stroke Frame in the Object Styles panel to apply the style to the frame.**

   Even though the object style is based on the selected object, you still have to manually apply the new style to the object. It's easy to forget this step.

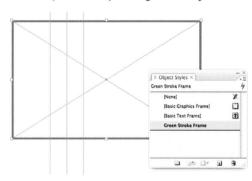

Note:

If you double-clicked Object Style 1 to open the Object Style Options dialog box, you don't need to complete this step since the style will be applied to the selected object when you double-click.

9. **Create three more graphics frames using the following parameters:**

Box 1:		Box 2:	
X: 9″	**W: 2.6″**	**X: 6.95″**	**W: 2.5″**
Y: 3.3″	**H: 1.7″**	**Y: 4.3″**	**H: 1.77″**

Box 3:	
X: 8.6″	**W: 2.65″**
Y: 5.4″	**H: 2″**

Note:

Object styles do not store the dimensions or position of the frame.

10. **Apply the Green Stroke Frame style to all three new frames.**

11. **Place images into the graphics frames, using the following image as a guide. Drag each picture within its frame so the main food item is roughly centered.**

When you place the images within the frames, keep an eye on the panel's left fold guide and the right page edge. Although the frames extend beyond these points, the frame area on the front panel is the "real" area that you have to work with.

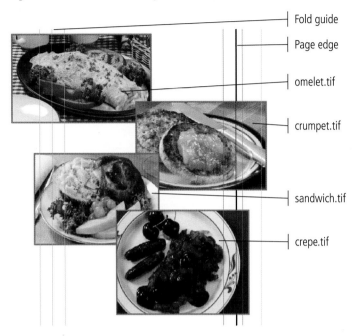

Fold guide

Page edge

omelet.tif

crumpet.tif

sandwich.tif

crepe.tif

12. **Control/right-click Green Stroke Frame in the Object Styles panel and choose Edit "Green Stroke Frame".**

13. **Click Stroke in the list of categories and change the stroke weight to 6 pt.**

Because you used an object style to format all four of these frames, you can easily change the attributes of all four frames by changing the style definition.

14. **Click the Drop Shadow option in the Effects area to add a drop shadow to the style.**

15. **Change the drop shadow Offset values to 0.04″, and then click OK.**

If the Preview option is checked, the new stroke weight and drop shadow automatically reflect in the document.

16. Create a new frame with a Paper fill that covers the parts of the graphics frames that extend into the mailing panel.

This type of "digital white-out" is the only way to create the effect you need — the frame stroke is visible on the tops, bottoms, and right sides but not on the outside edges. (For the two images that bleed off the right page edge, the stroke will be trimmed off, so you don't need to add the empty box on the right side.)

Note:

Some people advise against this technique of hiding objects with a paper-colored box, but it's the only way to achieve the desired effect in this project.

17. Save the file and continue to the next exercise.

 Edit the Basic Graphics Frame Style

You can edit object styles as you would edit a text-formatting style; changes to the style automatically apply to objects that use the style. In this exercise, you apply and change the Basic Graphics Frame style — which exists by default in every layout — so a number of frames can have the same basic settings with no stroke value and with a defined text-wrap attribute.

1. With Page 2 of cafe.indd showing, create a new empty graphics frame with the following dimensions:

    X: –0.125″   W: 5.5″
    Y: 5.3″   H: 3.325″

2. Open the Object Styles panel (Window>Object Styles).

3. With the new graphics frame selected, click [Basic Graphics Frame] in the Object Styles panel.

Note:

If the Object Styles panel isn't visible, you can apply an object style using the Object Style menu in the Control bar.

4. Create a second frame with the following dimensions, then apply the [Basic Graphics Frame] object style:

    X: 3.687″   W: 3.7″
    Y: –0.125″   H: 2.5″

5. Create a third frame with the following dimensions, then apply the [Basic Graphics Frame] object style:

X: 7.375″   W: 3.75″

Y: 3.825″   H: 4.8″

By default, the Basic Graphics Frame style has a 1-pt. black stroke and no text wrap. You're going to change the default settings so you can apply the same settings to all three graphics on the page.

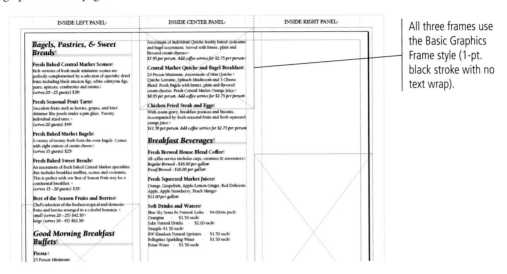

All three frames use the Basic Graphics Frame style (1-pt. black stroke with no text wrap).

6. In the Object Styles panel, Control/right-click [Basic Graphics Frame] and choose Edit [Basic Graphics Frame].

7. Click Stroke in the list of options and change the weight to 0 pt.

8. Click Text Wrap & Other in the list of options and apply a text wrap based on the object bounding box with a 0.1″ offset on all four sides.

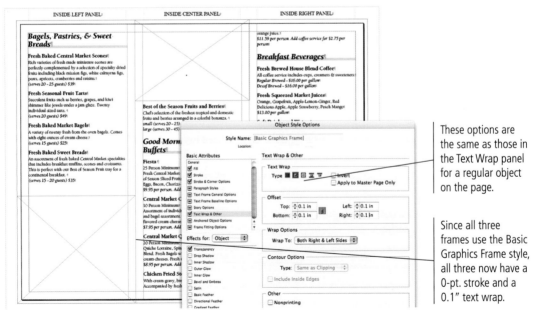

These options are the same as those in the Text Wrap panel for a regular object on the page.

Since all three frames use the Basic Graphics Frame style, all three now have a 0-pt. stroke and a 0.1″ text wrap.

9. Click OK to return to the layout.

10. Save the file and continue to the next exercise

INDESIGN FOUNDATIONS

Use the following chart as a reminder of exactly what can be stored in an object style definition, as well as where to find the equivalent in the application interface for a selected object.

Category	Options		Application Equivalent
General	Based on Reset to base	Shortcut	N/A
Fill	Color	Tint	Swatches panel
Stroke	Color	Tint	Swatches panel
	Weight Gap attributes	Type	Stroke panel
Stroke & Corner Options	Stroke alignment End cap End treatment (arrowheads)	Join Miter limit Corner effects (bevel, etc.)	Stroke panel
Paragraph Styles	Default paragraph style for frame		Paragraph Styles panel
Text Frame General Options	Columns Vertical justification	Inset spacing Ignore text wrap	Text Frame Options dialog box (Object>Text Frame Options)
Text Frame Baseline Options	First baseline	Custom baseline grid options	Text Frame Options dialog box (Object>Text Frame Options)
Story Options	Optical margin alignment		Story panel
Text Wrap & Other	Text wrap type Wrap options	Offset Contour options	Text Wrap panel
	Nonprinting check box		Attributes panel
Anchored Object Options	Position (Inline, Above Line, Custom) Prevent manual positioning		Anchored Object Options dialog box (Object>Anchored Object>Options)
Frame Fitting Options	Crop amount Fitting on empty frame	Alignment reference point	Frame Fitting Options dialog box (Object>Fitting>Frame Fitting Options)
Effects	Effect (including Transparency) for object, fill, stroke, or text		Effects panel

Access Embedded Clipping Paths and Alpha Channels

At times, you might want to show a specific part of an image instead of the entire image. You can accomplish this task in a number of ways, but the two most common involve using Alpha channels and clipping paths that are stored in the image.

A **clipping path** is a vector-based path that is used to mask (cover) specific parts of an image; areas inside the path are visible and areas outside the path are hidden. Because the clipping path is a vector-based object, clipping paths always result in hard edges on the clipped image.

An **Alpha channel** is a special type of image channel that masks specific parts of an image by determining the degree of transparency in each pixel. (In other words, a 50% value in the Alpha channel means that particular spot of the image will be 50% transparent). Alpha channels allow you to design with degrees of transparency; the soft edge created by a blended alpha channel means you can blend one image into another, blend one layer into another, or blend an entire image into a background in a page-layout application.

1. Continue working in the open file. Place the file muffins.tif into the frame at the top of the middle panel of Page 2.

2. Select the empty frame in the right panel. Open the Place dialog box and navigate to the file coffee.tif. Make sure the Show Import Options and Replace Selected Item boxes are checked and click Open.

3. In the Image tab of the Image Import Options dialog box, activate the Apply Photoshop Clipping Path option and click OK.

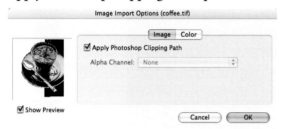

The clipping path hides the background area in the placed image.

4. With the placed file selected, choose Object>Clipping Path>Options.

5. In the Clipping Path dialog box, make sure the Preview option is checked and choose None in the Type menu.

Turning off the clipping paths shows the image background.

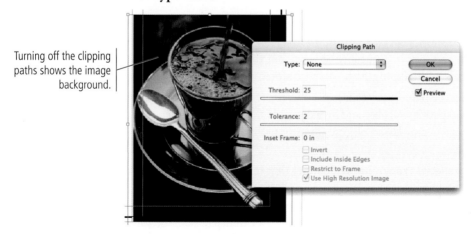

6. **Click Cancel to leave the clipping path in place.**

7. **Select the empty frame in the left panel. Open the Place dialog box and navigate to the file bread_bowl.psd. With the Show Import Options and Replace Selected Item boxes checked, click Open.**

8. **In the Image tab of the Image Import Options dialog box, choose Bowl in the Alpha Channel menu and click OK.**

   Although you can turn embedded clipping paths on and off in the application interface, this is the only way to access an embedded Alpha channel.

Note:

If this menu isn't available, the image doesn't include an Alpha channel.

9. **Scale the placed image (not the frame) to 85%.**

10. **In the Text Wrap panel, apply the Wrap Around Object Shape type of wrap and change the Offset value to 0.1″. In the Contour Options Type menu, choose Alpha Channel.**

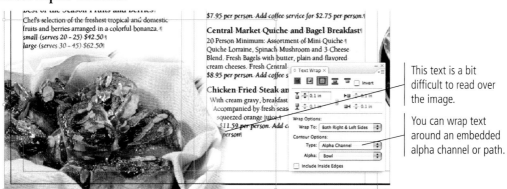

This text is a bit difficult to read over the image.

You can wrap text around an embedded alpha channel or path.

11. **Click the placed image with the Direct Selection tool so you can see the text-wrap boundary line.**

12. **Drag the anchor points of the text wrap boundary away from the right edge of the alpha channel, until you're satisfied with the position of text at the bottom of the center panel.**

Edit the boundary anchor points to move the text away from the image.

When you change the boundary, this menu defaults to User-Modified Path.

13. Add soft returns (Shift-Return/Enter) after the word "Pastries" in the first category heading, after the word "Morning" in the second category heading, and after the word "for" in the last paragraph of the center panel.

This final clean-up step fixes the **orphans** (single short words at the end of a paragraph that result in an unbalanced appearance in the paragraph) on Page 2.

14. Save the file and continue to the next exercise.

 IMPORT OBJECT STYLES

If you've already spent the time to build an element once, why not save yourself time and effort by reusing that same element? Object styles are not limited to the file in which you create them. As with text-formatting styles, you can import object styles from one InDesign file to another.

1. With cafe.indd open, choose Load Object Styles in the Object Styles panel options menu.

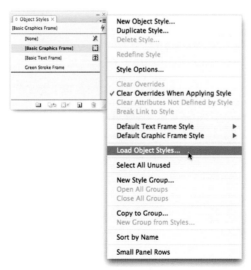

2. **Navigate to form_styles.indd in the RF_InDesign>Cafe folder and click Open.**

3. **Uncheck the two basic frame styles, leaving only the Form Box option checked.**

   If you change the Basic Graphics Frame style for a file (as you did in an earlier exercise), be careful when importing object styles from one InDesign file to another; you could inadvertently overwrite the changes you already made, meaning you would have to redo your earlier work.

   The Form Box style was not created based on the Basic frame style, so there should be no conflict if you import only the Form Box style.

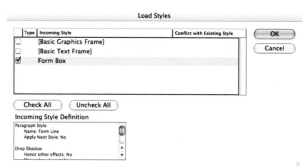

4. **Click OK to import the Form Box object style.**

The Form Box style is imported.

A new paragraph style, defined as part of the object style, is also imported into the InDesign file.

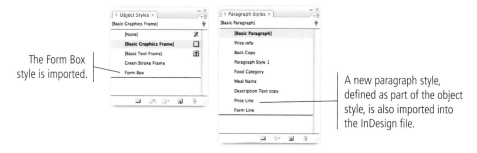

5. **Create a new text frame on Page 1 that fills the width of the left panel with a height of 2.25″. Position the frame at X: 0.25″, Y: 4.75″ based on the top-left reference point.**

6. **With the insertion point in the new text frame, click the [Basic Paragraph] style and then type:**

   Sign me up to win breakfast for my office!

   Name[Tab]

   Company[Tab]

   Address[Tab]

   City[Tab]

   State[Tab]

   Zip[Tab]

   Phone[Tab]

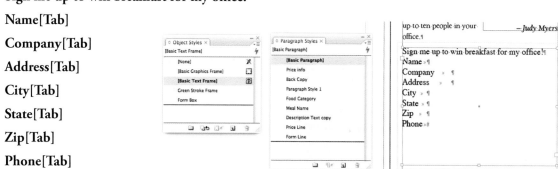

7. **Click the frame with the Selection tool, and then click Form Box in the Object Styles panel.**

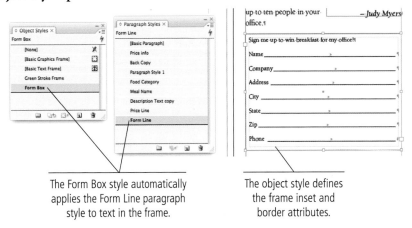

The Form Box style automatically applies the Form Line paragraph style to text in the frame.

The object style defines the frame inset and border attributes.

8. **Save the file and continue to the next exercise.**

 CREATE AN INDESIGN LIBRARY

Object styles allow you to apply the same attributes to a frame, considerably shortening your workload if you repeatedly use the same settings. In other cases, you might need to use the same content (such as a logo) or the same group of objects with different content (such as a graphics frame grouped with a text frame for the caption) throughout a document. Object styles don't manage placed graphics or grouped objects. In these situations, you can use an InDesign library to speed up the process.

1. **With cafe.indd open, place the file al_fresca.eps onto Page 1, scale it to 75%, and fit the frame to the content.**

   You can uncheck the Show Import Options box when you import this picture.

2. **Place the frame at the top of the right panel on Page 1.**

3. **Create a new text frame below the logo and type:**

   2218 Pacific Crest Highway
   Monterey Heights, CA 95313

4. **Apply the [Basic Paragraph] style to the text, and then change the formatting to 11-pt ATC Elm Normal with automatic leading, and with centered paragraph alignment.**

Note:

Again, you have to create the text frame outside the boundaries of existing text frames.

5. **Select the logo frame and the address frame and group them (Object>Group).**

The two grouped objects have a single bounding box.

6. **Choose File>New>Library.**

7. **Navigate to your WIP>Cafe folder as the target location. Change the file name to "alfresca.indl".**

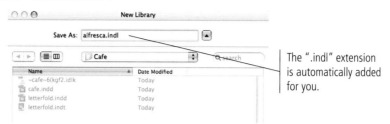

The ".indl" extension is automatically added for you.

Note:

Library items store the links to placed graphics files. The graphic is not embedded in the library item — you have to make sure the links are up to date before outputting the file.

8. **Click Save to create the new library.**

A library is a special type of file that stores objects (including the objects' content) for use in any InDesign file. Library files are not linked or specific to any individual layout (indd) file, so you can open and use items from an existing library in any layout you build.

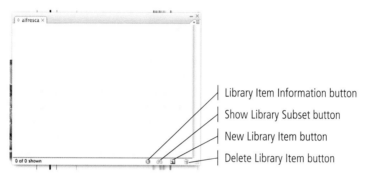

Library Item Information button
Show Library Subset button
New Library Item button
Delete Library Item button

Note:

Library items do not store fonts. If a library item uses a specific font, that font must be active on whatever system uses the library.

9. **With the grouped logo/address frame selected in the layout, click the New Library Item button in the alfresca panel.**

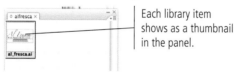

Each library item shows as a thumbnail in the panel.

Note:

You can also simply drag an object from the layout into the Library panel. This will have no effect on the object already placed in the layout.

Choose Add Items On Page [N] As Separate Objects in the Library panel options menu to add all the objects on the page as separate library items.

Choose Add Items On Page [N] in the Library panel options menu to add all objects on the page as a single library item.

10. **With the al_fresca.ai item selected, click the Library Item Info button at the bottom of the panel.**

11. **In the Item Information dialog box, change the Item Name field to "Logo with address" and click OK.**

You can also change the object type and add a description for any library item.

12. **Drag the Logo with address item from the Library panel into the layout.**

13. **Scale the new instance to 60% and rotate it 90° counterclockwise, and then drag it to the bottom-left corner of the center panel (it's the return-address info on the mailing panel).**

There is no dynamic link between items in the library and instances placed in a layout. Changing one placed instance has no effect on the original library item, or on other placed instances of the same item.

Note:

Deleting an object from the library has no effect on placed instances in the layout. Deleting a placed instance has no effect on the item in the library.

14. Drag another instance to the bottom of the inside flap panel, scale the instance to 70%, and center it horizontally in the panel area.

15. Click the Close button on the Library panel to close the library file.

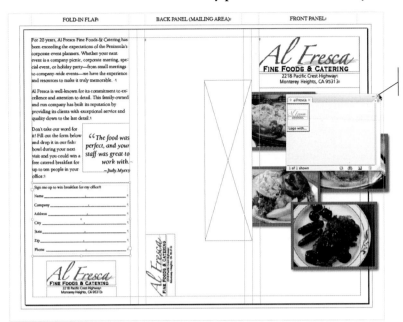

Click here to close the Library panel/file.

Note:

Styles in library items will be automatically added to any layout where you place an instance of that item. If a library item uses a style (text or object) that conflicts with a style in the document where you're placing an instance, the style definition from the document will override the style definition from the library item.

Of course, this project is only a two-page brochure and all the instances of the library item appear on the same page. But think of a layout with more than a few pages — a newsletter, a booklet, or even a multi-file multi-chapter book. You can use library items to easily access common graphics such as logos; maintain consistency between sidebars on Page 1 and Page 42; and even use the same graphic-and-text-frame structure for graphics with captions on every page of a 240-page book.

Now think about combining libraries with the other tools you've learned about. For example, let's say you create a library item with a graphics frame and a caption frame. The graphics frame is formatted with an object style and the caption frame has placeholder text that is formatted with a paragraph style. You can use the library to place and change the content in individual instances, then change the object and paragraph styles as necessary, and still maintain consistency throughout the document.

16. Save the file, preflight it, and create a final job package for the printer.

Managing Libraries

INDESIGN FOUNDATIONS

If you have a large collection of objects in a library, you can show a subset of the library by clicking the Show Library Subset button (or choosing Show Subset from the Library panel options menu). The Show Subset dialog box allows you to define what you want to find, based on the item name, creation date, object type, or description text. You can always restore the entire library by choosing Show All in the Library panel options menu.

Click here to add parameters to the search (up to five).

Click here to remove parameters from the search (the minimum is one).

Summary

This project built on the skills you learned in previous projects. To begin the letterfold layout, you built a technically accurate folding guide on a facing-page master layout, incorporating nonprinting fold guides and text frames into the slug area. To speed up the process for the next time you need to build one of these common letterfold jobs, you saved your initial work as a template.

Completing this project also required extensive work with imported text, specifically importing styles from a Microsoft Word file and then editing those styles. You also worked with several advanced text options, including nested styles and tab formatting, to fine-tune the text in this project.

You also learned about two more options for improving workflow. Object styles allow you to store and apply multiple frame-formatting options (including nested paragraph styles) in a single click. Libraries store entire objects or groups of objects (including their formatting and even contents) so you can place as many instances as necessary on any page of any file.

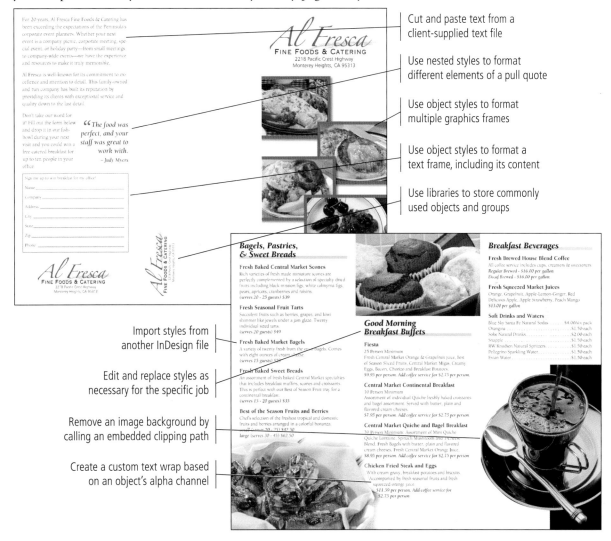

Cut and paste text from a client-supplied text file

Use nested styles to format different elements of a pull quote

Use object styles to format multiple graphics frames

Use object styles to format a text frame, including its content

Use libraries to store commonly used objects and groups

Import styles from another InDesign file

Edit and replace styles as necessary for the specific job

Remove an image background by calling an embedded clipping path

Create a custom text wrap based on an object's alpha channel

Portfolio Builder Project 4

The owner of Hollywood Sandwich Shoppe wants you to design new menus that can be printed every month at the local quick printer.

To complete this project, you should:

❏ Plan the overall layout of the piece using a letter-size sheet as the basic flat size, with no bleeds.

❏ If you decide to design the menu with folds, create a document grid that incorporates the necessary folding allowances.

❏ Import the client's text, then develop a text-formatting scheme (using styles) that will communicate the theme of the restaurant.

❏ Find supporting artwork or images that will support the restaurant's theme.

"A menu is the single most important tool that a restaurant can develop to promote the business. It's well known that large chains spend millions of dollars refining, measuring, and redesigning their menus each year. Be creative, but also be sure that the menu is readable.

"The cover needs to include the restaurant's logo, name, and address. We gave you the logo, and the address is in the menu text file (in the RF_Builders>Hollywood folder).

"Somewhere on the menu, you need to include space for a "special feature" that will include a description of the monthly special and a picture of the star that it's named after — we'll send this to you as soon as we finalize the first two months' specials. For now, can you just use placeholders?

"Since we have to print new menus every month, we just take them to the local quick printer. We want something we can print on letter-size paper — nothing fancy or overly expensive. We might be willing to print in color if it's important, but black-only is much cheaper so we'll probably stick with that."

Realty Collateral Booklet

Your client is the Southern California Realtors Association, which provides support materials for member realtors. They hired you to create a booklet with tips for sellers who want to make their homes more attractive to buyers. The booklet will be printed in very large quantities and distributed to agents' offices, so the individual realtors can use it as a tool when they are contacted about listing a home for sale. The ultimate consumer for this piece is the home seller (not the agent), so it needs to be visually inviting and easy to read.

This project incorporates the following skills:

❑ Understanding and controlling facing-page layouts

❑ Using master pages to apply repetitive layout elements

❑ Converting regular layout pages to master pages

❑ Automatically flowing text across multiple pages

❑ Using special characters, markers, and text variables

❑ Basing style sheets on other style sheets to improve consistency

❑ Applying bulleted list formatting

❑ Controlling page breaks with paragraph Keep options

❑ Controlling automatic hyphenation

❑ Printing a booklet using built-in imposition options

The Project Meeting

Client Comments

The idea behind this booklet is to give realtors something they can hand to potential sellers — kind of a tactful way to point out what a home-owner needs to do to prepare their house for selling. This way the agents don't have to blatantly say things like "scrub the mold off your bathtub before showing it." So really, the booklet is a tool for the agents to hand out, but ultimately it's for the sellers to use as a checklist of things to do before a big open house.

The text was created in Microsoft Word, using a custom template with all of the text formats that we use in a number of similar collateral pieces. We're also sending you some images from different agents' files; we have permission to use them in marketing materials without paying a specific licensing fee. Our research shows that a 5.5 × 8.5″ booklet is well received by most consumers, so we want the finished booklet to be that size.

Art Director Comments

This booklet was originally specified as 16 pages with a separate cover, but the client decided that a self-cover will work just as well. We had already designed the front and back covers for the initial client pitch meeting, so you can just import the existing cover layouts into the main booklet file.

Most marketing data shows that consumers don't like to read long blocks of body copy. This project has a considerable amount of text — but a lot of it will work well as bulleted lists, so you will use different kinds of bullets to break up most of the body text. Each spread in the booklet will also have a large picture and a callout box to add visual interest to the text.

This project will also require tighter control over the text flow than what you need when you're working with smaller bits of text. Long documents like this one are going to require some special attention to detail to prevent problems such as bad line breaks and bad page breaks.

Consistency is very important for any document with more than a few pages; the same basic grid should be used for most internal pages in the booklet. Completing this project will be much easier if you take the time to build the basic layout on master pages.

Project Objectives

To complete this project, you will:

❑ Use master pages with placeholders for the different elements of the layout

❑ Change the margin guides and text frame on a master layout

❑ Convert layout pages to master pages and import them into the main booklet file

❑ Place automatic page number characters

❑ Create a custom slug with text variables to keep track of the file status

❑ Automatically flow text into multiple layout pages based on the applied master layout

❑ Define styles that are based on other styles to improve consistency and facilitate changing multiple styles at once

❑ Format bulleted lists to improve readability

❑ Control paragraph positioning, widows, orphans, and automatic hyphenation to prevent bad line breaks

❑ Print the completed booklet as imposed printer's spreads

Stage 1 Working with Master Pages

In Project 3, you worked with the existing master pages in a newsletter template. In Project 4, you used master pages to build a technically accurate folding grid on facing pages of a spread. To complete this booklet project, you will dig much deeper into the capabilities and advantages of master pages.

CREATE THE BOOKLET FILE

Multi-page documents (such as the booklet you're building here) typically require special layout considerations so the pages will appear in the correct position when the job is finished. You'll deal with output considerations for long documents (called **imposition**) in Stage 3. For now, however, you need to understand two issues related to setting up this type of file:

- Books and booklets usually have facing pages, which means opposing left and right pages of a spread mirror each other.

- Files with facing pages can have different margin values on the inside (near the spread center) and outside (away from the spread center) edges.

1. **Choose File>New.**

2. **In the New Document dialog box, choose Letter – Half in the Page Size menu, using portrait orientation.**

   The 5.5 × 8.5″ document size is common enough to be included in the default InDesign settings.

3. **Make sure the Facing Pages and Master Text Frame options are checked.**

   The Master Text Frame option creates an automatic text frame that snaps to the defined margins, using the number of columns and gutter width defined in the Columns area of the dialog box. This frame is placed on the default master page layout, so it will also appear on every layout page associated with the default master page layout.

4. **In the Columns area, define 2 columns with a 0.2″ gutter.**

5. **In the Margins area, apply a 0.5″ margin to all four sides of the page.**

6. **Define a 0.125″ bleed and a 0.5″ slug on all four sides.**

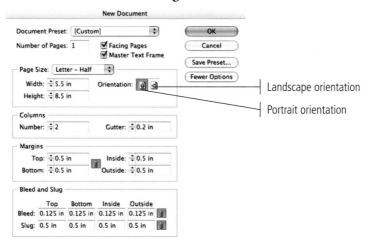

Landscape orientation

Portrait orientation

Note:

Before completing this project, copy the Realtors folder from the WIP folder on your Resource CD to your WIP folder where you are saving your work. When you save files for this project, save them in your WIP>Realtors folder.

Note:

If you can't see the Bleed and Slug options, click the More Options button below the Save Preset button.

Note:

The inside bleed and slug will be removed when the job is imposed to create a booklet (Stage 3).

7. **Click OK to create the new document.**

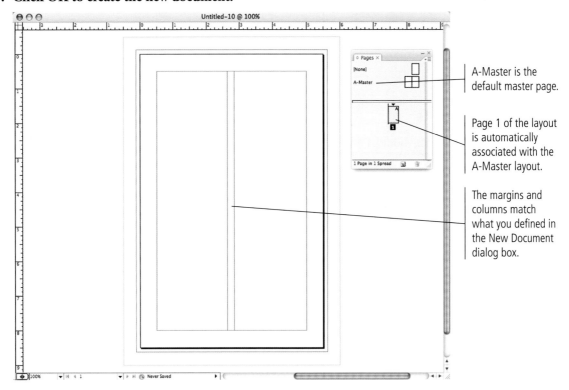

A-Master is the default master page.

Page 1 of the layout is automatically associated with the A-Master layout.

The margins and columns match what you defined in the New Document dialog box.

8. **Save the file as "booklet_working.indd" in your WIP>Realtors folder and continue to the next exercise.**

 CREATE MASTER PAGES FROM LAYOUT PAGES

This project was originally defined as a 16-page booklet "plus cover." In other words, the main booklet file would have 16 pages, but the cover would be created and printed as a separate file. Once printed, the two pieces would be combined and bound together into a single finished piece.

Based on the amount of text they created, your clients have decided to create the booklet as 16 pages "including self cover," which means the first and last pages of the main booklet file will be the front and back covers (respectively). The first step in completing this project is to bring the cover pages into the main layout.

1. **Open the file Cover.indd from the RF_InDesign>Realtors folder.**

2. **If you get a message that some links are missing, click the Fix Links Automatically button and locate the missing images. Both images used in this file are in the RF_InDesign>Realtors folder.**

This layout includes two pages — the front cover and the back cover. Like too many projects, however, these pages were not created using master pages.

Although you could simply copy the page contents from this file into your main file, it is a better idea to work with master pages whenever possible. Doing so gives you the most flexibility and control over the different layouts. If the layouts are created as master pages, you can easily import them into other files and apply them to specific document pages as necessary.

INDESIGN FOUNDATIONS

When you are working with facing pages, the default master page is actually a spread. In the Pages panel, the A-Master layout icon shows two pages, representing the two pages in the master page spread. Depending on your needs, you can also create master pages with a single page instead of a spread.

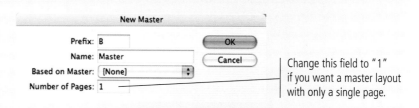

Change this field to "1" if you want a master layout with only a single page.

If you double-click the name of a master page in the Pages panel, you select the entire page or spread that makes up that master layout. You can select only one page of a master page spread by clicking the left or right page icon for that master.

In a facing-page document, the default A-Master has two pages — a spread.

You can add a single-page master layout to a facing-page document.

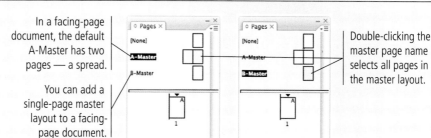

Double-clicking the master page name selects all pages in the master layout.

If an entire master page spread is already selected (both page icons are highlighted), you have to first deselect the spread to select only one page of the spread. You can do this by simply clicking any other page icon — master page or regular page — in the panel.

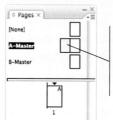

Single-click either page icon in a master page spread to select only that page, rather than the entire spread.

When you add pages to the layout by dragging a master page, the selected page icons determine what will be added. If both pages of a master page spread are highlighted, dragging the selected icons into the lower half of the panel will add the entire master page spread. If only one page of the master spread is selected, you can add a single page to the layout.

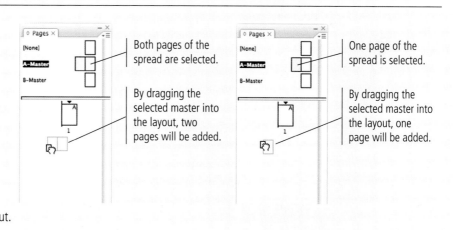

Both pages of the spread are selected.

By dragging the selected master into the layout, two pages will be added.

One page of the spread is selected.

By dragging the selected master into the layout, one page will be added.

Fortunately, it is very easy to create a master page layout from a regular page layout.

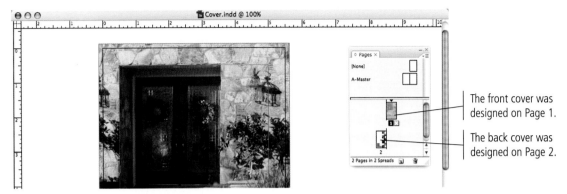

The front cover was designed on Page 1.

The back cover was designed on Page 2.

3. In the Pages panel, Control/right-click the Page 1 icon and choose Save as Master from the contextual menu.

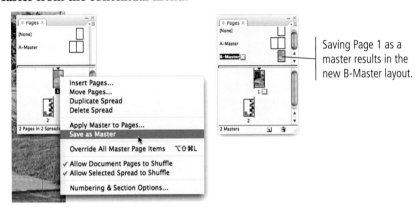

Saving Page 1 as a master results in the new B-Master layout.

4. Control/right-click the new B-Master and choose Master Options for "B-Master" from the contextual menu.

5. In the Master Options dialog box, change the name to "Front Cover" and click OK.

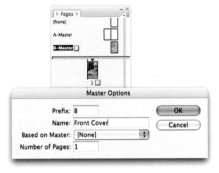

6. Repeat this process to convert the Page 2 layout to a master page layout named "Back Cover".

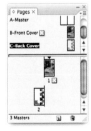

7. **In the top section of the Pages panel, Control/right-click the A-Master layout name and choose Delete Master Spread "A-Master" from the contextual menu.**

The default master layout in this file was never used, so you can simply delete it.

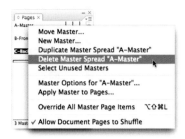

8. **Save the file as "cover_masters.indd" in your WIP>Realtors folder and close the file.**

9. **Continue to the next exercise.**

IMPORT MASTER PAGES

Now that the front and back covers are saved as master pages, you can easily import and apply them in the booklet file you created.

1. **With booklet_working.indd open, choose Load Master Pages from the Pages panel options menu.**

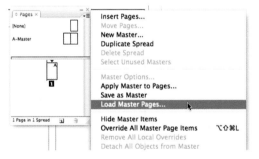

2. **In the resulting dialog box, navigate to the file cover_masters.indd in your WIP>Realtors folder and click Open.**

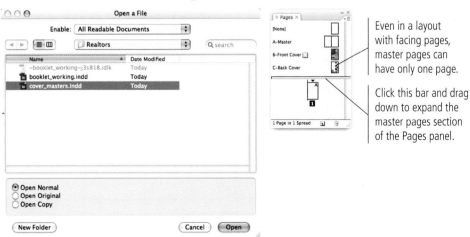

Even in a layout with facing pages, master pages can have only one page.

Click this bar and drag down to expand the master pages section of the Pages panel.

3. Open the Swatches and Paragraph Styles panels.

Loading master pages from one file to another is an all-or-nothing process. Both master pages from the cover_masters.indd file are now part of the new file.

When you load a master page from one file to another, all the required assets (styles, swatches, etc.) are also imported. One color and one gradient have been added to the Swatches panel; two paragraph styles have been added to the Paragraph Styles panel.

Note:

There is no dynamic link between the master pages now in the booklet file and the master pages in the original cover file. Changing one version of the front cover master (for example) will not affect the other version.

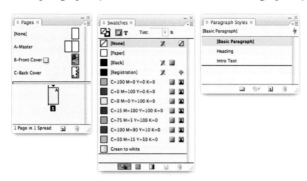

4. In the Pages panel, drag the B-Front Cover icon onto the Page 1 icon.

By default, Page 1 of any new file is associated with the A-Master layout. You can change this by simply dragging a different master onto the page icon.

Note:

You can also Control/ right-click a page icon in the lower section of the Pages panel and choose Apply Master to Page from the contextual menu.

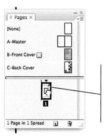

A dark black outline indicates that you are dragging the B-Front Cover master onto the existing page icon.

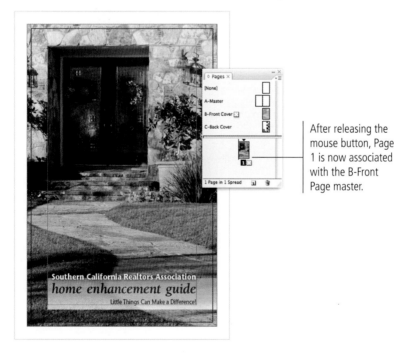

After releasing the mouse button, Page 1 is now associated with the B-Front Page master.

5. **In the Pages panel, select only the left page of the A-Master spread and drag it below the Page 1 icon.**

   Using facing pages, new pages are added to the left and right of the spread center. When you release the mouse button, the new Page 2 is automatically added on the left side of the spread center.

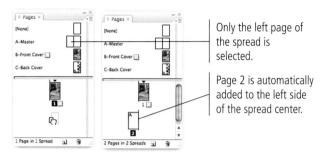

Only the left page of the spread is selected.

Page 2 is automatically added to the left side of the spread center.

Note:

*Pages on the left side of the spread center are called **left-facing** or **verso** pages.*

*Pages on the right side of the spread center are called **right-facing** or **recto** pages.*

6. **Double-click the Page 2 icon in the Pages panel to show that page in the document window.**

7. **Drag the C-Back Cover icon onto the Page 2 icon to change the associated master.**

Note:

By convention, odd-numbered pages are right-facing and even-numbered pages are left-facing.

8. **Make sure guides (View>Grids & Guides>Show Guides) and frame edges (View>Show Frame Edges) are visible.**

   Two objects now appear on Page 2 — a text frame and a graphics frame. The frame edges appear as dotted lines instead of solid lines. This indicates that the objects are from the associated master page; you can't select them on the layout page unless you override the master page items for that layout page.

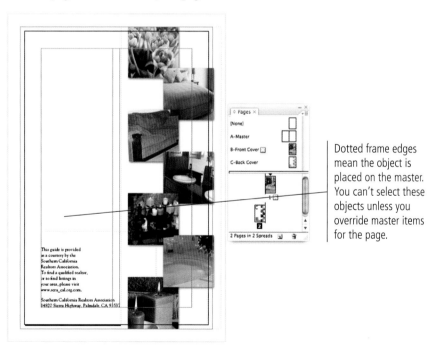

Dotted frame edges mean the object is placed on the master. You can't select these objects unless you override master items for the page.

9. **In the Pages panel, drag the left page of the A-Master spread to the left of the Page 2 icon.**

Before you release the mouse button, a vertical black bar indicates the potential position of the new page.

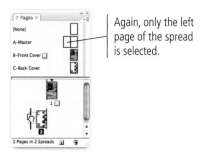

Again, only the left page of the spread is selected.

After you release the mouse button, the new page is automatically added before Page 2. Because this is a facing-page layout, the new Page 2 becomes the left-facing page and the old Page 2 — now Page 3 — moves to the right side of the spread.

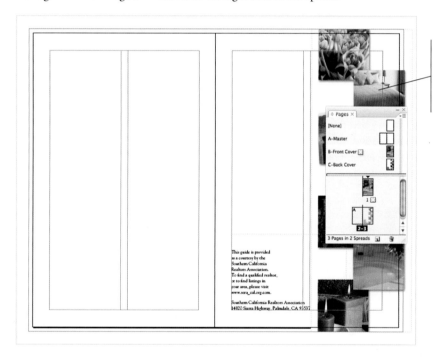

Objects from the C-Back Cover master still appear in the same position relative to the page.

10. **Save the file and continue to the next exercise.**

 ## EDIT THE DEFAULT MASTER PAGE

The main body of the booklet will be fourteen pages in seven spreads; each spread will have the same basic layout:

- A large image, which fades to white, fills the background of each left-facing page.

- A heading and introductory paragraph sits at the bottom of each left-facing page.

- The right-facing page of each spread has two columns of body copy.

- Each right-facing page has a callout box of related checklist items.

- The right-facing page of each spread should include the page number and the words "Home Enhancement Guide."

Because these elements are common to most pages in the layout, it makes sense to create them on a master page layout. You could either create a new master page for the body spread or simply edit the existing default master page.

1. **With booklet_working.indd open, double-click the words "A-Master" in the top section of the Pages panel.**

   Double-clicking a master page navigates to that master layout in the document window.

   Each page of the A-Master spread has the margin and column settings you defined in the New Document dialog box.

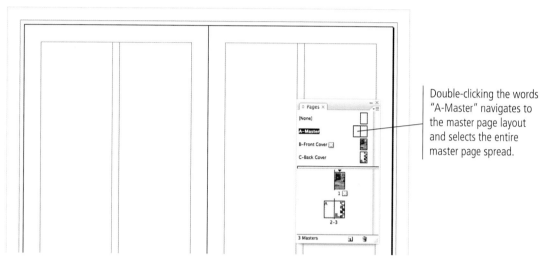

Double-clicking the words "A-Master" navigates to the master page layout and selects the entire master page spread.

   Based on the specified elements of the main pages, each page in this spread has different margin and column requirements. Fortunately, InDesign allows you to modify those settings for individual pages in the spread.

2. **Click once on any page other than the A-Master spread in the Pages panel.**

   When you double-click the master page name in the Pages panel, the entire spread is selected (highlighted) in the panel. To change the setting for only one page of the spread, you have to first deselect the spread (by selecting some other page), and then select the specific page you want to modify.

   You can click a regular page or a master page icon; the important point is to deselect the A-Master spread.

Note:

Clicking a page icon once selects that page without changing the visible page in the document window.

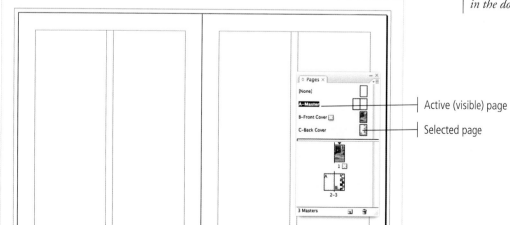
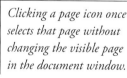

Active (visible) page

Selected page

Understanding Relative Object Positioning

You need to understand the difference between spread master pages and single-page master pages, especially when working with facing pages. In the booklet file you're building now, you have both kinds of master pages— the covers are both single-page masters and the A-Master layout is a spread of two facing pages.

In the previous exercise, you added a page in front of the back cover page. The back cover page, which had been Page 2, moved to Page 3, and the objects on the page stayed in the same position relative to the page (in other words, they also moved from Page 2 to Page 3). This happened because the back page master is a single page, so the objects on the master (and the associated layout pages) are positioned relative to the single page.

When you work with a spread master page, the objects on the master page layout are positioned relative to the entire spread. Objects on regular layout pages, however, are positioned relative to the page on which they are created.

Understanding this concept is particularly important if:

• You are working with objects that bleed off the left or right side of a page

• You override the master page items on a specific page

When you move a page from one side of a spread to the other (e.g., from left to right) any bleed object will continue to bleed past the same edge of its new page position — possibly interfering with the other page of the spread.

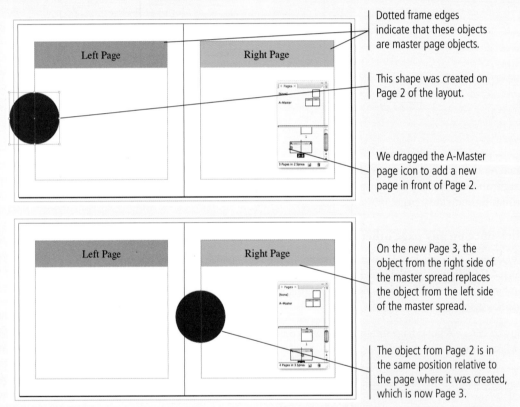

Dotted frame edges indicate that these objects are master page objects.

This shape was created on Page 2 of the layout.

We dragged the A-Master page icon to add a new page in front of Page 2.

On the new Page 3, the object from the right side of the master spread replaces the object from the left side of the master spread.

The object from Page 2 is in the same position relative to the page where it was created, which is now Page 3.

INDESIGN FOUNDATIONS

A related problem occurs when you override and change master page items on regular layout pages. When you override master page items, they become regular layout page items. Adding pages to the middle of a layout moves those items relative to their new page position; the original master page objects are added directly behind the overridden objects. If necessary, you can choose Remove All Local Overrides from the Pages panel options menu, or you can select specific objects and choose Remove Selected Local Overrides.

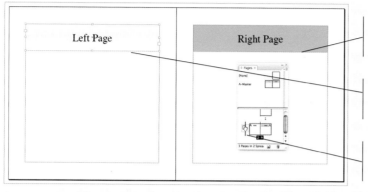

Dotted frame edges indicate that this object is a master page object.

We overrode master page items for Page 2, then changed the object fill color from magenta to yellow.

We then dragged the A-Master page icon to add a new page in front of Page 2.

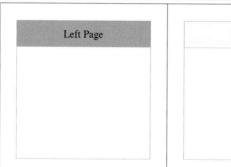
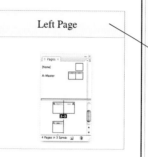

Because overriding master page items converts them into regular page items, the overridden object moves relative to the page on which it is placed (the moved Page 2).

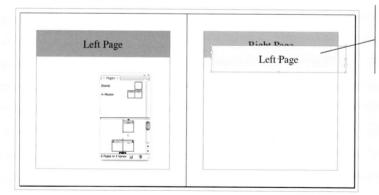

Moving the overridden object shows that the correct master page object has been added to the page, directly behind the overridden object.

3. **In the Pages panel, click once on the left page icon of the A-Master spread.**

4. **With the left page of the A-Master layout selected, choose Layout>Margins and Columns.**

5. **With the Preview option checked, change the top margin to 3″, change the outside margin to 2″, and change the number of columns to 1.**

   Unfortunately, changing the margins and columns does not automatically change the settings of the master text frame. You have to change those separately.

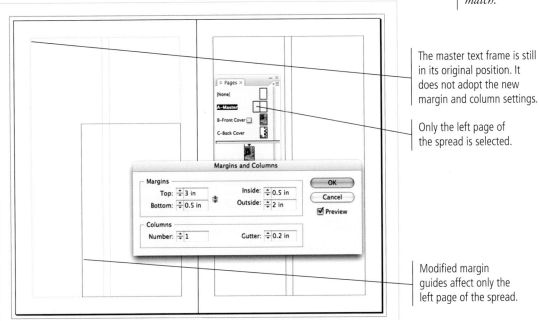

Note:

Make sure the lock icon between the margin fields is a broken chain. If the icon shows an unbroken chain, changing one margin field will change the other three fields to match.

The master text frame is still in its original position. It does not adopt the new margin and column settings.

Only the left page of the spread is selected.

Modified margin guides affect only the left page of the spread.

6. **Click OK to apply the changes.**

7. **In the document window, use the Selection tool to resize the master text frame to match the new margin guides.**

8. **Control/right-click the frame, choose Text Frame Options from the contextual menu, and change the number of columns to 1. In the Vertical Justification area, change the align menu to Bottom. Click OK.**

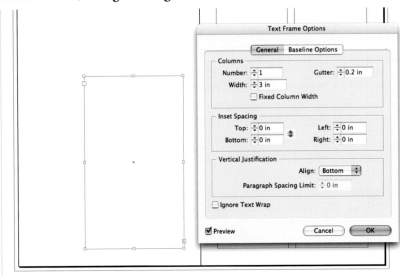

9. **In the Pages panel, select only the right page of the A-Master spread. Choose Layout>Margins and Columns and change the bottom margin to 3.25". Click OK.**

10. **Using the Selection tool, drag the bottom edge of the text frame to match the new bottom margin guide on the right page of the spread.**

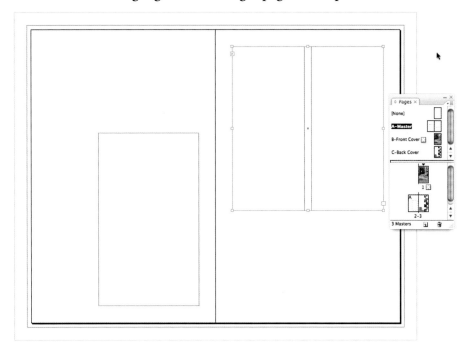

11. **Save the file and continue to the next exercise.**

 ## ADD COMMON ELEMENTS TO A MASTER PAGE LAYOUT

In addition to the master text frame, you need several other elements to appear on every body spread: the graphics frame on the left side of the spread, as well as the callout box and page footer on the right page of the spread. Again, it makes sense to create master page placeholders for these objects rather than to recreate the objects on individual layout pages. Doing so reduces the number of repetitive tasks as much as possible to maximize your productivity.

The client's content is supplied in a single file, and the callout text for each spread appears within the main body of the text. Each callout has the heading "Through the Buyers Eyes," so you can identify the appropriate text.

1. **With the file booklet_working.indd open, make sure the A-Master layout is showing in the document window.**

2. **Create a new text frame with the following dimensions (based on the top-left reference point):**

> X: 7.375"   W: 3.75"
>
> Y: 5.7"   H: 2.25"

Note:

By default, InDesign measurements reflect an object's position relative to the entire spread; the X: 7.375" position is actually 1.875" from the left edge of the right page. You can change this behavior by changing the Ruler Units origin in the Units & Increments pane of the Preferences dialog box.

3. **Fill the new text frame with the Green to White gradient swatch, and use the Gradient panel to change the gradient angle to 90°.**

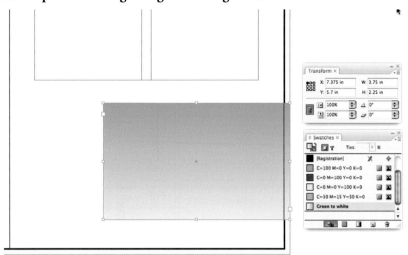

4. **Control/right-click the new frame and choose Text Frame Options from the contextual menu.**

5. **Change the Top, Bottom, and Left Inset Spacing fields to 0.125″, and change the Right Inset field to 0.625″.**

Because the frame bleeds off the page edge, you need to adjust the frame inset on only the bleed side to match the rest of the layout. Instead of overlaying two frames — one with the bleeding gradient and one with the text frame, you can use uneven inset spacing to achieve the same goal.

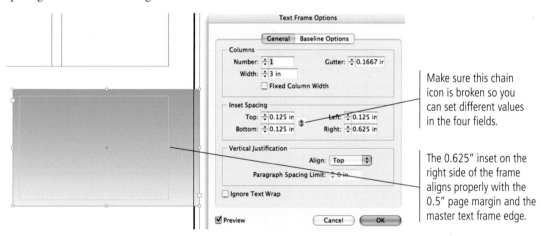

Make sure this chain icon is broken so you can set different values in the four fields.

The 0.625″ inset on the right side of the frame aligns properly with the 0.5″ page margin and the master text frame edge.

6. **Click OK to apply the changes.**

7. **Create another text frame immediately above the one you just created.**

8. **Type "through the buyers eyes" in the frame, and then change the formatting to 15-pt ATC Laurel Bold Italic using the C=50, M=15, Y=50, K=0 swatch.**

9. **Using either the Text Frame Options dialog box or the Control bar, change the frame's vertical justification to bottom.**

10. **Align the left edges of the two frames, and then move the heading frame vertically so the bottoms of the heading descenders are just above the top edge of the larger frame.**

11. Using the Selection tool, click the master text frame on the right page of the spread.

12. Click the Out port of the master text frame, and then immediately click the gradient-filled text frame to link the two frames.

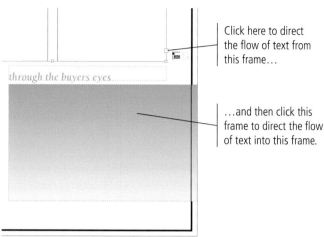

Click here to direct the flow of text from this frame…

…and then click this frame to direct the flow of text into this frame.

13. Choose View>Show Text Threads.

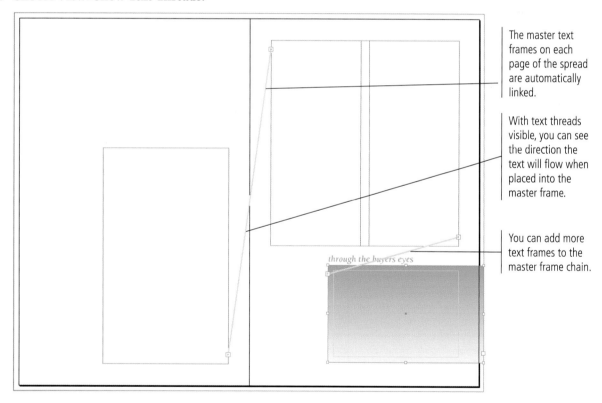

The master text frames on each page of the spread are automatically linked.

With text threads visible, you can see the direction the text will flow when placed into the master frame.

You can add more text frames to the master frame chain.

14. Turn off the text threads (View>Hide Text Threads).

15. Create an empty graphics frame with the following dimensions:

    X: –0.125"   W: 5.625"

    Y: –0.125"   H: 8.75"

16. Choose Object>Effects>Gradient Feather.

By applying the Gradient Feather effect to the placeholder, the effect will automatically be applied to each picture when you place the files into the main layout pages — one more way you can improve productivity by automating repetitive tasks.

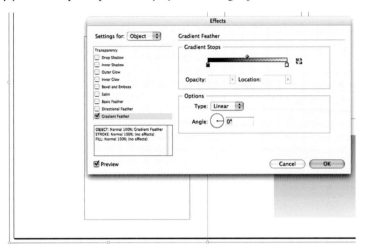

17. Click OK to apply the change, and then make sure the frame edges are visible (View>Show Frame Edges).

When frame edges are visible, empty picture frames have crossed diagonal lines. Because this frame has a defined Gradient Feather effect, the diagonal lines become less visible toward the right side of the frame.

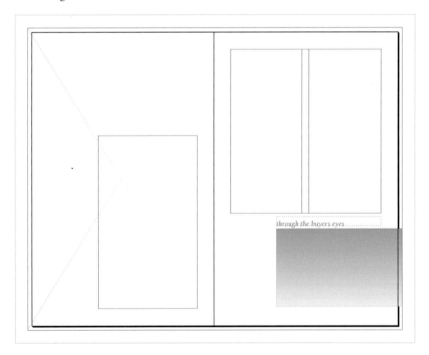

18. With the graphics frame selected, choose Object>Arrange>Send to Back to move the graphics frame behind the text frame.

19. Save the file and continue to the next exercise.

PLACE AUTOMATIC PAGE NUMBER MARKERS

The last item to add to the master page layout is the page footer information — the page number and the name of the booklet. Rather than manually numbering each page in the booklet — which can be time consuming and invites human error — you can use special characters to automatically number the pages in any layout.

1. **With booklet_working.indd open, make sure the A-Master layout is showing.**

2. **Create a new text frame with the following dimensions (based on the top-left reference point):**

   X: 6″   W: 4.5″

   Y: 8.125″   H: 0.25″

3. **Type "Home Enhancement Guide", and then change the formatting to 12-pt ATC Laurel Bold Italic with right paragraph alignment.**

The Glyphs Panel

ASCII is a text-based code that defines characters with a numeric value between 001 and 256. The standard alphabet and punctuation characters are mapped from 001 to 128. **Extended ASCII characters** are those with ASCII numbers higher than 128, including symbols (bullets, copyright symbols, etc.) and some special characters (en dashes, accent marks, etc.). Some of the more common extended characters can be accessed in the Type>Insert submenus.

OpenType fonts can store more than 65,000 **glyphs** (characters) in a single font — far beyond what you could access with a keyboard (even including combinations of the different modifier keys). The large glyph storage capacity means that a single OpenType font can replace the multiple separate "Expert" fonts that contain variations of fonts (Minion Swash, for example, is no longer necessary when you can access the Swashes subset of the Minion Pro font).

Unicode fonts include two-bit characters that are common in some foreign language typesetting (e.g., Cyrillic, Japanese, and other non-Roman or pictographic fonts).

The Glyphs panel (Window>Type & Tables>Glyphs or Type>Glyphs) provides access to individual glyphs in a font, including basic characters in regular fonts, extended ASCII and OpenType character sets, and even pictographic characters in Unicode fonts.

Using the Glyphs panel is simple: make sure the insertion point is flashing where you want a character to appear, and then double-click the character you want to place. You can view the character set for any font by simply changing the menu at the bottom of the panel. By default, the panel shows the entire font, but you can show only specific character sets using the Show menu.

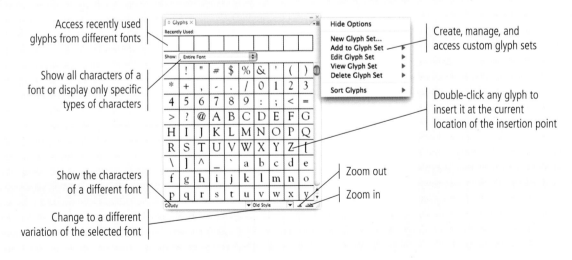

Access recently used glyphs from different fonts

Show all characters of a font or display only specific types of characters

Show the characters of a different font

Change to a different variation of the selected font

Create, manage, and access custom glyph sets

Double-click any glyph to insert it at the current location of the insertion point

Zoom out

Zoom in

4. **Place the insertion point immediately after the word "Guide" and press the Spacebar once.**

Because the text is right-aligned, the Space character is not visible; a space at the end of a line is not considered in the line length or type position when paragraphs are aligned.

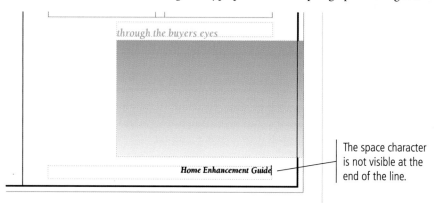

The space character is not visible at the end of the line.

Special Characters and White Space

A number of special characters can be accessed in the Type submenus. Use the following chart as a how-and-why guide for accessing these characters.

Menu			What it's used for
Insert Special Character	Markers	Current Page Number	Places the current page number
		Next Page Number	Places the page number of the next frame in the same story
		Previous Page Number	Places the page number of the previous frame in the same story
		Section Marker	Places a user-defined text variable that is specific to the current layout section (You'll work with section numbering in Project 8.)
		Footnote Number	Inserts a number character based on the options defined in the Footnote Options dialog box
	Hyphens and Dashes	Em Dash	Places a dash equivalent to the width of a capital M in the applied font
		En Dash	Places a dash equivalent to one-half an em dash
		Discretionary Hyphen	Allows you to hyphenate a word in a location other than what is defined by the currect dictionary, or hyphenate a word when automatic hyphenation is turned off. The discretionary hyphen only appears if the word is hyphenated at the end of a line.
		Nonbreaking Hyphen	Places a hyphen character that will not break at the end of a line; used to keep both parts of a phrase on the same line of the paragraph
	Quotation Marks	Double Left Quotation Marks	"
		Double Right Quotation Marks	"
		Single Left Quotation Mark	'
		Single Right Quotation Mark	'
		Straight Double Quotation Marks	"
		Straight Single Quotation Mark	'
	Other	Tab	Forces following text to begin at the next defined or default tab stop
		Right Indent Tab	Forces following text to align at the right edge of the column or frame
		Indent to Here	Creates a hanging indent by forcing all following lines in the paragraph to indent to the location of the character
		End Nested Style Here	Interrupts nested style formatting before the defined character limit
		Non-joiner	Prevents adjacent characters from being joined in a ligature or other alternate character connection

5. **With the insertion point flashing after the space character (which you can't see), choose Type>Insert Special Character>Markers>Current Page Number.**

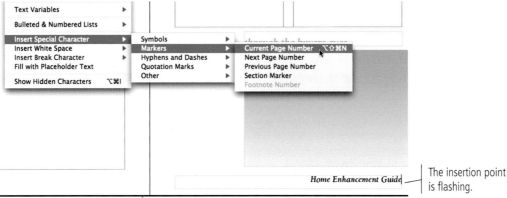

The insertion point is flashing.

Special Characters and White Space (continued)

Menu		What it's used for
Insert White Space	Em Space	Space equivalent to the width of a capital M in the applied type size
	En Space	One-half of an em space
	Nonbreaking Space	Places a space character the same width as pressing the Spacebar; this character prevents a line break from occurring, which allows you to keep related words together on the same line.
	Nonbreaking Space (Fixed Width)	Same as the regular nonbreaking space, but does not change size when a paragraph uses justified alignment.
	Hair Space	One-twenty-fourth of an em space
	Sixth Space	One-sixth of an em space
	Thin Space	One-eighth of an em space
	Quarter Space	One-fourth of an em space
	Third Space	One-third of an em space
	Punctuation Space	Same width as a period in the applied font
	Figure Space	Same width as a number in the applied font
	Flush Space	Variable space in a justified paragraph placed between the last character of the paragraph and a decorative character (called a "bug") used to indicate the end of a story
Insert Break Character	Column Break	Forces text into the next available column (or frame, if used in a one-column frame or the last column of a multi-column frame)
	Frame Break	Forces text into the next available frame
	Page Break	Forces text into the first available frame on the next page, skipping any available frames or columns on the same page
	Odd Page Break	Forces text into the first available frame on the next odd-numbered page
	Even Page Break	Forces text into the first available frame on the next even-numbered page
	Paragraph Return	Creates a new paragraph (same as pressing Return/Enter)
	Forced Line Break	Creates a new line without starting a new paragraph (called a "soft return")
	Discretionary Line Break	Creates a new line if the character falls at the end of the line; if the character falls in the middle of the column, the line is not broken

INDESIGN FOUNDATIONS

6. **If the hidden characters are not visible, choose Type>Show Hidden Characters.**

The Current Page Number command inserts a special character that reflects the correct page number of any page where it appears. Because you placed this character on the A-Master page, the character shows as "A" in the text box.

Now that the Space character is no longer the last character in the line, you can see it — as long as hidden characters are showing.

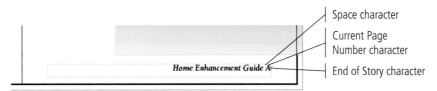

Space character

Current Page Number character

End of Story character

Home Enhancement Guide A

In this case, the single, regular Space character is not enough to separate the booklet name from the page number. InDesign provides a number of options for increasing (and decreasing) white space without simply pressing the Spacebar numerous times.

7. **Highlight the Space character before the Page Number character.**

Keyboard Shortcuts for Special Characters

Character	Keyboard Shortcut	
	Macintosh	**Windows**
Current page number	Command-Option-Shift-N	Control-Alt-Shift-N
Em dash	Option-Shift-Hyphen (-)	Alt-Shift-Hyphen (-)
En dash	Option-Hyphen	Alt-Hyphen
Discretionary hyphen	Command-Shift-Hyphen	Control-Shift-Hyphen
Nonbreaking hyphen	Command-Option-Hyphen	Control-Alt-Hyphen
Double left quotation marks	Option-[	Alt-[
Double right quotation marks	Option-Shift-[	Alt-Shift-[
Single left quotation mark	Option-]	Alt-]
Single right quotation mark	Option-Shift-]	Alt-Shift-]
Straight double quotation marks	Control-Shift-'	Alt-Shift-'
Straight single quotation mark	Control-'	Alt-'
Tab	Tab	Tab
Right indent tab	Shift-Tab	Shift-Tab
Indent to here	Command-\	Control-\
Em space	Command-Shift-M	Control-Shift-M
En space	Command-Shift-N	Control-Shift-N
Nonbreaking space	Command-Option-X	Control-Alt-X
Thin space	Command-Option-Shift-M	Control-Alt-Shift-N
Column break	Enter (numeric keypad)	Enter (numeric keypad)
Frame break	Shift-Enter (numeric keypad)	Shift-Enter (numeric keypad)
Page break	Command-Enter (numeric keypad)	Control-Enter (numeric keypad)
Paragraph return	Return	Enter
Forced line break	Shift-Return	Shift-Enter

INDESIGN FOUNDATIONS

8. **Choose Type>Insert White Space>Em Space.**

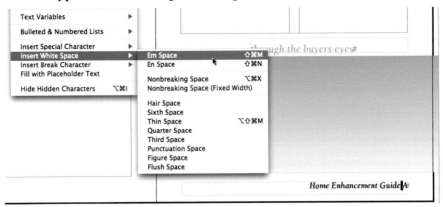

An **em** is a typographic measure equivalent to the width of the capital letter M in a specific typeface. For example, an em is ten points wide in 10-pt. type and twelve points wide in 12-pt. type. An em space is white space equal to one em.

9. **Add a second Em Space character immediately after the first.**

10. **Select all the text in the footer and change the type size to 10 pt.**

    Special and hidden characters are still characters; changing the type formatting affects these characters in the same way as regular characters.

Em Space characters

11. **Save the file and continue to the next exercise.**

 ## CREATE TEXT VARIABLES

The last thing you are going to add on the master page is a custom slug, which is file information that will be printed outside the trim and bleed areas. You already defined the slug area in the first exercise of this project; you can now use text variables to place the same information on each of the three master pages in the layout.

1. **With booklet_working.indd open, make sure the A-Master layout is showing.**

2. **Create a new text frame in the slug area above the left page of the spread.**

3. **With the insertion point flashing in the new text frame, choose Type>Text Variables>Insert Variable>Modification Date.**

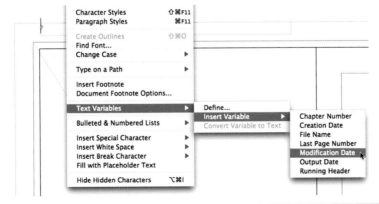

InDesign includes several common default variables, including the Modification Date variable, which places the date and time when the file was last saved.

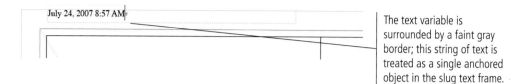

July 24, 2007 8:57 AM

The text variable is surrounded by a faint gray border; this string of text is treated as a single anchored object in the slug text frame.

4. **Choose Type>Text Variables>Define.**

This dialog box allows you to change the built-in text variables, or you can define your own text variables to meet the specific needs of a project.

In this case, you're going to create a "status" variable that reflects the current stage of the file. This information should appear over every spread, which means it needs to be placed on all three master page layouts. You could accomplish the same thing by simply typing the stage in the slug of each master page; however, you would have to make the same change on each of those three master pages in each stage of the project.

By defining a text variable that you will place on all three master pages, you can simply change the variable definition for each stage of the project, and then all instances of the placed variable will automatically reflect the same change.

Note:

Even though you can't select the actual characters within the placed text variable instance, you can still change the formatting of variables by highlighting the instance in the layout and making whatever changes you want.

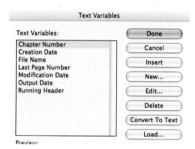

5. **In the Text Variables dialog box, click the New button.**

6. **In the Name field of the New Text Variable dialog box, type "File Status".**

7. **In the Type menu, choose Custom Text.**

Eight of these options place specific text (using the formatting you can define in this dialog box). These variable types are the same as the ones that already appear in the Text Variables>Insert Variables submenu. You can, however, define more than one variable for a single type. For example, you can define two different modification date variables — one that shows the day, month, year, and time; and one that shows only the day and month.

Note:

You can convert text variable instances to regular text by selecting an instance in the layout and choosing Type>Text Variables>Convert Variable to Text. You can convert all instances of a specific variable to regular text by opening the Text Variables dialog box, selecting a specific variable, and clicking the Convert to Text button.

Note:

If you delete a variable that is used in the layout, you can choose to replace placed instances with a different variable, convert the instances to regular text, or simply remove the placed instances.

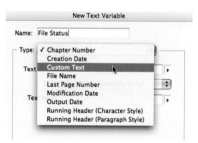

8. **Click the menu to the right of the Text field.**

   Using the Custom Text option, you can determine what text appears in the variable. The menu provides access to common special characters (these are the same characters that you can access in the Type>Insert Special Character submenus).

9. **Choose Ellipsis from the menu.**

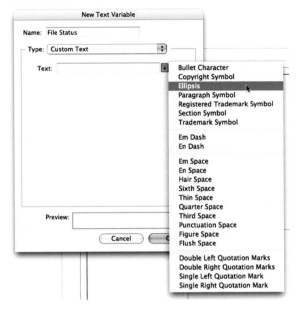

10. **With the insertion point after the code for the Ellipsis character, type "Stage 1".**

    This type of variable could be used in a client job to show the stage of the file, such as "First Round Comp" or "Sent for Approval".

11. **Click OK to close the New Text Variable dialog box.**

    The new File Status variable now appears in the list.

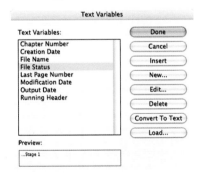

12. **Click Done to close the Text Variables dialog box.**

13. **With the insertion point flashing after the Modification Date text variable in the slug text frame, press Tab and then choose Type>Text Variables>Insert Text Variable>File Status.**

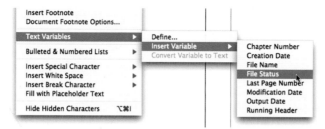

The variable text you defined is placed immediately after the Tab character. Because it is a variable instance, it is surrounded by a gray border.

14. **Click the Selection tool in the Tools panel.**

Because the slug text frame was already active, it is automatically selected.

15. **Press Command/Control-C to copy the frame.**

16. **In the Pages panel, double-click the B-Front Cover master page.**

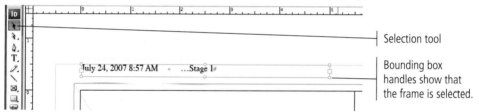

Selection tool

Bounding box handles show that the frame is selected.

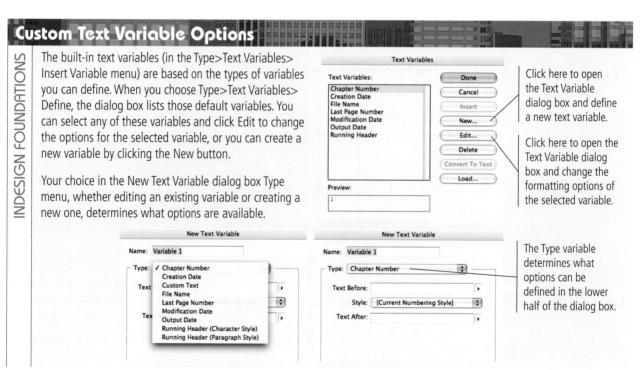

For all but the Custom Text variable, you can define the characters that precede (Text Before field) or follow (Text After field) the variable information. You can type specific information in either of these fields, or you can use the associated menus to place symbols, em or en dashes, white-space characters, or typographer's quotation marks.

The **Chapter Number** variable inserts the chapter number based on the file's position in a book document (you will work with InDesign books in Project 8). You can use the Style menu to format the chapter number as lowercase or uppercase letters, lowercase or uppercase Roman numerals, or Arabic numbers.

The **Creation Date** variable inserts the time the document is first saved. The **Modification Date** variable inserts the time the document was last saved. The **Output Date** variable inserts the date the document was last printed, exported to PDF, or packaged. You can use the **Date Format** menu to modify the date format for all three of these variables. You can either type a format directly into the field, or you can use the associated menu to choose the options you want to include. If you want to simply type the format into the field, you have to use the correct abbreviations.

The **File Name** variable inserts the name of the open file. You can use the check box options to include the entire folder path and the file extension. (The path and extension will not appear until you save the file at least once.)

Abbreviation	Description	Example
M	Month number	1
MM	Month number (two digits)*	01
MMM	Month name (abbreviated)	Jan
MMMM	Month name (full)	January
d	Day number	3
dd	Day number (two digits)	03
E	Weekday name (abbreviated)	Wed
EEEE	Weekday name (full)	Wednesday
yy	Year number (last two digits)	07
yyyy	Year number (four digits)	2007
G	Era (abbreviated)	AD
GGGG	Era (full)	Anno Domini
h	Hour	1
hh	Hour (two digits)	01
H	Hour (24-hour format)	16
HH	Hour (two digits, 24-hour format)	16
m	Minute	9
mm	Minute (two digits)	09
s	Second	2
ss	Second (two digits)	02
a	AM or PM	AM
z	Time zone (abbreviated)	PST
zzzz	Time zone (full)	Pacific Standard Time

*The two-digit formats force a leading zero in front of numbers lower than 10 (for example, 9/25/07 would appear as 09/25/07 if you use the two-digital Month format).

The **Last Page Number** variable can be used to create a "Page x of y" notation. This variable can indicate the last page number of the entire document or the current section (in the Scope menu). You can also determine the numbering style (with the same options as in the Chapter Number variable).

The **Running Header** variables can be used to find content on the page based on applied paragraph or character styles.

In the Style menu, you can choose the paragraph or character style to use as the variable content. The Use menu identifies which instance of the defined style (first or last on the page) to use as the variable content. For example, say you have a glossary page and all the terms are formatted with the Glossary Term character style. You could define two Running Header (Character Style) variables — one that identifies the first use of the Glossary Term style and one that identifies the last use of the Glossary Term style on the current page. You can then place the two variables in a text frame to create a running header that shows the first and last terms on the page — e.g., [First Term] – [Last Term].

The Delete End Punctuation option identifies the text without punctuation. For example, you can identify a Bold Run-In character style that is applied to text that always ends with a period. When the style is identified as the variable, the period will not be included in the variable text.

The Change Case options determine capitalization for the variable text:

• Upper Case capitalizes the entire variable.

• Lower Case removes all capitalization.

• Title Case capitalizes the first letter in every word.

• Sentence Case capitalizes only the first word.

The **Custom Text** variable inserts whatever text you define in the associated field.

17. Press Command/Control-V to paste the copied frame, and then drag the frame into the slug area above the page.

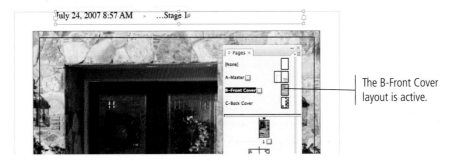

The B-Front Cover layout is active.

18. Navigate to the C-Back Cover layout and paste the copied text frame into the slug area above the page.

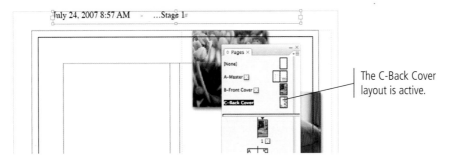

The C-Back Cover layout is active.

19. In the top section of the Pages panel, Control/right-click the A-Master layout name and choose Master Options for "A-Master" from the contextual menu.

20. In the Master Options dialog box, change the Name field to "Body Spread" and click OK.

It's always a good idea to use a meaningful name for any element you define in InDesign, including a master page.

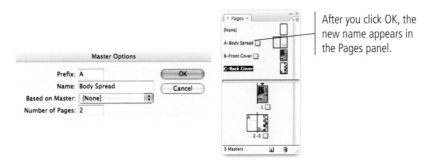

After you click OK, the new name appears in the Pages panel.

21. Save the file and continue to the next stage of the project.

Stage 2 Controlling Text Flow

Because you imported the covers as master pages and built a spread layout to hold the different body elements, all the necessary pieces are in place to import the client's provided text and graphics. The time you spent building effective master pages will significantly improve your ability to quickly place the layout content and create a multi-page document, speeding up the development process by eliminating the need to create these elements manually on individual pages.

CHANGE THE CUSTOM TEXT VARIABLE

The File Status variable you defined in the previous exercise allows you to monitor the status of the project while you work. As you begin the second stage of the project, you should change the variable to reflect the new status.

1. **With booklet_working.indd open, double-click the Page 2 icon in the Pages panel to navigate to that page.**

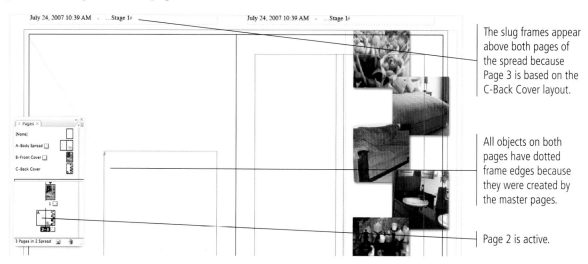

The slug frames appear above both pages of the spread because Page 3 is based on the C-Back Cover layout.

All objects on both pages have dotted frame edges because they were created by the master pages.

Page 2 is active.

2. **Choose Type>Text Variables>Define.**

3. **Select File Status in the list and click Edit.**

4. **In the Text field, change Stage 1 to "Stage 2".**

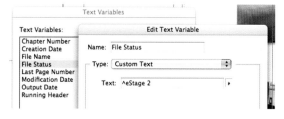

5. **Click OK, and then click Done to return to the layout.**

   Because you placed the File Status variable on each master page layout, changing the variable definition automatically changes all placed instances. And by placing the variable instances on the master page layouts, the same change automatically reflects on the associated layout pages.

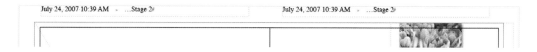

6. **Save the file and continue to the next exercise.**

IMPORT AND AUTO-FLOW CLIENT TEXT

You are building a document with 16 facing pages. You could manually insert the necessary pages, and then manually link the text from one page to the next. But anytime you see the word "manually," you should look for ways to automate some or all of the process. The ability to automate work is one of the defining characteristics of professional page-layout software such as InDesign.

1. **With Page 2 of booklet_working.indd visible, choose File>Place.**

2. **Navigate to the file named booklet.doc in the RF_InDesign>Realtors folder. Make sure the Show Import Options box is checked and click Open.**

3. **In the Import Options dialog box, make sure the Preserve Styles and Formatting option is selected.**

4. **In the Manual Page Breaks menu, choose No Breaks.**

    This command removes any page and section breaks that exist in the client's Word file.

5. **Select the Import Styles Automatically option, and choose Auto Rename in both conflict menus.**

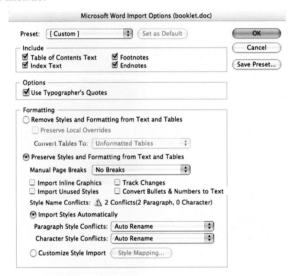

6. **Click OK to import the text.**

    When you see the Missing Fonts warning, click OK. You're going to change the style definitions for the booklet text, so you don't have to worry about finding the missing fonts.

    This is a very common workflow issue when you work with client-supplied files. Every situation is different, but we find it best to import the client's formatting so we can review the editorial priority, and then edit or define styles as necessary to complete the page layout.

7. **Press Shift, and then click the loaded text cursor inside the margin guides on Page 2.**

Pressing Shift converts the loaded text cursor into the automatic-flow text cursor.

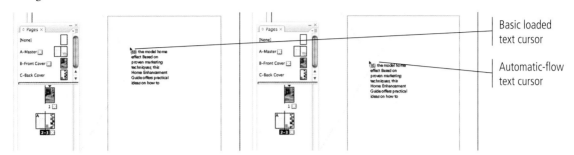

Basic loaded text cursor

Automatic-flow text cursor

When you Shift-click to place text inside the margin guides on a page with a master text frame, the entire story is automatically placed; enough pages are added to the end of the layout to accommodate the entire story.

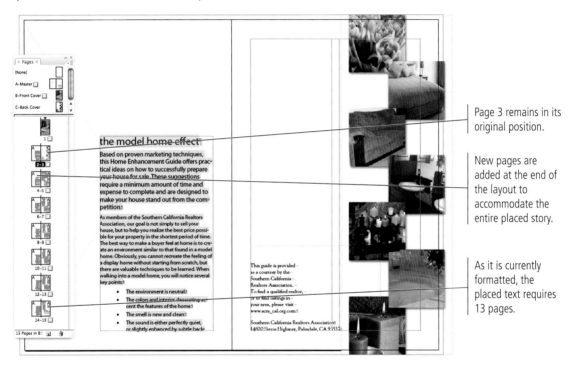

Page 3 remains in its original position.

New pages are added at the end of the layout to accommodate the entire placed story.

As it is currently formatted, the placed text requires 13 pages.

8. **Click the Page 3 icon and drag it to the right of Page 15. When you see the vertical black bar, release the mouse button.**

When you release the mouse button, Page 3 (the back cover) becomes Page 15. The previous Pages 4–15 become Pages 3–14; each page moves to the appropriate side of the spread.

Although you did not manually override the master page items for the body pages, placing content into the pages' master frames means those text frames are automatically detached from the associated master frames.

As we explained earlier, regular page objects (the current state of the text frames) are positioned relative to the page on which they exist. When the previous Page 4 (a left-facing page) becomes Page 3 (a right-facing page), the text frame from the left-facing page moves along with the page; items from the right page of the master layout are added behind the text frame.

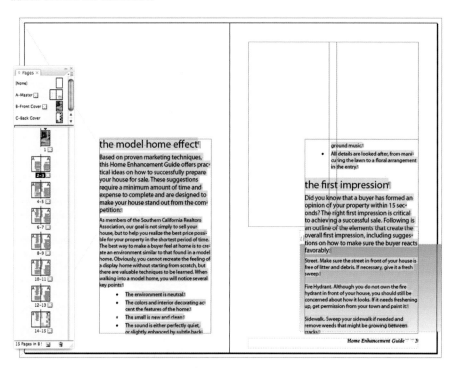

9. **In the Pages panel, click the Page 2 icon, press Shift, and then click the Page 15 icon to select all but the first page.**

Note:

Page 15 is the back page. You are also deleting that page in this step.

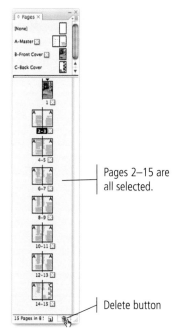

Pages 2–15 are all selected.

Delete button

10. **Click the Pages panel Delete button to delete the selected pages.**

Rather than trying to manually fix all of the problems caused by changing the right- and left-facing positions of fifteen different pages, it is easier to simply reflow the text. Because you have complete master layouts for the back cover and body spreads, this is very easy to accomplish.

11. **Click OK in the resulting warning.**

12. **In the Pages panel, drag the left page icon of the A-Body Spread below the Page 1 icon to add a second page to the layout.**

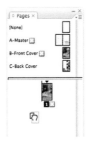

13. **Place the file booklet.doc again with the Show Import Options box checked.**

14. **In the Import Options, make sure the Preserve Styles option is selected and No Breaks is selected in the Manual Page Breaks menu. Activate the Import Styles Automatically option and choose Use InDesign Style Definition in both Conflict menus.**

When you deleted the pages, you also deleted the contents of those pages. However, styles and other assets are not objects; the styles from the first text import remain in the InDesign file.

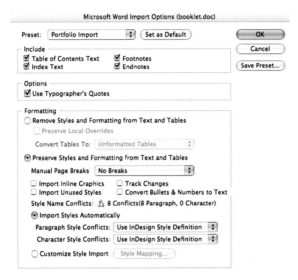

15. **Click OK to import the document, and then click OK to dismiss the Missing Font dialog box.**

16. Shift-click the loaded text cursor inside the margin guides on Page 2.

The text automatically flows through 13 pages that are based on the A-Body Spread layout.

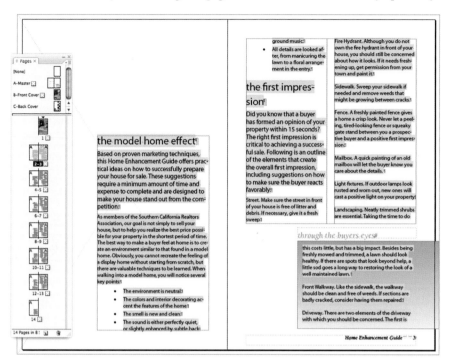

Note:

You will add the back cover again later in the project. Because is created on its own master page, you can easily place it where necessary when you are finished with the body of the project.

17. Save the file and continue to the next exercise.

REVIEW, REPLACE, AND EDIT IMPORTED STYLES

As you can see in the current booklet file, the text is just a long block with little to distinguish the different elements of editorial priority (e.g., headings, subheadings, and so on). Fonts used in the client's file aren't available, as indicated by the pink "missing font" highlight. This type of situation occurs frequently. When it does, you should begin by reviewing the text to see if applied styles can provide any clues about which elements belong where.

1. With Page 2 of booklet_working.indd showing, click the Type tool in the first paragraph ("the model home effect").

2. Look at the Paragraph Styles panel.

The first paragraph is formatted with the Section Head style. You can also assume that other text with the same basic appearance is also a section head.

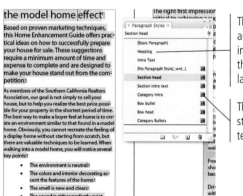

These two styles — Heading and Intro Text —were imported when you loaded the cover master page layouts into the booklet file.

The disc icon shows that the style was imported with the text file.

3. **Press the Down Arrow key to move the insertion point to the next paragraph.**

The second paragraph is formatted with the Section Intro Text style. Again, you can assume that other text with the same appearance is also the introductory text for a section.

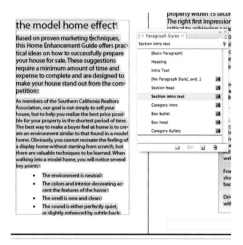

4. **In the Paragraph Styles panel, Control/right-click the Section Head style and choose Delete Style from the contextual menu.**

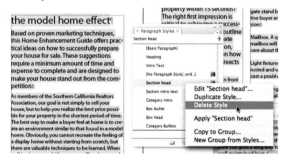

Note:

You can also edit a style by double-clicking the style in the panel. However, double-clicking a style in the panel applies the style to the current text and then opens the Paragraph Style Options dialog box.

By Control/right-clicking the style in the panel, you can edit the style without it being applied to the currently selected text.

5. **In the Delete Paragraph Style dialog box, choose Heading in the Replace With menu and click OK.**

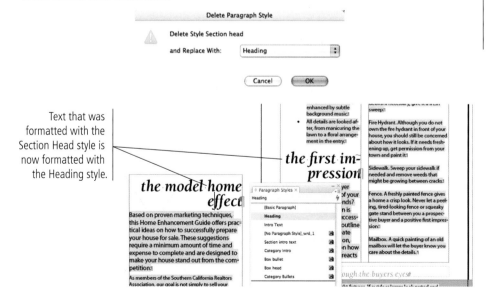

Text that was formatted with the Section Head style is now formatted with the Heading style.

6. **Using the same process, replace the Section Intro Text style with the Intro Text style.**

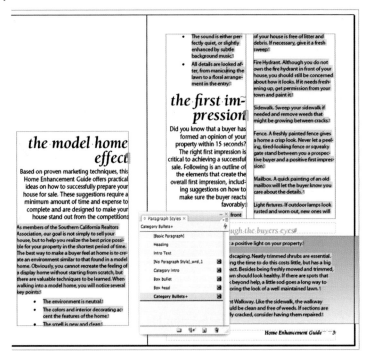

7. **Place the insertion point in the third paragraph.**

   This paragraph is formatted with the Category Intro style.

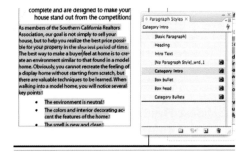

8. **Control/right-click the Category Intro style and choose Edit "Category Intro" from the contextual menu.**

9. **In the Basic Character Formats options, change the style to 9.5-pt ATC Pine Normal.**

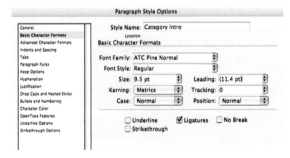

10. In the Indents and Spacing options, change all the Indent fields to 0. Change the Space Before field to 0.1″, and change the Space After field to 0.

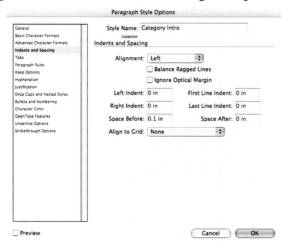

Note:

Remember, if you check the Preview box in the Paragraph Style Options dialog box, you can see the effect of your changes before you decide to click OK.

11. Click OK to change the style definition.

Much of the text in this layout is formatted with the Category Intro style. That text now reflects the changed definition.

12. Save the file and continue to the next exercise.

DEFINE PARENT-CHILD STYLE RELATIONSHIPS

Two points about designing long documents are particularly important to remember. First, changing the definition of a style changes all text formatted with that style. Second, text should be consistently formatted from one page to the next; body copy and similar styles (such as bulleted lists) should use the same basic font throughout the entire layout.

These two points are related — consider, for example, what happens if you decide to change the font for the main body copy from Times New Roman to Adobe Garamond. Changing the main body font means you should also change any related styles that are variations of the main body text, such as bulleted or numbered lists.

The best way to manage this type of situation is to create secondary styles that are based on the main style. This way, changes to the main style also reflect in styles that are based on the main style.

1. **With Page 2 of booklet_working.indd visible, place the insertion point in the first bulleted paragraph where the font is still missing.**

    This text is formatted with the Category Bullets style. The plus sign to the right of the style name indicates that some formatting other than the style definition has been applied to the selected paragraph — called a **local formatting override**.

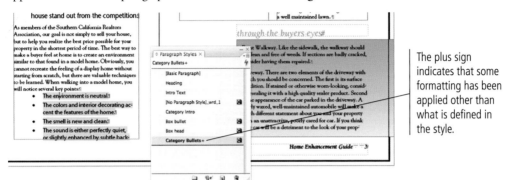

The plus sign indicates that some formatting has been applied other than what is defined in the style.

2. **Control/right-click the Category Bullets style in the Paragraph Styles panel and choose Edit "Category Bullets" from the contextual menu.**

3. **In the General options, choose Category Intro in the Based On menu.**

    When you redefine an existing style to be based on another style, InDesign tries to maintain the formatting of the original style instead of the one it is being based on. In the Style Settings area, you can see the style will be Category Intro +. Everything after the plus sign is different than the style defined in the Based On menu (called the **parent style**).

Note:

Local formatting overrides are very common when you import text from a client-supplied Microsoft Word file.

[Paragraph Style Options dialog — Style Name: Category Bullets; Based On: Category Intro; Next Style: [Same style]; Style Settings show: Category Intro + next: [Same style] + ATC Colada + size: 10 pt + left indent: 0.7 in + first indent: –0.25 in + tabs: count = 1, [position: 0.7 in, alignment: left] + space after: 0.0417 in]

4. **Click the Reset to Base button above the Style Settings pane.**

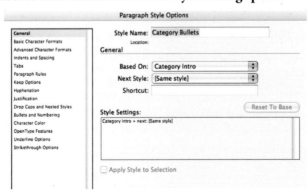

5. In the Indents and Spacing options, change the Space Before field to 0.05″ and click OK.

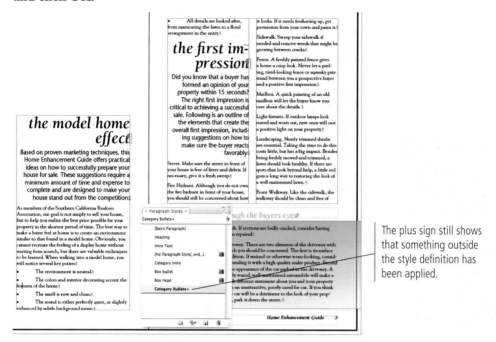

The plus sign still shows that something outside the style definition has been applied.

6. With the insertion point anywhere in the selected text, choose Edit>Select All to select the entire story.

You can clear overrides for any selected text, whether for a single character or for an entire story. In this case, all the overrides were created in the original Word file; rather than manually clearing overrides in each paragraph, you can simply select the entire story and clear all overrides at once.

7. At the bottom of the Paragraph Styles panel, click the Clear Overrides button.

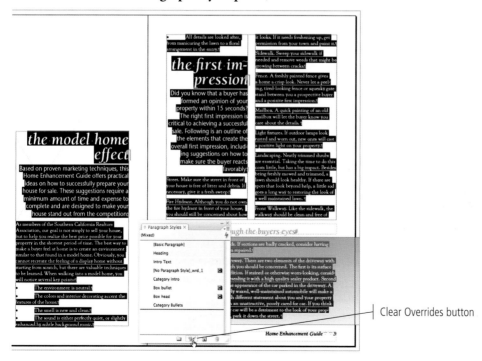

Clear Overrides button

By clearing overrides, the bullet characters have been removed from the Category Bullets style. You will add these back in later by editing the style definition.

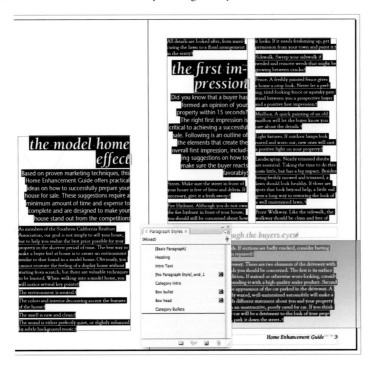

8. **Deselect all the text, navigate to Page 4, and place the insertion point in the first indented paragraph with the missing font highlight.**

This text is formatted with the Box Bullet style. You can ignore the first line with missing text; since you placed the box heading in its own frame on the master page, you are going to delete the redundant text heading from the imported text.

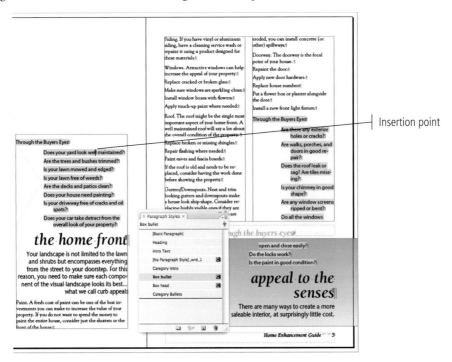

Insertion point

9. **Using the same method from Steps 2–5, change the Box Bullet style to be based on the Category Intro text style with a 0.05″ Space Before value.**

You could actually base this style on the Category Bullet style, but we try to avoid too many levels of nested styles. More levels of nesting equals greater complexity when you need to make changes.

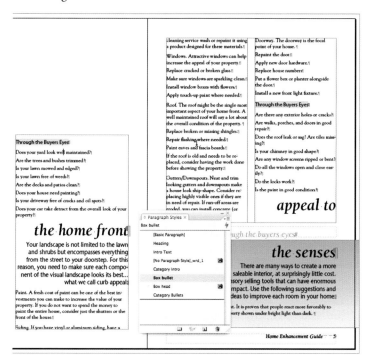

10. **Save the file and continue to the next exercise.**

DEFINE BULLETS AND NUMBERING OPTIONS

By changing the style definitions in the previous exercise, you removed the bullets from two different types of lists (the category bulleted lists and the box bulleted lists); these bullets need to be replaced. You're also going to convert the Category Intro text paragraphs to bullets to create improved visual separation.

You could manually type the characters at the beginning of each line, but it's much easier and more efficient to use the Bullets and Numbering paragraph formatting options.

1. **With booklet_working.indd open, Control/right-click Category Intro in the Paragraph Styles panel and choose Edit "Category Intro" from the contextual menu.**

2. **In the Paragraph Style Options dialog box, display the Bullets and Numbering options.**

3. In the List Type menu, choose Bullets.

By default, you can apply the Bullets or Numbers type of lists.

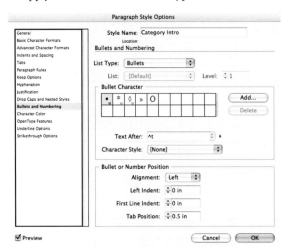

Note:

You can also define custom lists by choosing Type>Bulleted & Numbered Lists>Define Lists. If you've defined a custom list type, it will be available in the List Type menu of the Paragraph Style Options dialog box.

4. Click the Add button to the right of the Bullet Character list.

The Add Bullets dialog box allows you to choose the character you want to use for the bullet. This character defaults to the same font used in the style, but you can choose any font and font style from the menus at the bottom of the dialog box.

5. In the Add Bullets dialog box, find and select the Tilde (~) character.

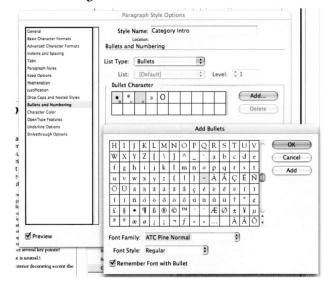

6. Make sure the Remember Font with Bullet option is checked and click OK to return to the Paragraph Style Options dialog box.

The selected bullet character is added to the list of available bullet characters. If you don't check the Remember Font with Bullet option, the character will be applied in whatever font is used for the style.

7. Click the Tilde character in the grid of available characters to select it.

8. Leave the Text After field to the default (^t, or the special code for a Tab character).

Note:

The Remember Font with Bullet option can be important if you use extended characters or decorative or dingbat fonts as bullet characters. If you select the solid square character in the Zapf Dingbats font (■), for example, changing to a different font would show the letter "n" as the bullet character.

9. **In the Bullet or Number Position area, change the Left Indent value to 0.125″, change the First Line Indent to –0.125″, and change the Tab Position field to 0.125″.**

This negative first-line indent is called a **hanging indent**.

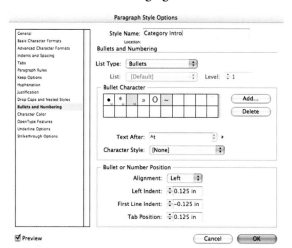

Note:

Changing these fields also changes the same fields in the Indents and Spacing options.

10. **Click OK to change the style definition and return to the layout.**

Because the two bullet styles are based on the Category Intro style, virtually all text in the layout (except the heading and intro text) now has the initial Tilde character and the hanging indent you just defined.

11. **Control/right-click the Category Bullets style and choose Edit "Category Bullets" in the contextual menu.**

12. **In the Bullets and Numbering options, click the Double-Chevron (») character from the default Bullet Character list.**

13. **Change the Left Indent field to 0.25″ and click OK.**

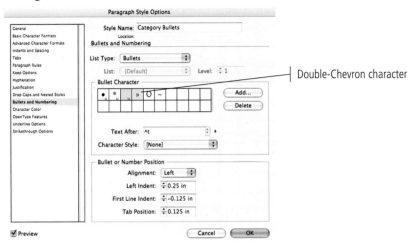

Double-Chevron character

14. **Navigate to Page 5 to review the effect of changing the character and indent options for the secondary bulleted list.**

The Category Bullet paragraphs are indented 0.125″ from the column edge because the negative first line indent was not equal to the first line indent value. In other words:

Left Indent   +   First Line indent   =   Indent location of the first line

0.25   +   (−0.125)   =   0.125

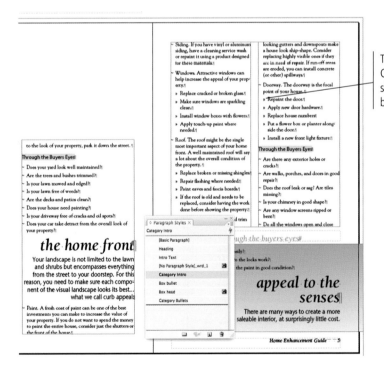

Text formatted with the Category Bullet style now shows the double-chevron bullet character.

15. **Edit the Box Bullet style to use a check box-like character as the bullet character, with a 0.2" hanging indent.**

    For the bullet character, try the "o" character from the Zapf Dingbats (Macintosh) or Wingdings (Windows) fonts. If you don't have one of these fonts, use any character from any font that you think works well as a bullet character.

    To format this style as a hanging indent, set the left indent to 0.2" and the first-line indent to –0.2".

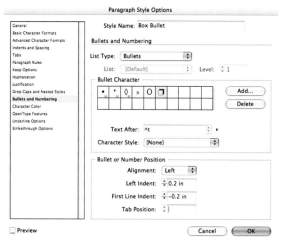 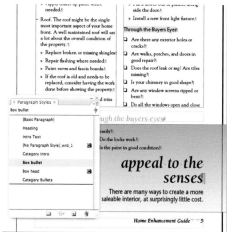

16. **Save the file and continue to the next exercise.**

 ## CONTROL PAGE AND FRAME BREAKS

In the completed booklet, each spread will have a single section heading followed by a section intro on the left page. The main and secondary bullet points will all appear on the right side, and the "Through the Buyers Eyes" bullets will appear in the gradient-filled frame. Rather than manually placing page breaks, you can use styles and paragraph formatting options to automatically place text in the correct frame on the correct side of the page.

1. **With Page 2 of booklet_working.indd visible, Control/right click Heading in the Paragraph Styles panel and choose Edit "Heading" from the contextual menu.**

2. **Display the Keep options.**

3. **In the Start Paragraph menu, choose On Next Even Page.**

    Each section heading should appear on the left page of a spread, and left-facing pages are even-numbered.

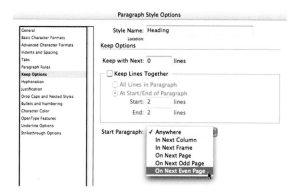

4. Click OK to change the style definition.

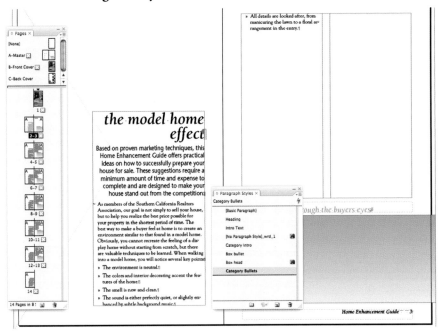

5. Navigate to Page 4 of the layout.

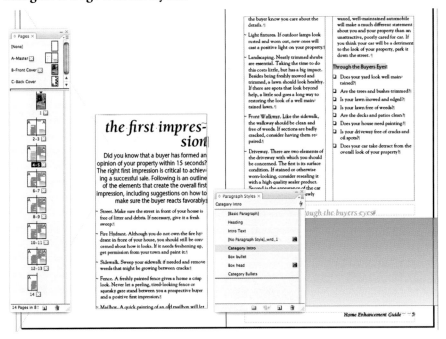

6. Control/right click Category Intro in the Paragraph Styles panel and choose Edit "Category Intro" from the contextual menu.

7. Display the Keep options.

In addition to determining where a paragraph can start, the Keep options are also used to control **orphans** (single lines of a paragraph at the end of a column) and **widows** (single lines of a paragraph that fall at the top of a column). Typography conventions suggest that at least two lines of a paragraph should be kept together at the beginning and end of a column or frame. (Headings at the end of a frame or column are also sometimes considered orphans.)

8. **Activate the Keep Lines Together check box and choose the All Lines in Paragraph option.**

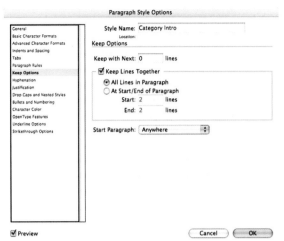

Note:

These same options can be applied to any specific paragraph by choosing Keep Options from the Paragraph panel options menu.

9. **Click OK to change the style definition.**

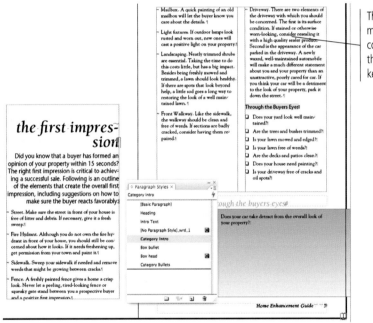

This entire paragraph moves to the next column so all lines in the paragraph can be kept together.

10. **Control/right-click the Category Intro style and choose Duplicate Style from the contextual menu.**

The left page of the spread should contain only the heading and the intro text; you need to force all remaining text onto the right side of the spread. You could do this manually, but a new style can handle the formatting for you.

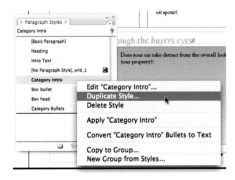

11. **Change the Style Name field to "Category Intro – First" and choose Category Intro in the Based On menu.**

As with the bulleted lists, it's a good idea to base the new style on the existing style so that later changes will reflect in the duplicate style.

12. **In the Keep options, choose In Next Column from the Start Paragraph menu and click OK.**

The Column option moves a paragraph to the next column in the same frame or to the next frame if the text is already in the last (or only) column of a frame.

13. **Place the insertion point in the first Category Intro paragraph on Page 4 (the first paragraph with a tilde as the bullet character), and then click the Category Intro – First style in the Paragraph Styles panel.**

As soon as you apply the style, the paragraph automatically moves to the next available frame in the text chain.

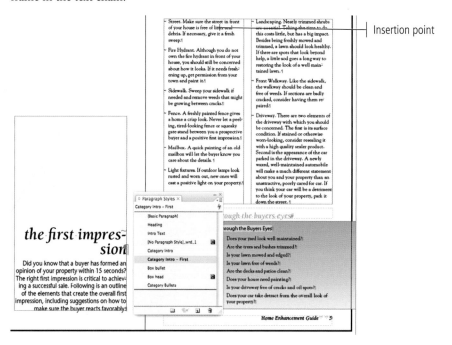

14. **Using the same method, create another style sheet so the first boxed bullet in each list starts in the next available frame.**

- **Duplicate the Box bullet style, and base the duplicate on the original style.**

- **Change the new style name to indicate its use.**

- **Change the Keep options of the new style so the paragraph starts in the next available frame.**

15. **Navigate through the layout and apply the two new styles where appropriate.**

- **As you move to each spread, delete the redundant instances of the paragraph "Through the Buyers Eyes" in the body copy.**

- **The third paragraph on each spread should be formatted with the Category Intro – First style.**

- **The first paragraph after the inline "Through the Buyers Eyes" heading should be formatted with the Box bullet – First style.**

16. **When you get to Page 14, add another page based on the A-Body Spread master and flow the overset text onto the next page.**

17. **Apply the "first" paragraph styles and delete the extra heading from this final spread.**

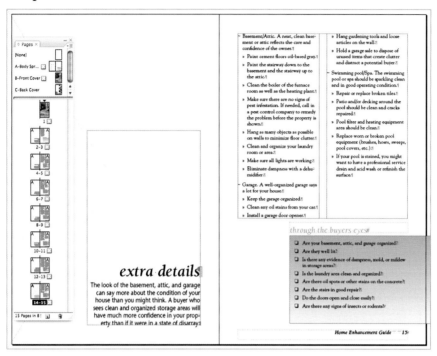

18. **Navigate to Page 7.**

   Despite all the available automation and productivity options, some things simply must be resolved manually. There is no way to tell InDesign, for example, "If only one secondary bullet fits in the first column, move the preceding primary bullet to the next column." Resolutions to issues such as these, which add polish to a professional layout, must be determined and applied manually.

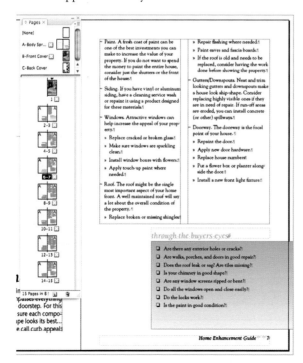

19. **Place the insertion point in the "Roof" Category Intro paragraph, and then click the Category Intro – First style.**

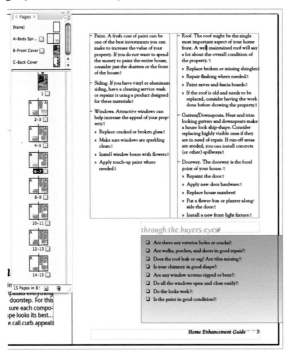

20. **Navigate through the layout and apply the same change wherever you think it is necessary.**

   We applied the formatting on Pages 11 and 15.

21. **Save the file and continue to the next exercise.**

CONTROL AUTOMATIC HYPHENATION

Automatic hyphenation is another key to professional page layout. Typographic conventions recommend no hyphenation in headings, no more than three hyphens in a row, and at least three characters before or after a hyphen. Some people have stricter rules, such as not hyphenating proper nouns, and others prefer to not hyphenate at all. Whatever your requirements, you can control the hyphenation of any paragraph, whether locally or in a style definition.

1. **With Page 4 of booklet_working.indd visible, Control/right-click the Heading style and choose Edit "Heading" from the contextual menu.**

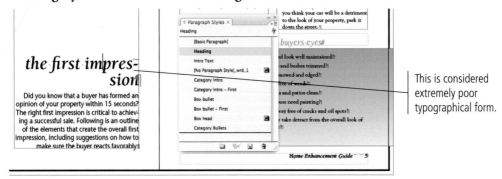

This is considered extremely poor typographical form.

2. **In the Paragraph Style Options dialog box, show the Hyphenation options.**

3. **Uncheck the Hyphenate option and click OK.**

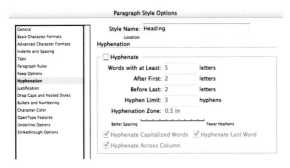 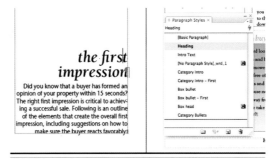

4. **Control/right-click the Category Intro style and choose Edit "Category Intro" from the contextual menu.**

   Remember, most of the other styles are based on this style; by changing the hyphenation options for this style, you also change the options for all styles based on this one.

Note:

Unchecking the Hyphenate check box turns off automatic hyphenation.

5. **In the Hyphenation options, change the After First and Before Last fields to "3". Click OK to change the style definition.**

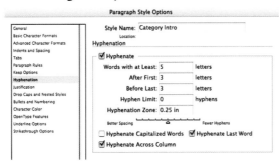

The Hyphenation options allow you to control the way in which InDesign hyphenates text. (If the Hyphenate box is unchecked, InDesign will not hyphenate text in the paragraph.)

- **Words With At Least _ Letters** defines the minimum number of characters that must exist in a hyphenated word.

- **After First _ Letters** and **Before Last _ Letters** defines the minimum number of characters that must appear before or after a hyphen.

- **Hyphen Limit** defines the maximum number of hyphens that can appear on consecutive lines. (Remember, you are defining the limit here, so zero means there is no limit — allowing unlimited hyphens.)

- **Hyphenation Zone** defines the amount of white space allowed at the end of a line of unjustified text before hyphenation begins.

- If **Hyphenate Capitalized Words** is checked, capitalized words (proper nouns) can be hyphenated.

- If **Hyphenate Last Word** is checked, the last word in a paragraph can be hyphenated.

- If **Hyphenate Across Column** is checked, the last word in a column or frame can be hyphenated.

Note:

These same options can be applied to any specific paragraph by choosing Hyphenation from the Paragraph panel options menu.

6. Navigate to Page 2.

As with balancing columns, there is some subjective element to balancing lines of copy — especially headlines.

7. Place the insertion point before the word "home" in the heading and press Shift-Return/Enter.

This character, called a **soft return**, forces a new line without starting a new paragraph.

Line break character

8. Navigate through the layout and add soft returns wherever you think they are necessary to balance the two lines of the headings.

We adjusted the headings on Pages 8, 10, and 12.

9. Save the file and continue to the next exercise.

INDESIGN FOUNDATIONS

Paragraph Composition Options

InDesign offers two options for controlling the overall flow of text (called **composition**) within a paragraph: **Adobe Paragraph Composer** (the default) and **Adobe Single-Line Composer**. Both methods create breaks based on the applied hyphenation and justification options for a paragraph.

You can change the composition method for an individual paragraph in the Paragraph panel options menu or the Justification dialog box; or change the composition method for a paragraph style in the Justification pane of the Paragraph Style Options dialog box.

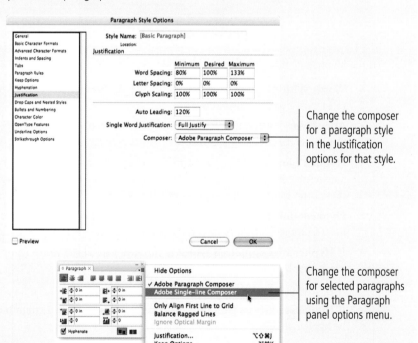

Change the composer for a paragraph style in the Justification options for that style.

Change the composer for selected paragraphs using the Paragraph panel options menu.

The Adobe Paragraph Composer evaluates the entire paragraph as a unit so changing one line of a paragraph might alter other lines in the paragraph (including earlier lines) to create what the software defines as the "best" overall paragraph composition. For example, adding a manual line break on Line 6 to eliminate a hyphen might also cause Lines 2 through 5 to reflow if InDesign determines the shift will create a better overall paragraph. (Although primarily a matter of personal preference, Adobe Paragraph Composer can be annoying for anyone who wants tight or exact control over the text in a layout.)

The Adobe Single-Line Composer is a better choice if you prefer to control your own text flow. Using Single-Line Composer, adding a manual line break on Line 6 will not affect preceding lines in the paragraph.

InDesign applies automatic hyphenation based on the defined language dictionary. You can override the hyphenation as defined in the dictionary by choosing Edit>Spelling>Dictionary.

If you highlight a word before opening the dictionary, it automatically appears in the Word field. Clicking the Hyphenate button shows the possible hyphenation locations as defined in the dictionary. You can override the automatic hyphenation by adding or deleting the consecutive Tilde characters in the Word field. When you change the hyphenation of a word, you have to click the Add button to add the new hyphenation scheme to the dictionary.

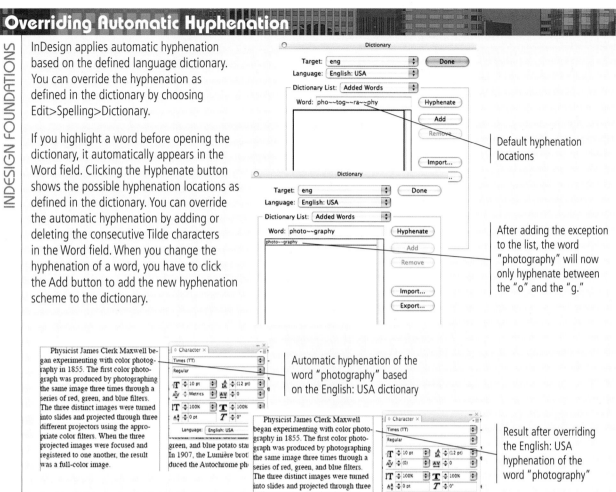

Default hyphenation locations

After adding the exception to the list, the word "photography" will now only hyphenate between the "o" and the "g."

Automatic hyphenation of the word "photography" based on the English: USA dictionary

Result after overriding the English: USA hyphenation of the word "photography"

FINALIZE THE FILE

For all intents and purposes the booklet text is finished; the final task you need to complete is to place the images. Because you placed the graphics frame on the master page layout, you can simply place most of these images into the existing frames without any additional intervention.

1. **With booklet_working.indd open, navigate to Page 2 of the layout and choose File>Place.**

2. **Navigate to the file named front.tif (in the RF_InDesign>Realtors folder) and turn off the Show Import Options and Replace Selected Item options.**

3. **Click Open to load the image into the cursor, and then click inside the graphics frame on Page 2 to place the image.**

   Because you applied the Gradient Feather effect to the graphics frame on the master page, the placed image automatically fades from full strength to white.

4. **Place the remaining images on the left page of each layout spread:**

Page 4	doorway_outside.tif
Page 6	doorway_inside.tif
Page 8	candles.tif
Page 10	flowers.tif
Page 12	bathroom.tif
Page 14	storage.tif

5. **Navigate to Page 3 of the layout.**

6. **Using the Selection tool, select and delete the gradient-filled text frame.**

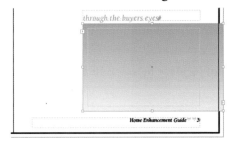

Note:

As with placing text into the master text frame, you don't have to override the master page to be able to place the image into the graphics frame. InDesign assumes that clicking inside an existing frame — even one from the master page — means you want to place the image inside that frame.

7. **Command/Control-Shift-click the text frame that is still linked to the master page (the one with the "through the buyers eyes" heading), and then delete the frame.**

   By pressing Command/Control-Shift, you can detach a single master page item without detaching the entire page from the master page.

8. **Place the file named squares.tif onto Page 3 and position the file as shown in the following image.**

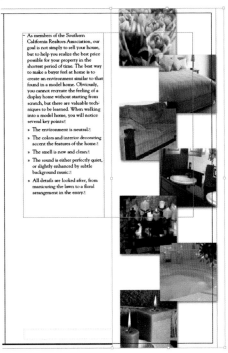

9. **Deselect the squares.tif image.**

10. **Command/Control-Shift-click the text frame at the bottom of the page, and then choose Object>Arrange>Bring to Front.**

11. **Delete the words "Home Enhancement Guide" from the text frame, leaving only the page number.**

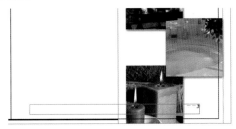

12. **In the Pages panel, drag the C-Back Cover master page icon below the Page 15 icon to add the back cover page at the end of the layout.**

    Because the cover is entirely designed on a master page, adding the cover into the file is as simple as adding a page to the layout.

13. **Save the file and continue to the next stage of the project.**

Stage 3 Understanding Multi-Page Output

When a page is printed, it is typically output on a larger sheet than the job's trim size. Multiple pages are often **imposed** (arranged) on a single press sheet, and the printed pieces are later cut from the press sheet and trimmed to their final size. In some cases, entirely different jobs can be **ganged** (combined) together to make the best use of available space on the press sheet. Multi-page documents that use facing pages have special output requirements; understanding these requirements means you will also be able to see how your design might be affected by output processes after the file leaves your desk.

Note:

*A **reader's spread** is a set of two pages that appear next to each other in a printed document — Page 2 faces Page 3, and so on.*

*A **printer's spread** refers to the way pages align on a press sheet, so after a document is folded and cut, the reader's spreads are in the correct locations.*

CREATE A FOLDING DUMMY

When multiple-page books and booklets are produced, they are not printed as individual pages. Instead, they are printed in signatures of eight, sixteen, or more pages at a time. Each signature is composed of two flats. (The term **flat** is a relic of the days when film was manually stripped together on a light table; it is still sometimes used to describe one side of one signature.)

Layouts are designed in reader's spreads, but arranged into printer's spreads on the printing plate. **Imposition** refers to the arrangement of a document's pages on a printing plate to produce the final product. A **signature** consists of multiple pages of a document that are all printed on the same press sheet, which is later folded and cut to the final trim size.

Understanding Imposition

INDESIGN FOUNDATIONS

If you fold a piece of paper in half twice, numbered the pages, and then unfold the paper, you will see the basic imposition for an eight-page signature.

If you look at your folded piece of paper, you can see that the tops of all the pages are folded together. If elements bleed to the top of a page, given the inaccuracy of folding machines (±0.03125"), that ink would appear on the edge of the page against which it abutted on the signature (as an example, see Pages 12 and 13 in the following illustration).

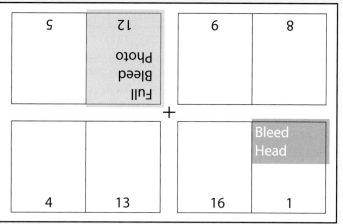

The pages of a signature must be cut apart at the top, which requires at least 1/8" at the top of the page for the trim. The outside edge of half the pages also must be cut apart (this is called a **face trim**) so the pages of the finished piece can be turned. This face trim also requires 1/8" around the page edge. That trim would shorten an 8.5 × 11" book to 8.375 × 10.875". This shorter size might be fine, but it could also ruin a design and layout. There's a better solution.

On the press-sheet layout, space is added between the tops of the printer's spreads to allow room for bleed and for cutting the pages apart. This separation is probably all that will be required for a 16-page saddle-stitched booklet printed on a 70# text-weight paper. If you use a heavier paper (for example, a 100# coated sheet for an annual report), or if you have more than one 16-page signature, you need to allow room for **creep**, which is the progressive extension of interior pages of the folded signature beyond the trim edge of the outside pages.

If you have questions about folds or imposition, you should always call your service provider. Somebody there will be able to advise you on the best course to take. In most cases these issues will be handled entirely by the service provider, often using software specifically designed for the prepress workflow. If you try to do too much, you might cause them extra work (and yourself extra expense).

1. **Fold a piece of paper in half, and then in half again.**

2. **While the paper is still folded, write the sequential page numbers 1 through 8 on the folded sections.**

3. **Unfold it and you will see the printer's spreads for an eight-page document.**

   The dummy unfolds to show how an eight-page signature is laid out. Page 8 and Page 1 create a single printer's spread.

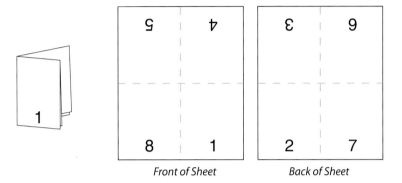

Front of Sheet   Back of Sheet

Note:

When arranged in printer's spreads, the sum of pairs of page numbers always totals the number of pages in the signature, plus 1. For example, in a 16-page signature, Page 4 faces Page 13, Page 16 faces Page 1, and so on.

If a saddle-stitched (stapled) book is made up of multiple signatures, the page numbers on printer's spreads equal the total number of pages in the publication, plus 1. For example, a saddle-stitched booklet is 32 pages, made up of two 16-page signatures. The page numbers on each printer's spread total 33: Page 16 faces Page 17, Page 22 faces Page 11, and so on.

PRINT A BOOKLET PROOF

You probably don't want to (and really, you shouldn't) think about creating full impositions for a press. At times, however, you might want to print proofs in printer's spreads to show clients. You could work through a complicated manual process of rearranging pages, but the InDesign Print Booklet command is far easier — and it's non-destructive.

1. **With booklet_working.indd open, choose File>Print Booklet.**

   This dialog box shows only the output options related to printing printer's spreads. You can't even directly change the printer that will be used for output.

2. **In the Setup pane of the dialog box, make sure 2-up Saddle Stitch is selected in the Booklet Type menu.**

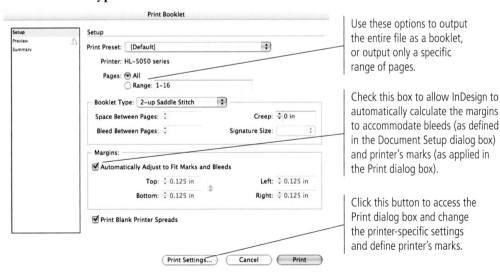

Use these options to output the entire file as a booklet, or output only a specific range of pages.

Check this box to allow InDesign to automatically calculate the margins to accommodate bleeds (as defined in the Document Setup dialog box) and printer's marks (as applied in the Print dialog box).

Click this button to access the Print dialog box and change the printer-specific settings and define printer's marks.

In the Booklet Type menu, you can choose what kind of imposition to create.

- **2-up Saddle Stitch** creates two-page printer's spreads from the entire layout or selected page range. If the layout doesn't have enough pages to create the necessary printer's spreads, InDesign automatically adds blank pages at the end of the layout.

- **2-up Perfect Bound** creates two-page printer's spreads that fit within the specified signature size (4, 8, 12, 16, or 32 pages). If the number of layout pages to be imposed is not divisible by the selected signature size, InDesign adds blank pages as needed to the end of the finished document.

- **Consecutive** creates a two-, three-, or four-page imposition appropriate for a foldout brochure.

You can also define settings to adjust for imposition issues related to printer's spreads versus reader's spreads.

- **Space Between Pages** defines the gap between pages in the printer's spread. This option is available for all but saddle-stitched booklet types.

- **Bleed Between Pages** defines the amount that page elements can bleed into the space between pages in a printer's spread (from 0 to half the defined space between the pages) for perfect-bound impositions.

- **Creep** defines the amount of space necessary to accommodate paper thickness and folding on each signature.

- **Signature Size** defines the number of pages in each signature for perfect-bound impositions.

- **Print Blank Printer Spreads** determines whether any blank pages that are added to fill out a signature will be printed.

3. **Click the Print Settings button.**

4. **In the Print dialog box, choose the printer and PPD you will use to output the booklet.**

5a. **If you have a printer that can output to tabloid-size paper, output the job at 100% using landscape orientation. In the Marks and Bleeds options, activate the All Printer's Marks and Use Document Bleed Settings options.**

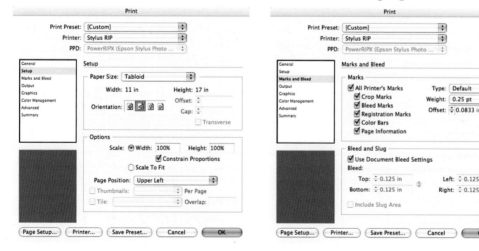

5b. If you can output to letter-size paper only, output the job at 100% using landscape orientation. In the Marks and Bleeds section, turn off all printer's marks and uncheck the Use Document Bleed Settings option.

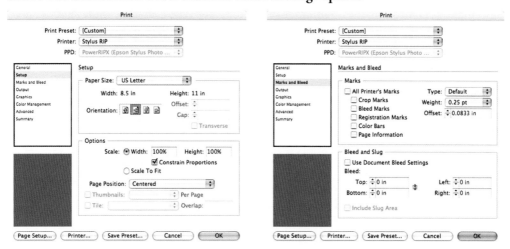

6. Click OK to return to the Print Booklet dialog box.

7. In the Print Booklet dialog box, click Preview in the list of options.

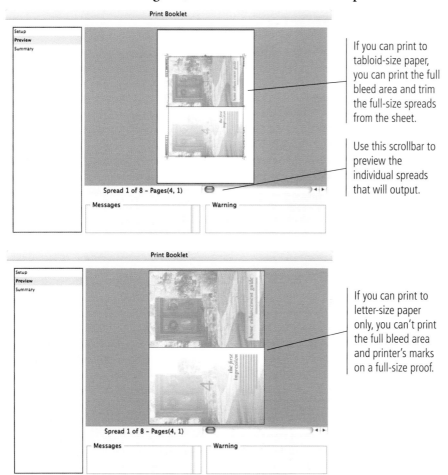

If you can print to tabloid-size paper, you can print the full bleed area and trim the full-size spreads from the sheet.

Use this scrollbar to preview the individual spreads that will output.

If you can print to letter-size paper only, you can't print the full bleed area and printer's marks on a full-size proof.

8. Click Print.

9. When the file is finished spooling to the printer, save it as "booklet_final.indd" in your WIP>Realtors folder, and then close the file.

Summary

Controlling the flow of text in a document — especially for documents with more than one or two pages — is just as important as controlling the appearance of the different type elements. InDesign provides powerful tools that let you control virtually every aspect of document design, from the exact position of individual paragraphs to entire blocks of text to automatic page numbers based on the location of special characters in the layout.

Changing the master page settings for this booklet allowed you to automatically flow a single story into multiple pages. Using the Keep options for the applied styles, you were able to position each element in the appropriate frame on the appropriate spread, which significantly reduced the amount of manual evaluation and adjustment that would have been required without these features.

Using effective master pages also allowed you to place repeating elements to appear on every spread in the layout. Combining that functionality with special characters and variable text elements, you were also able to eliminate a number of unnecessarily repetitive tasks, such as individually applying the gradient feather efffect to each picture and manually numbering the pages.

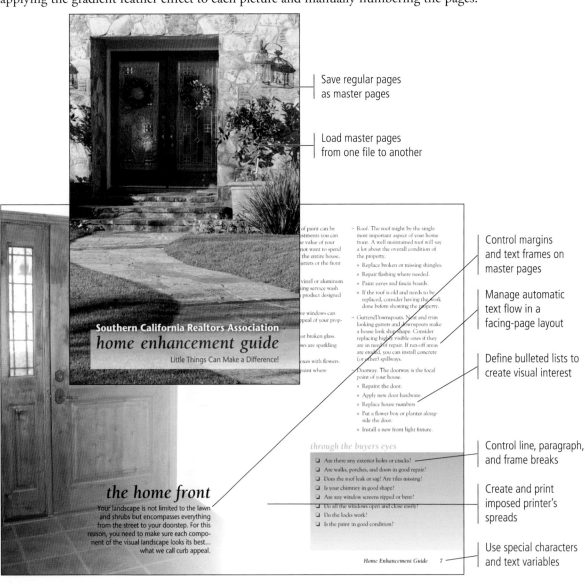

Save regular pages as master pages

Load master pages from one file to another

Control margins and text frames on master pages

Manage automatic text flow in a facing-page layout

Define bulleted lists to create visual interest

Control line, paragraph, and frame breaks

Create and print imposed printer's spreads

Use special characters and text variables

Portfolio Builder Project 5

Your clients are very happy with the finished Home Enhancement Guide. They would like you to create another collateral booklet that they can provide to prospective home buyers, providing contact information for agents in specific geographic areas.

To complete this project, you should:

❏ Create a 16-page booklet using the same document size as the Home Enhancement Guide.

❏ Design a facing-page layout that is aesthetically pleasing, which clearly presents the necessary information.

❏ Find or create supportive images for each spread that match the overall theme of the project.

"This booklet is one of our contractual obligations with our member realtors. It will list each agent based on their general geographic location, including their name and photo, phone number, street address, and the types of properties in which they specialize.

"We've sent you a text file with a short blurb for the inside front page, as well as the realtor information that we exported from our database (in the RF_Builders>Realtors folder). We don't have the agents' photos yet; we'll forward them as soon as possible. Just make sure you leave space for them in the layout.

"For the covers, use the same layout as the Home Enhancement Guide. For the front cover, use a different picture — maybe a similar shot, but of a more contemporary-style house. The title for the booklet is 'Buyer's Resource Guide', so make sure you change the text. On the back cover, replace the checkerboard image with pictures that you use in this booklet.

"We want the first spread in the booklet to include only the introductry text blurb — which should be prominent — and some kind of graphics. We thought a montage of different home styles would be a good visual.

"One last thing. For now, leave the center spread open. We might want to add something different there, but we haven't figured out what yet."

Versioned Product Brochure

Your client produces a monthly brochure that is mailed to consumers throughout the eastern United States and Canada. The brochures used to list two different prices for each product: one in U.S. dollars and one in Canadian dollars. The client now wants to produce two separate versions of the piece — one version with the U.S. prices and one version with the Canadian prices.

This project incorporates the following skills:

❏ Managing color in placed images and layout files

❏ Controlling import options for a variety of image file types

❏ Controlling the language and checking the spelling in layout text

❏ Searching and replacing text and special characters

❏ Searching and changing object attributes

❏ Creating multiple versions of a file using layers

❏ Outputting a color-managed PDF file

We print and mail a new brochure every month with a few featured products and sale information, which is mailed to a variety of lists that we buy from consumer list houses. The brochures drive a lot of traffic to our Web store, where we close the sales without needing to maintain a brick-and-mortar storefront.

Every issue is printed five-color — CMYK plus one of the three spot colors in our logo. We always use the same layout for brand recognition, but we cycle through the different spot colors; this issue should use the blue spot color.

We do a lot of business with consumers in Canada. We used to print one version of each brochure with both prices, but that caused a lot of confusion from people who didn't understand why Canadians had to "pay more." We've decided to use two different versions this year so customers in each country will see only the prices that apply to their currency.

After two years in business, we're starting to branch out beyond the East Coast. Our company used to be named VermontKids, but we changed it to ToyTrends so the company didn't seem so regional. We've included our new logo with the files for this issue.

We build each issue of the brochure from a standard template to maintain the brand consistency that the client prefers; since they just changed their logo, you should replace the logo in the template and save a new template so you won't have to make the same changes next month.

The client has provided all of the pieces for the job — a text file with this issue's copy, as well as all the different product images. As the production artist, your job is to assemble all the pieces, check the text and images for errors or technical problems, and create the final printable files. You are ultimately creating two different products: one U.S. version and one Canadian version.

- ❑ Define file color settings
- ❑ Replace an existing image and save a new template
- ❑ Place and control a variety of file types, including native Illustrator, native Photoshop, EPS, TIFF, PDF, JPEG, and native InDesign layouts
- ❑ Place multiple images at one time
- ❑ Check and correct spelling in the entire document and linked files
- ❑ Search and replace basic text and special characters, text formatting, and object attributes
- ❑ Control paragraph composition options
- ❑ Create and manage multiple layers
- ❑ Proof colors and separations on screen
- ❑ Export a color-managed PDF file

Stage 1 **Controlling Color for Output**

You can't accurately reproduce color without a basic understanding of color theory, so we present a very basic introduction to color theory in the following pages. We highly recommend that you read this information. Be aware that there are entire, weighty books written about color science; we're providing the condensed version of what you absolutely must know to work effectively with files in any color mode.

While it's true that color management science can be extremely complex and beyond the needs of most graphic designers, applying color management in InDesign is more intimidating than difficult. We believe this foundational knowledge on color management will make you a more effective and practically grounded designer.

Additive vs. Subtractive Color Models

The most important thing to remember about color theory is that color is light, and light is color. You can easily prove this by walking through your house at midnight; you will notice that what little you can see appears as dark shadows. Without light, you can't see — and without light, there is no color.

The **additive color** model (RGB) is based on the idea that all colors can be reproduced by combining pure red, green, and blue light in varying intensities. These three colors are considered the **additive primaries**. Combining any two additive primaries at full strength produces one of the **additive secondaries** — red and blue light combine to produce magenta, red and green combine to produce yellow, and blue and green combine to produce cyan. Although usually considered a "color," black is the absence of light (and, therefore, of color). White is the sum of all colors, produced when all three additive primaries are combined at full strength.

Printing pigmented inks on a substrate is a very different method of reproducing color. Reproducing color on paper requires **subtractive color** theory, which is essentially the inverse of additive color theory. Instead of adding red, green, and blue light to create the range of colors, subtractive color begins with a white surface that reflects red, green, and blue light at equal and full strength. To reflect (reproduce) a specific color, you add pigments that subtract or absorb only certain wavelengths from the white light. To reflect only red, for example, the surface must subtract (or absorb) the green and blue light.

Remember that the additive primary colors (red, green, and blue) combine to create the additive secondaries (cyan, magenta, and yellow). Those additive secondaries are also called the **subtractive primaries** because each subtracts one-third of the light spectrum and reflects the other two thirds:

- Cyan absorbs red light, reflecting only blue and green light.

- Magenta absorbs green light, reflecting only red and blue light.

- Yellow absorbs blue light, reflecting only red and green light.

A combination of two subtractive primaries, then, absorbs two-thirds of the light spectrum and reflects only one-third. As an example, a combination of yellow and magenta absorbs both blue and green light, reflecting only red.

Note:

Additive color theory is practically applied when a reproduction method uses light to reproduce color. A television screen or computer monitor is black when turned off. When the power is turned on, light in the monitor illuminates at different intensities to create the range of colors you see.

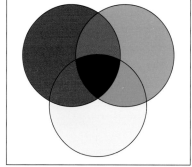

Subtractive color model

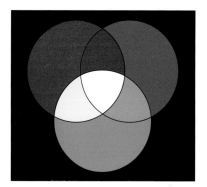

Additive color model

Color printing is a practical application of subtractive color theory. The pigments in the cyan, magenta, yellow, and black inks are combined to absorb different wavelengths of light. To create the appearance of red, the green and blue light must be subtracted or absorbed, thus reflecting only red. Magenta absorbs green light, and yellow absorbs blue light; combining magenta and yellow inks on white paper reflects only the red light. By combining different amounts of the subtractive primaries, it's possible to produce a large range (or gamut) of colors.

Because white is a combination of all colors, white paper should theoretically reflect equal percentages of all light wavelengths. However, different papers absorb or reflect varying percentages of some wavelengths, thus defining the paper's apparent color. The paper's color affects the appearance of ink colors printed on that paper.

Understanding Gamut

Different color models have different ranges or **gamuts** of possible colors. A normal human visual system is capable of distinguishing approximately 16.7 million different colors. Color reproduction systems, however, are far more limited. The RGB model has the largest gamut of the output models. The CMYK gamut is far more limited; many of the brightest and most saturated colors that can be reproduced using light cannot be reproduced using pigmented inks.

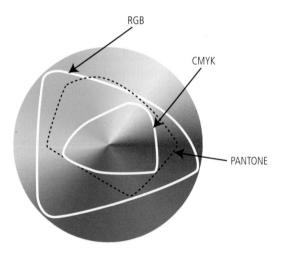

This difference in gamut is one of the biggest problems graphic designers face when working with color images. Digital image-capture devices (including scanners and digital cameras) work in the RGB space, which, with its larger gamut, can more closely mirror the range of colors in the original scene. Printing, however, requires images first to be converted or **separated** into the CMYK space.

The usual goal in color reproduction is to achieve a color appearance equivalent to the original. Depending on the images, at least some colors in the RGB model likely cannot be reproduced in the more limited gamut of the CMYK color model. These **out-of-gamut** colors pose a challenge to faithfully reproducing the original image. If the conversion from RGB to CMYK is not carefully controlled, **color shift** can result in drastic differences between the original and the printed images.

Color Management in Brief

Color management is intended to preserve color predictability and consistency as a file is moved from one color mode to another throughout the reproduction process. Color management can also eliminate ambiguity when a color is only specified by some numbers. For example, you might create a royal purple in the Color Picker; but without color management, that same set of RGB numbers might look more lilac (or even gray) when converted to CMYK for printing. A well-tuned color management system can translate the numbers that define a color in one space to numbers that can better represent that same color in another space.

It's important to have realistic expectations of color management, and to realize that color management isn't a replacement for a thorough understanding of the color-reproduction process. Even at its best, color management can't fix bad scans or bad photos — all it can do is provide consistency and predictability to a process that otherwise rarely has either.

Note:

Color shift can also result when converting from one type of CMYK to another, or (though less likely) from one version of RGB to another. Whatever models are being used, color management gives you better control over the conversion process.

Color management relies on **color profiles**, which are simply data sets that define the reproduction characteristics of a specific device. A profile is essentially a recipe that contains the ingredients for reproducing a specific color in a given color space. The color recipes in profiles are known as **look-up tables** (LUTs), which are essentially cross-reference systems for finding matching color values in different color spaces.

Source profiles are the profiles of the devices (scanners, digital cameras, etc.) used to capture the image. **Destination profiles** are the profiles of output devices. **LAB** (or L*a*b*, or CIELAB) is a device-independent, theoretical color space that represents the entire visible spectrum. The color management engine uses LAB as an intermediate space to translate colors from one device-dependent space to another.

The mechanics of color-managed conversions are quite simple. Regardless of the specific input and output spaces in question, the same basic process is followed for every pixel in the image:

1. The Color Management Module (CMM) looks up the color values of a pixel in the input-space profile to find a matching set of LAB values.

2. The CMM looks up the LAB values in the output-space profile to find the matching set of color values that will display the color of that pixel as accurately as possible in the output space.

Note:

Color profiles are sometimes called "ICC profiles," named after the International Color Consortium (ICC), which developed the standard for creating color profiles.

Color Management in Theory and Practice

INDESIGN FOUNDATIONS

RGB and CMYK are very different entities. The two color models have distinct capabilities, advantages, and limitations. There is no way to exactly reproduce RGB color using the CMYK gamut because many of the colors in the RGB gamut are simply too bright or too saturated. Rather than claiming to produce an exact (impossible) match from your monitor to a printed page, the true goal of color management is to produce the best possible representation of the color using the gamut of the chosen output device.

A theoretically ideal color-managed workflow looks like this:

- Image-capture devices (scanners and digital cameras) are profiled to create a look-up table that defines the device's color-capturing characteristics.

- Images are acquired using a profiled device. The profile of the capturing device is tagged to every image captured.

- You define a destination (CMYK) profile for the calibrated output device that will be used for your final job.

- InDesign translates the document and embedded image profiles to the defined destination profiles.

Two of the "ideal workflow" steps mention a form of the word "calibrate." Calibration is an essential element in a color-managed workflow; it is fundamentally important to consistent and predictable output. To **calibrate** something means to check and correct the device's characteristics.

Taking this definition a step further, you cannot check or correct the color characteristics of a device without having something to compare the device against. To calibrate a device, a known target — usually a sequence of distinct and varying color patches — is reproduced using the device. The color values of the reproduction are measured and compared to the values of the known target. Precise calibration requires adjusting the device until the reproduction matches the original.

As long as your devices are accurately calibrated to the same target values, the color acquired by your RGB scanner will match the colors displayed on your RGB monitor and the colors printed by your CMYK desktop printer. Of course, most devices (especially consumer-level desktop devices that are gaining a larger market share in the commercial graphics world) are not accurately calibrated, and very few are calibrated to the same set of known target values.

Keeping in mind these ideals and realities, the true goals of color management are to:

- Compensate for color variations in the different devices
- Accurately translate one color space to another
- Compensate for limitations in the output process
- Better predict the final outcome when a file is reproduced

DEFINE COLOR SETTINGS

InDesign's color management options allow you to integrate InDesign into a color-managed workflow. This includes managing the color profiles of placed images, as well as previewing potential color problems on screen before the job is actually output.

There are two primary purposes for managing color in an InDesign file: previewing colors based on the intended output device before the file is output, and converting colors to the appropriate color space when a file is output (whether to PDF or to an imagesetter for commercial printing).

1. **With no file open in InDesign, choose Edit>Color Settings.**

    The Color Settings dialog box defines default working spaces for RGB and CMYK colors, as well as general color management policies.

    The RGB working space defines the default profile for RGB colors and images that do not have embedded profiles.

    The CMYK working space defines the profile for the device or process that will be used to output the job.

2. **Choose North America Prepress 2 in the Settings menu.**

    InDesign includes a number of common option groups, which you can access in the Settings menu. You can also make your own choices and save those settings as a new preset by clicking Save, or you can import settings files created by another user by clicking Load.

    A working space is a specific profile that defines color values in the associated mode. Using Adobe RGB (1998), for example, means new RGB colors in the InDesign file and imported RGB images without embedded profiles will be described by the values in the Adobe RGB (1998) space.

3. **In the CMYK menu, choose U.S. Sheetfed Coated v2.**

    There are many CMYK profiles — and each different printer and press has a gamut unique to that individual device. This is a United States industry-standard profile for a common type of printing (sheetfed printing on coated paper). In a truly color-managed workflow, you would actually use a profile for the specific printing press/paper combination being used for the job. (We're using one of the default profiles to show you how the process works.)

Note:

Before completing this project, copy the Toys folder from the WIP folder on your Resource CD to your WIP folder where you are saving your work. When you save files for this project, you will save them in your WIP>Toys folder.

Note:

The Adobe RGB (1998) space is a neutral color space that isn't related to a specific monitor's display capabilities. Using this space assumes you are basing color decisions on numeric values, not by what you see on your monitor.

Note:

The Working Spaces menus identify exactly which version of each space defines color within that space.

4. **In the Color Management Policies area, make sure Preserve Embedded Profiles is selected for RGB, and Preserve Numbers (Ignore Linked Profiles) is selected for CMYK.**

   These options tell InDesign what to do when you open existing files, or if you copy elements from one file to another.

   - When an option is Off, color is not managed for objects or files in that color mode.

   - **Preserve Embedded Profiles** maintains the profile information that is saved in the file; files with no profile use the current working space.

   - If you choose **Convert to Working Space**, files are automatically converted to the working space defined at the top of the Color Settings dialog box.

   - For CMYK colors, you can choose **Preserve Numbers (Ignore Linked Profiles)** to maintain raw CMYK numbers (ink percentages) rather than adjusting the colors based on an embedded profile.

5. **Check all three options under the Color Management Policies menus.**

   The check boxes control InDesign's behavior when you open an existing file or paste an element from a document with a profile other than the defined working space (called a **profile mismatch**), or when you open a file that does not have an embedded profile (called a **missing profile**).

6. **If it is not already checked, activate the Advanced Mode check box.**

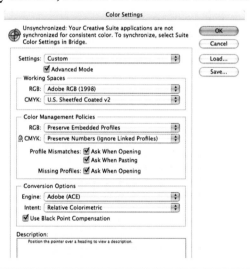

Note:

As soon as you choose U.S. Sheetfed Coated v2 in the CMYK menu, the Settings menu automatically switches to Custom.

Understanding Rendering Intents

INDESIGN FOUNDATIONS

LAB color has the largest gamut, RGB the next largest, and CMYK the smallest. If you need to convert an image from RGB to a more limited CMYK space, you need to tell the CMS (color management system) how to handle any colors that exist outside the CMYK space. You can do this by specifying the **rendering intent** that will be used when you convert colors.

- **Perceptual** presents a visually pleasing representation of the image, preserving visual relationships between colors. All colors in the image — including those available in the destination gamut — are shifted to maintain the proportional relationship within the image.

- **Relative Colorimetric** maintains any colors in both the source and destination profiles. Any source colors outside the destination gamut are shifted to fit into the destination gamut. The Relative Colorimetric method is a good choice, especially when most source colors are in-gamut. This method adjusts for the whiteness of the background media.

- **Absolute Colorimetric** maintains colors in both the source and destination profiles. Any colors outside the destination gamut are shifted to a color within the destination gamut, based on the color's appearance on white paper.

- **Saturation** compares the saturation of colors in the source profile and shifts them to the nearest possible saturated color in the destination profile. Saturation is a good method for images with high levels of saturation, such as pie charts and graphs. The focus is on saturation instead of actual color value, which means this method can produce drastic color shift.

The **Engine** option determines the system and color-matching method for converting between color spaces:

- Adobe (ACE) stands for Adobe Color Engine; this is the default, and it is Adobe's recommendation for most users.
- Apple CMM (Macintosh only) uses the Apple ColorSync engine and the CMM management system.
- Microsoft ICM (Windows only) uses the Microsoft ICM engine and its default color-matching methods.

The **Intent** menu defines how the engine translates source colors outside the gamut of the destination profile.

When the **Use Black Point Compensation** option is selected, the full range of the source space is mapped into the full-color range of the destination space. This method can result in blocked or grayed-out shadows, but it is most useful when the black point of the source is darker than that of the destination.

7. **Click OK to apply your settings.**

8. **Continue to the next stage of the project.**

Assigning and Converting Color Profiles

If you need to change the working RGB or CMYK space in a document, you can use either the **Assign Profiles dialog box** (Edit>Assign Profiles) or the **Convert to Profile dialog box** (Edit>Convert to Profile). Although these two dialog boxes have slightly different appearances, most of the functionality is exactly the same.

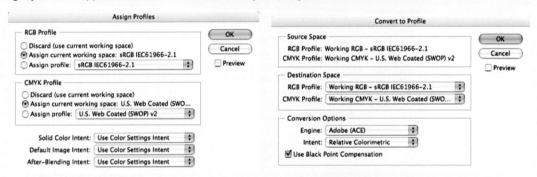

In the Assign Profiles dialog box:

- **Discard (Use Current Working Space)** removes the current profile from the document. This is useful if you do not want to color-manage the document. Colors will be defined by the current working space, but the profile is not embedded in the document.
- **Assign Current Working Space** embeds the working space profile in the document.
- **Assign Profile** allows you to define a specific profile for the document other than the working space profile. However, colors are not converted to the new space, which can dramatically change the appearance of the colors as displayed by your monitor.

You can also define different rendering intents for solid colors, placed raster images, and transparent elements that result from blending modes, effects, or transparency settings. All three of the Intent menus default to use the intent defined in the Color Settings dialog box, but you can change any or all of the menus to a specific intent.

In the Convert to Profile dialog box, the menus can be used to change the RGB and CMYK destination spaces. This is basically the same as using the Assign Profile options in the Assign Profiles dialog box. You can also change the color management engine, rendering intent, and black point compensation options.

Stage 2 Placing and Controlling Images

Adobe InDesign supports a variety of graphics formats. The specific type of graphics you use depends on your ultimate output goal. For print applications such as the brochure you're building in this project, you should use only high-resolution raster image files or vector-based graphics files. (Refer to Project 1 for an explanation of resolution requirements for print images.)

Note:

InDesign supports the following graphics file formats: TIFF, PSD, GIF, JPEG, BMP, AI, EPS, DCS, PICT, WMF, EMF, PCX, PNG, Scitex CT, and SWF.

REPLACE A NATIVE ILLUSTRATOR FILE

As part of the Adobe Creative Suite, InDesign supports native Adobe Illustrator files (with the ".ai" extension) that have been saved to be compatible with the PDF format. Illustrator files can include both raster and vector information (including type and embedded fonts), as well as objects on multiple layers in a variety of color modes (including spot colors, which are added to the InDesign Swatches panel).

Note:

You can also copy objects in Illustrator and paste them into InDesign as a group.

1. **Open the file toys.indt from the RF_InDesign>Toys folder.**

   The existing template file does not have a defined RGB or CMYK profile. Because you activated the Ask When Opening option in the Color Settings dialog box, InDesign asks how you want to handle color in the file.

2. **In the Profile or Policy Mismatch dialog box for RGB settings, select the second option.**

   This option assigns the existing color settings to the new file (you are creating a new file by opening the template file).

3. **Leave the remaining options at their default values and click OK.**

   Again, your choices in the Color Settings dialog box said to Ask When Opening if a file was missing a CMYK profile. Because the template file does not have a defined CMYK profile, you now see that warning in a second dialog box.

4. **Choose the second radio button to adjust the document to match the current color settings and click OK.**

This template contains the layout for a four-page brochure. The layout is designed with a 17 × 11″ page size; the flat size is 8.5 × 11″ when folded in the middle.

Although you could design this file as four 8.5 × 11″ pages, this layout is a good example of a file that can be safely built with printer's spreads instead of reader's spreads. On Page 1 of the layout, the back (Page 4) faces the front (Page 1) of the brochure; on Page 2 of the layout, Page 2 of the brochure faces Page 3 of the brochure.

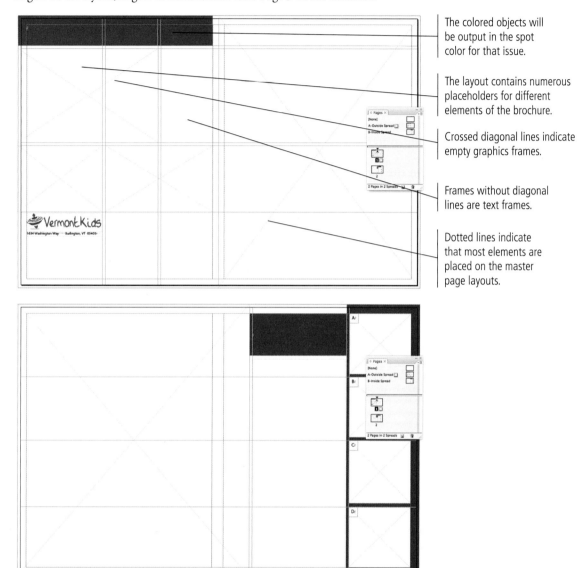

The colored objects will be output in the spot color for that issue.

The layout contains numerous placeholders for different elements of the brochure.

Crossed diagonal lines indicate empty graphics frames.

Frames without diagonal lines are text frames.

Dotted lines indicate that most elements are placed on the master page layouts.

5. **Double-click the A-Outside Spread icon in the Pages panel to show that layout.**

   Your client sent a new logo, which you need to use in the layout and template.

6. **Using the Direct Selection tool, click the logo on the page.**

7. **Open the Transform panel (Window>Object & Layout>Transform).**

   This graphic is scaled to 46.5% proportionally.

Note:

Make sure you select the logo with the Direct Selection tool. If you use the Selection tool, the Transform panel shows the values for the frame instead of the graphic that is placed in the frame.

8. **With the graphic still selected, choose File>Place and navigate to the file ToyTrends Logo.ai in the RF_InDesign>Toys folder.**

9. **At the bottom of the Place dialog box, check the Replace Selected Item and Show Import Options boxes.**

   When the Replace Selected Item option is checked, the file you choose will replace the selected item in the layout.

10. **Click Open.**

    When Show Import Options is checked, the Place [Format] dialog box opens with the options for the relevant file format. (Every file format has different available options.)

    When you place a native Illustrator file, the dialog box shows the Place PDF options because the PDF format is the basis of Illustrator files that can be placed into InDesign. (For an Illustrator file to be placed into InDesign, it must be saved from Illustrator with the Create PDF Compatible File option checked in the Illustrator Options dialog box.)

Note:

If nothing is selected in the layout, the file you select will simply be loaded into the cursor so you can click to place it.

11. **In the General tab, choose Art in the Crop To menu.**

    The Crop To menu determines what part of the file will be imported:

    - **Bounding Box** places the file based on the minimum area that encloses the objects on the page.
    - **Art** places the file based on the outer dimensions of actual artwork in the file.
    - **Crop** places the file based on the crop area defined in the file. If no crop area is defined, the file is placed based on the defined Artboard dimensions.
    - **Trim** places the file based on trim marks defined in the placed file. If no trim marks are defined, the file is placed based on the defined Artboard size.
    - **Bleed** places the file based on the defined bleed area. If no bleed area is defined, the file is placed based on the defined Artboard size.
    - **Media** places the file based on the physical paper size (including printer's marks) on which the PDF file was created. This option is not relevant for native Illustrator files.

Note:

In the General tab, you can also define the specific page of the file to place. These options are irrelevant for native Illustrator files, which can only have a single page.

When the **Transparent Background** option is checked, background objects in the layout will show through empty areas of the placed file. If this option is not checked, empty areas of the placed file will knock out underlying objects.

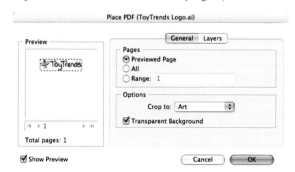

Note:

Artwork in the Illustrator file must be entirely within the bounds of the Artboard (page) edge. Anything outside the Artboard edge will not be included when you place the file into InDesign

12. **Click the Layers tab to display those options.**

PDF and native Illustrator files can include multiple layers. You can determine which layers to display in the placed file by toggling the eye icons on or off in the Show Layers list. In the Update Link Options menu, you can determine what will happen if you have to update the link to the placed file.

- **Keep Layer Visibility Overrides** maintains your choices regarding which layers will be visible in the InDesign layout.

- **Use PDF's Layer Visibility** restores the layer status as saved in the placed file.

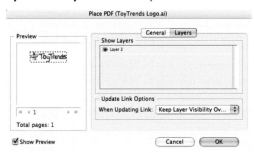

Note:

To learn about the different elements and options for Adobe Illustrator files, we recommend the book **Adobe Illustrator CS3: The Professional Portfolio** *from Against The Clock.*

13. **Click OK to place the file.**

When you replace a selected file, the new file maintains the same transformations that were applied to the original. In this case, the replaced file is also scaled to 46.5%.

14. **Choose File>Save.**

15. **Save the file in your WIP>Toys folder as an InDesign template named "toys_revised.indt".**

Because the new logo should be used in all future versions of the catalog mailer, you are resaving the template. In the next exercise, you will create a new document from the template for the current issue of the catalog.

16. **Close the template file and continue to the next exercise.**

 PLACE A NATIVE PHOTOSHOP FILE

Like Illustrator, Adobe Photoshop is part of the Adobe Creative Suite; you can place native Photoshop files (with the extension ".psd") into an InDesign layout. You can control the visibility of Photoshop layers and layer comps, as well as access embedded paths and Alpha channels in the placed file. If a Photoshop file includes spot color channels, the spot colors are added to the InDesign Swatches panel.

1. **Open the file toys_revised.indt from your WIP>Toys folder and make sure Page 1 of the layout is showing.**

Because this is a template file, it opens as a new untitled document.

2. **Make sure nothing is selected in the layout, and then choose File>Place. If necessary, navigate to the RF_InDesign>Toys folder.**

If you continued directly from the previous exercise, the Place dialog box defaults to the last-used location.

Note:

To learn about the different elements and options for Adobe Photoshop files, we recommend the book **Adobe Photoshop CS3: The Professional Portfolio** *from Against The Clock.*

3. **In the Place dialog box, select the file clowns.psd.**

4. **Make sure the Show Import Options and Replace Selected Item options are checked.**

    These check boxes default to the last-used settings. If you continued directly from the previous exercise, they should still be selected.

5. **Click Open.**

6. **In the Image Import Options dialog box, click the Image tab and review the options.**

    If the Photoshop file includes clipping path or Alpha channel information, you can activate those options when the file is placed.

7. **Click the Color tab and review the options.**

    The Profile menu defaults to the profile that was embedded in the file. If the file was not saved with an embedded profile, the menu defaults to Use Document Default. You can use the Profile menu to change the embedded profile (not recommended) or assign a specific profile if one was not embedded.

    The Rendering Intent menu defaults to Use Document Image Intent; you can also choose one of the four built-in options for this specific image.

Note:

When you export the finished layout to PDF, you will use the PDF engine to convert the RGB images to CMYK. This profile tells InDesign how the RGB color is described in the file so it can be properly translated to the destination (CMYK) profile.

Reviewing Image Color Settings

INDESIGN FOUNDATIONS

You can review and change the profile associated with a specific image by selecting the image in the layout and choosing Object>Image Color Settings. Keep in mind, however, that just because you *can* change the profile doesn't mean you *should*. If an image has an embedded profile, you should assume that the embedded profile is the correct one; don't make random profile changes in InDesign.

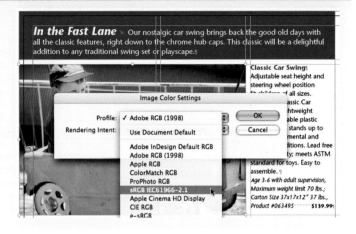

8. Click the Layers tab and review the options.

Photoshop files can include multiple layers and layer comps (saved versions of specific layer position and visibility). You can turn off specific layers by clicking the eye icon for that layer. If the file includes layer comps, you can use the Layer Comp menu to determine which comp to place.

The Update Link Options here are the same as those in the Place PDF dialog box.

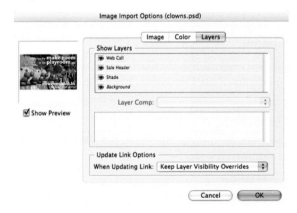

Note:

Unless you know what the different layers contain, it is difficult to decide what you want to place, based on the very small preview image.

9. Click OK.

Even though you checked the Replace Selected Item option in the Place dialog box, the image is loaded into the cursor because nothing was selected in the layout (in other words, there is nothing to replace).

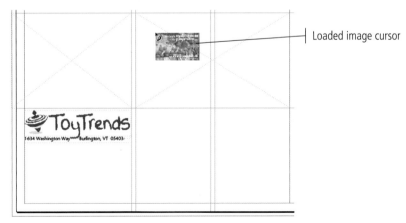

Loaded image cursor

10. **Click the loaded cursor in the middle frame on the page to place the image (as shown in the following image).**

11. **With the placed file selected, choose Object>Object Layer Options.**

    This dialog box has the same options as the Layers tab in the Image Import Options dialog box.

12. **Activate the Preview option, and then click the eye icon for the Web Call layer to turn off that layer.**

    Because you aren't relying on the small preview in the dialog box, this method is easier for experimenting with different layer visibility options.

Note:

You're turning off the Web Call layer because the client changed its company name, and got a new Web address to match the new name.

13. **Click OK to close the Object Layer Options dialog box.**

14. **Create a text frame with bottom vertical alignment over the bottom part of the clowns image. Inset the edges of the frame about 1/8″ (0.125″) from the edge of the image.**

15. **Type:**

    Go to www.toytrends.biz [line break]
    for more great savings!"

16. **Apply right paragraph alignment to the text. Open the Character Styles panel and apply the Call to Action small text style to the entire paragraph. Apply the Call to Action large text style to only the Web address.**

17. **Look at the Links panel.**

    The red eye icon indicates that layer visibility in the original file has been overridden in the placed file.

18. **Save the file as "toys_working.indd" in your WIP>Toys folder and continue to the next exercise.**

 PLACE AN EPS FILE

The EPS (Encapsulated PostScript) format is commonly used for exporting vector graphics from Adobe Illustrator or other vector-based applications. This format uses an adaptation of the PostScript page-description language to produce a "placeable" file for PostScript-based artwork.

Many vector graphics are saved as EPS files, but not all EPS files are vector graphics; the format supports both vector and raster information. Some Photoshop files — specifically, those with embedded clipping paths or spot color channels — also use the EPS format.

When you place an EPS file into InDesign, you can use or ignore an embedded file preview. You can also manage OPI (Open Prepress Interface) image links, as well as embedded clipping paths for Photoshop EPS files. Spot colors in an EPS file are added to the InDesign Swatches panel.

Because InDesign supports native Illustrator and Photoshop files, as well as PDF files, the EPS format is slowly disappearing from the graphics workflow. QuarkXPress, which does not yet support native Illustrator files, still requires the EPS format to read artwork created in Adobe Illustrator or Photoshop files that include spot color channels.

1. **With toys_working.indd open, select the placed clowns image.**

2. **Choose File>Place and select the file sand.eps.**

3. **With the Show Import Options and Replace Selected Item options both checked, click Open.**

Note:

If you print a page with an EPS file to a non-PostScript printer, only the screen-resolution preview will print.

Note:

Photoshop files with spot color information might also be saved using the DCS (Desktop Color Separation) format, which is a modification of the EPS format. DCS files are not particularly common in modern design and print workflows.

4. **Review the options in the EPS Import Options dialog box.**

The **Read Embedded OPI Image Links** option tells InDesign to read links from OPI comments for images included in the graphic. (OPI is a workflow that allows designers to work with low-resolution placement-only images in the layout; when the file is output, high-resolution versions of the images are merged into the output stream in place of the low-resolution proxies.)

The **Apply Photoshop Clipping Path** option is used to apply a defined clipping path in a Photoshop EPS file. (If you turn off this option, you can later apply the clipping path by choosing Object>Clipping Path>Options.)

The Proxy Generation options determine how the placed file will be viewed in the layout:

- **Use TIFF or PICT Preview** shows the preview that is embedded in the file. If the file doesn't have an embedded preview, InDesign generates a low-resolution bitmap after rasterizing the PostScript data.

- **Rasterize the PostScript** discards the embedded preview.

5. **Activate the Use TIFF or PICT Preview option and click OK to place the file.**

Because the clowns image was selected and the Replace Selected Item option was checked, the sand image is placed into the selected frame.

6. **Choose Edit>Undo Replace.**

If you accidentally replace a selected item, undoing the placement loads the last-placed image into the cursor.

7. **Click the loaded cursor in the empty frame to the left of the clowns image.**

This is an easy fix if you accidentally replace an image — simply use the Undo command, and then click to place the loaded image where you want it.

Note:

The Undo command undoes the single last action. In this case, placing the image into the frame — even though it happened automatically — was the last single action.

8. **Save the file and continue to the next exercise.**

By default, files display in the document window using the "Typical" display performance settings. In the Display Performance pane of the Preferences dialog box, you can change the default view settings (Fast, Typical, or High Quality), as well as change the definition of these view settings.

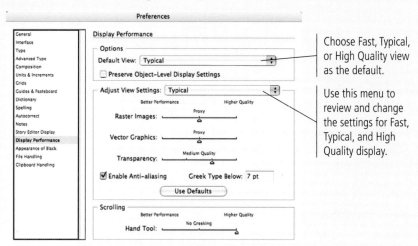

Choose Fast, Typical, or High Quality view as the default.

Use this menu to review and change the settings for Fast, Typical, and High Quality display.

In the Adjust View Settings section, individual sliders control the display of raster images, vector graphics, and objects with transparency. You can change the individual settings for any of the view settings (for example, you may want to view vector graphics at high resolution even for the Typical view).

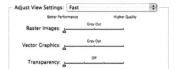

In the layout, you can change the document display performance using the View>Display Performance menu. Using the default settings for each view:

If Allow Object-Level Display Settings is checked in the View>Display Performance menu, you can also change the preview for a single image in the layout (in the Object>Display Performance menu or using the object's contextual menu).

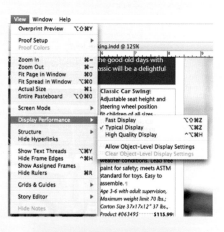

You can turn object-level display settings on and off using the Allow Object-Level Display Settings toggle. To remove object-level settings, choose Clear Object-Level Display Settings. (Object-level display settings are only maintained while the file remains open; if you want to save the file with specific object-level display settings, check the Preserve Object-Level Display Settings option in the Preferences dialog box.)

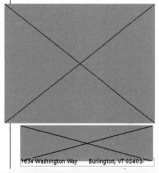

Fast turns off images and graphics, displaying only gray boxes.

Typical shows the low-resolution proxy images.

High Quality shows the full resolution of placed files.

PLACE A **TIFF** FILE

The TIFF format is used only for raster images such as those from a scanner or digital camera. These files can be one-color (bitmap or monochrome), grayscale, or continuous-tone images. When you place a TIFF file into InDesign, you can access the clipping paths and Alpha channels saved in the file. InDesign does not allow access to different layers in a TIFF file; all layers are flattened in the placed file.

1. **With toys_working.indd open, make sure the placed sand image is selected in the layout and choose File>Place.**

2. **In the Place dialog box, select the file car.tif and uncheck the Replace Selected Item option.**

3. **Make sure the Show Import Options box is checked and click Open.**

   In the Image Import Options dialog box, the Image and Color options for placing TIFF files are the same as the related options for placing native Photoshop files.

4. **Click OK.**

   Although the placed sand image was selected when you reopened the Place dialog box, the car image is loaded into the cursor because you unchecked the Replace Selected Item option.

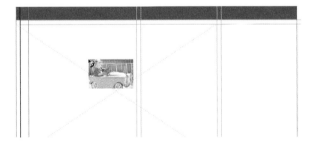

5. **Click the loaded cursor in the empty frame above the sand image to place the loaded file.**

6. **Save the file and continue to the next exercise.**

PLACE A PDF FILE

PDF (Portable Document Format) files save layout, graphics, and font information in a single file, which means those files do not need to be present for the job to output correctly. The format was created to facilitate cross-platform file sharing so one file could be transferred to any other computer, and the final layout would print as intended. This benefit, though originally meant for Internet use, is now a standard in the graphics industry for submitting ads, artwork, or even completed jobs to an output provider.

You can place a PDF file into an InDesign layout, just as you would any other image. You can determine which page is placed (if the file contains more than one page), which layers are visible (if the file has more than one layer), and the specific file dimensions (bounding box) to use when the file is placed.

1. **With toys_working.indd open, choose File>Place.**

2. **In the Place dialog box, select the file Car Cover.pdf.**

3. **Make sure Show Import Options is checked and Replace Selected Item is not checked, and then click Open.**

   The options in the Place PDF dialog box are exactly the same as the ones you saw when you placed the native Illustrator file. However, the options in the General tab will typically be more important for PDF files than for Illustrator files.

   PDF files can contain multiple pages; you can review the different pages using the buttons below the preview image. You can place multiple pages at once by choosing the All option, or you can select specific pages using the Range option.

   The Crop To options are also significant when placing PDF files. If the file was created properly, it should include a defined bleed of at least 1/8 inch and trim marks to mark the intended trim size.

4. **Choose Bleed in the Crop To menu and click OK.**

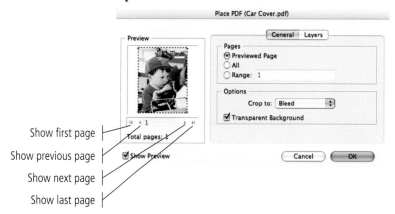

Show first page
Show previous page
Show next page
Show last page

5. **Click the loaded cursor in the empty frame on the right side of Page 1 to place the loaded file.**

Note:

Placing PDF files can destroy your job if they were not created and optimized for commercial printing. Internet-optimized PDF files do not have sufficient resolution to print cleanly on a high-resolution output device.

Note:

If you place multiple pages of a PDF file, each page is loaded into the cursor as a separate object.

Note:

Import continuous pages by defining a page range, using a hyphen to separate the first page and the last page in the range. Import non-continuous pages by typing relevant page number, separated by commas.

6. **Click the placed image with the Direct Selection tool and look at the Transform panel.**

   This file was created with 1/8″ bleeds on all four sides. In this layout, however, the left bleed allowance is not necessary. When you place the image into the frame, the bleed area on the left side causes the image to appear farther to the right than it should.

Note:

Remember, the Selection tool selects the frame; the Direct Selection tool selects the frame content.

   When selected with the Direct Selection tool, you can see the image edge beyond the frame edge.

   The image is placed at X:0, Y:0, based on the top-left reference point in relation to the frame.

7. **With the placed file still selected, make sure the top-left reference point is selected and change the picture position to X: –0.125″.**

   The image bounding box now shows the extra bleed allowance extending beyond the left edge of the graphics frame.

8. **Save the file and continue to the next exercise.**

Place an InDesign File

In addition to the different types of image files, you can also place one InDesign layout directly into another InDesign file. As with PDF files, you can determine which page is placed (if the file contains more than one page), which layers are visible (if the file has more than one layer), and the specific file dimensions (bounding box) to use when the file is placed. Placed InDesign pages are managed as individual objects in the file where they are placed.

1. **Copy the file slide.indd from the RF_InDesign>Toys folder to your WIP>Toys folder.**

   You are going to edit this file, so it has to be in a location where you can make changes and save the file.

2. **With toys_working.indd open, navigate to Page 2 of the layout.**

3. **Choose File>Place. Navigate to the slide.indd file in your WIP>Toys folder in the Place dialog box.**

4. **With the Show Import Options box checked, click Open.**

5. **In the General tab of the Place InDesign Document dialog box, choose Bleed Bounding Box in the Crop To menu.**

   The options for placing an InDesign file are mostly the same as for placing PDF files, except for the options in the Crop To menu. When you place InDesign files into other InDesign files, you can place the pages based on the defined page, bleed, or slug, as defined in the Document Setup dialog box.

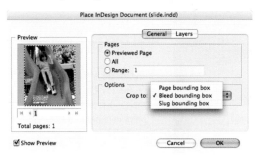

5. **Click OK. Read the resulting warning message and click OK.**

   To output properly, image links need to be present and up to date. Images placed in nested InDesign layouts are still images, so the link requirements apply in those files as well.

6. **Click the loaded cursor in the empty frame on the left side of Page 2 to place the loaded file.**

   When you place one InDesign file into another, the Links panel lists images placed in the InDesign file (indented immediately below the placed InDesign file).

The file slide.tif, which is placed in the slide.indd file, is missing.

7. **Save the file and continue to the next exercise.**

EDIT A LINKED FILE

The InDesign Links panel provides valuable information about the status of placed files. More than just an informational tool, however, the Links panel also allows you to navigate to and edit selected images, as well as locate links.

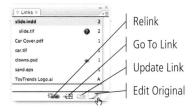

- The **Relink** button opens a navigation dialog box, where you can locate a missing file or link to a different file.

- The **Go To Link** button displays the selected file, centered in the document window.

- The **Update Link** button updates modified links. If the selected image is missing, this button opens a navigation dialog box so you can locate the missing file.

- The **Edit Original** button opens the selected file in its native application. When you save the file and return to the InDesign layout, the placed file is automatically updated.

1. **With toys_working.indd open, click slide.indd in the Links panel, and then click the Edit Original button.**

   The Edit Original function opens the file selected in the Links panel. Because slide.indd is a placed InDesign file, that document opens in a new document window in front of the toys_working.indd file.

2. **In the Profile or Policy Mismatch dialog box, choose the Adjust option and click OK.**

   This file was created with the U.S. Web Coated (SWOP) v2 CMYK working space. You are working with the U.S. Sheetfed Coated v2 working space, so you are converting this file to the same CMYK working space as the main brochure file.

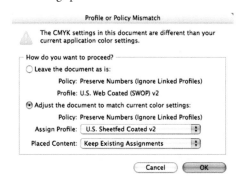

Note:

The Edit Original option works for any type of placed file (as long as your computer recognizes the file type), including native Illustrator and Photoshop files, TIFF files, JPEG files, EPS files, and so on.

Note:

You can also Control/ right-click a specific image in the layout and choose Edit Original from the contextual menu.

3. **Click Don't Fix in the warning message.**

   When the file opens, you see a warning message about the missing image link — the reason you are editing the file.

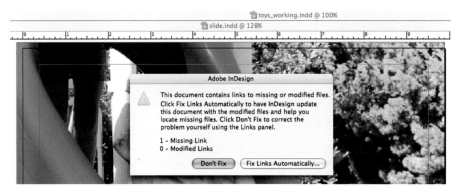

4. **In the Links panel for slide.indd, click the missing file to select it, and then click the Relink button at the bottom of the panel.**

5. **Navigate to the file slide_revised.tif in the RF_InDesign>Toys folder and click Open.**

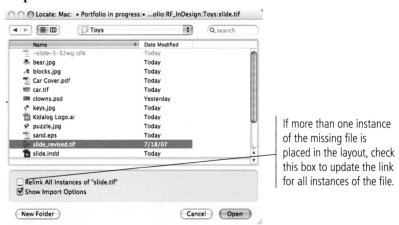

   If more than one instance of the missing file is placed in the layout, check this box to update the link for all instances of the file.

6. **When you see a message asking if you want to replace the old file with the new one, click Yes.**

   Because the new file does not have the same name as the original file, InDesign asks you to confirm the replacement.

7. **If the Image Import Options dialog box opens, click OK.**

8. **Save the file and close it.**

   When you save and close the slide.indd file, the Links panel for the file toys_working.indd automatically reflects the new placed file.

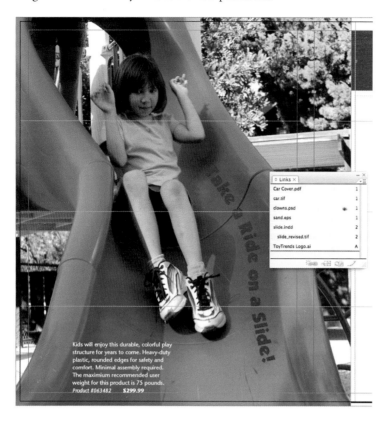

Note:

If you change a placed file without using the Edit Original option, the Links panel will show a Modified icon. You have to manually update the link.

9. **Save toys_working.indd and continue to the next exercise.**

 ## Place Multiple JPEG Images

The JPEG format is commonly used for raster images, especially images that come from consumer-level digital cameras. Originally used for Web applications only, the JPEG format is now supported by most commercial print design applications (including InDesign).

   The JPEG format can be problematic, especially in print jobs, because it applies a lossy compression scheme to reduce the image file size. If a high-resolution JPEG file was saved with a high level of compression, you might notice blockiness or other artifacts in the printed image. If you must use JPEG files in your work, save them with the lowest possible amount of compression.

1. **With toys_working.indd open, choose File>Place.**

2. **Navigate to the RF_InDesign>Toys folder and click bear.jpg to select it.**

3. **Press Shift, and then click blocks.jpg to select that file as well.**

4. **Press Command/Control, and then click keys.jpg and puzzle.jpg.**

   In many cases, you might need to place more than one image from the same location into the same InDesign layout. Rather than placing images one at a time, you can speed up the process by loading multiple images into the cursor at once, and then clicking and placing each image where it needs to go.

Key Command:

Press Shift to select multiple contiguous files in the dialog box.

Press Command/Control to select multiple non-contiguous files.

5. **With the Show Import Options box checked, click Open.**

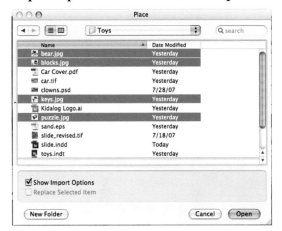

6. **Click OK in each of the four Image Import Options dialog boxes.**

   When you place multiple files, you can define different import options for each selected file. Because you had four files selected in the Place dialog box, you see four separate Image Import Options dialog boxes.

   When the last Import Options dialog box closes, the cursor is loaded with the selected pictures. A number in the cursor shows the number of files that are loaded; the cursor thumbnail and the LP in the Links panel indicate which loaded file will be placed when you click.

Note:

The Import options for JPEG files are the same as those available for TIFF files.

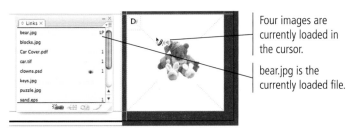

Four images are currently loaded in the cursor.

bear.jpg is the currently loaded file.

7. **Click the bottom empty frame on the right side of the page to place the bear.jpg file.**

   As soon as you place the bear file, the next loaded image appears in the cursor thumbnail.

8. **Click in the empty frame at the top of the page to place the loaded blocks image.**

9. **Place the loaded keys image into the second frame, and then place the final loaded image (puzzle) into the third frame.**

When all the images are placed, you might notice two problems. First, the images don't fit perfectly into the available frames. Second, the letters that were in the top-left corner of each frame are missing.

10. **Click the top image to select it, and then Control/right-click the image. Choose Fitting>Fit Content Proportionally from the contextual menu.**

11. **Control/right-click the image again and choose Fitting>Center Content.**

12. **Repeat Steps 10 and 11 for the remaining three images on the right edge of the page.**

The Fitting options resize content relative to the containing frame, or resize the containing frame to match the placed content.

- **Fit Content To Frame** resizes content to fit the dimensions of the containing frame, even if that means scaling the content out of proportion (stretched in one direction or another).

- **Fit Frame To Content** resizes the frame to the dimensions of the placed content.

- **Center Content** centers content within its containing frame, but neither the frame nor the content is resized.

- **Fit Content Proportionally** resizes content to fit entirely within its containing frame, maintaining the current aspect ratio of the image. Some empty space might result along one dimension of the frame.

- **Fill Frame Proportionally** resizes content to fill the entire frame while preserving the content's proportions.

Fitting proportionally places the entire image into the frame; some areas of the frame might be empty.

Filling proportionally fills the frame; some areas of the image might be cropped.

13. **In the Pages panel, Control/right-click the Page 2 icon and choose Override All Master Page Items.**

When you placed images into the four graphics frames, they were automatically detached from the master layout; the Override All Master Page Items option brings those items to the top of the stacking order, above anything that is still placed by the master page. The four text frames with the letters were not detached from the master, so they are now behind the placed images.

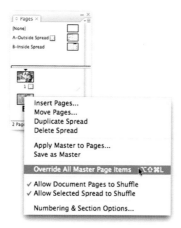

14. **Using the Selection tool, select the four frames with the placed graphics, as well as the red frame in the background, and choose Object>Arrange>Send to Back.**

When you overrode the master page for Page 2, the letters became part of the layout page. Those text frames are again on the top of the layers stack.

15. **Save the file and continue to the next stage of the project.**

Stage 3 Controlling and Checking Text

As you already learned in an earlier project, InDesign gives you extremely tight control over virtually every aspect of the text in a layout. You can control the appearance and precise position of every single character to create high-quality typographic elements. This level of precision separates the amateur from the professional designer. Some text issues, however, have little to do with typography and more to do with "user malfunction" — common errors introduced by the person who creates the text. Regardless of how knowledgeable or careful you are, some problems will inevitably creep into your text. Fortunately, InDesign gives you the tools to correct those issues.

PLACE AND CUT TEXT

If you completed the earlier projects in this book, you already learned about the options that are available when you import a text file. Whenever you work with client-supplied text, we recommend that you maintain text formatting when the file is imported, and then make the necessary adjustments once you have reviewed the different editorial elements of the imported text.

1. **With toys_working.indd open, choose File>Place.**

2. **Select the file toys.doc, make sure the Show Import Options box is checked, and click Open.**

3. **In the Microsoft Word Import Options dialog box, choose the Preserve Styles and Formatting option.**

4. **Make sure the Import Styles Automatically option is selected, and both conflict menus are set to Use InDesign Style Definition.**

5. **Click OK to import the text into the cursor. If you get a missing font warning, click OK to dismiss it.**

6. **Click the loaded text cursor in the empty red frame at the top of Page 2.**

   When the text is placed, it automatically flows from the red frame into the white frame below. Using a responsibly designed InDesign template, coupled with a Microsoft Word template that has the correct style names for this project, the imported text is automatically placed and correctly formatted — at least, most of the text is correctly formatted.

   Despite the best intentions when you set up files, some items will need to be fixed — especially when dealing with client-supplied text. In the placed text, the words "Outside Text" are not part of the actual brochure copy. The client also separated every paragraph with an extra return, and placed two spaces after every period in the text (relics of traditional typing techniques that remain, even though many people have never used a manual typewriter). These issues are very common, and they must be fixed.

7. **Select the text from the beginning of the story to the paragraph return before the words "Inside Text."**

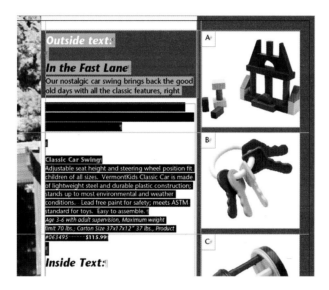

8. **Cut the selected text and navigate to Page 1 of the layout (the "outside" of the brochure).**

9. **In the Pages panel, Control/right-click the Page 1 icon and choose Override All Master Page Items.**

   You can't access the text frames from the master page until you detach the pages from the master.

10. **Place the insertion point in the red frame at the top of the page and paste the text that you cut in Step 8.**

11. **Delete the words "Outside Text" and the two following paragraph returns from the beginning of the pasted story.**

    The frame should begin with the words "In the Fast Lane."

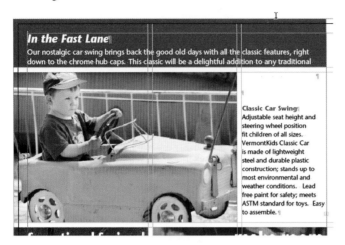

12. **On Page 2, delete the words "Inside Text" and the following paragraph returns from the beginning of the story.**

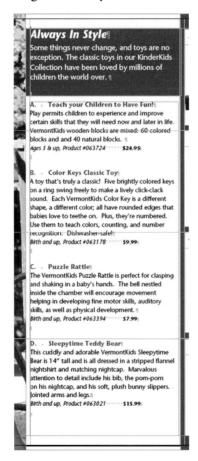

13. **Save the file and continue to the next exercise.**

FIND AND CHANGE LAYOUT TEXT

There will be many cases when you need to search for and replace specific elements in a layout — a word, a phrase, a formatting attribute, or even a specific kind of object. InDesign's Find/Change dialog box allows you to easily locate exactly what you need, whether your layout is two pages or two hundred. For this brochure, you can use the Find/Change dialog box to correct the client's typing errors.

1. **With toys_working.indd open, choose Edit>Find/Change.**

2. **Place the insertion point in the Find What field and press the Spacebar twice.**

3. **Press Tab to highlight the Change To field and press the Spacebar once.**

4. **In the Search menu, choose Document.**

   You can use the Search menu to search an entire document, all documents, the selected story, or all text following the insertion point in the selected story (To End of Story).

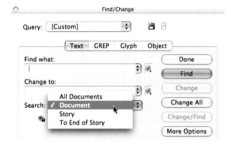

5. **Click Change All. When you see the message that 14 replacements were made, click OK.**

6. **Highlight the content of the Find What field (the two space characters).**

   Because you can't see the space characters in the field, it can be easy to forget about them. If you forget to highlight the space characters, the new content will be added to the characters instead of replacing them.

7. **Open the menu to the right of the Find What field and choose End of Paragraph.**

   This menu is used to place common special characters into the dialog box fields. When you choose a special character in the menu, the special code for that character is entered into the field.

Note:

You can also type the special codes directly into a dialog box field. The caret character is accessed by pressing Shift-6.

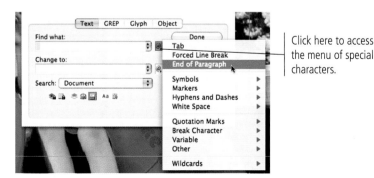

Click here to access the menu of special characters.

8. **Choose End of Paragraph from the menu again to search for all instances of two consecutive paragraph returns.**

9. **Highlight the Change To field and choose End of Paragraph from the associated menu.**

   You are replacing all instances of two paragraph returns with a single paragraph return.

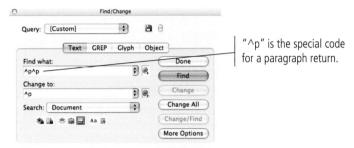

"^p" is the special code for a paragraph return.

10. **Click Change All, and then click OK to close the message dialog box.**

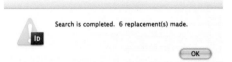

Search is completed. 6 replacement(s) made.

11. **Change all instances of the word "VermontKids" to "ToyTrends".**

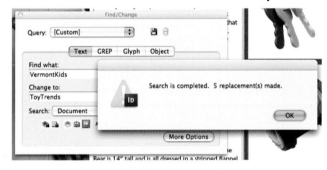

Search is completed. 5 replacement(s) made.

12. **Click Done to close the Find/Change dialog box.**

13. **On Page 2, place the insertion point in the last line of the white text and press the Down Arrow key to move the insertion point into the next paragraph. Open the Keep options (from the Paragraph panel options menu) for the paragraph and force the selected paragraph to begin in the next available frame. Click OK.**

There is a paragraph of red text on top of the red frame; it's impossible to see (except hidden characters), but it is there.

You can use special characters in InDesign dialog boxes using the following special codes (called metacharacters).

Character	Code (Metacharacters)
Symbols	
Bullet (•)	^8
Caret (^)	^^
Copyright (©)	^2
Ellipsis (…)	^e
Paragraph	^7
Registered Trademark (®)	^r
Section (§)	^6
Trademark (™)	^d
Dashes and Hyphens	
Em Dash (—)	^_
En Dash (–)	^=
Discretionary hyphen	^-
Nonbreaking hyphen	^~
White Space Characters	
Em space	^m
En space	^>
Third space	^3
Quarter space	^4
Sixth space	^%
Flush space	^f
Hair space	^| (pipe)
Nonbreaking space	^s
Nonbreaking space (fixed width)	^S
Thin space	^<
Figure space	^/
Punctuation space	^.
Quotation Marks	
Double left quotation mark	^{
Double right quotation mark	^}
Single left quotation mark	^[
Single right quotation mark	^]
Straight double quotation mark	^"
Straight single quotation mark	^'
Page Number Characters	
Any page number character	^#
Current page number character	^N
Next page number character	^X
Previous page number character	^V

Character	Code (Metacharacters)
Break Characters	
Paragraph return	^p
Forced line break (soft return)	^n
Column break	^M
Frame break	^R
Page break	^P
Odd page break	^L
Even page break	^E
Discretionary line break	^j
Formatting Options	
Tab character	^t
Right indent tab character	^y
Indent to here character	^i
End nested style here character	^h
Nonjoiner character	^k
Variables	
Running header (paragraph style)	^Y
Running header (character style)	^Z
Custom text	^u
Last page number	^T
Chapter number	^H
Creation date	^S
Modification date	^o
Output date	^D
File name	^l (lowercase L)
Markers	
Section marker	^x
Anchored object marker	^a
Footnote reference marker	^F
Index marker	^I
Wildcards	
Any digit	^9
Any letter	^$
Any character	^?
White space (any space or tab)	^w
Any variable	^v

14. **On Page 1, replace the paragraph return at the end of the first paragraph with a tab character.**

15. **Save the file and continue to the next exercise.**

FIND AND CHANGE FORMATTING ATTRIBUTES

In addition to finding and replacing specific text or characters, you can also find and replace formatting attributes for both text and objects. For this project, you need to use the blue spot color as the accent, replacing the red spot color from the template. However, you can't just delete the red from the Swatches panel because the red color is used in the placed logo file. The Find/Change dialog box makes this kind of replacement a relatively simple process.

1. **With toys_working.indd open, choose Edit>Find/Change.**

2. **Highlight the Find What field. Click the associated menu and choose Any Character from the Wildcards submenu.**

   Wildcards allow you to search for formatting attributes, regardless of the actual text. In addition to searching for Any Character, you can also narrow the search to Any Digit, Any Letter, or Any White Space characters.

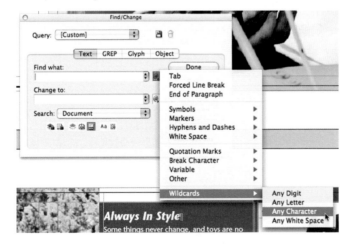

3. **Remove all characters from the Change To field.**

   You only want to change the formatting, not the text that is formatted. To accomplish this result, you have to delete all characters from the Change To field.

4. **Click the More Options button to show the expanded Find/Change dialog box.**

When more options are visible, you can find and replace specific formatting attributes of the selected text.

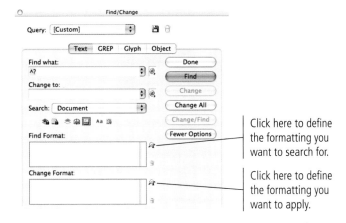

Click here to define the formatting you want to search for.

Click here to define the formatting you want to apply.

5. **Click the button for the Find Format field to open the Find Format Settings dialog box.**

You can search for and replace any character formatting option (or combination of options) that can be applied in the layout.

6. **Show the Character Color options and click the Pantone 186 C swatch.**

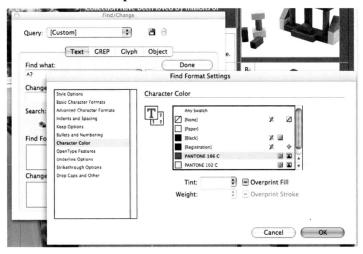

7. **Click OK to return to the Find/Change dialog box.**

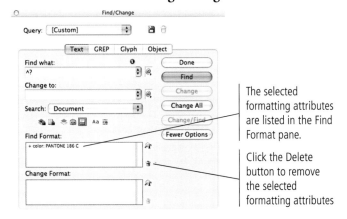

The selected formatting attributes are listed in the Find Format pane.

Click the Delete button to remove the selected formatting attributes

8. **Click the button for the Change Format field to open the Change Format Settings dialog box.**

9. **Highlight the Character Color options and click the Pantone Blue 072 C swatch. Click OK.**

10. **Make sure Document is selected in the Search menu and click Change All. Click OK to close the message about the number of replacements.**

11. **Click the Object tab in the Find/Change dialog box.**

    As with text formatting options, you can also find and replace specific object formatting attributes.

12. **Make sure Document is still selected in the Search menu.**

    When you search objects, you can search the current document, all documents, or the current selection.

13. **In the Type menu, choose All Frames.**

    This menu allows you to limit your search to specific kinds of frames or search all frames.

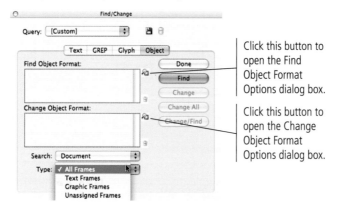

Click this button to open the Find Object Format Options dialog box.

Click this button to open the Change Object Format Options dialog box.

14. **Click the button to open the Find Object Format Options dialog box.**

    You can find and change any formatting attributes that can be applied to a frame.

15. **Display the Fill options and click the Pantone 186 C swatch.**

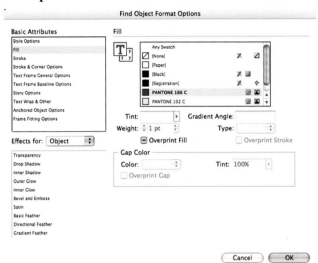

Note:

Selected formatting options are cumulative. If you added the stroke color to the Find options, the search would only identify objects that have a red fill and a red stroke. To find either of these options, you have to perform two separate searches.

16. **Click OK to return to the Find/Change dialog box.**

17. **Open the Change Object Format Options dialog box and choose the Pantone Blue 072 C swatch in the Fill options.**

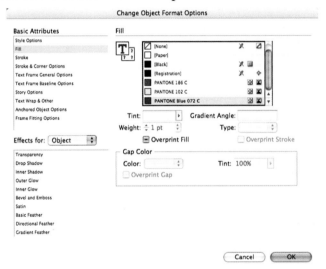

18. **Click OK to return to the Find/Change dialog box, and then click Change All.**

19. **Click OK to dismiss the message about the number of changes.**

20. **Close the Find/Change dialog box, and then review the layout.**

Elements of placed Illustrator and EPS artwork are not affected by the Find/Change function.

Placed InDesign files are only affected by the search if those files are also open when you initiate the search. Because the slide.indd file was not already open, the red spot color text in the placed InDesign file was not affected; you now have to open the placed InDesign file and manually change the red text.

21. **Control/right-click the placed slide.indd file and choose Edit Original from the contextual menu. In the linked file, change the red text (along the curved path) to a fill of Paper. Save the file and close it.**

It makes more visual sense to change the red type to white ("Paper") rather than placing blue type on a blue image. When you return to the toys_working file, the change will automatically reflect in the placed file.

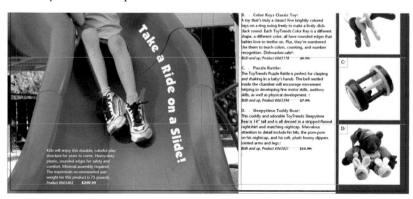

22. **Save the toys_working.indd file and continue to the next exercise.**

In addition to the tools you use in this project, the Find/Change dialog box has a number of options for narrowing or extending a search beyond the basic options.

The buttons below the Search menu are toggles for specific types of searches:

- When **Include Locked Layers** is active, the search will locate text on locked layers; you can't replace text on a locked layer unless you first unlock the layer.

- When **Include Locked Stories** is active, the search will locate text that is locked; you can't replace locked text unless you first unlock it.

- When **Include Hidden Layers** is active, the search will include text frames on layers that are not visible.

- When **Include Master Pages** is active, the search will include text frames on master pages.

- When **Include Footnotes** is active, a search will identify instances within footnote text.

- When **Case Sensitive** is active, a search will only find text with the same capitalization as the text in the Find What field. For example, a search for "InDesign" will not identify instances of "Indesign," "indesign," or "INDESIGN."

- When **Whole Word** is active, a search will only find instances where the search text is an entire word (not part of another word). For example, if you search for "old" as a whole word, InDesign will not include the words "gold," "mold," or "embolden."

As you have seen, the Text tab allows you to search for and change specific character strings, with or without specific formatting options. The Object tab identifies specific combinations of object formatting attributes, such as fill color or applied object effects.

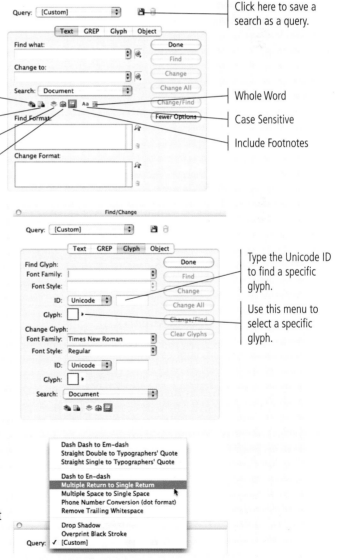

Include Locked Layers
Include Locked Stories
Include Hidden Layers
Include Master Pages

Click here to save a search as a query.

Whole Word
Case Sensitive
Include Footnotes

Type the Unicode ID to find a specific glyph.

Use this menu to select a specific glyph.

The GREP tab is used to search with pattern-based search techniques, such as finding phone numbers in one format (e.g., 800.555.1234) and changing them to the same phone number with a different format (e.g., 800/555-1234). Adobe's video-based help system (www.adobe.com) provides some assistance in setting up an advanced query.

The Glyph tab allows you to search for and change glyphs using Unicode or GID/CID values. This is useful for identifying foreign language and pictographic characters, as well as characters from extended sets of OpenType fonts.

You can also save specific searches as queries, and call those queries again using the Query menu at the top of the Find/Change dialog box. This option is useful if you commonly make the same modifications, such as changing Multiple Return to Single Return (this particular search and replacement is so common, in fact, that the query is built into the application).

CHECK DOCUMENT SPELLING

In Project 3 you learned about preflighting and how to verify that required elements (graphics and fonts) are available. This simple process prevents potential output disasters such as font replacement or low-resolution preview images in the final print.

Many designers understand these issues and carefully monitor the technical aspects of a job. It is all too common, however, to skip another important check — for spelling errors. Misspellings and typos creep into virtually every job despite numerous rounds of content proofs. These errors can ruin an otherwise perfect print job.

You might not (and probably won't) create the text for most design jobs, and you aren't technically responsible for the words your client supplies. However, you can be a hero if you find and fix typographical errors before a job goes to press; if you don't, you will almost certainly hear about it after it's too late to fix. Remember the cardinal rule of business: the customer is always right. You simply can't brush off a problem by saying, "That's not my job" — at least, not if you want to work with that client in the future.

1. **With toys_working.indd open, open the Dictionary pane of the Preferences dialog box.**

   InDesign checks spelling based on the defined language dictionary — by default, English USA. You can choose a different language dictionary in the Language menu.

Note:

Remember, preferences are accessed in the InDesign menu on Macintosh or in the Edit menu on Windows.

2. **Make sure English: USA is selected in the Language menu and click OK.**

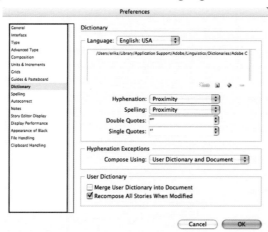

3. **Choose Edit>Spelling>Dictionary.**

   When you check spelling, you are likely to find words that, although spelled correctly, are not in the selected dictionary. Proper names, scientific terms, corporate trademarks, and other custom words are commonly flagged even though they are correct. Rather than flagging these terms every time you recheck the spelling, you can add these words to a custom user dictionary so InDesign will recognize them the next time you check spelling.

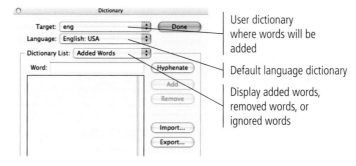

User dictionary where words will be added

Default language dictionary

Display added words, removed words, or ignored words

4. **In the Target menu, choose toys_working.indd.**

   By default, the user dictionary is associated with all documents. You can define custom words for a specific file using the Target menu; when you change the user dictionary for a specific file, words you add for that file will still be flagged in other files.

5. **In the Word field, type "ToyTrends".**

   Your client's name is not a real word (even though it is a combination of two real words). If you know certain words will be flagged, you can manually add those words to the user dictionary at any time.

   You're adding this word to the file's dictionary. Doing so prevents a potential error if you ever work on a different project with the term used in a more generic sense. For example, a magazine article about "Toy Trends in Middle America" should result in an error if the first two words are not separated by a space.

6. **Check the Case Sensitive option at the bottom of the dialog box, and then click Add.**

   If Case Sensitive is not checked, InDesign will not distinguish between ToyTrends (which is correct) and toytrends (which is wrong).

7. **Click Done to close the Dictionary dialog box.**

8. **With nothing selected in the layout, choose Edit>Spelling>Check Spelling.**

As soon as you open the Check Spelling dialog box, the first flagged word is highlighted in the layout. The same word appears in the Not in Dictionary field of the Check Spelling dialog box.

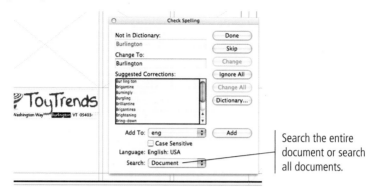

Search the entire document or search all documents.

The flagged word (Burlington) is the name of a city. Although it is not in the dictionary, it is spelled correctly.

9. **Activate the Case Sensitive option and click Add to add the word "Burlington" to the user dictionary.**

The layout immediately changes to show the next flagged word — the sole capital letter "B." Many single letters will be flagged when you check spelling.

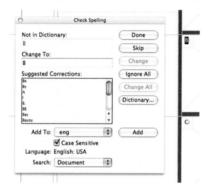

Note:

If the insertion point is currently placed in a story, the Search menu also includes options to search the selected story or the selected story after the insertion point.

Note:

Never simply click Change when checking spelling. Review each flagged word carefully and make the correct choices within the context of the layout.

10. **Click Skip.**

In context, this single letter is used as an identifier, so it is correct. However, other instances of the single letter B might be errors. Clicking Skip moves to the next flagged word without adding the word to the user dictionary.

11. **Review the next flagged word (the company's Web address), and then click Ignore All.**

Web addresses are almost always flagged as potential errors. In this case, you don't want to add it to the user dictionary, but you also don't want InDesign to flag it as an error.

12. **Review the next flagged word.**

"KinderKids" is the name of a product line, and it is spelled correctly.

13. Click the Dictionary button in the Check Spelling dialog box. Choose toys_working.indd in the Target menu and click Add.

When you add words in the Check Spelling dialog box, the words are added to the default user dictionary. When you open the Dictionary dialog box from the Check Spelling dialog box, you can choose the file-specific dictionary in the Target menu and click Add to add the word to the dictionary for the selected file only.

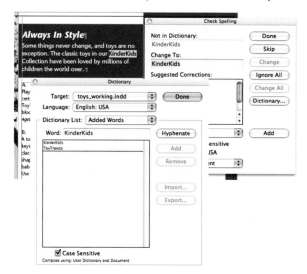

14. Click Done to close the Dictionary dialog box and return to the Check Spelling dialog box, and then click Skip.

When you return to the Check Spelling dialog box, KinderKids still appears in the Word field. You have to click Skip to find the next suspect word.

15. Continue checking the spelling in the document:

Not in Dictionary:	_Action to take:_
and and	Click "and" in the Suggested Corrections list and click Change
Sleepytime	Add to toys_working.indd dictionary
Marvalous	Click "Marvelous" in the Suggested Corrections list and click Change
playscape	Add to toys_working.indd dictionary
ASTM	Skip
lbs	Ignore all

16. Click Done to close the Check Spelling dialog box.

17. Using the Edit Original function in the Links panel, open slide.indd and check the spelling in the linked file. Correct any errors, and then save and close the file.

As with the Find/Change function, the Check Spelling function only interacts with nested files if those nested files are already open and the All Documents option is selected in the Search menu.

18. Save the toys_working.indd file and continue to the next stage of the project.

Note:

InDesign checks spelling based on the defined language dictionary. In addition to misspellings, however, InDesign also identifies repeated words (such as "the the"), uncapitalized words, and uncapitalized sentences. These options can be turned off in the Spelling pane of the Preferences dialog box.

Using Dynamic Spelling

You can turn on dynamic spelling (Edit>Spelling>Dynamic Spelling) to underline potential spelling and capitalization errors in the document without opening the Check Spelling dialog box. You can use the Spelling pane of the Preferences dialog box to assign a different-colored underline for each of the four potential problems.

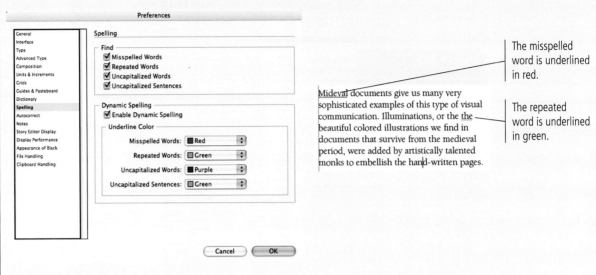

Mideval documents give us many very sophisticated examples of this type of visual communication. Illuminations, or the the beautiful colored illustrations we find in documents that survive from the medieval period, were added by artistically talented monks to embellish the hand-written pages.

The misspelled word is underlined in red.

The repeated word is underlined in green.

Enabling Autocorrect

If you type directly into InDesign, you can turn on the Autocorrect feature (Edit>Spelling>Autocorrect) to correct misspelled words as you type. Of course, automatic corrections are not always correct; software can't always select the correct word within the context of the layout, and it might produce some very strange results for words that aren't in the active dictionary (technical or corporate terms, for example). To avoid the potential for fixing "errors" that aren't really errors, you can define what misspellings to replace and what spelling should replace those specific errors.

In the Autocorrect pane of the Preferences dialog box, you can click Add to define a specific misspelling, as well as the correct spelling to use. The Autocorrect List is maintained for the specified language dictionary.

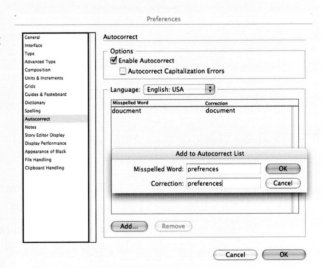

Stage 4 Creating Multiple Layers

One of the advantages of using a professional page layout application is the ability to create and manage complex layouts with a large number of elements. The InDesign Layers utility is a powerful option for controlling the objects that compose your layouts. In addition to managing individual elements, you can also use the Layers utility to create multiple versions of the same layout. This is particularly useful if:

- You are working with multiple overlapping objects on a page. Layers help you manage the stacking order of the different objects.

- You are working with multiple versions of the same layout, such as two versions of the same layout in different languages or several versions with different images in the same position for regional publications.

- You are creating a special die-cut layout using a template created in an illustration application.

Note:

Die-cut documents are cut in an odd, nonrectangular (page) shape or contain an area cut out within the page. The tab on a manila folder and a folded carton are two examples of die-cut jobs.

CREATE A NEW LAYER

When you create multiple versions using layers, you first need to determine how many layers you need. You should decide which elements (if any) will be included in all versions; those should exist on one layer. Elements that will change from one version to the next should be placed on their own layers.

This project requires three separate layers: one for the images that are the same for the U.S. and Canadian brochures; one for the text elements with U.S. prices; and one for the text elements with Canadian prices.

1. **With toys_working.indd open, navigate to Page 1 of the layout.**

2. **Display the Layers panel (Window>Layers).**

   Even if you have never opened the Layers panel before, every file has one layer named "Layer 1" by default.

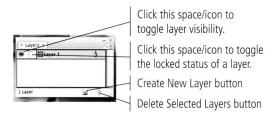

Click this space/icon to toggle layer visibility.

Click this space/icon to toggle the locked status of a layer.

Create New Layer button

Delete Selected Layers button

3. **Click the Create New Layer button at the bottom of the panel.**

   New layers are added above the currently selected layer; each new layer is added as Layer [N] (where "N" is just a sequential number). In this case, the new layer is "Layer 2" because "Layer 1" already exists.

The Pen icon indicates the layer where new objects will be created.

4. **In the Layers panel, double-click the Layer 2 name to open the Layer Options dialog box.**

5. Change the Name field to "American Prices" and review the other options.

- The **Color** menu determines the color of frame edges and bounding box handles for objects on that layer. You can choose a different color from the menu, or you can choose Custom at the bottom of the menu and define your own color.

- If **Show Layer** is checked, the layer contents are visible in the document window. You can also change this attribute by toggling the eye icon in the Layers panel.

- If **Lock Layer** is checked, you can't select or change objects on that layer.

- If **Print Layer** is checked, the layer will output when you print or export to PDF.

- The **Show Guides** option allows you to create and display different sets of guides for different layers; this is a more versatile option than showing or hiding *all* guides (which occurs with the View>Grids & Guides>Show/Hide Guides toggle).

- The **Lock Guides** option allows you to lock or unlock guides on specific layers only.

- If **Suppress Text Wrap When Layer is Hidden** is checked, text on underlying layers will reflow when the layer is hidden.

Controlling Text Wrap on Different Layers

INDESIGN FOUNDATIONS

Text wrap attributes of an object affect all text frames that touch that wrap object (unless Ignore Text Wrap in the Text Frame Options dialog box is checked for a specific text frame). The wrap object's position in the object's stacking order, as well as a layer's position within in the layer stack, are both irrelevant.

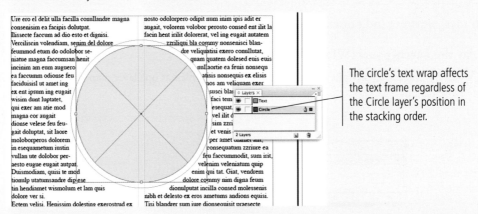

The circle's text wrap affects the text frame regardless of the Circle layer's position in the stacking order.

If Suppress Text Wrap When Layer is Hidden is checked in the Layer Options dialog box, text on other layers will reflow when the layer is hidden. The text wrap attributes of objects on the layer will only be applied when the layer is visible.

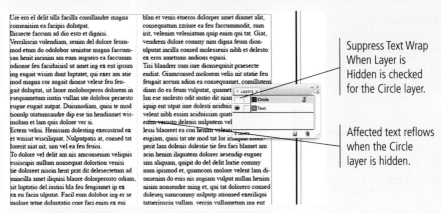

Suppress Text Wrap When Layer is Hidden is checked for the Circle layer.

Affected text reflows when the Circle layer is hidden.

6. **Click OK to close the Layer Options dialog box.**

The layer shows its new name.

7. **Double-click Layer 1 in the Layers panel. Change the layer name to "Common Elements" and click OK.**

8. **Save the file and continue to the next exercise.**

 ## CONTROL OBJECTS AND LAYERS

The only variation from one version to the next is the prices, so only text boxes containing prices need to be moved to the variation layers. Rather than create the Canadian Prices layer immediately, it makes more sense to move the varying elements to the American Prices layer, and then duplicate that layer with the elements already in place.

1. **With toys_working.indd open, navigate to Page 1 of the layout.**

2. **Using the Selection tool, select the text frame that contains the description of the classic car swing.**

   If you remember from the previous exercise, this text frame is actually threaded from the blue text frame at the top of the page.

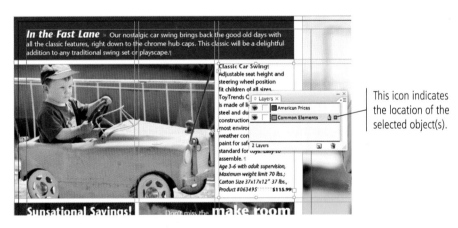

This icon indicates the location of the selected object(s).

3. **Shift-click the blue text frame at the top of the page to add it to the selection.**

Note:

Although you can thread text from one layer to another, we don't recommend doing so. Whenever possible, place all frames in the same thread on the same layer.

4. **In the Layers panel, drag the Selected Items icon from the Common Elements layer to the American Prices layer.**

Drag the Selected Items icon to another layer to move objects from one layer to another.

Note:

Selected objects can exist on multiple layers; in this case, the Layers panel shows icons to the right of all layers that contain selected objects.

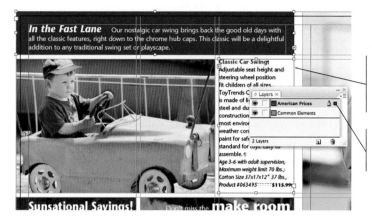

Red frame edges and bounding box handles match the red color of the American Prices layer.

The two selected items are now on the American Prices layer.

5. **On Page 2, move the two threaded text frames to the American Prices layer.**

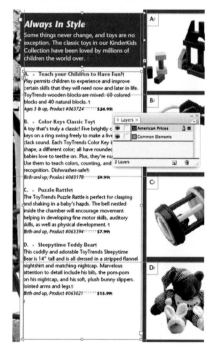

The last item to move is the description copy for the sliding board, which exists in a separate file. You could accomplish this using several methods:

- Move the entire placed slide file and create multiple versions of the slide.indd file to place on each layer in the brochure file.

- Create multiple layers in the slide.indd file and use the Object Layer Options to control which layers are visible on which layer of the brochure file.

- Simply copy the varying text frame from the placed file into the main brochure.

Every project will have different requirements. In this case, you're going to use the simplest method — copying and pasting the text frame from one file into another.

Note:

Unfortunately, there is no way to break the placed InDesign file into its component elements from within the brochure file. If you want those elements to be part of the brochure, you have to simply copy and paste.

6. **Control/right-click the placed slide.indd file in the layout and choose Edit Original from the contextual menu.**

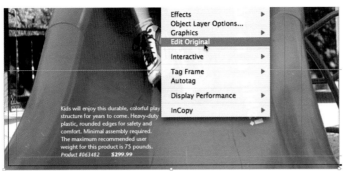

7. **In the external file, select the text frame with the Selection tool and choose Edit>Cut.**

8. **Save the external file and close it.**

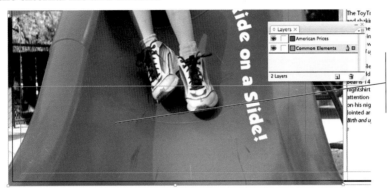

The placed file on the Common Elements layer no longer has a description text frame.

9. **In the toys_working.indd file, make sure the American Prices layer is the target layer and choose Edit>Paste.**

10. **Move the frame to the same approximate location where it appeared in the original slide.indd file.**

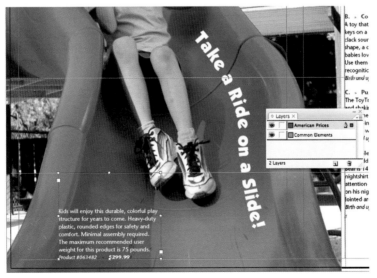

11. **Save the file and continue to the next exercise.**

USE A DUPLICATE LAYER TO CREATE DIFFERENT VERSIONS

Now that all of the varying text elements are in place on the American Prices layer, it is a simple process to duplicate the layer and create the second version.

1. **With toys_working.indd open, Control/right-click the American Prices layer and choose Duplicate Layer "American Prices" from the contextual menu.**

2. **In the resulting dialog box, change the layer name to "Canadian Prices".**

3. **Choose a color other than red from the Color menu, and then click OK.**

Because you duplicated the existing layer, the new layer defaults to red frame edges and handles.

Note:

Two layers of the same color defeat the purpose of unique layer identifiers. When you duplicate a layer, it's a good idea to also change the layer color for the duplicate.

4. **With the Canadian Prices layer selected in the Layers panel, find and highlight the product price on Page 1 of the layout.**

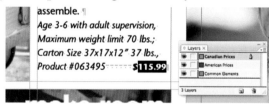

5. **Change the highlighted price to "139.99".**

Because the same text frame exists on both Prices layers, you can immediately see the problem — with both prices visible, neither is legible.

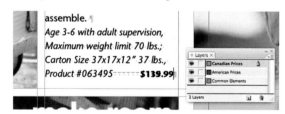

6. **In the Layers panel, click the eye icon to hide the American Prices layer.**

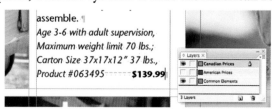

Note:

By default, hidden layers do not print. You will learn how to control layer output at the end of this project.

7. **Navigate to Page 2 of the layout.**

8. **Find and change each price in the brochure (there are five prices on Page 2):**

Slide	$359.99
Blocks	$29.99
Keys	$11.99
Rattle	$9.99
Teddy bear	$18.99

9. **Save the file and continue to the next exercise.**

 PREVIEW SEPARATIONS

To be entirely confident in your color output, you should also check the separations that will be created when your file is output to an imagesetter. InDesign's Separations Preview panel makes this easy to accomplish from directly within the application workspace.

1. **With toys_working.indd open, choose Window>Output>Separations Preview.**

2. **In the View menu, choose Separations.**

    When Separations is selected in the View menu, all separations in the current file are listed in the panel. You can turn individual separations on and off to preview the different ink separations that will be created:

    - To view a single separation and hide all others, click the name of the separation you want to view. By default, areas of coverage appear in black; you can preview separations in color by toggling off the Show Single Plates in Black command in the panel options menu.

    - To view more than one separation at the same time, click the empty space to the left of the separation name. When viewing multiple separations, each separation is shown in color.

    - To hide a separation, click the eye icon to the left of the separation name.

    - To view all process plates at once, click the CMYK option at the top of the panel.

3. **Click Pantone 186 C in the Separations panel, and then click the empty space to the left of Pantone 102 C to review where those two colors are used in the layout.**

The placed logos on Page 1 use both of the selected Pantone colors.

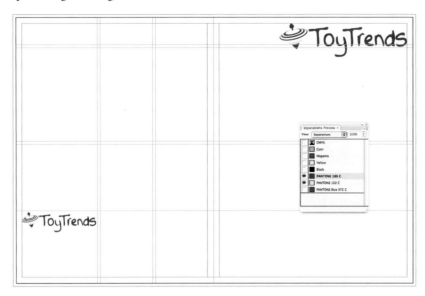

Monitoring Ink Limits

In CMYK color, shades of gray are reproduced using combinations of four printing inks. In theory, a solid black would be printed as 100% of all three inks, and pure white would be 0% of all three inks. This, however, does not take into consideration the limitations of mechanical printing.

Paper's absorption rate, the speed of the printing press, and other mechanical factors limit the amount of ink that can be placed on the same area of a page. If too much ink is applied, the result is a dark blob with no visible detail; heavy layers of ink also result in drying problems, smearing, and a number of other issues.

Total area coverage (also called **total ink coverage**) is the largest percentage of ink that can be safely printed on a single area. This number varies according to the ink/paper/press combination being used for a given job. The Specifications for Web Offset Printing (SWOP) indicates a 300% maximum. Many sheetfed printers require 280% maximum, while the number for newspapers is usually around 240% because the lower-quality paper absorbs more ink.

In the Separations Preview panel, you can choose Ink Limit in the View menu and define the TAC value for the file. You can then preview the layout to find elements that exceed the defined limit; if color is critical, those images should be corrected in Photoshop to be within the defined CMYK working space and ink limits.

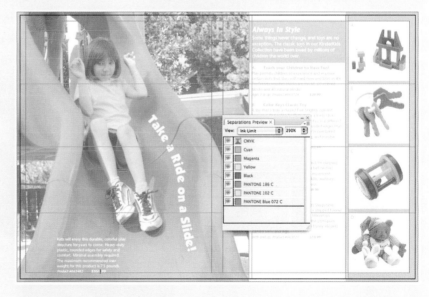

4. Click Pantone Blue 072 C in the Separations panel to see where that color is used.

As your client stated, the brochure should only use a single spot color — for this issue, the blue spot color in the logo. By reviewing the separation, you can see that the same blue from the logo is used for the accent elements on both pages of the layout.

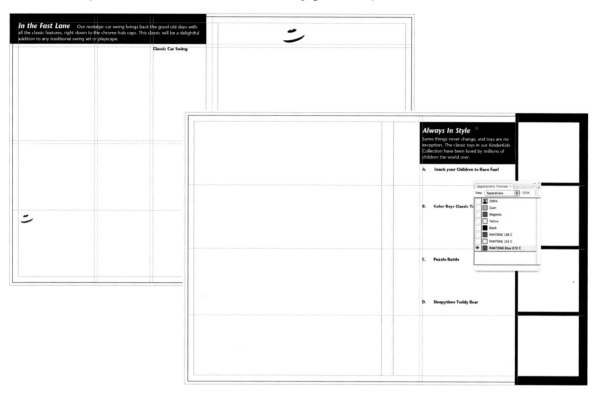

5. Click the empty space left of CMYK in the Separations panel to view the CMYK separations in addition to the Pantone Blue 072 C separation.

You can't simply delete the spot colors because they are used elsewhere in the document. You could convert them for output only, but if you need to output more than once you would have to convert the colors again each time you output the file. The most efficient option, in this case, is to convert the unwanted spot colors to process colors before you output the file.

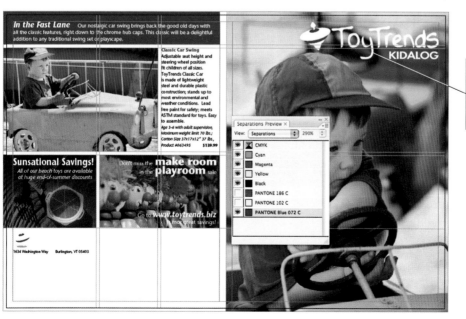

The red and yellow elements from the two hidden spot separations are not visible.

6. **In the Swatches panel, Control/right-click Pantone 186 C and choose Swatch Options from the contextual menu.**

7. **Change the Color Type menu to Process and click OK.**

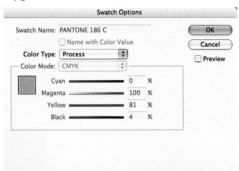

Note:

Be very careful when changing spot colors to process. One reason for using spot colors is to reproduce colors that are outside the CMYK gamut; when spot colors are converted to the nearest possible CMYK equivalent, some (possibly drastic) color shift will occur.

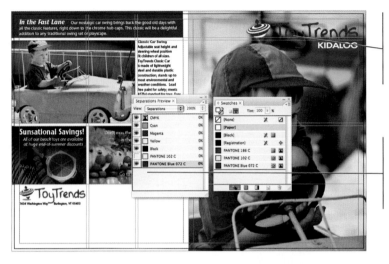

The missing red elements now appear because they are CMYK builds instead of spot colors.

After converting the Pantone 186 C swatch to process color, the separation is removed from the Separations panel.

8. **Repeat Steps 6–7 for the Pantone 102 C swatch.**

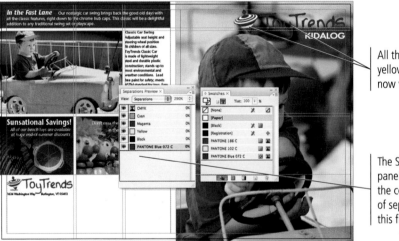

All the red and yellow elements are now visible.

The Separations panel now shows the correct number of separations for this file.

9. **Save the file and continue to the final exercise.**

EXPORT COLOR-MANAGED PDF FILES

The file is now complete and ready for output. To create the two versions of the file, you have to output the same file twice, selecting different layers for each version.

1. **With toys_working.indd open, create a final job package with all the elements of the job (document, pictures, and fonts).**

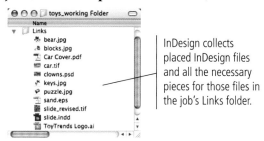

InDesign collects placed InDesign files and all the necessary pieces for those files in the job's Links folder.

2. **Choose File>Export. Navigate to your WIP>Toys folder as the destination and choose Adobe PDF in the Format menu.**

3. **Change the file name to "toys_canadian.pdf" and click Save.**

4. **Choose [High Quality Print] in the Preset menu.**

5. **In the General options, make sure Visible & Printable Layers is selected in the Export Layers menu.**

   When you output a file with layers, you can choose All Layers (including hidden and non-printable layers), Visible Layers (regardless of printable status), or Visible & Printable Layers.

Note:

These same options are available in the Print dialog box.

6. **In the Marks and Bleeds pane, turn on Crop Marks and activate the Use Document Bleed Settings option.**

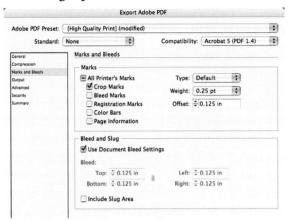

7. **In the Output pane, choose Convert to Destination in the Color Conversion menu.**

   You have several options for converting colors when you output a file:

   - **No Color Conversion** maintains all color data (including placed images) in its current space.

   - **Convert to Destination** converts colors to the profile selected in the Destination menu.

   - **Convert to Destination (Preserve Numbers)** converts colors to the destination profile if the applied profile does not match the defined destination profile. Objects without color profiles are not converted.

   The **Destination** menu defines the gamut for the output device that will be used. (This menu defaults to the active destination working space.) Color information in the file (and placed images) is converted to the selected Destination profile.

8. **Choose Include Destination Profile in the Profile Inclusion Policy menu.**

   The **Profile Inclusion Policy** menu determines whether color profiles are embedded in the resulting PDF file. (Different options are available, depending on what you selected in the Color Conversion menu.)

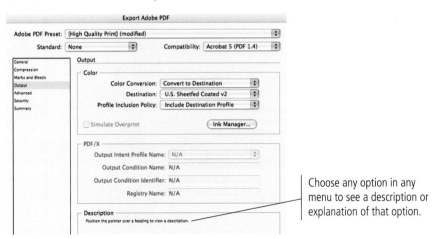

Choose any option in any menu to see a description or explanation of that option.

9. **Click the Save Preset button. In the Save Preset dialog box, name the preset "Toy Brochure PDF" and click OK.**

   Because you're going to export this file twice, saving a preset eliminates the need to make the same set of choices more than once.

Note:

Spot color information is preserved when colors are converted to the destination space.

10. **Click Export to create the PDF file.**

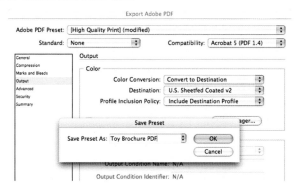

Note:

If you continued directly from the previous exercise, the Toy Brochure PDF preset will already be selected. If you (or someone else) did other work since completing the last exercise, you might have to manually select the preset again.

11. **When you return to the layout, hide the Canadian Prices layer and show the American Prices layer.**

12. **Export the file to PDF again, this time with the name "toys_american.pdf". In the Export Adobe PDF dialog box, call the Toy Brochure PDF preset and click Export.**

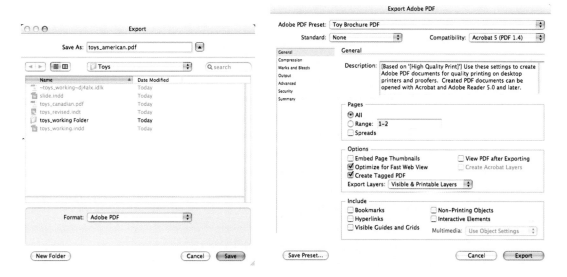

13. **Close the toys_working file without saving.**

Using the Ink Manager

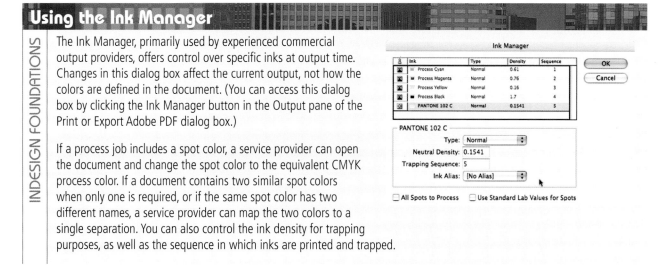

The Ink Manager, primarily used by experienced commercial output providers, offers control over specific inks at output time. Changes in this dialog box affect the current output, not how the colors are defined in the document. (You can access this dialog box by clicking the Ink Manager button in the Output pane of the Print or Export Adobe PDF dialog box.)

If a process job includes a spot color, a service provider can open the document and change the spot color to the equivalent CMYK process color. If a document contains two similar spot colors when only one is required, or if the same spot color has two different names, a service provider can map the two colors to a single separation. You can also control the ink density for trapping purposes, as well as the sequence in which inks are printed and trapped.

INDESIGN FOUNDATIONS

Although trapping should typically be left to experienced professionals in the output provider's prepress department, knowledge is proverbial power. If you understand these concepts, you will be better able to prevent potential output problems when you build a layout.

Trapping Theory and Terminology

In process-color printing, the four process colors (Cyan, Magenta, Yellow, and Black) are imaged or separated onto individual printing plates; each color separation is printed on a separate unit of a printing press. When printed on top of each other in varying percentages, the semitransparent inks produce the range of colors in the CMYK gamut. Spot colors are printed using specially formulated inks as additional color separations.

Because printing is a mechanical process, some variation between the different units of the press is possible (if not likely). Paper moves through the units of a press at considerable speed, and some movement from side to side is inevitable. Each printing plate has one or more registration marks (crosshairs) that are used to monitor the registration of each color. If the units are in register, the cross hairs from each color plate print exactly on top of each other.

Misregistration can cause a noticeable gap of uninked paper between adjacent elements, particularly when these elements are comprised of different ink colors. When a press is out of register, the individual overlapping colors are discernible.

Misregister results in a visible gap between objects.

Misregister

If any misregister occurs, type can become blurry or virtually unreadable. Any time multiple inks are placed on top of each other, you run the risk of misregister.

Trapping is the compensation for misregister of the color plates on a printing press. Trapping minimizes or eliminates these errors by artificially expanding adjacent colors so small areas of color on the edge of each element overlap and print on top of one another. If sufficiently large, this expansion of color, or trap, fills in the undesirable inkless gap between elements. Trapping procedures differ based upon your workflow; most service providers will perform trapping before generating film or plates. The specific amount of trapping to be applied varies, depending on the ink/paper/press combination that will be used for the job.

A **knockout** is an area of background color that is removed so a lighter foreground color is visible. To achieve white (paper-colored) type on a black background, for example, the black background is removed wherever the type overlaps the black. Any time a lighter color appears on top of a darker color, the area of the lighter color is knocked out of the background.

Overprint	Knockout

When a color is set to knock out, anything beneath that color will not be printed. If the black knocks out the Cyan, any misregistration can result in a paper-colored gap where the two objects meet. Setting black to overprint eliminates the possibility of a gap caused by misregistration. (The dashed lines in the graphic are for illustration only.)

Overprint is essentially the opposite of knockout. A darker-color foreground object is printed directly on top of a lighter-color background, which means that slight variation in the units of the press will not be as noticeable, especially if the darker color is entirely contained within the lighter color. Black is commonly set to overprint other colors, as are some special colors that are printed using opaque inks. Black is particularly effective when overprinted since it becomes visually richer when other process colors — especially cyan — are mixed with it.

A **choke** means that the edge of the background color is expanded into the space in which the foreground color will be printed. A **spread** means that the edge of the foreground color is expanded to overprint the edge of the background color. As a general rule, the lighter object should be trapped into the darker area. This rule helps determine whether you should choke or spread.

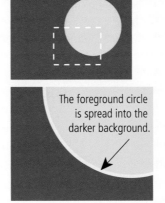
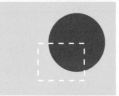
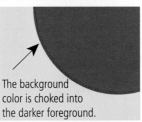

- If the background is darker than the foreground object, the lighter color of the foreground object should be spread to overprint the darker background.

- If the foreground color is darker than the background color, the lighter background color is choked so that it overprints the darker foreground color.

The foreground circle is spread into the darker background.

The background color is choked into the darker foreground.

If adjacent elements share a large percentage of one or more common colors, trapping between those elements is unnecessary. If both elements contain a lot of magenta, for example, the continuity of the magenta between the two objects will mask any gaps that occur between the other process colors in the two images; this makes trapping unnecessary. The general rule is that if two adjacent elements share one process color that varies by less than 50%, or if two elements share two or more process colors that vary by less than 80%, don't bother with trapping — the continuous layer of the inks common to both elements will effectively mask any gaps.

C: 85
M: 50
Y: 0
K: 0

C: 0
M: 50
Y: 80
K: 0

Cyan plate

Yellow plate

Magenta plate

Controlling the Appearance and Overprint Attributes of CMYK Black

The black inks that are used in process-color printing might not produce a pure opaque black. (You used a rich black in Project 2 to improve the appearance of solid black areas.) On screen or on a desktop inkjet printer, however, 100% black typically looks as black as black can be. This discrepancy can cause problems when you don't get what you expect in the final printed job. To solve the problem, you can change the appearance of black in the Appearance of Black preferences.

You can define how blacks appear on-screen and in output.

- **Display All Blacks Accurately** shows 100% CMYK black as dark gray on screen.

- **Display All Blacks As Rich Black** shows 100% CMYK black as pure black (R=0 G=0 B=0).

- **Output All Blacks Accurately** outputs CMYK blacks based on the actual numbers in the color definition. This allows you to see the difference between pure black and rich black on non-PostScript desktop printers.

- **Output All Blacks As Rich Black** outputs all blacks as pure black (R=0 G=0 B=0) when printing to a non-PostScript desktop printer.

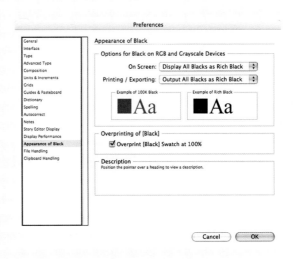

By default, [Black] is set to overprint other colors. If you want to knock out [Black] elements, you have to uncheck the Overprint [Black] Swatch at 100% option.

Controlling Trapping in InDesign

INDESIGN FOUNDATIONS

InDesign applies trapping using Trap Presets, or defined collections of trapping settings. The Trap Presets panel (Window>Output>Trap Presets) allows you to create, edit, and apply trap presets to specific pages in a layout. If you don't apply a specific trap preset to a page, that page will use the [Default] trap preset.

If you choose Assign Trap Preset in the panel options menu, you can assign an existing preset to all pages or a specific range of pages. Clicking Done simply closes the dialog box; you have to click the Assign button to change the preset for the selected pages.

If you edit the Default trap preset, you open the Modify Trap Preset Options dialog box. If you create a new trap preset, you open the New Trap Preset dialog box. In either case, you have the same choices; the only difference is the availability of the Name field (you can't rename the Default trap preset option).

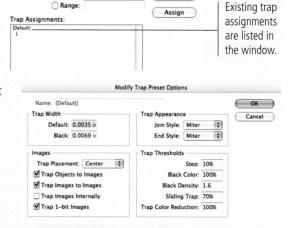

Existing trap assignments are listed in the window.

Trap Width. Different types of paper and inks, as well as different output devices, require different amounts of trapping. The two fields in this section define the amount of overlap that will be created in the traps.

- **Default** defines the trap width for all colors except those with 100% Black. The default value is 0.0035" (1/4 point).
- **Black** defines the distance that other colors will spread into colors with 100% Black. The default is 0.0069" (1/2 point).

Trap Appearance. These menus determine the shape of joins (where two trap edges meet) and ends in trap lines.

- **Join Style** controls the shape of the outside join of two trap segments (Miter, Round, and Bevel).
- **End Style** determines how the ends of lines appear when three different trap lines intersect.

Images. InDesign is able to trap placed raster images; each option handles imported graphics differently.

- **Trap Placement** determines where the trap falls when you trap vector objects to bitmap images. Center creates a trap that straddles the edge between objects and images. Choke causes objects to overlap abutting images. Neutral Density applies the same trapping rules as used elsewhere in the document. Spread causes images to overlap abutting objects.
- **Trap Objects To Images** forces vector objects (e.g., frame strokes) to trap to images using the Trap Placement settings.
- **Trap Images To Images** enables trapping along the edges of two overlapping raster images.
- **Trap Images Internally** enables trapping within an individual raster image. This option should be used with caution for only high-contrast images; it does not produce good results for photographic (continuous-tone) images.
- **Trap 1-Bit Images** enables trapping for 1-bit (bitmap or line art) images.

Trap Thresholds. These values determine when trapping will be applied.

- **Step** specifies the threshold at which a trap is created, or the percentage that adjacent component colors must be different before trapping occurs. Higher Step percentages require greater variance in adjacent colors; lower percentages make the application more sensitive to color differences, resulting in more traps.
- **Black Color** defines the minimum percentage of black ink required before the Black trap-width setting is applied.
- **Black Density** defines a neutral density value at which InDesign treats an ink as black. Any inks with a neutral density at or above this value will use the Black trap-width setting.
- **Sliding Trap** determines when traps start to straddle the centerline of the color edges. The value refers to the proportion of the lighter color's neutral density to that of adjacent darker colors; using the default value (70%), the trap will be applied at the centerline when the lighter color's neutral density is more than 70% of the darker color's neutral density (lighter color's neutral density divided by darker color's neutral density > 0.70).
- **Trap Color Reduction** defines the degree to which components from adjacent colors are used to reduce the trap color. A Trap Color Reduction lower than 100% lightens the color of the trap; Trap Color Reduction of 0% makes a trap with the same neutral density as the darker color.

Summary

As you have seen, placing pictures into an InDesign layout is a relatively easy task, whether you place them one at a time or load multiple images at once and then simply click to place the loaded images into the appropriate spots. InDesign allows you to work with all of the common image formats (including PDF), as well placing one InDesign layout directly into another. The Links panel is a valuable tool for managing images, from updating file status to replacing one image with another to opening an external file in its native application so you can easily make changes in placed files.

Fine-tuning a layout requires checking for common errors — both technical (such as low-resolution images) and practical (such as spelling errors). You learned in Project 3 how to use InDesign's preflighting tools; the Check Spelling utility is just as important in creating high-quality, professional designs.

The InDesign Layers utility makes it very easy to create versioned documents. Once you have determined which elements will change, you can simply move elements to the appropriate layers and make the necessary changes. This might be as basic as changing some prices, or it might involve entirely new text (for example, a Spanish translation). Regardless of how much content will change, layers are the easiest way to create and manage multiple versions of the same file.

Place and control a PDF file

Place and control a TIFF file

Place and control a layered Photoshop file

Place and control an EPS file

Place and control a native Illustrator file

Place and control a native InDesign file

Load and place multiple images at one time

Edit a placed image using the Links panel

Find and replace elements with specific formatting attributes

Find and replace text strings, with and without specific formatting attributes

Check for and correct spelling errors

Create multiple versions of the layout using layers

Portfolio Builder Project 6

Your client, the Miami/Equatorial Travel Agency, wants to create a graphics-rich brochure to promote travel and tourism in Costa Rica.

To complete this project, you should:

❏ Design two versions of the brochure using the client's die-cut template. Make sure to incorporate bleed allowance outside the template edges.

❏ Flip the template horizontally on the second page so the front and back of the piece line up properly.

❏ Create different layers for the English and Spanish versions of the brochure.

❏ Use the die template, images, and text for both languages from the RF_Builders>Travel folder.

"We want to create a special brochure to encourage travel to Costa Rica. We want this brochure to be unique, to really stand out. Our printer gave us a die-cut template that we'd like to use for this job. The printer's CSR said to just place the file as a template on its own layer in the file, and treat the template lines like page edges.

"We want the brochure to focus on images — beautiful sunsets, beaches... the kind of image that makes someone say, 'I want to go there.' We've given you some of those, but feel free to find other images that will convey this same message.

"There is very little text. The words 'Costa Rica' should appear on the front, back, and inside of the brochure. Otherwise, we have a two-line blurb about how to contact us, which has to be included in the final piece, and some quotes that you can use in whatever way you think best.

"It wouldn't make sense to promote a primarily Spanish-speaking country using only English; besides, here in Miami, a large segment of our customers are fluent in Spanish. Even though there is very little text for the brochure, we're going to create two versions of the brochure — one in English and one in Spanish."

National Parks Info Pieces

Your client is a marketing manager for the National Parks Service (NPS). She wants to create a series of collateral pieces that can be distributed to tourism centers as a lure to potential visitors. The entire project includes a one-sheet flyer that will be distributed in print and online, a rack card that can be placed in area hotels, and a postcard that will be given away to park visitors.

This project incorporates the following skills:

- ❏ Using placeholder objects and text to design a layout concept
- ❏ Adjusting a layout concept to suit content provided by the client
- ❏ Creating an XML file using tagged frames and content
- ❏ Building a layout from imported XML content
- ❏ Controlling the structure of a layout to merge XML content into tagged frames
- ❏ Defining hyperlinks to link layout elements to an external Web page
- ❏ Creating interactive buttons with multiple states
- ❏ Exporting PDF files without interactive elements for print distribution
- ❏ Exporting PDF files with interactive elements for digital distribution

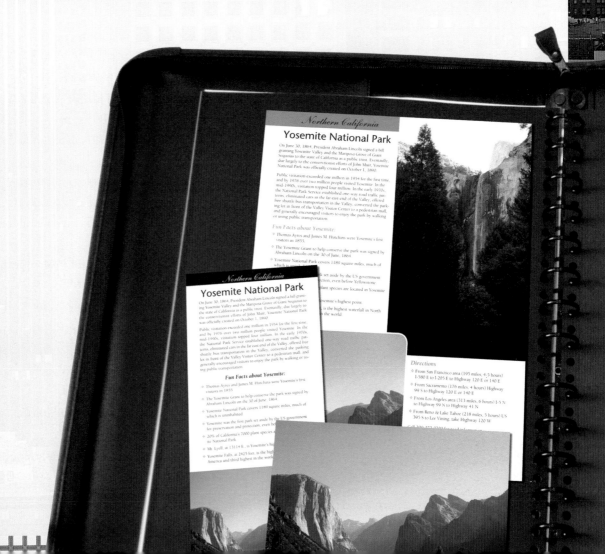

The Project Meeting

We want to create several short informational pieces to promote tourism in the national parks. Each piece should include two images, which we will provide as soon as we decide which ones we want to use. We haven't written any of the content yet, but we can tell you it will include the park name, the park location (as in, "California State Parks"), two paragraphs of historical copy, a list of six or seven "fun facts" about the park, and directions to the park from all four compass points.

For each park, we want two different layouts — a flyer and a rack card — with the same content. The flyer will be sent to tourism boards and agencies as a handout; the rack card will be placed in hotels near the park for potential visitors. We also want to create a postcard that we can give away as a free souvenir to visitors; this piece will have some (but not all) of the same content as the other two pieces.

We would also like to offer the flyers digitally, both as downloads from our Web site and as attachments to promotional emails. In the digital version, we would like to add buttons that link to the park's home page on the NPS Web site and to our basic informational email address.

The client promised to give us actual content for at least one park by the end of the week. While you're waiting, I want you to start experimenting with a layout concept. You know all of the elements that need to be included, so you can use placeholders to play with various options.

There are more than 350 national parks, monuments, and other protected areas in the national park system. When the flyer layout is finalized, save it as a template so you can use it again later when we get the content for the different parks.

Because each of these pieces is going to include the same content, you can use InDesign's XML tools to share the content between the pieces. This will make it much easier in case the client decides to change something — you'll need to change only one instance, and then update the XML file in the other documents.

For the interactive elements, you can build them into the same file that will be used for print. InDesign makes it easy to control whether those elements will be included in a PDF file, so there is no need to create two different versions of the flyer.

To complete this project, you will:

- ❏ Use text and picture placeholders to design a layout concept
- ❏ Experiment with glyphs to find suitable bullet characters
- ❏ Create styles based on formatting in the layout
- ❏ Redefine styles based on local formatting overrides
- ❏ Sample colors from a placed image to unify the completed layout
- ❏ Tag frames and content for XML
- ❏ Generate a structured XML file from layout content
- ❏ Create additional layouts from imported XML content
- ❏ Create hyperlinks and buttons to add user interactivity
- ❏ Export multiple PDF files for different distribution methods

Stage 1 Experimenting with Layout Options

Many InDesign projects start with little more than an idea. Although templates, master pages, and styles are invaluable tools when implementing a layout, in many cases you simply need to open a blank document and start experimenting. When you have to design a project from scratch, InDesign makes it easy to create and format objects and experiment with different options, and then create masters and styles when you are satisfied with your work.

Use Placeholders to Structure a Layout

It's always a good idea to begin a project as soon as possible after getting the assignment. When working with clients, however, you will often find that the idea for a project comes before the actual content — sometimes *long* before the client has finalized the text or provided the promised images. Rather than waiting until the client's content is ready — which is sometimes the day before a project is due — you can design a layout using placeholders to mark the location of pictures and text frames, and even experiment with the appearance of different elements of the text.

The pieces in this project will include the same basic information:

- Two images

- The location of the park

- The park name

- Two paragraphs of descriptive copy about the park

- A short list of "fun facts" about the park

- Directions to the park from four major landmarks (one in each compass direction)

The main piece of this project is the so-called "one-sheet," or a single-page flyer printed on one side of the sheet. Because this is the primary piece of the project, you'll create that file first.

1. **Create a new letter-size file using portrait orientation. Define 1/2″ margins on all four sides and 1/8″ bleeds on all four sides. Use non-facing pages and no master text frame.**

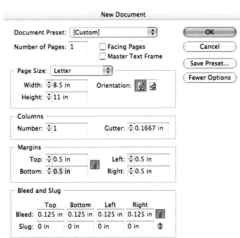

Note:

Before completing this project, copy the Parks folder from the WIP folder on your Resource CD to your WIP folder where you are saving your work. When you save files for this project, you will save them in your WIP>Parks folder.

2. **Drag a vertical page guide to mark the center of the page.**

3. **Create a text frame that fills the left side of the page, snapping to the top, left, and bottom margin guides.**

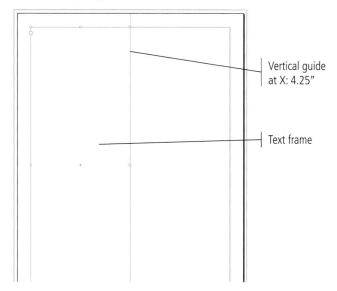

Vertical guide
at X: 4.25″

Text frame

4. **Place the insertion point in the text frame on the left side of the page.**

5. **Choose Type>Fill with Placeholder Text.**

This command fills the entire text frame with nonsense or **lorem text** (so called because it is Greek nonsense) using the default text-format settings.

Lorem placeholder text is valuable for experimenting with the appearance of paragraph text; these random words give you a better idea of what text will look like when real content is placed in the layout.

Note:

If a text frame is linked to other text frames, the placeholder text will fill the entire series of linked text frames.

Note:

The placeholder text is randomly generated, so the exact words in your layout will probably not match what you see in our screen shot. However, the exact words are not important; the important issue is that you have some placeholder text to work with while you experiment with formatting options.

6. **Create a new text frame at the top of the page. Bleed the frame past the left and top edges, snap the right edge to the vertical center guide, and snap the bottom edge to the top margin guide.**

7. **With the insertion point in the new frame, type "South Carolina State Parks". Change the text to center paragraph alignment.**

In some cases, certain text elements will be made clear in the initial project description. Your client stated that the one-sheets should identify the location of the park, so you can use actual text to plan the appearance of this element. The words "South Carolina" have the most characters of all fifty states, so this is a good representation of the possible text that can appear in this area.

8. **Fill the text frame with the C=100, M=0, Y=0, K=0 swatch.**

You aren't going to leave this frame filled with cyan, but it will have a colored fill. You're using cyan simply as a representation that some color will fill the frame.

9. **Control/right-click the new text frame and choose Text Frame Options from the contextual menu.**

10. **Apply a 0.625″ inset to the left edge and a 0.125″ inset to the bottom edge of the frame. Change the Align menu to Bottom and click OK.**

The left inset allows you to center the frame content in the space above the main text frame. The left edge of the main text frame is 0.5″ from the left edge of the page. You have to add the bleed (0.125″), so the left inset value needs to be 0.625″.

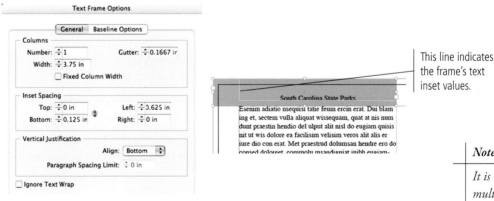

This line indicates the frame's text inset values.

Note:

It is unnecessary to place multiple text frames on top of one another to achieve this effect.

11. **Choose Layout>Margins and Columns. Change the Top margin field to 0.625″ and click OK.**

You can change the margins on any regular layout page, just as you changed the master page margins in Project 5.

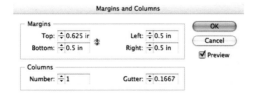

12. **Drag the top edge of the main text frame down to match the new top margin guide.**

Revised top margin guide

13. **Save the file as "Flyer Concept.indd" in your WIP>Parks folder and continue to the next exercise.**

 ## EXPERIMENT WITH TEXT FORMATTING

The best place to begin experimenting is to define the basic font for the majority of the layout. Rather than simply selecting the text in a frame and adjusting it locally, you can change the [Basic Paragraph] style to affect the default appearance of all text in the layout.

As you design a layout, the important thing to realize is that nothing is permanent — including styles — until the job is printed. Of course, some methods for changing a design are better than others. Because changing a style applies the same change to any text formatted with that style, it's better to do as much of your work as possible with styles.

1. **With Flyer Concept.indd open, Control/right-click [Basic Paragraph] in the Paragraph Styles panel and choose Edit "[Basic Paragraph]" from the contextual menu.**

2. **In the Basic Character Formats options, change the font to the Book variant of ATC Laurel, and change the type size to 10 pt. Click OK to apply the change.**

By changing the default text formatting, the placeholder text no longer fills the frame.

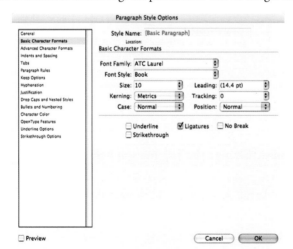

Note:

If you edit the [Basic Paragraph] style with no file open, the adjusted text formatting options will be the default settings in all new files.

3. **Place the insertion point at the end of the text in the main frame and choose Type>Fill with Placeholder Text.**

More lorem text is placed, filling the available space in the frame.

4. **Make sure hidden characters are visible (Type>Show Hidden Characters).**

5. **Place the insertion point at the top of the frame and press Return/Enter to add a new paragraph.**

6. **Place the insertion point in the new empty paragraph at the top of the frame, and then type "Black Canyon of the Gunnison National Park".**

Just as "South Carolina" is the longest state name, this is the longest name in the list of national parks. When you're working with placeholders, it's always a good idea to design around the longest possible content.

7. **Select the entire first paragraph (the park name) and change the font to ATC Oak Normal. Apply centered paragraph alignment.**

Note:

It isn't always possible to determine the longest possible content for a particular editorial element. In this case, use your judgment when planning a layout. In other words, don't try to format a main heading with only one or two words of placeholder text.

Note:

A bit of creative thinking might be required to find the longest possible text for a specific element. To identify the longest national park name, we searched the Internet for a list of all parks, formatted the list in a monospace font, and simply looked for the one that extended farthest to the right.

8. **Press Command/Control-Shift-period to enlarge the text size by 2 points. Continue pressing this shortcut until the paragraph extends to a third line.**

 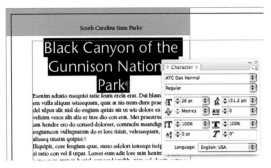

9. **Press Command/Control-Shift-comma to reduce the text size by 2 points.**

   The text should now fit on two lines.

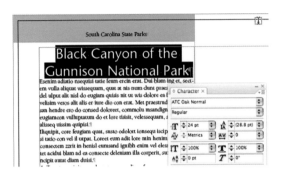

Note:

By default, the key command for increasing and decreasing type size changes the size by 2 points. You can change this increment in the Units and Increments pane of the Preferences dialog box.

10. **Highlight the first two paragraphs of the body copy (below the park name). Change the space before the selected paragraphs to 0.125".**

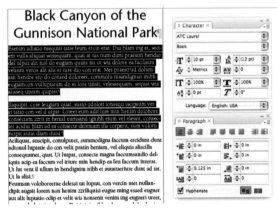

Note:

Add Option/Alt to the basic keyboard shortcut to increase or decrease the type size by five times the defined increment.

Note:

By default, leading is only applied to selected text. To apply leading changes to entire paragraphs, activate the Apply Leading to Entire Paragraphs option in the Type pane of the Preferences dialog box.

11. **Place the insertion point at the end of the second body paragraph and press Return/Enter to start a new paragraph.**

12. **Type "Fun Facts about Black Canyon of the Gunnison".**

    You know the basic structure of the text that will be used in the piece, including this heading (or other words to the same effect).

Because you pressed Return/Enter from the end of the previous paragraph, the Space Before value is also applied to the new paragraph.

INDESIGN FOUNDATIONS

Keyboard shortcuts can be helpful, especially in early stages when you are still experimenting with text formatting options.

	Macintosh	Windows
Bold type style	Command-Shift-B	Control-Shift-B
Italic type style	Command-Shift-I	Control-Shift-I
Normal type style	Command-Shift-Y	Control-Shift-Y
Underline type style	Command-Shift-U	Control-Shift-U
Strikethrough type style	Command-Shift-/	Control-Shift-/
All Caps type style (on/off)	Command-Shift-K	Control-Shift-K
Small Caps type style (on/off)	Command-Shift-H	Control-Shift-H
Superscript type style	Command-Shift-Plus sign	Control-Shift-Plus sign
Subscript type style	Command-Option-Shift-Plus sign	Control-Alt-Shift-Plus sign
Reset horizontal scale to 100%	Command-Shift-X	Control-Shift-X
Reset vertical scale to 100%	Command-Option-Shift-X	Control-Alt-Shift-X
Align left	Command-Shift-L	Control-Shift-L
Align right	Command-Shift-R	Control-Shift-R
Align center	Command-Shift-C	Control-Shift-C
Justify all lines (all but last line)	Command-Shift-J	Control-Shift-J
Justify all lines (all lines)	Command-Shift-F	Control-Shift-F
Increase point size*	Command-Shift->	Control-Shift->
Decrease point size*	Command-Shift-<	Control-Shift-<
Increase point size by 5 times the defined increment*	Command-Option-Shift->	Control-Alt-Shift<
Decrease point size by 5 times the defined increment*	Command-Option-Shift-<	Control-Alt-Shift->
Increase leading*	Option-Up Arrow	Alt-Up Arrow
Decrease leading*	Option-Down Arrow	Alt-Down Arrow
Increase leading by 5 times the defined increment*	Command-Option-Up Arrow	Control-Alt-Up Arrow
Decrease leading by 5 times the defined increment*	Command-Option-Down Arrow	Control-Alt-Down Arrow
Auto leading	Command-Option-Shift-A	Control-Alt-Shift-A
Align to grid (on/off)	Command-Option-Shift-G	Control-Alt-Shift-G
Auto-hyphenate (on/off)	Command-Option-Shift-H	Control-Alt-Shift-H
Increase kerning and tracking	Option-Left Arrow	Alt-Left Arrow
Decrease kerning and tracking	Option-Right Arrow	Alt-Right Arrow
Increase kerning and tracking by 5 times	Command-Option-Left Arrow	Control-Alt-Left Arrow
Decrease kerning and tracking by 5 times	Command-Option-Right Arrow	Control-Alt-Right Arrow
Increase kerning between words*	Command-Option-\	Control-Alt-\
Decrease kerning between words*	Command-Option-Delete	Control-Alt-Backspace
Clear all manual kerning and reset tracking to 0	Command-Option-Q	Control-Alt-Q
Increase baseline shift**	Option-Shift-Up Arrow	Alt-Shift-Up Arrow
Decrease baseline shift**	Option-Shift-Down Arrow	Alt-Shift-Down Arrow
Increase baseline shift by 5 times	Command-Option-Shift-Up Arrow	Control-Alt-Shift-Up Arrow
Decrease baseline shift by 5 times	Command-Option-Shift-Down Arrow	Control-Alt-Shift-Down Arrow

* Using the default settings the keyboard shortcut changes the selected setting by 2 points. You can change this value in the Units & Increments pane of the Preferences dialog box.

13. **Highlight the entire paragraph and change the text to 13.5-pt. ATC Laurel Bold Italic.**

    Subheads like this should typically be related to either the body copy or the main headings. Remember that professional-looking designs do not use 15 different fonts on a page. Try to stick with two or three primary fonts, and use variants of those fonts for emphasis and visual interest. (Of course, rules were made to be broken, but don't break from design conventions unless you have a good reason for doing so.)

14. **Highlight the text in the cyan-filled frame and change it to ATC Jacaranda. Enlarge the text as much as possible until the top edge of the character ascenders is still at least 1/8″ from the page edge.**

15. **Save the file and continue to the next exercise.**

Navigating and Selecting Text with Keyboard Shortcuts

Keyboard shortcuts can be helpful, especially in early stages when you are still experimenting with text formatting options.

	Macintosh	Windows
Move left one character*	Left Arrow	Left Arrow
Move right one character*	Right Arrow	Right Arrow
Move up one line*	Up Arrow	Up Arrow
Move down one line*	Down Arrow	Down Arrow
Move left one word*	Command-Left Arrow	Control-Left Arrow
Move right one word*	Command-Right Arrow	Control-Right Arrow
Move to start of line*	Home	Home
Move to end of line*	End	End
Move to previous paragraph*	Command-Up Arrow	Control-Up Arrow
Move to next paragraph*	Command-Down Arrow	Control-Down Arrow
Move to start of story*	Command-Home	Control-Home
Move to end of story*	Command-End	Control-End
Select current line	Command-Shift-\	Control-Shift-\
Select characters from insertion point	Shift-click	Shift-click
Select entire story	Command-A	Control-A
Select previous frame	Command-Option-Page Up	Control-Alt-Page Up
Select next frame	Command-Option-Page Down	Control-Alt-Page Down
Select first frame	Command-Option-Shift-Page Up	Control-Alt-Shift-Page Up
Select last frame	Command-Option-Shift-Page Down	Control-Alt-Shift-Page Down
Delete word in front of insertion point (Story Editor)	Command-Delete	Control-Backspace
* Add Shift to select text between the previous and new location of the insertion point.		

EXPERIMENT WITH GLYPHS

The Glyphs panel offers an easy way to review and select specific characters in available fonts. When experimenting with type formatting, the Glyphs panel is an excellent way to search through extended, symbol, and pictographic characters that you can't easily preview in the document layout.

1. **With Flyer Concept.indd open, choose Window>Type & Tables>Glyphs.**

2. **In the text after the subheading you created in the previous exercise, break up the paragraph into seven individual paragraphs of two lines each.**

   In the experimentation phase, these paragraphs represent the "fun facts" paragraphs that will appear in the final copy. The actual text in these lines (including capitalization) is irrelevant because you are using them for formatting purposes only.

   > **Fun Facts About Black Canyon of the Gunnison**
   > Aciliquat, suscipit, conulputet, summodigna faccum ercidunt dunt adionul luptatie do con velit pratin heniam, ¶
   > vel eliquis aliscilla consequamet, quat. Ut lutpat, consecte magna faccumsandio deliquis acip ea faccum vel iriure ¶
   > min hendip ea feu faccum iurerat. Ut lut vent il ullum in hendignim nibh et autatueriure dunt ad tat. Ut la alisi.¶
   > Feumsan voloboreetue delessi tat luptat, con vercin utet nullandipit augait lorem non henim zzriliquisi eugue ¶
   > ming essed euguer aut alit luptatio odip et velit wis nonsenit venim ing eugueri ureet, commodo lutatie vel utat. ¶
   > Duisit ipit nibh et laorer sed do el euis eugiamconse dolendre diam, quipsustio dolorper in ex exerosto ex ea ¶
   > faccum do con velis acilla ad deliquat. Venim in hent lummy nim do ex ex endio exer illa feu feuipit autatue tie ¶

3. **Place the insertion point at the beginning of the first two-line paragraph.**

4. **In the menu at the bottom of the Glyphs panel, choose a pictographic font such as Zapf Dingbats or Wingdings.**

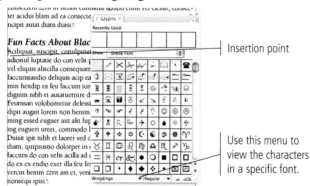

Insertion point

Use this menu to view the characters in a specific font.

5. **Scroll through the panel and find a character that matches the theme of the document.**

   We found a character in the Wingdings font that looks like a compass crosshair. You can use any character from any font that you feel works with the "outdoors" theme of national parks.

   The important point to remember is that you can use the Glyphs panel to look at all of the available characters in the selected font. This is an excellent way to explore and experiment when you want to use type characters to create visual interest.

Note:

You can also open the Glyphs panel by choosing Type>Glyphs.

Note:

Decorative fonts can be useful for adding visual interest without the need for linked graphics.

6. **When you find a character you want to use, double-click that glyph in the panel.**

   Double-clicking inserts the selected character at the location of the insertion point.

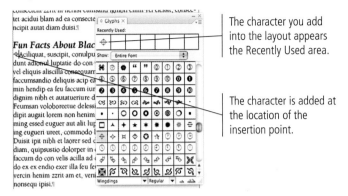

The character you add into the layout appears the Recently Used area.

The character is added at the location of the insertion point.

7. **Make note of the font that includes the character you selected.**

8. **Select all seven of the "fun facts" paragraphs. In the Paragraph panel options menu, choose Bullets and Numbering.**

   These are the same options you used to define styles with bullets in Project 5. Anything that can be applied in a style can also be applied as a local formatting option.

9. **Apply the Bullets list type with a 0.15″ hanging indent and a 0.15″ tab position.**

   Remember, a hanging indent is a negative first-line indent; set the Left indent field to 0.15″ and the First Line Indent field to –0.15″.

10. **Click the Add button. In the Add Bullets dialog box, select the same font you noted in Step 7. Find and select the character you decided to use as a bullet and click OK.**

    You could have skipped Steps 4–6; however, we believe it's easier to use the Glyphs panel for exploring and experimenting with different characters. Once you know what you want to use, it's easy to add that character in the formatting of a bulleted list.

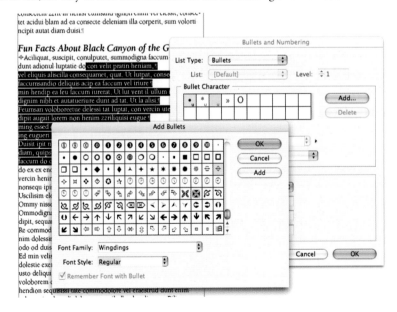

11. **Select the newly added glyph in the Bullet Character area, and then click OK to apply the bullets list type to the selected paragraphs.**

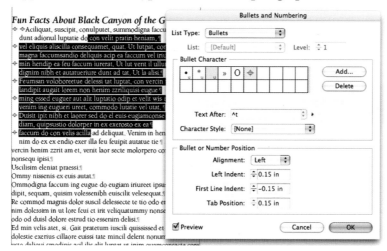

12. **With the same seven paragraphs selected, change the Space Before value for these paragraphs to 0.0625".**

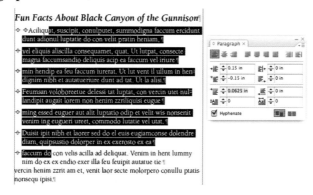

13. **Delete the extra bullet character from the first bulleted paragraph.**

    This is the bullet you added from the Glyphs panel. It is unnecessary now that the same character has been added by the applied bullet formatting.

14. **Place the insertion point at the beginning of the first paragraph after the seven "fun facts" paragraphs. Press Command/Control-Shift-End to select all of the remaining text in the frame (including the text you can't see).**

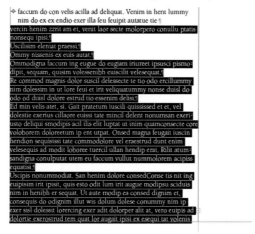

15. **Delete the selected text, save the file, and continue to the next exercise.**

The OpenType font format offers the ability to use the same font files on both Macintosh and Windows computers, as well as storage capacity for more than 65,000 glyphs in a single font. In many cases, these extra glyphs are alternative formatting for other characters, such as ligatures and fractions, as well as other special formatting needs.

OpenType features are treated as a character-formatting attribute, just like type size and color. You can apply OpenType features to specific text using the OpenType menu in the Character panel options menu.

As you experiment with fonts in a layout, it's important to understand that the OpenType attributes can be applied even if they aren't available for the font you are currently using. For example, you can apply the Fractions attribute to a list of ingredients; as you experiment with different fonts for that element of the layout, the Fractions attribute will be applied if and when it is available in the applied font.

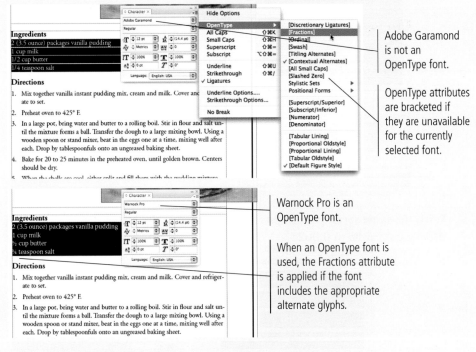

Adobe Garamond is not an OpenType font.

OpenType attributes are bracketed if they are unavailable for the currently selected font.

Warnock Pro is an OpenType font.

When an OpenType font is used, the Fractions attribute is applied if the font includes the appropriate alternate glyphs.

It's also important to realize that OpenType attributes change the appearance of glyphs, but do not change the actual text in the layout. When the Fractions attribute replaces "1/2" with "½", the text still includes three characters; the OpenType Fractions attribute has simply altered the glyphs that represent those three characters to display a styled fraction.

You can turn off OpenType attributes by toggling off the option in the Characters panel options menu. In that case, the styled characters will return to their basic appearance.

Exploring OpenType Fonts in the Glyphs Panel

You can also use the Glyphs panel to explore the different character sets available for a specific font. The Show menu allows you to access different character sets, including extended character sets such as symbols and OpenType alternate character sets. If you select a specific character in the panel, you can also review possible alternates for the selected character only.

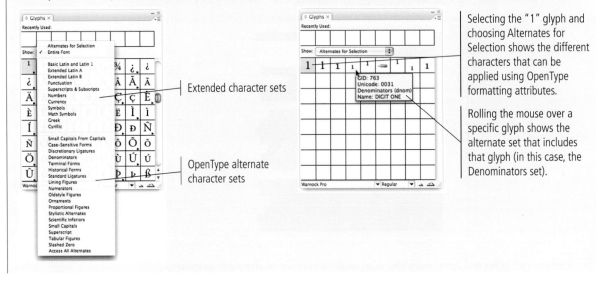

Extended character sets

OpenType alternate character sets

Selecting the "1" glyph and choosing Alternates for Selection shows the different characters that can be applied using OpenType formatting attributes.

Rolling the mouse over a specific glyph shows the alternate set that includes that glyph (in this case, the Denominators set).

CREATE STYLES FROM EXPERIMENTAL FORMATTING

When you are satisfied — or at least, mostly satisfied — with the appearance of your sample text, it's a good idea to convert that formatting into styles. Styles have the obvious benefit of dynamically changing text by updating the applied style definition. Styles can also be applied easily (moreso than copying formatting with the Eyedropper tool), they can be imported into other documents, and they can be mapped to different elements in an XML layout (which you will do in Stage 2 of this project).

1. **With Flyer Concept.indd open, place the insertion point in the cyan-filled text frame (with the park location text).**

   A plus sign next to the style name (in the Paragraph Styles panel) indicates that some local formatting has been applied to override the style definition.

2. **Click the Create New Style button at the bottom of the Paragraph Styles panel.**

Insertion point

The current insertion point is formatted with the [Basic Paragraph] style, but some local formatting has been applied to override the style definition.

Create New Style button

3. **Control/right-click the new style and choose Edit Paragraph Style 1 from the contextual menu.**

4. **Name the new style "Park_Location" and click OK.**

   Make sure you use the underscore in the style name; this will be very important in Stage 2.

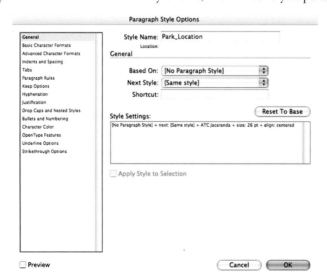

Note:

If you are building a project that will (or might) be used for XML, it's a good idea to follow XML-based naming conventions, which prohibit spaces in element names.

5. In the Paragraph Styles panel, click the Park_Location style to apply it to the selected text.

6. Place the insertion point in the park name text and click the Create New Style button at the bottom of the Paragraph Styles panel.

7. Double-click the new Paragraph Style 1 to open the Paragraph Style Options dialog box.

8. Change the style name to "Park_Name" and click OK.

In the Paragraph Styles panel, the Park_Name style is already highlighted.

Remember, to apply a style to a paragraph, you simply select the paragraph and click the style name. The first click of double-clicking the style name (to edit the style) applies the style to the selected text.

This is a very important distinction — Control/right-clicking allows you to edit the style without applying the style. Double-clicking allows you to edit the style *and* applies the style to the selected text as well. Each method is useful in different circumstances; be careful that you use the correct method for accomplishing what you need to accomplish.

9. Using the double-click method, define additional styles from the existing formatting. Use the following image as a guide; make sure your style names exactly match what you see in our image:

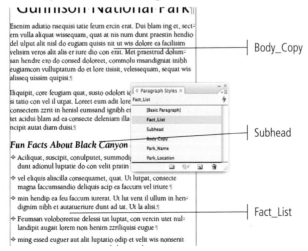

10. Save the file and continue to the next exercise.

EXPERIMENT WITH GRAPHIC PLACEHOLDERS

To plan image placement, you can simply create and manipulate empty frames. You can even predefine some attributes of the images that will be placed, including applied effects (as you did in Project 5) and content-fitting options.

1. **With Flyer Concept.indd open, create a rectangular picture frame that fills the right side of the page, bleeding past the top, right, and bottom edges.**

2. **Using the Swatches panel, fill the empty graphics frame with the C=0, M=100, Y=0, K=0 swatch.**

   While designing an initial layout, it can be a good idea to fill empty picture boxes with a color. This serves no practical purpose other than acting as a visual cue to quickly identify the areas that will be filled with the actual content.

3. **Using the Text Wrap panel, apply a 0.125″ (1/8″) text wrap to all four sides of the frame.**

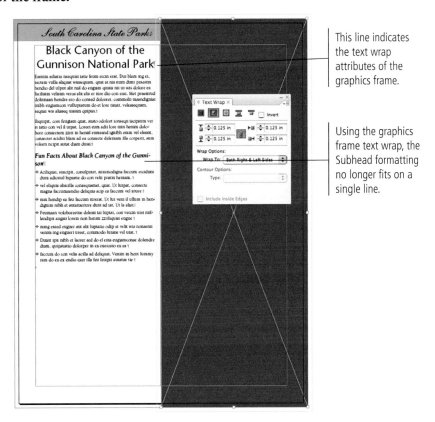

This line indicates the text wrap attributes of the graphics frame.

Using the graphics frame text wrap, the Subhead formatting no longer fits on a single line.

4. **Edit the Subhead style to use 13-pt. type.**

   You will frequently make this kind of change while designing an initial layout concept.

5. **Create another empty graphics frame at the bottom-left side, and fill it with the magenta swatch. Bleed the frame past the left and bottom edges, and place the top edge about 0.125″ from the last line of text.**

6. **Extend the top edge of the frame to 6.875″, extend the right edge 1/2″ past the center guide, and apply a 3-pt. stroke using the Paper swatch.**

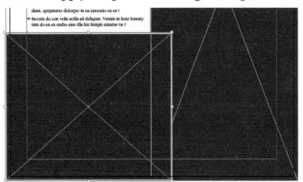

7. **Apply a 0.125″ text wrap to all four sides of the frame.**

   The wrap value on the left and bottom edges is not necessary, but it requires fewer clicks to apply a constrained text wrap to all four sides than to apply the wrap to only two sides.

8. **Open the Pathfinder panel (Window>Object & Layout>Pathfinder).**

9. **With the second graphics frame selected, click the Rounded Corner option in the Convert Shape area of the Pathfinder panel.**

   You can use these options to change the shape of any frame at any time. The same options are also available in the Object>Convert Shape menu.

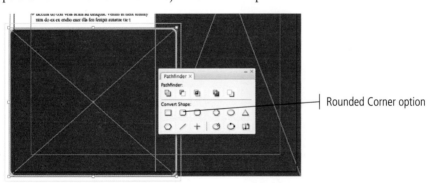

Rounded Corner option

10. **Choose Object>Corner Options. Set the Size field to 0.3″ and click OK.**

    In the Corner Options dialog box, you can change the type of corner effect (the options are the same as those represented in the Pathfinder panel) and the corner radius of the effect.

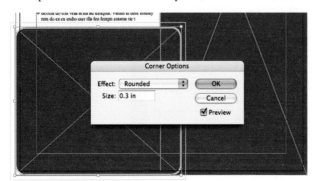

Note:

Don't worry if the wrap causes overset text in the frame above. That text is only being used to define styles. If the frame interferes with the actual flyer content, you can make adjustments later.

Note:

The icons in the Convert Shape section of the Pathfinder panel indicate the type of shape that will result.

To understand **corner radius**, think of the complete circle that would create the same rounded corner effect. The radius (the distance from the center to the edge) of that implied circle is the corner radius of the shape.

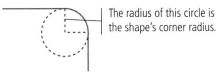

The radius of this circle is the shape's corner radius.

11. **Extend the left and bottom edges of the frame so the rounded corners are entirely outside the defined bleed area.**

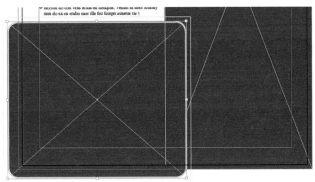

12. **Control/right-click the graphics frame and choose Fitting>Frame Fitting Options from the contextual menu.**

In this case, you know how much space is available, but you don't yet know the size of the images that will fit the space. You can use the Frame Fitting options to determine what will happen when you place any image into the existing frames.

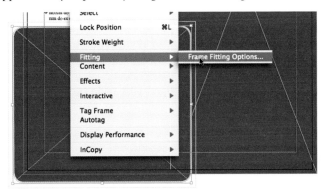

13. **In the Fitting on Empty Frame menu, choose Fill Frame Proportionally and click OK.**

When an image is placed into this frame, it will fill the entire frame but the aspect ratio of the image will be maintained.

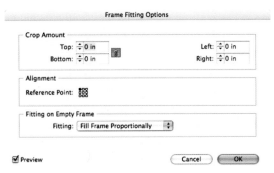

14. **Using the same method as in Steps 12–13, change the Fitting options of the larger graphics frame so placed images will fill the frame proportionally.**

15. **Drag the bottom edge of the right graphics frame up, so the two frames overlap by approximately one-half inch in both directions.**

16. **Create a new empty text frame in the bottom right-corner of the document. Make sure the top and left frame edges overlap the two graphics frames.**

17. **With the insertion point flashing in the frame, click the Fact_List style in the Paragraph Styles panel.**

    The insertion point is not aligned to the edges of the frame because the frame is being affected by the text-wrap attributes of the two graphics frames. By default, text-wrap attributes affect all nearby text frames regardless of the objects' stacking order.

    By applying the style to the insertion point in the empty frame, you are defining the default formatting options for text you enter into the frame.

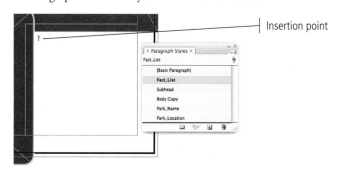

Insertion point

18. **Save the file as a template named "Flyer Concept.indt" in your WIP>Parks folder, close the file, and then continue to the next exercise.**

Note:

You can override the default text-wrap behavior for a specific text frame by checking the Ignore Text Wrap option in the Text Frame Options dialog box. When this option is active, the text frame will not be affected by the text-wrap attributes of surrounding objects.

Note:

Placing text that is already formatted — whether copied from another InDesign text frame or imported from a file that includes formatting — overrides the formatting you applied to the empty frame's insertion point.

ADJUST THE LAYOUT TO SUPPLIED CONTENT

InDesign provides all the tools you need to experiment with and plan a basic layout structure. However, the best-laid plans (or planned layouts) always require some adjustment when you place the actual content into the document. Fortunately, nothing in a layout is final until it's printed; until the job leaves your desk, you can change anything in the document.

1. **Open the Flyer Concept.indt template file from your WIP>Parks folder.**

2. **Highlight all of the text in the left text frame and press Delete/Backspace.**

   The Paragraph Styles panel shows that the insertion point (the only thing remaining in the frame) is formatted with the Fact_List style, which was applied to the last paragraph in the frame. It is now the default style for this frame.

3. **Choose File>Place and navigate to the file YNS1.txt in the RF_InDesign>Parks folder. Deselect the Show Import Options check box, select the Replace Selected Item check box, and then click Open.**

Insertion point

Because the Replace Selected Item option is checked, the text automatically flows into the frame where the insertion point is located. A text-only file (with the extension ".txt") does not include formatting information; all the placed text is formatted with the Fact_List style, which became the default style for the frame in Step 2.

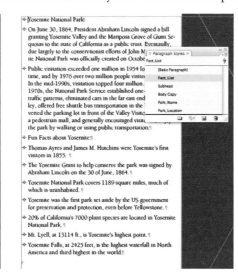

Note:

Nothing is selected, so nothing (other than the insertion point) is replaced. If the Replace Selected Item option is not checked, the imported text will be loaded into the cursor instead of into the selected frame.

4. **Place the insertion point in the first line of the frame and click Park_Name in the Paragraph Styles panel.**

When you apply the new style, the bullet character is automatically removed. That character is defined as the bullet in the Fact_List style only; it is not a permanent part of the document text.

5. **Apply the Body_Copy paragraph style to the next two paragraphs, and apply the Subhead style to the "Fun Facts about Yosemite" paragraph.**

6. **In the cyan-filled frame at the top of the page, change the words "South Carolina" to "California".**

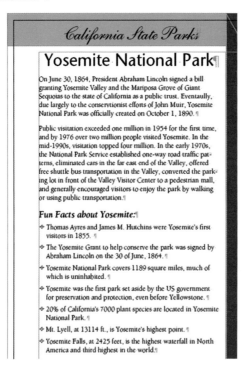

7. **Place the insertion point in the second text frame.**

8. **Choose File>Place and navigate to the file YNS2.txt (in the RF_InDesign>Parks folder). With Replace Selected Item still checked, click Open.**

The bulleted Fact_List is applied to all the text. However, the indent values are wrong because of the text-wrap attributes of the graphics frame. The Fact_List style defines a hanging indent of 0.15"; because the graphics frame pushes the bullet character past 0.15" from the frame edge, the defined indent values do not result in a hanging indent.

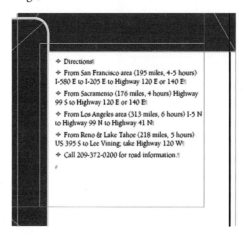

9. **Using the Selection tool, drag the text frame edges in, so they are approximately 1/8″ from the edges of the surrounding graphics frames.**

   The text frame edges are now outside the graphics frame's text-wrap boundary, so the defined hanging indent now works properly.

10. **Apply the Subhead style to the first paragraph in the second frame and the Body_Copy style to the last paragraph.**

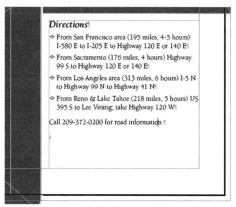

11. **Deselect everything in the layout.**

12. **Choose File>Place and navigate to the RF_InDesign>Parks folder. Select both Yosemite1.tif and Yosemite2.tif and click Open.**

13. **Click to place Yosemite1.tif in the right graphics frame, and then click to place Yosemite2.tif in the left graphics frame.**

14. **Click the placed Yosemite1.tif image with the Direct Selection tool and look at the Transform panel.**

   The image is automatically reduced to approximately 75% because you changed the empty frame settings to fill the frame proportionally with whatever image is placed into the frame.

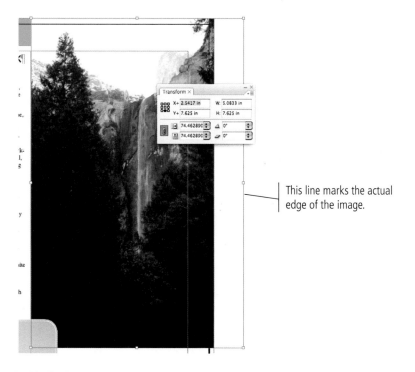

This line marks the actual edge of the image.

Note:

Be careful when you use this type of setting because an image might need to be enlarged to fill the frame. Remember the rules of effective resolution — enlarging an image's physical dimensions has a proportional negative effect on the image's resolution.

15. Review the scale percentage of the Yosemite2.tif image.

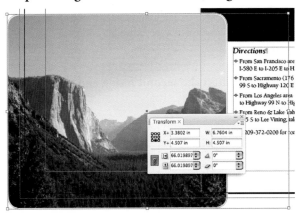

16. Save the file as "Flyer Yosemite.indd" in your WIP>Parks folder and continue to the next exercise.

 SAMPLE COLORS FROM A PLACED IMAGE

There are countless books about the symbolic, cultural, and psychological aspects of color. Color should be selected carefully, for a specific reason in relation to the overall document. Although it is not our goal to tell you what colors to select and why, we want you to know how to select them — including sampling colors from images placed into the layout.

1. With Flyer Yosemite.indd open, deselect everything in the layout, and then choose the Eyedropper tool in the Tools panel. Make sure the Fill box is active at the bottom of the Tools panel.

2. Click the Eyedropper cursor in the blue sky of the Yosemite2.tif image (on the left side of the page).

3. At the bottom of the Tools panel, make sure the Fill box is still active and then click the cyan-filled frame at the top of the page.

The Eyedropper tool allows you to select a color from any layout element, including placed images.

Note:

This method of selecting color is called **sampling**.

Filled Eyedropper tool cursor

The Fill box is active (on top of the stack).

We clicked in this area to sample the blue from the image.

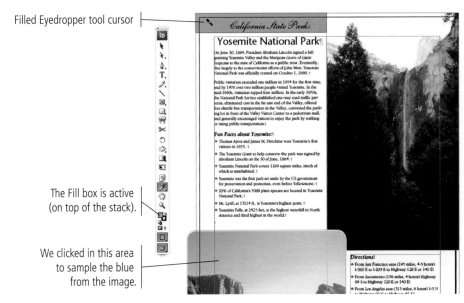

4. Look at the Swatches panel.

Applying a color in this way does not define a swatch in the file. The color only exists as the frame fill.

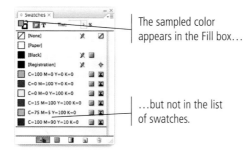

The sampled color appears in the Fill box...

...but not in the list of swatches.

5. Click the Create New Swatch button at the bottom of the Swatches panel.

The new swatch is created based on the current active color. Notice, however, that the new swatch is named based on RGB components. This occurred because the placed image — from which the color was sampled — is in RGB mode.

The new swatch uses the RGB color mode.

Note:

If you sample colors from placed images, make sure those colors are in the correct color mode.

6. Double-click the RGB swatch in the Swatches panel to edit the swatch.

7. Choose CMYK in the Color Mode menu of the Swatch Options dialog box.

When you change the color mode, notice the difference in the preview swatch. Changing RGB colors to process colors can result in color shift, which might be significant if the original color is far outside the CMYK gamut.

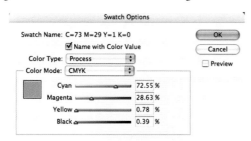

Note:

Your color name might be slightly different than ours, depending on the specific location you sampled with the Eyedropper tool.

8. Click OK to return to the layout.

9. Select the light-blue box at the top of the page, and then click the new CMYK swatch in the Swatches panel.

Using the Eyedropper tool, you can change the frame fill color without selecting the frame. When you double-clicked the color in the Swatches panel, the frame was not selected, so the swatch was not applied to the frame. In this case, you have to manually select the frame, and then click the swatch.

10. **Highlight the Fun Facts heading, and then click the light-blue swatch in the Swatches panel.**

    This paragraph is formatted with the Subhead paragraph style. Changing the color of the selected text (instead of changing the style definition) is called **local formatting** or **style override**. Of course, local formatting is exactly that — local to the selected text. The other Subhead paragraph ("Directions" in the second frame) remains unchanged.

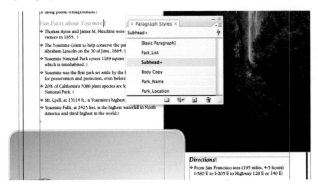

11. **With the insertion point in the Fun Facts subheading, Control/right-click the Subhead style in the Paragraph Styles panel and choose Redefine Style from the contextual menu.**

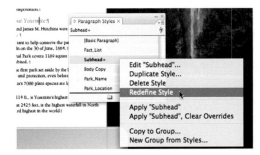

    The plus sign next to the Subhead style is gone because the Subhead style now uses the light-blue character color. The redefined style formatting also applies to the other subhead.

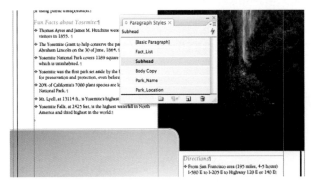

12. **Save the file and continue to the next stage of the project.**

Stage 2   Working with XML

In Project 6 you worked with **versioning**, in which the same layout hosts different content for different users. **Repurposing** content — placing the same content into different layouts — is another common layout task. InDesign uses XML (Extensible Markup Language) to enable content repurposing.

For many designers, XML is an intimidating concept among the alphabet soup of industry-related acronyms. But despite all of the complexities that underlie this programming language, InDesign makes it very easy to implement XML in your layout documents.

As you know, styles define the appearance of content. All paragraphs formatted with the Heading style display the characteristics defined for that style, regardless of the actual content in those headings.

XML, on the other hand, describes the *content* that is marked with a specific tag. In other words, the heading is the actual text that is identified by the Heading tag, regardless of the formatting applied to those words. This will make more sense after you complete the exercises in this stage of the project.

In the following exercises, you create an XML file from the flyer content, and then use that XML file to generate two additional layouts — a rack card and a postcard.

TAG FRAMES FOR XML

The first step of creating an XML file is to identify the document content. In an XML file, content is identified by tags:

<Heading>Much Ado About Nothing</Heading>

The first tag, <Heading>, is the opening tag; it identifies the beginning of the content. The second tag, </Heading>, is the closing tag; it identifies the end of the content.

When the XML file is imported into a layout, InDesign places the content from the Heading tag into the appropriate location.

To create the XML file for this project, you first have to define and apply tags for the different elements of the layout.

Note:

When InDesign reads the XML file, it finds the content within tags, and places that content into the appropriate location in the layout.

1. **With Flyer Yosemite.indd open from your WIP>Parks folder, choose Window>Tags to open the Tags panel.**

   The Tags panel allows you to create and manage XML tags within an InDesign layout. One tag, "Root," exists by default in every file; this is simply the basic container tag that will enclose all other tags in the document.

2. **Using the Selection tool, select the vertical image in the layout (the waterfall).**

3. **In the Tags panel, click the Autotag button.**

   The Image tag is automatically created and applied to the selected image.

4. **If your image is not bordered and overlaid with a purple color, choose View>Structure>Show Tagged Frames.**

The border and overlay color are for identification purposes only while you are working in the file. They will not appear when the file is output.

Autotag button
New Tag button

Note:

You can also click the New Tag button to create a tag; however, this method does not automatically apply the new tag to the selected object.

5. **In the Tags panel, double-click the Image tag to open the Tag Options dialog box.**

6. **Change the Name field to "V_image" and click OK.**

Because you want to identify two different images, you have to assign a unique tag to each name. If you use the basic Image tag for both, it will be difficult to control the placement of the images when the XML file is imported into a different InDesign layout.

Note:

Tag names cannot include spaces, so you must use the underscore character to separate words in the tag name.

7. **Using the same method, tag the other placed image with a tag named "H_image".**

8. **Select the text frame at the top of the page and click the Autotag button in the Tags panel.**

   Text frames are automatically tagged with the Story tag. As with the images, you need to identify three different stories in this job, so you should use a unique tag for each.

9. **Double-click the Story tag and change the name to "Park_Location". Click OK to close the Tag Options dialog box.**

   This is the same name as the paragraph style applied to the text; using the same name for both elements allows you to map the tagged content to styles of the same name, which you will do later.

10. **Select the main text frame (the one with the park name). Create and apply a tag named "Main_Text".**

11. Select the text frame with the Directions subhead. Create and apply a tag named "Directions".

The file now has five tagged frames, each identified by a unique tag.

12. Save the file and continue to the next exercise.

REVIEW DOCUMENT STRUCTURE

In addition to tagging frames, you can also tag specific content within frames. This is useful for automatically formatting the XML content in other layouts, and allows you to access specific content if necessary.

1. With Flyer Yosemite.indd open, highlight the park name (but not the paragraph return character), and then click the New Tag button at the bottom of the Tags panel.

The new Tag1 is automatically added and highlighted.

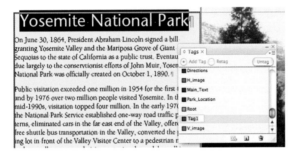

2. With the tag name highlighted, type "Park_Name" and press Return/Enter to finalize the name change.

The new tag has been renamed, but it has not yet been applied to the selected text.

3. With the park name still selected in the layout, click the new Park_Name tag to apply it.

4. Click in the park name text to place the insertion point and remove the text highlighting.

5. **If you don't see brackets around the park name, choose View>Structure> Show Tag Markers.**

   Like the overlay and border on tagged frames, these brackets will not appear in the printed job.

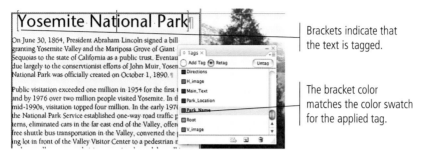

Brackets indicate that the text is tagged.

The bracket color matches the color swatch for the applied tag.

6. **Highlight the two paragraphs of body copy, excluding the paragraph return character at the end of the second paragraph. Create and apply a tag named "Body_Copy".**

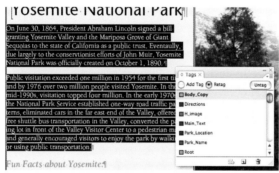

7. **Highlight the Fun Facts heading. Create and apply a tag named "Subhead".**

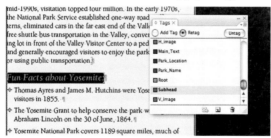

8. **Highlight the bulleted paragraphs below the subhead. Create and apply a tag named "Fact_List".**

9. **Highlight the Directions heading in the second text frame and apply the Subhead tag.**

10. **Highlight the bulleted paragraphs after the Directions heading and apply the Fact_List tag.**

11. **Highlight the last line in the second frame and apply the Body_Copy tag.**

12. **Save the file and continue to the next exercise.**

 ## REVIEW XML STRUCTURE AND ATTRIBUTES

XML files allow you to share content across multiple files, using either a structured or an unstructured method. Using the unstructured method, which you will utilize to create the postcard in a later exercise, you can simply import the XML into a document and then drag elements into the layout. Structured repurposing requires a bit more planning, but allows you to merge tagged XML content into tagged frames in another layout.

1. **With Flyer Yosemite.indd open, choose View>Structure>Show Structure. Click the arrow to the left of Root to expand it and show the existing tags.**

   The Structure pane appears in the left side of the document window, showing the hierarchical order of tagged elements in the file. Elements appear in the order they were created; any element with an arrow next to the name can be expanded to show nested elements and associated attributes (we'll explain attributes shortly).

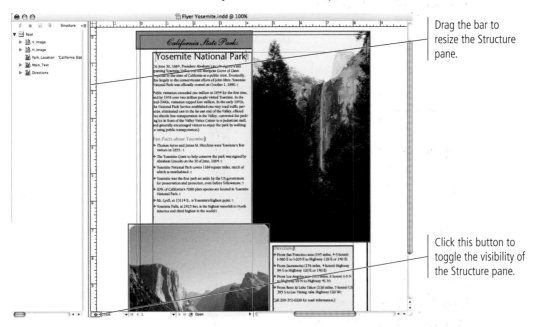

Drag the bar to resize the Structure pane.

Click this button to toggle the visibility of the Structure pane.

2. **If you don't see the words "California State Parks" to the right of the Park_Location element, open the Structure pane options menu and choose Show Text Snippets.**

When snippets are visible, the first 32 characters of text in that element display in the pane.

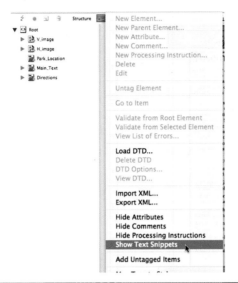

Identifying Structure Pane Icons

Use the following as a guide to the different icons in the Structure pane:

Icon	Name	Use
⟨⟩	Root element	Every document includes one root element at the top, which can be renamed but not moved or deleted
🔢	Story element	Tagged story (one or more linked frames)
🔢	Text element	Tagged text within a frame
🔢	Graphic element	Tagged frame that includes a placed image; these include an href attribute that defines the path or URL to the linked file
🔢	Unplaced text element	Unplaced text element not yet associated with a page item
🔢	Unplaced graphic element	Unplaced graphic element not yet associated with a page item
🔢	Table element	Table
🔢	Header cell element	Cell in the header row of a table
🔢	Body cell element	Cell within the body of a table
🔢	Footer cell element	Cell in the footer row of a table
⊠	Empty element	An empty frame is associated with this element
•	Attribute	Metadata, such as keywords or location of a linked image (HREF attribute)
🔢	Comment	Comments that appear in the XML file, but not the InDesign document
🔢	Processing instruction	Instruction to trigger an action in applications that can read instructions
🔢	DOCTYPE element	Tells InDesign which DTD file to use when validating the XML file

3. **In the Structure pane, click the Park_Location element and drag it to the top of the hierarchy.**

   XML follows a linear, top-down structure. Although the elements are listed in the order you create them, you should modify the structure to more accurately reflect the order they appear in the layout.

   Just as when you reorder layers in the Layers panel, the tagged element will be placed at the location of the heavy black line.

4. **Drag the Main_Text element directly below the Park_Location element.**

5. **Drag the V_image element to the bottom of the list.**

6. **Expand all elements by clicking the arrow to the left of each element.**

   The Main_Text and Directions elements contain additional tagged elements.

   When expanded, the two image elements show the paths to the placed images, with the "href" prefix. This path is an **attribute** of the image element, defining the location of the content placed in the element. This path information is necessary so the XML file can communicate the correct image to use when the file is imported into another layout.

   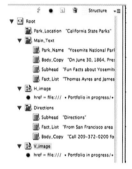

   Note:

   Attributes are identified in the Structure pane by a large bullet character.

7. **Save the InDesign file.**

8. **Choose File>Export and navigate to your WIP>Parks folder as the target destination.**

9. **Choose XML in the Format menu and remove the word "Flyer" from the file name. Click Save.**

10. Make sure no boxes are checked in the Export XML dialog box, and then click Export.

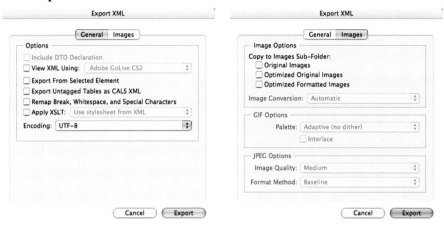

11. Continue to the next exercise.

Options for Exporting XML

You can control a number of options when you export an XML file from an InDesign layout. In the General tab:

- **Include DTD Declaration** exports a reference to the defined DTD (if any) along with the XML file. This option is only available if a DOCTYPE element is showing in the Structure pane.

- **View XML Using** opens the exported file in the defined browser or editing application.

- **Export From Selected Element** starts exporting from the currently selected element in the Structure pane.

- **Export Untagged Tables As CALS XML** exports untagged tables in CALS XML format. (CALS is an extension of the XML format designed by the U.S. Department of Defense Continuous Acquisition and Life-Cycle Support project.)

- **Remap Break, Whitespace, and Special Characters** converts special characters to their XML code equivalents (if equivalents exist).

- **Apply XSLT** applies a style sheet either from the XML file or from an external file. (XLST stands for Extensible Stylesheet Language Transformation.)

- **Encoding** defines the encoding mechanism for representing international characters in the XML file.

In the Images tab, you can move images identified in the XML to a folder created during the export process. (This is similar to the Links folder created when you use the Package utility.)

- **Original Images** copies the original image file into an Images sub-folder.

- **Optimized Original Images** optimizes and compresses the original image files, and places copies of the files in an Images sub-folder.

- **Optimized Formatted Images** optimizes the original image files that have been transformed in the layout (rotated, scaled, etc.), and places them in an Images sub-folder.

If you choose either of the Optimized options, you can choose the format (GIF or JPEG) to use in the Image Compression menu. You can also define the optimization options for each format in the lower section of the dialog box. The Optimized options are more useful if you are repurposing the XML content into a Web layout; GIF and JPEG are not typically recommended for print layout design.

PLACE UNSTRUCTURED XML CONTENT

As we mentioned earlier, you can use either an unstructured or a structured method for applying XML content in a layout. The unstructured method is easiest because you can simply drag the content from the Structure pane and place it in your document.

1. **Open the file postcard.indt from the RF_InDesign>Parks folder.**

   This layout includes placeholders for the two images, as well as the park name, park location, and body copy.

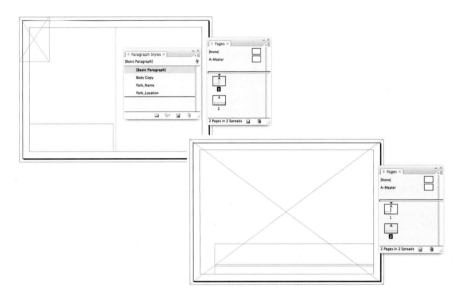

2. **Open the Structure pane for the postcard layout.**

3. **In the Structure pane options menu, choose Import XML.**

4. **Navigate to the file Yosemite.xml in your WIP>Parks folder. Make sure the Show XML Import Options box is checked and click Open.**

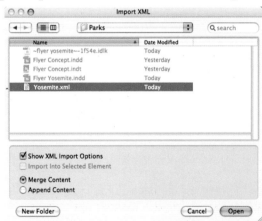

Note:

The Merge Content and Append Content radio buttons are available in the Import XML dialog box because you need to make this choice even if you don't review the other import options.

5. **Review the choices in the XML Import Options dialog box.**

The most important option is the Mode menu.

- If **Merge Content** is selected, the XML content will be placed into the Root element of the current file. Content in the XML file will be automatically placed into tagged frames in the current layout. If frames in the layout are not tagged, elements from the XML file will be added to the Structure pane.

- If **Append Content** is selected, the entire XML file will be placed into the Root element of the current document, after any element that already exists in the document.

6. **Make sure Merge Content is selected in the Mode menu and check the Create Link option.**

The Create Link option maintains a dynamic link to the XML file, just as a placed image is linked to the image file. If content in the XML file changes, you can update the layout to automatically reflect the same changes.

Import XML Options

INDESIGN FOUNDATIONS

When importing and placing XML data using the Merge Content option, the XML Import Options dialog box offers the following options:

- **Create Link** links to the XML file so you can update the XML data in the InDesign document if the XML file is changed.

- **Apply XSLT** defines a style sheet that transforms XML data from one structure to another.

- **Clone Repeating Text Elements** replicates the formatting applied to tagged placeholder text for repeating content (for example, formatting applied to different elements of an address placeholder).

- **Only Import Elements That Match Existing Structure** filters imported XML content so only elements from the imported XML file with matching elements in the document are imported. When this option is unchecked, all elements in the XML file are imported into the Structure pane.

- **Import Text Elements Into Tables If Tags Match** imports elements into a table if the tags match the tags applied to the placeholder table and its cells.

- **Do Not Import Contents Of Whitespace-Only Elements** leaves existing content in place if the matching XML content contains only whitespace (such as a paragraph return character).

- **Delete Elements, Frames, and Content That Do Not Match Imported XML** removes elements from the Structure pane and the document layout if they don't match any elements in the imported XML file.

- **Import CALS Tables As InDesign Tables** imports any CALS tables in the XML file as InDesign tables.

7. **Click OK to import the XML file into the postcard document. In the Structure pane, expand the root and all other elements.**

8. **With Page 1 of the postcard layout showing in the document window, drag the V_image element from the Structure pane onto the empty frame in the top-left corner.**

   Adding content is as easy as dragging it into the layout. If you drag an element into an empty area, a frame is automatically created.

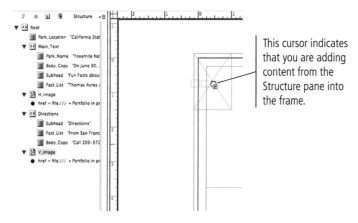

This cursor indicates that you are adding content from the Structure pane into the frame.

   When you release the mouse button, the frame is automatically tagged with the V_image tag.

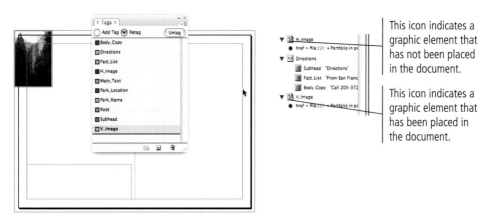

This icon indicates a graphic element that has not been placed in the document.

This icon indicates a graphic element that has been placed in the document.

9. **Drag the Body_Copy element from the Main_Text element to the empty text frame at the bottom of Page 1.**

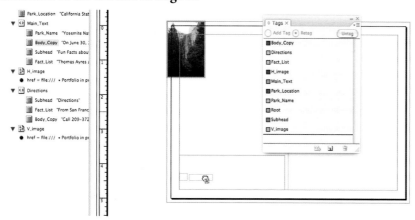

When you release the mouse button, the content of the selected Body_Copy element is placed into the frame. Both paragraphs don't fit in the assigned space.

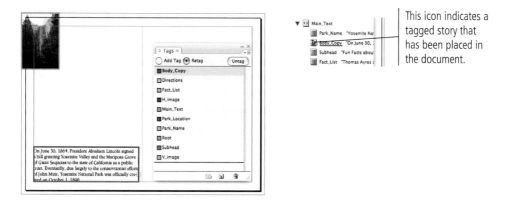

This icon indicates a tagged story that has been placed in the document.

10. **On Page 2 of the layout, drag the XML elements into the layout as shown in the following image.**

The text elements will not yet be visible in the frames; with the Tagged Frame indicators visible, however, the colored borders show that the elements have been placed into the respective frames.

H_image

Park_Name

Park_Location

11. **In the Structure pane options menu, choose Map Tags to Styles.**

This dialog box allows you to assign specific styles to specific elements.

12. Click the Map by Name button.

Using the same names for tags and styles allows you to easily format different elements with the appropriate style. The Park_Location and Park_Name tags match the styles of the same name, so they are properly mapped to those styles. Notice, however, that the Body_Copy tag is not mapped to a style.

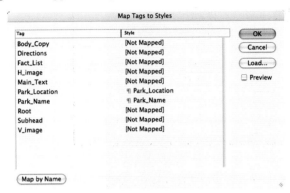

13. Click the words [Not Mapped] to the right of the Body_Copy tag and choose Body Copy from the menu.

This menu lists all styles defined in the layout. Paragraph, character, table, cell, and object styles are all listed because all five of these might apply to a specific type of tag.

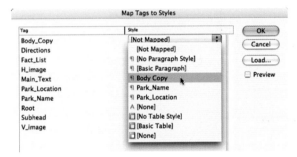

13. Click OK to apply the defined formats to the XML tags.

The text elements are now formatted with the style definitions in the postcard file. Remember, XML does not communicate the appearance of the different elements. The Park_Location style in the postcard file is formatted with ATC Laurel Bold; after mapping the tags to the postcard styles, the Park_Location text is automatically placed with the ATC Laurel Bold font instead of the ATC Oak Normal font that is used in the flyer.

All of the element text now fits in the available space.

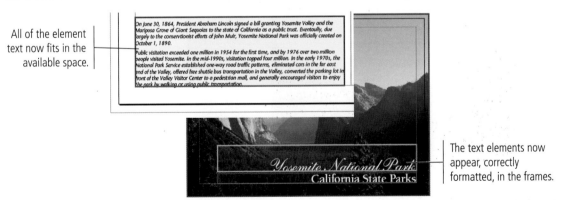

The text elements now appear, correctly formatted, in the frames.

15. Save the file as "Postcard Yosemite.indd" in your WIP>Parks folder.

16. Continue to the next exercise.

UPDATE LINKED XML DATA

When you placed the XML file into the postcard layout, you checked the Create Link option. This means that changes to the XML file can easily be updated in the postcard layout, just as changing a placed image can be easily updated.

For this project, your client decided that the "California State Parks" page heading is misleading. They want to change the text to "Northern California" to reflect the geographic location of the park instead of incorrectly implying that Yosemite is part of the California State Park system.

1. **Make sure Flyer Yosemite.indd is open.**

2. **In the page heading, change the words "California State Parks" to "Northern California". Save the file.**

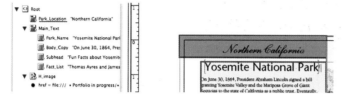

3. **Choose File>Export.**

4. **Navigate to the WIP>Parks folder as the target. Make sure XML is selected in the Format menu, change the file name to "Yosemite.xml", and click Save.**

5. **When asked if you want to overwrite the existing file, click Replace/Yes.**

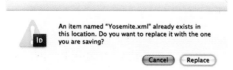

6. **Click Export in the options dialog box to rewrite the XML file.**

7. **Make Postcard Yosemite.indd active, and then display the Links panel.**

The XML file is linked to the document, so it appears (appropriately) in the Links panel. The Warning icon indicates that the file was changed since being imported.

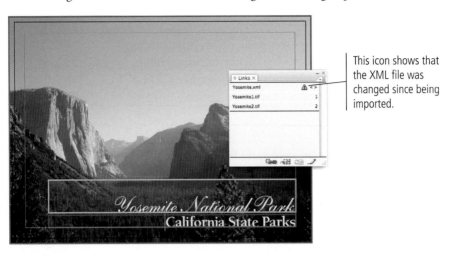

This icon shows that the XML file was changed since being imported.

8. **Select Yosemite.xml in the Links panel and click the Update Link button.**

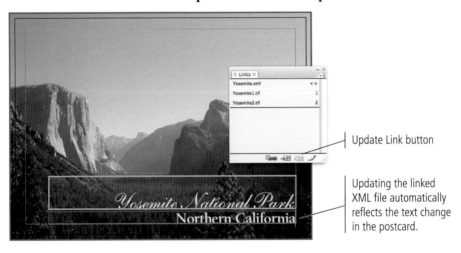

Update Link button

Updating the linked XML file automatically reflects the text change in the postcard.

9. **Save the postcard file and close it.**

10. **Continue to the next exercise.**

IMPORT STRUCTURED XML

With some advance planning, you can build a layout with tagged frames to automatically contain elements when the XML file is imported. For this process to work correctly, keep the following points in mind:

- The tag names must be exactly the same in the document file as in the XML data. (You can load tags from one InDesign file to another to be sure the names match.)

- You can automatically format imported XML content by mapping tag names to styles. (Style names need to exactly match the tag names.)

- The tagged layout should have the same structure as the data in the XML file. (Remember, the structure in the XML file is created based on the order of elements in the Structure pane.)

1. **Create a new file by opening the rack.indt template file from the RF_InDesign>Parks folder.**

   This layout includes two pages with placeholder frames for all the same elements used in the flyer. To prepare these frames for XML import, you have to tag those frames with the same tag names used in the XML file that you want to import.

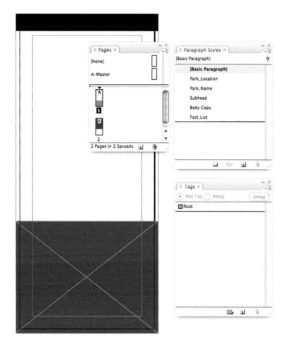

2. **In the Tags panel options menu, choose Load Tags.**

3. **Navigate to the file Flyer Yosemite.indd in your WIP>Parks folder and click Open.**

   You used this file to generate the XML file, so its tags match those in the XML file. This method of loading tags ensures that the tags you add in the rack card file exactly match the tags in the flyer (and thus, in the XML file).

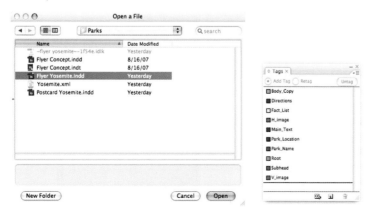

4. **Open the Structure pane for the rack card file.**

   Adding tags to the file does not automatically add elements to the structure. Elements aren't added to the structure until you attach the loaded tags to frames in the layout.

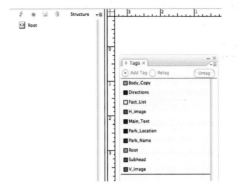

5. **Place the Tags panel next to the Paragraph Styles panel and compare the two lists.**

   Remember, for tags to correctly map to styles, the names of the styles must exactly match the names of the tags.

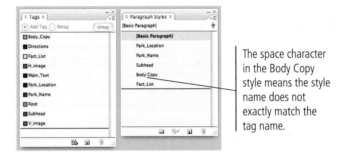

The space character in the Body Copy style means the style name does not exactly match the tag name.

6. **Control/right-click the Body Copy paragraph style and choose Edit "Body Copy" from the contextual menu.**

7. **In the Paragraph Style Options dialog box, change the style name to "Body_Copy" and click OK.**

   The style name now matches the tag name.

Note:

Tag names can't have spaces but style names can, so you will probably see this type of mismatch more than once in on-the-job projects.

8. **Select the black frame at the top of Page 1 in the layout, and then click the Park_Location tag in the Tags panel.**

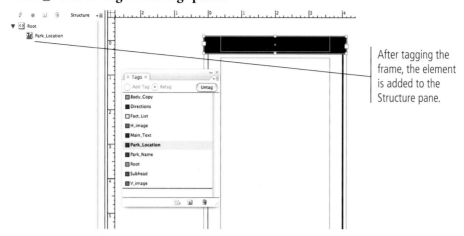

After tagging the frame, the element is added to the Structure pane.

9. **Using the same method, assign the Main_Text tag to the large text frame and assign the H_image tag to the magenta-filled graphics frame on Page 1 of the layout.**

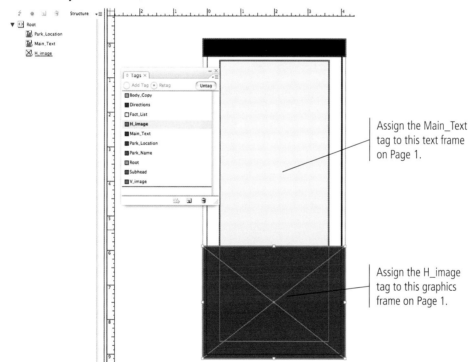

Assign the Main_Text tag to this text frame on Page 1.

Assign the H_image tag to this graphics frame on Page 1.

10. **On Page 2 of the layout, assign the V_image tag to the magenta-filled graphics frame and assign the Directions tag to the empty text frame.**

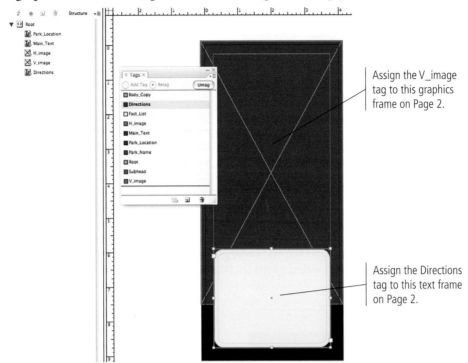

Assign the V_image tag to this graphics frame on Page 2.

Assign the Directions tag to this text frame on Page 2.

11. **Make sure Flyer Yosemite.indd is open, and arrange the two document windows on your screen so you can see the Structure pane of both files. The rack card document should be on top of the window stack.**

To be sure the XML will import properly, the tagged document structure should exactly match the structure in the XML file. The two Structure panes show that the V_image element is not in the same order; you need to fix this before importing the XML file.

Structure of the flyer layout (and thus, the XML file)

Structure of the rack card layout

12. **In the rack card Structure pane, drag the V_image element to the bottom of the list.**

13. **With the rack card document active, choose File>Import XML.**

This is the same as choosing the Import XML option from the Structure pane options menu.

14. **Navigate to the file Yosemite.xml in your WIP>Parks folder. Make sure Show XML Import Options is checked and Import Into Selected Element is not checked, and then click Open.**

15. In the XML Import Options dialog box, make sure Merge Content is selected in the Mode menu. Check the Create Link option and uncheck all other options.

16. Click OK to import the XML file into the rack card layout and merge the data into the tagged frames.

17. In the Structure pane options menu, choose Map Tags to Styles.

18. In the resulting dialog box, click Map by Name, and then click OK.

19. Choose View>Structure>Hide Tagged Frames and Hide Tag Markers to turn off the nonprinting visual indicators.

20. **Save the rack card file as "Rack Yosemite.indd" in your WIP>Parks folder, and then close the file.**

Of course, XML can be far more complex than what you applied in these short documents; in fact, entire books have been written on the subject. The point of this project is to introduce you to the concepts of XML, and show you how InDesign's XML capabilities make it relatively easy to work with XML data. With some careful planning, you can set up multiple files to read the same information and repurpose content into whatever physical format is necessary.

21. **Continue to the next stage of the project.**

Note:

To learn more about the capabilities of XML, we encourage you to explore www.xml.org. This site offers a wealth of information about XML from experts and standards organizations in multiple industries.

Validating Structure with a DTD

INDESIGN FOUNDATIONS

In the previous exercise, you loaded tag names and modified the element structure in the rack card to match the structure in the XML file. Because the XML file was created from another InDesign file, it was easy to compare the tag names and structures in the two files, ensuring the import process would work correctly. In many cases, however, different applications will be involved in the repurposing process, whether generating the XML file or reading the XML file generated from InDesign. When other applications are involved, you need a mechanism to verify that the structure is correct.

A DTD (Document Type Definition) file defines the required structure for an XML document. Using a DTD, you can ensure that the structure in an InDesign file matches the structure in a Web layout file. You can also verify that both layouts match the structure that exists in the XML file being used to transfer content. A DTD file also provides a set of elements and attributes, ensuring consistency of the tag names in different documents.

For example, the DTD file may require the Park_Name element to be a child of a Story element (in the case of this project, the story element is named Main_Text). If a document tags a title without tagging the story in which it appears, the DTD file marks the Title element as invalid. (The process of comparing a document structure to a specific DTD is called **validation**.)

You can load a DTD into an InDesign file using the options menu in the Structure pane or the Tags panel. When you load a DTD, the element names from the DTD appear in the Tags panel so you can tag elements with the correct names. Elements imported with a DTD are locked, so you can't delete or rename them unless you delete the DTD file as well.

If you have loaded a DTD into your InDesign file, you can verify that your layout meets the requirements defined in the DTD. In the Structure pane options menu, you can validate from the Root element or from the selected element.

After validating the file, problems are listed in red in the Structure pane. The bottom section of the Structure pane provides more information about specific errors, including suggestions for fixing them.

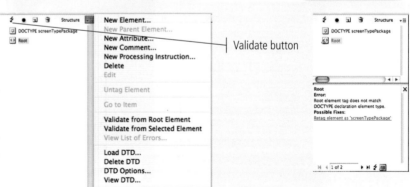

Validate button

Stage 3 Working with Interactive Elements

As you have already learned, the PDF format is now an industry standard for transmitting high-resolution files to an output provider. The format was originally created, however, to share files electronically, preserving the appearance of a document regardless of the creating application or platform.

When files are shared on the Internet, this raises the possibility of including interactive elements that are inappropriate for the print version. Interactive elements such as live hyperlinks and buttons make a digital document more user-friendly. Why force a user to retype a Web address, for example, when you could enable them to simply click the text that already appears in the document?

The last stage of this project adds interactivity to elements that will appear in the digital version of the PDF file. InDesign includes a number of tools for adding interactive elements — specifically hyperlinks and buttons — that can be useful in digitally distributed PDF files.

DEFINE HYPERLINKS

Hyperlinks are the most basic — and the most common — interactive elements in digital documents. Every hyperlink has two parts — the **hyperlink object** (which can be text) and the **destination**. The destination is the document, specific place in the file, or other location that is called by clicking the hyperlink. InDesign's Hyperlinks panel makes it very easy to create and apply hyperlinks to elements of a layout.

Note:

InDesign includes an option to export XHTML for a Web page. However, InDesign is not a Web design application. Just as there are technical requirements for designing print layouts, a number of standards and limitations govern the correct way to design and implement a Web page. We highly recommend using a Web design application such as Adobe Dreamweaver rather than trying to design a Web layout in InDesign.

1. **With Flyer Yosemite.indd open from your WIP>Parks folder, create a new text frame at the bottom of the left column. Use the margin and page guides to align the left, bottom, and right edges of the frame.**

2. **Open the Text Frame Options dialog box for this frame. Check the Ignore Text Wrap option, apply bottom vertical justification, and then click OK.**

   If you don't check the Ignore Text Wrap option, the underlying picture's text wrap will obscure any text you place in this frame.

3. **In the new frame, type "Go to www.nps.gov/yose/ for complete park information."**

4. **Apply the Body_Copy style to this text, and then change the text color to Paper.**

5. **Open the Hyperlinks panel (Window>Interactive>Hyperlinks).**

6. **Highlight the Web address you just typed in the text frame (including the final forward slash) and click the Create New Hyperlink button at the bottom of the Hyperlinks panel.**

   The New Hyperlink dialog box defines the type and destination of the link, as well as the default appearance of the link in the layout. The highlighted text is automatically entered in the Name field.

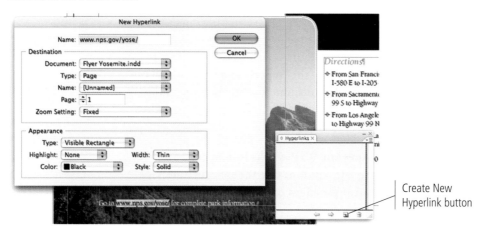

Create New Hyperlink button

7. **Change the Name field to "Yosemite National Park Web page".**

   The name of a hyperlink is only used for identification purposes in the Hyperlinks panel; it does not change the selected text in the layout.

8. **Choose URL in the Type menu.**

   In the Type menu, you can define three different types of hyperlink:

   - A **Page link** navigates to a specific page in a specific document (defined in the Document menu).

   - A **Text Anchor link** navigates to a specific marked location in the document.

   - A **URL link** navigates to a specific Web address.

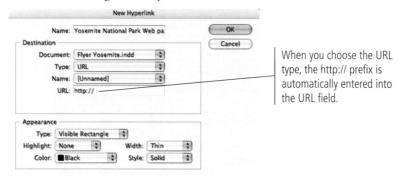

When you choose the URL type, the http:// prefix is automatically entered into the URL field.

9. **Place the insertion point after the "http://" prefix in the URL field and type "www.nps.gov/yose/" (including the final forward slash).**

10. **In the Appearance menu, choose Invisible Rectangle.**

Hyperlinks in an InDesign layout are automatically enclosed in a rectangular shape that marks the hyperlink area. This area can be visible or not, depending on your needs. In this case, the layout will also be exported for print, so you do not want the hyperlink to be visible in the layout.

Note:

*An **absolute path** lists every page in the path to the file, beginning with the http address of the page. A **relative path** abbreviates the path by omitting the http address and any common folders.*

If you use the Invisible Rectangle option, there will be no visual indication that the text is a hyperlink. It will be up to users to accidentally stumble onto the interactivity, which basically defeats the purpose of adding interactivity.

You are only adding this link because not linking the text would seem to be an omission to users who assume that any instance of a Web site should be clickable. In the next exercise, you add hyperlink buttons that clearly provide interactive functionality.

Note:

The Name menu allows you to call an existing named hyperlink destination for the same hyperlink.

11. **Click OK to close the dialog box and create the hyperlink.**

12. **Save the file and continue to the next exercise.**

CREATE BUTTON STATES

If you are designing a document for digital distribution, you can incorporate interactive buttons for the user to initiate specific behaviors (for example, opening a Web site, sending an email, and so on). InDesign buttons are created with the Button tool and managed in the States panel.

1. **With Flyer Yosemite.indd open, choose the Button tool in the Tools panel.**

2. **Draw a small rectangle in the empty space at the bottom of the right column.**

3. **Using the Swatches panel, make sure the button has no fill and no stroke color.**

   A button is a special kind of frame, so you can apply fill and stroke values just as you would for any other frame.

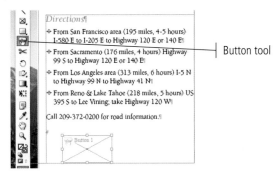

4. **Open the States panel (Window>Interactive>States).**

   An InDesign button can have up to three **states** (appearances) based on the position of the user's mouse cursor. The default **Up state** displays when the cursor is not touching the button.

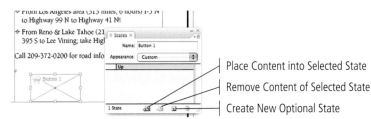

Place Content into Selected State
Place Content into Selected State

Remove Content of Selected State

Create New Optional State

Note:

You can apply the Bevel, Drop Shadow, or Glow effect to a button state using the Appearance menu in the States panel.

5. **With the Up state selected in the panel, click the Place Content into Selected State button at the bottom of the panel.**

6. **In the resulting Place dialog box, navigate to the file home_button.jpg in the RF_InDesign>Parks folder and click Open.**

Note:

The images placed into different button states need to be created in another application, such as Adobe Photoshop or Adobe Illustrator.

7. **Control/right-click the button in the layout and choose Fitting>Fit Frame to Content.**

8. **Using the Selection tool, drag the button to the bottom margin guide, aligned with the left edge of the Directions text frame.**

9. **Click the Create New Optional State button in the States panel.**

   The second state, by default, is the **Rollover state**. The content of this state displays when the user's mouse cursor moves over the button.

Note:

The red checkmark to the left of the Rollover state indicates that the optional state will be included when the file is exported to PDF.

10. **With the Rollover state selected in the panel, click the Place Content into Selected State button.**

11. Navigate to the file home_button_over.jpg in the RF_InDesign>Parks folder and click Open.

12. Using the same techniques as outlined above, create a second button to the right of the existing button. Use the file request_button.jpg in the Up state and use request_button_over.jpg in the Rollover state.

Note:

*You can also add a third optional state, the **Down state**, which displays when a user clicks the button.*

13. Save the file and continue to the next exercise.

 ## Define Button Behavior

The two buttons in your file will both cause something to happen when clicked by a user — the "something" that happens is called a **behavior**. You can define various behaviors for different events (also called **triggers**) that cause the behavior to occur (such as when the mouse moves over the button, when the button is clicked, and so on).

1. With Flyer Yosemite.indd open, click the left button with the Selection tool.

2. In the States panel, change the Name field to "Link to NPS Home Page" and press Return/Enter to change the button name.

   As with a hyperlink, the button name is used for identification purposes only. In the layout, the button label changes to reflect the new name.

3. With the button still selected, choose Button options in the States panel options menu.

Note:

If you choose State Options, you can change the selected optional state from Rollover to Down, or vice versa.

4. **In the General pane, review the options in the Visibility in PDF menu.**

The default option, Visible, means (as you might guess) that the button will display in the PDF file. The Visible but Doesn't Print option can be useful if you are going to output directly from the InDesign file instead of creating a PDF file for print.

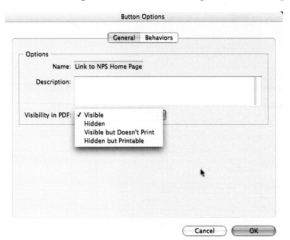

Note:

The description field can be used to add text that will be available to search engines or other applications that read metadata.

5. **Click the Behaviors tab to show those options.**

In this tab, you define what will happen when a certain event occurs.

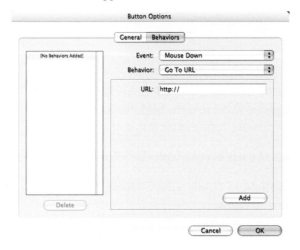

6. **Choose Mouse Up in the Event menu.**

InDesign supports six different types of events:

- The **Mouse Up** event triggers an action when the mouse button is released after clicking.

- The **Mouse Down** event triggers an action as soon as the mouse button is clicked.

- The **Mouse Enter** event triggers an action when the mouse cursor enters the button area.

- The **Mouse Exit** event triggers an action when the mouse cursor leaves the button area.

- The **On Focus** event triggers an action when pressing the Tab key highlights the button (called being **in focus**).

- The **On Blur** event triggers an action when pressing the Tab key moves the focus to the next button in the tab order.

7. **Make sure Go To URL is selected in the Behavior menu.**

When the user clicks and then releases the mouse button, an action will occur. The specific action that occurs is defined in the Behavior menu.

- **Close** closes the PDF file.
- **Exit** quits the application being used to display the PDF file.
- **Go To Anchor** navigates to the specified bookmark or anchor.
- **Go To [page]** navigates to the first, last, previous, or next page in the PDF file.
- **Go To Previous View** navigates to the most recently viewed page in the PDF file, or returns to the last used zoom size (similar to the Back button in a browser).
- **Go To Next View** navigates to a page after going to the previous view (similar to the Forward button in a browser).
- **Go To URL** opens a specific Web page in the user's default browser.
- **Movie** allows you to play, pause, stop, or resume a movie file that is placed in the document.
- **Open File** opens the specified file in the file's native application (if possible).
- **Show/Hide Fields** toggles the visibility of specific buttons (fields) in the PDF file.
- **Sound** allows you to play, pause, stop, or resume a sound file that has been added to the document.
- **View Zoom** displays the page according to the zoom option you specify.

8. **In the URL field, place the insertion point after the "http://" prefix and type "www.nps.gov/yose/".**

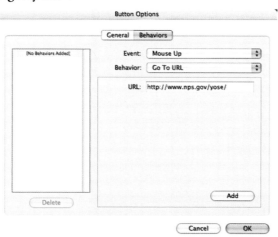

Note:

You can place QuickTime (".mov") or Microsoft AVI video files, as well as animated Flash files that have been exported to the SWF format, into the layout just as you would place any other picture. You can also control the properties of placed movie files by choosing Object>Interactive> Movie Options.

Note:

You can place Apple AIFF or Microsoft WAV sound files into a layout. You can also control the properties of placed sound files by choosing Object>Interactive> Sound Options.

9. **Click the Add button.**

   The Mouse Up behavior has been added to the selected button. If necessary (or if you want to), you can add different behaviors to each event.

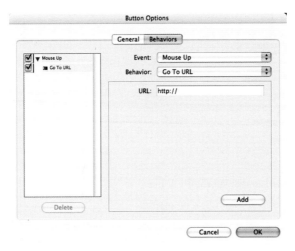

10. **Click OK to return to the layout.**

11. **Select the second button and change its name to "Contact NPS at Yosemite".**

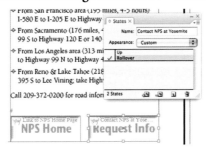

12. **Open the button options for the second button. Define a Mouse Up event with the Go To URL behavior.**

13. **In the URL field, delete the "http://" prefix and type "mailto:information@ yosemite.gov".**

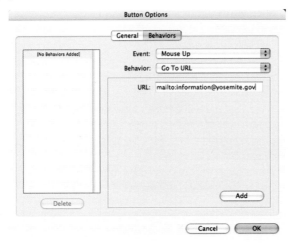

Note:

The "mailto:" prefix is the correct code to open a new message that is already addressed to the defined email address.

14. **Click Add to add the behavior to the button, and then click OK to return to the layout.**

15. **Save the file and continue to the next exercise.**

EXPORT MULTIPLE PDF FILES

Your layout now has two interactive buttons and one hyperlink that is not visually identified in the layout, although it will work if a user clicks the address text. The final step of this project is to output your files to the necessary formats.

1. **With Flyer Yosemite.indd open, choose File>Export.**

2. **Choose Adobe PDF in the Format/Save as Type menu.**

3. **Navigate to your WIP>Parks folder, and change the file name to "Flyer Yosemite Print.pdf".**

4. **Click Save.**

5. **In the Export Adobe PDF dialog box, choose [High Quality Print] in the Adobe PDF Preset menu.**

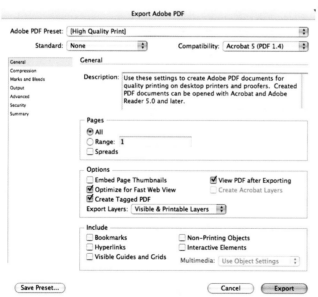

6. **In the Marks and Bleeds options, add crop marks with a 0.125″ offset, and include a 0.125″ bleed.**

7. **Click the Save Preset button, and save these settings as "Print with Bleed".**

   You need to export two other layouts using the same settings; creating a preset will save time later.

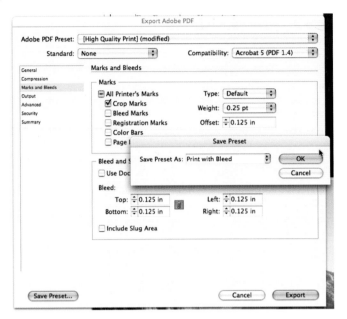

8. **Click OK to close the Save Preset dialog box, and then click Export to create the PDF file for print.**

9. **When the export process is complete, choose File>Export again.**

10. **Change the file name to "Flyer Yosemite Web.pdf".**

11. **In the Export Adobe PDF dialog box, choose [Smallest File Size] in the Adobe PDF Preset menu.**

12. In the General tab, check the Hyperlinks and Interactive Elements options in the Include area.

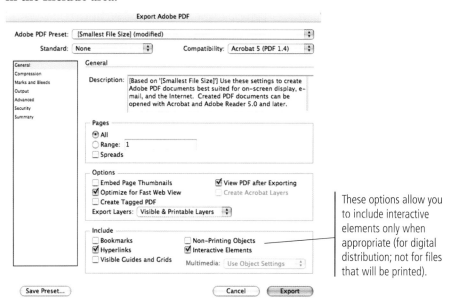

These options allow you to include interactive elements only when appropriate (for digital distribution; not for files that will be printed).

13. Click Export. When the export process is complete, open the Flyer Yosemite Web.pdf file in Adobe Acrobat Reader (if possible) and test the buttons.

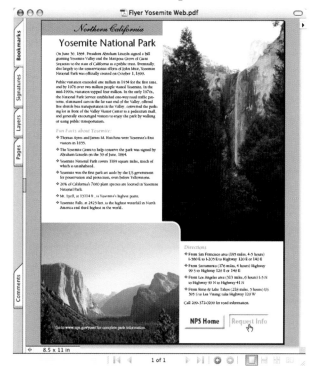

14. Close the PDF file and return to InDesign. Save and close the flyer file.

15. Open the postcard and rack card files from your WIP>Parks folder. Export PDF files for print using the Print with Bleed preset.

16. Save and close both files.

Summary

To complete this project, you started with the very basics — defining a new document — and worked all the way through complex content repurposing using XML. You should realize that you have virtually unlimited creative control as you experiment with an initial layout concept, but that creating a unified design sometimes requires minor adjustments based on the actual content that will be placed in the layout.

You used unstructured XML to drag specific types of content into a layout, and you used a more structured approach to automatically create place content into tagged frames of a different layout. By maintaining a link to the XML file, you were able to automatically update the placed content to reflect changes in the text. Repurposing the same content in multiple different layouts — both for print and digital distribution — is becoming increasingly common in the design world; using InDesign's XML capabilities makes the process far easier than manually creating each different version.

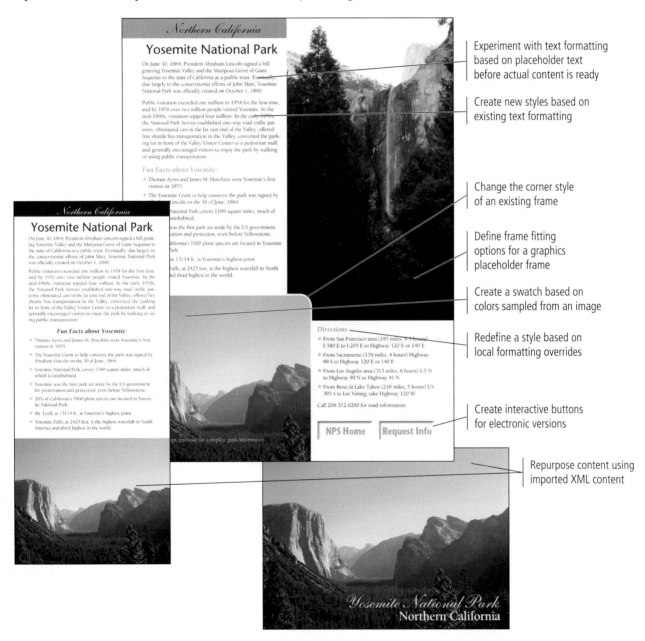

Experiment with text formatting based on placeholder text before actual content is ready

Create new styles based on existing text formatting

Change the corner style of an existing frame

Define frame fitting options for a graphics placeholder frame

Create a swatch based on colors sampled from an image

Redefine a style based on local formatting overrides

Create interactive buttons for electronic versions

Repurpose content using imported XML content

Portfolio Builder Project 7

The client is very pleased with the pieces you have designed to promote tourism in the national parks. Before she presents the project to her director for approval, she would like to have the same pieces for at least one other park.

To complete this project, you should:

❏ Create the flyer, rack card, and postcard layouts for Bryce Canyon National Park. Use the images and text that are provided in the RF_Builders>Parks folder.

❏ Create one additional layout for a letterfold brochure that will include the same content as the other pieces. The inside of the brochure should have only the park name and space for a map of the park.

"These pieces are exactly what I had in mind. I would like to see one additional layout — redesigning our park map brochure to include this same content, but also a large map of the specific park. We already have the maps, but I'll have to find the files for you; for now just leave space on the inside of the brochure.

"When I pitch the project to my superiors, I want to be able to show them the pieces for at least two different parks. That way the committee will see how different colors and pictures will affect the individual pieces, but still have a consistent look and feel. I've sent you the text and images for Bryce Canyon in Utah for this second set of files.

"I'm thinking about combining the flyers for all the parks (when they're done) into a booklet that we might be able to sell. I'm going to include this in my presentation as a potential source of income to justify the cost of the overall project. Having more than one flyer finished will help to explain this part of the project.

"I have a meeting scheduled for late next week. Can you have everything finished by then?"

Multi-Chapter Book Excerpts

Your client, Against The Clock (ATC), publishes books relating to the computer graphics industry. In addition to application-specific books, they are also creating a series of "companion" titles that discuss the concepts underlying the use of digital software — basic design principles, type, color, and so on. You have been hired to use the existing book chapters to build an "excerpt" booklet that can be used for marketing purposes.

This project incorporates the following skills:

❏ Combining multiple InDesign files into a single book

❏ Synchronizing the assets in multiple files to ensure consistency from one piece to the next

❏ Building a unified table of contents for the entire book

❏ Building an index that comprises all chapters of the book

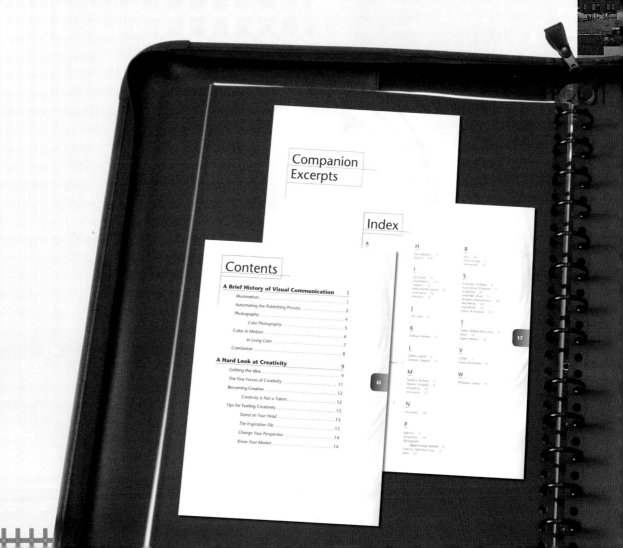

Client Comments

We are launching a new series of companion books that will complement our application-specific books. The companion books are already being printed, but we want to use the InDesign files to create a sample excerpt booklet that we can use in digital and print advertising.

We provided you with the files for the first chapter in two of the books. Unfortunately, the file from the *Color Companion* seems to be one version behind — we can't find the version that was tagged for the book's index. We want the sample booklet to include a representative index, though, so we'd like you to tag a few entries in the *Color Companion* chapter and build a mini-index for the sample. The booklet should also have its own self-cover/title page, as well as a table of contents.

The first set of these booklets will be printed and mailed to 50 clients we selected from our database. We're asking these 50 clients to review the sample chapters and provide quotes that we can use in our marketing materials. (We've also selected these 50 clients as the ones we think are most likely to purchase the Companion books.) We provided you with the letter in an InDesign file, as well as the data file that was exported from our database.

One final thing: each book in the Series uses a distinct highlight color. The *Color Companion* is orange, the *Design Companion* is blue, etc. We'd like to use purple as the highlight color for all files in the excerpt booklet.

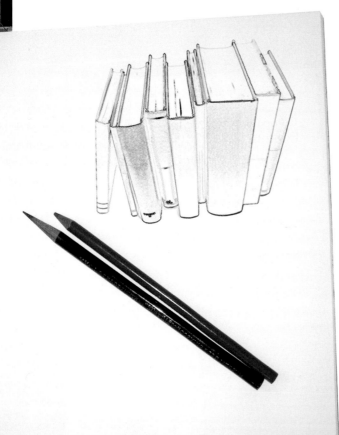

Art Director Comments

Long documents like books — especially non-fiction books — require several special elements, including a table of contents and an index. A lot of publishers spend many hours manually composing these elements; they literally flip through pages and hand-write every entry in a spreadsheet. Fortunately, InDesign has built-in tools that make this process far easier.

When you consistently (and correctly) use style sheets, you can build a table of contents based on the styles in the chapters, once you've combined all the chapters together. Unfortunately, the index is a bit more complicated. Although the tools for tagging and compiling an index make the process a bit easier, indexing is still a largely manual process; you have to decide exactly *what* to include in the index — there is no software smart enough to complete that job for you. Of course, after you've tagged the entries, compiling the final index is far easier using InDesign's built-in tools.

The advantage of using these tools is that you complete the process only once. Using the old methods, changes late in the process — which happen almost every time — meant manually re-compiling the table of contents and index. Using InDesign's built-in tools, you can easily re-compile either element as often as necessary, and you can format them automatically using other style sheets.

Project Objectives

To complete this project, you will:

❏ Create an InDesign book file

❏ Manage different files as chapters of a single book

❏ Control section and page numbering across multiple chapter files

❏ Synchronize assets in all files of the book

❏ Build a table of contents based on style sheets

❏ Tag index entries in each file of the book

❏ Compile the index for all book chapters at once

❏ Create a variable-data letter addressed to previous ATC clients

Stage 1 Combining Documents into Books

Publication design is a unique subset of graphic design. Attention to detail is critical. You must ensure that subhead formatting in early chapters matches the subhead formatting in later chapters, the captions are all set in the same font, the body copy is the same size throughout the document, and so on. Regardless of whether one or several designers work on the project, consistency is essential from the first page of the book to the last. To make long-document design easier, InDesign includes a special type of Book file for combining and managing multiple chapters as a single unit.

Long documents are frequently split into multiple files during the conception and design phases, and then combined at the end of the process to create the final job. This workflow offers several advantages:

- Layouts with numerous images can become very large; breaking these layouts into pieces helps to keep the file size smaller.

- If a long document is broken into multiple stand-alone files, several designers can work on different files of the same book without the risk of accidentally overwriting another designer's work.

- If a long document is split into several files, you won't lose the entire job if a single file becomes corrupt.

Before digital book-building utilities were introduced, multiple files were combined in the prepress department at the output provider. Working with multiple files required extreme care and attention to detail to maintain consistency from one file to the next. InDesign's book-building tools make the process much easier by automating many of the tasks that were previously done manually, including comparing proofs of every page in the document. (Even though the Book utilities automate much of the process, you must still — and always — pay close attention to the details of your work.)

 BUILD AN INDESIGN BOOK

An InDesign book is simply a container file, into which multiple InDesign files are placed for easier organization and file management. The InDesign Book utility offers several benefits, including:

- Synchronizing styles, colors, and other assets to the book's master file

- Monitoring page and section numbering of each individual file in the book, and of the book as a whole

- Easily adding or removing pages, or moving entire chapters, and automatically renumbering pages according to the book order

- Building a table of contents and index from all book files at once

- Printing or exporting the entire book at once, or only selected chapters

1. **Copy the contents of the RF_InDesign>Companions folder into your WIP>Companions folder.**

    When you work with book files, you frequently open, save, and close the chapters of the book files; in fact, some operations happen without your direct intervention. For this process to work properly, book chapter files must be unlocked — which means you can't work directly from the Resource CD.

> *Note:*
>
> *When a single design project is composed of several files, it is even more important to maintain consistency from one file to the next. If the font is slightly different from one issue of a newsletter to the next, few people are likely to spot much of a difference. That difference is far more noticeable, however, when two or more files are bound together in the same publication.*

> *Note:*
>
> *For the exercises in this project to work properly, the resource files must be in a location where you can save them without choosing Save As. Make sure you are working with the files in your WIP folder and not the files on your Resource CD.*

2. With nothing open in InDesign, choose File>New>Book.

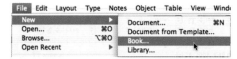

3. Navigate to your WIP>Companions folder as the target location.

Unlike creating a new file, creating a new book requires you to immediately name and save the book file.

4. Change the book name to "Excerpts.indb" and click Save.

The correct extension is automatically added for you, but if you accidentally remove it, type it back into the file name.

Clicking Save opens the Book panel; the file name you define is listed in the panel tab.

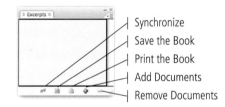

Synchronize
Save the Book
Print the Book
Add Documents
Remove Documents

Note:

If you open other book files, they will open in the same panel group as other open book files.

Note:

You can open a book file the same way you open a regular document file (File>Open).

5. Continue to the next exercise.

ADD BOOK CHAPTERS

Once the book file has been defined, adding chapters is easy. The first chapter you add is (by default) the Style Source chapter, to which other chapters can be synchronized.

1. With the excerpts book file open, click the Add Documents button at the bottom of the Book panel.

2. Navigate to the file Color1.indd in your WIP>Companions folder and click Open.

Depending on the size of the selected chapter, it might take a few seconds to process the file.

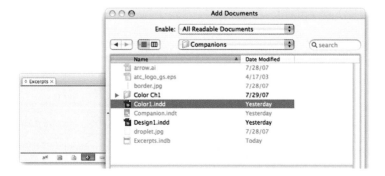

3. When InDesign is finished processing the file, it appears in the Book panel.

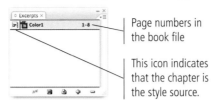

Page numbers in the book file

This icon indicates that the chapter is the style source.

Note:

You can change the style source for the book by clicking the empty space to the left of a specific chapter.

4. Click the Add Documents button again. Navigate to Design1.indd in your WIP>Companions folder and click Open.

New files are automatically added below the previously selected chapter. If no chapter is selected in the panel, new files are added to the end of the book.

If you haven't changed the section or page numbering options for the files you add, new book chapters are automatically numbered sequentially from one file to the next.

Note:

You can remove a file from a book by clicking the Remove Documents button at the bottom of the Book panel. Once you remove a chapter from a book, you can't undo the deletion. The file still exists in its original location, however, so you can simply add the file back into the book, if necessary.

5. Open the file Companion.indt from your WIP>Companions folder.

This is the template from which the companion chapters were created. Although the two excerpt chapters are already laid out, you need to create a front matter document that will hold a title page and the table of contents for the combined excerpts.

Note:

If you get a Profile or Policy Mismatch warning at any point in this project, select the option to leave the document as is and click OK.

6. In the Pages panel, drag the F-Title Page master page icon onto the Page 1 icon.

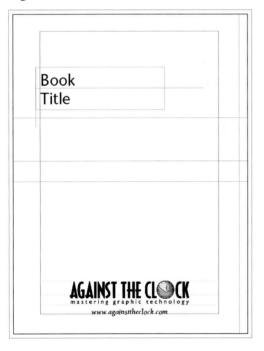

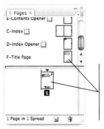

Drag the F-Title Page master onto the Page 1 icon in the lower section of the Pages panel.

7. Control/right-click the Page 1 icon and choose Override Master Page Items from the contextual menu.

The text frame for the book title is placed on the master page; to change the text and enter the actual book title, you have to either make the change on the master page or detach the master items on the regular layout page.

8. Highlight the text "Book Title" in the text frame and type "Companion Excerpts".

9. Drag the right-center handle of the text frame until the word "Excerpts" moves to the second line and the right edge of the frame is approximately 1/8″ from the edge of the text.

10. Drag the right end of the bisecting line until the end is approximately 1/2″ from the right edge of the text frame.

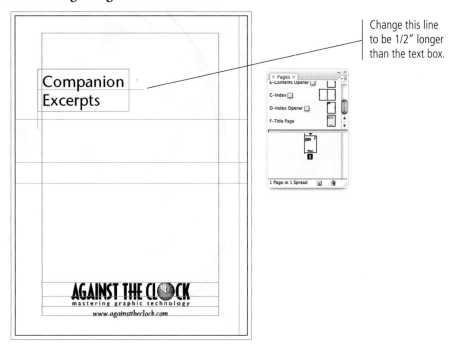

Change this line to be 1/2″ longer than the text box.

Companion Excerpts

11. Save the file as "Excerpts Front.indd" in your WIP>Companions folder, and then close the file.

12. In the Excerpts Book panel, click the Add Documents button.

13. Navigate to the Excerpts Front.indd file you just created and add it to the book file.

14. **Click Excerpts Front in the panel and drag up until a heavy black line appears above Color1 in the panel.**

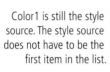

This line indicates the new position of the chapter (when you release the mouse button).

When you release the mouse button, Excerpts Front becomes the first chapter in the book.

Color1 is still the style source. The style source does not have to be the first item in the list.

Note:

You can save a book with a different name by choosing Save Book As from the panel options menu.

15. **Click the Save Book button at the bottom of the panel.**

16. **Continue to the next exercise.**

Managing Book Chapters

INDESIGN FOUNDATIONS

When you place a file into a book, the book file acts as a container; this process is very similar to placing an image into a layout. An InDesign layout stores the path to a placed image as a reference. Books use the same technique, storing references to the files contained within the book.

If the chapter files have been moved since being added to the book, the Book panel shows a missing-link warning icon. When you double-click a missing book chapter, InDesign asks if you want to replace the missing file; clicking Yes opens a navigation dialog box so you can locate the missing file or identify a replacement file. (You can also select a missing file in the panel and choose Replace Document from the Book panel options menu.)

Remember, when you change a placed image using the Edit Original option, the changes automatically reflect when you return to the main InDesign layout. The same concept applies with book chapters: when you open a chapter using the Book panel, changes automatically reflect in the containing book. When you open a book chapter outside the context of the book, the Book panel displays a modified-link icon for that file.

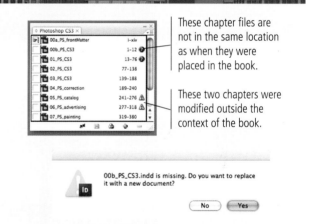

These chapter files are not in the same location as when they were placed in the book.

These two chapters were modified outside the context of the book.

00b_PS_CS3.indd is missing. Do you want to replace it with a new document?

No   Yes

You can update a modified book chapter by simply double-clicking the file in the panel to open it. When you save the chapter and close it, InDesign updates the book chapter link to reflect the most current version of the file. Once a chapter has been added to a book file, it is best to make changes only within the context of the book.

CONTROL SECTION AND PAGE NUMBERING

After moving the front matter chapter above the color chapter, the page numbers for each chapter automatically change to reflect their new positions. The problem, however, is that the second file (Color1) begins on Page 2 and the third file (Design1) begins on Page 10. Even-numbered pages are left-facing pages, but book design conventions typically dictate that chapters begin on right-facing (odd-numbered) pages.

1. **With the Excerpts book file open, choose Book Page Numbering Options from the Book panel options menu.**

2. **In the Book Numbering Options dialog box, choose the Continue on Next Odd Page option.**

   Although some book designs intentionally break from convention and begin chapters on left-facing pages, this is not the norm. Right-facing chapter-starts are so common, in fact, that InDesign's long-document tools include the ability to easily force chapters to begin on the right side of the spread.

   You can use this dialog box to control exactly where new chapter files begin:

   - **Continue from Previous Document**, the default option, allows new chapters to pick up numbering from the end of the previous file. This option allows new chapters to begin on odd- or even-numbered pages.

   - **Continue on Next Odd Page** forces new chapter files to begin on odd-numbered pages. If your layouts use facing pages, this means new chapters will always begin on right-facing pages.

   - **Continue on Next Even Page** forces new chapter files to begin on even-numbered pages. If your layouts use facing pages, this means new chapters will always begin on left-facing pages.

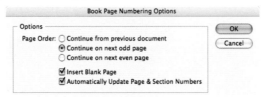

3. **Check the Insert Blank Page option and leave the Automatically Update option checked.**

   The Insert Blank Page option adds a blank page into any file where the defined page order leaves a blank space in the page numbering. When the Automatically Update option is checked (as it is by default), files in the book will automatically adjust to reflect your other choices in this dialog box.

4. Click OK to apply your changes.

The second and third files in the book now begin on odd-numbered (right-facing) pages. Blank pages have been added as necessary to fill in empty spaces caused by moving the chapters to the appropriate side of the spread.

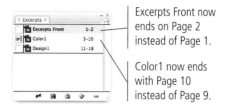

Excerpts Front now ends on Page 2 instead of Page 1.

Color1 now ends with Page 10 instead of Page 9.

5. In the Book panel, click the Excerpts Front file to select it.

6. In the panel options menu, choose Document Numbering Options.

In addition to controlling the page numbering from one file to another, you can also control the page numbering for a specific file. This is useful if, for example, you want the front matter of a book to be numbered separately from the main body of the document.

To change document-specific settings such as page numbering and sections, the document must be open. When you choose Document Numbering Options in the Book panel options menu, the selected file automatically opens so you can make changes.

Note:

Front matter *typically refers to the information that precedes the main content of a book, including a title page, copyright information, table of contents, acknowledgements, and other important elements.*

Understanding Book Page Numbering

INDESIGN FOUNDATIONS

If you had not checked Insert Blank Pages in the Book Page Numbering Options dialog box, each chapter in your book would begin on a right-facing (odd-numbered) page. However, the last page in each file would remain unchanged. The image here shows the original pagination (on the left) in comparison to the renumbered pages; the first page of each file is highlighted in pink. In the middle version — the result of the steps you just took — blank pages are highlighted in yellow.

The third version (on the right) shows what would have happened if you had not selected the Insert Blank Pages option. Although the second and third files would have begun on odd-numbered (right-facing) pages, the blank pages would not have been added to fill in the space. This could cause significant problems when the book is imposed into printer's spreads for commercial printing. (Refer to Project 5 for an explanation of printer's spreads.)

Original pagination:

	1
2	3
4	5
6	7
8	9
10	11
12	13
14	15
16	

Pagination after modifying book numbering (inserting blank pages):

	1
2	3
4	5
6	7
8	9
10	11
12	13
14	15
16	17
18	

Pagination after modifying book numbering (without inserting blank pages):

	1
	3
4	5
6	7
8	9
10	11
	13
14	15
16	17
18	

7. **In the Document Numbering Options dialog box, choose the lowercase Roman numerals in the Style menu.**

This is another common convention in book design and layout — the front matter is numbered separately from the main part of the book, commonly in lowercase Roman numerals.

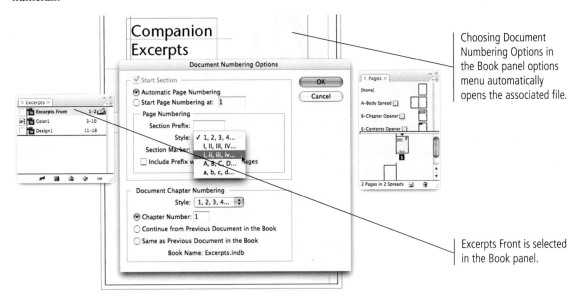

Choosing Document Numbering Options in the Book panel options menu automatically opens the associated file.

Excerpts Front is selected in the Book panel.

8. **Click OK to apply the change, save the open layout, and then close the file.**

In the Book panel, the Excerpts Front file reflects the new numbering style. The problem, however, is that the first content chapter still begins on Page 3 (even though this file is still numbered with Arabic numerals).

Note:

You could also select the page icon in the panel and choose Numbering & Section Options from the Pages panel options menu.

9. **Double-click Color1 in the Book panel.**

Double-clicking a file in the Book panel automatically opens that file.

10. **Control/right-click the Page 3 icon in the Pages panel and choose Numbering & Section Options.**

This command opens a dialog box very similar to the Document Numbering Options dialog box. The primary difference is that you are controlling the options for a specific page (Page 3, which you Control/right-clicked to access the dialog box).

When you use the Document Numbering Options command, InDesign automatically applies your choices, beginning with the first page of the selected file. Using the Numbering & Section Options command, you can change the options for any page in the document.

11. In the Numbering & Section Options dialog box, choose the Start Page Numbering At option, and change the number in the field to "1".

InDesign's default behavior — the Automatic Page Numbering option — causes pages to number sequentially from one file to the next in the book. By choosing the Start Page Numbering At option, you can override the default page numbering and determine the exact page number of any file in the book.

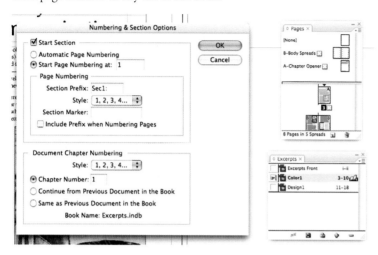

Note:

If you are using facing pages, changing an even-numbered page to an odd-numbered page will move the page to the other side of the spread. Remember from earlier chapters that this can cause objects to appear out of position in relation to the page's new position.

12. Click OK to apply the new page number to the first page of the Color1 file.

Because you haven't changed the numbering options for the Design1 file (or for any specific page in that file), it is still automatically numbered in sequence with the Color1 file.

The page numbering of a book relies on using the Current Page Number marker in the InDesign files. If you use the Current Page Number marker in book chapter files, those markers will reflect the correct page number in relation to the entire book.

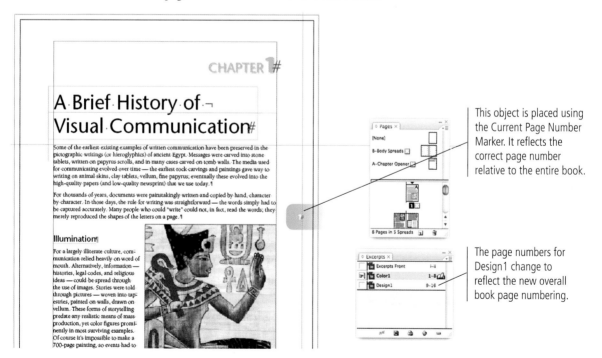

This object is placed using the Current Page Number Marker. It reflects the correct page number relative to the entire book.

The page numbers for Design1 change to reflect the new overall book page numbering.

13. Save the open document (Color1) and close it.

14. In the Book panel, click the Save the Book button, and then continue to the next exercise.

Section and Page Numbering in a Single File

Although there are distinct advantages to maintaining long documents in numerous separate files, there are times when you want to work with an entire booklet or other project in a single InDesign file. In that case, it is important to realize that you can change the page and section numbering options for any page in a layout; these options are not restricted to files placed in an InDesign book.

Sections allow you to create different page numbering sequences within a single file. For any section start page, you can restart page numbering at a specific page number, change the style of page numbers in the section, define a section marker for the section, and/or include the section prefix in the page number.

You can change the page and section options for any specific page by Control/right-clicking the page in the Pages panel and choosing Numbering & Section Options from the contextual menu.

When you choose Numbering & Section Options for any page that isn't already a section start, the Section Options dialog box opens. The Start Section option is automatically checked, so clicking OK will create a new section for the selected page.

If you choose Numbering & Section Options for an existing section start page, the Numbering & Section Options dialog box opens. The choices in these two dialog boxes are exactly the same; the only difference is the title bar, and the choices that are already selected when you open the dialog box. When you click OK in the New Section dialog box, the selected page is designated as a section start.

Pages between two section starts are part of the preceding section.

The first page in the file is a section start by default.

The triangle above the page icon indicates a section start.

Adding Section Prefixes

If you use the Page Number markers (Type>Insert Special Character>Markers>Current/Next/Previous Page Number), you can add a section prefix to page numbers in the layout by checking the **Include Prefix when Numbering Pages** option. Whatever you type in the Section Prefix field will be added in front of the page number.

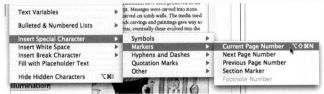

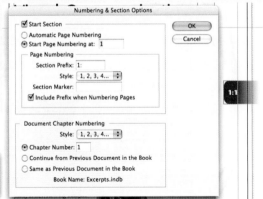

INDESIGN FOUNDATIONS

Adding Section Markers

Section markers are a type of variable. You can define the Section Marker text for a specific section, and then place the marker into the layout (Type>Insert Special Character>Markers>Section Marker). The defined Section Marker text for the section where the marker is placed will appear at the location of the marker.

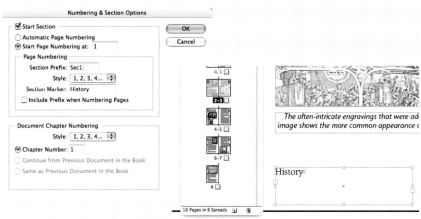

The Section Marker character displays the text in the Section Marker field of the Numbering & Section Options dialog box. If a section has no defined Section Marker text, the special character displays nothing. You can also change all instances of the section marker within a section by re-opening the dialog box for the section start page and changing the text in the Section Marker field.

Chapter Numbering

When you work with book files, you can also define Document Chapter Numbering options, which is basically section numbering for files. If you define a specific chapter number in the Numbering & Section Options dialog box, you can place the built-in Chapter Number variable (Type>Text Variables>Insert Variable>Chapter Number) in the layout to reflect the current chapter number.

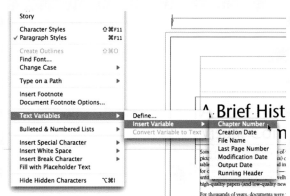

If nothing appears in the Insert Variable submenu, the document was probably created in an earlier version of InDesign. The several predefined variables, including Chapter Number, were added in InDesign CS3. In this case, you can either define your own Chapter Number variable (see Project 5) or load the variables from a file created in InDesign CS3.

SYNCHRONIZE BOOK FILES

An advantage of using style sheets for text layout is that a style can be changed easily and universally. This is also a disadvantage of using style sheets, particularly when combining multiple files into a single publication. Layout designers frequently manipulate, tweak, and even cheat to force-fit text into a desired amount of space, to make a runaround work correctly, or to achieve a specific effect. When the files are combined into the final book, these adjustments can cause problems if the variation is noticeable from one file to the next.

A primary advantage of using the InDesign book-building function is the ability to easily synchronize various assets across multiple chapter files. In the Synchronize Options dialog box, you can choose which types of assets you want to synchronize.

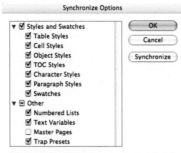

When a book is synchronized, elements of the Style Source file are added to the other files if they don't already exist in those files. If an element already exists in the other files, the element definition from the Style Source file is applied to the same-named element in the other files. The synchronization process does not affect elements that are not in the Style Source file.

For example, say you reduced the leading in the Caption style in a file that is not the Style Source file. Synchronizing the book overwrites the modified Caption style with the Caption style settings that exist in the Style Source file.

1. **With the Excerpts book file open, double-click the file Excerpts Front to open that document.**

2. **Open the Swatches panel, and then open the Swatch Options dialog box for the Companion Color swatch.**

3. **Change the swatch definition to C=70, M=100, Y=0, K=0 and make sure the Name with Color Value is not checked.**

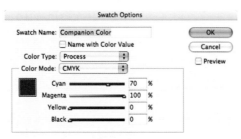

4. **Click OK to close the Swatch Options dialog box, save the document and close it, but leave the book file open.**

Note:

The tool tip name for the Synchronize button — Synchronize Styles and Swatches with the Style Source — is deceptively non-inclusive. Because you can synchronize far more than just these two elements, we refer to this button as simply "Synchronize."

Note:

Synchronizing a book does not delete any element from any file, but can override changes you made to a particular file.

Note:

If you change a style sheet — to fit text onto a page, for example — synchronizing the book to the master file overwrites the changes, and the text will no longer fit in the same way.

Note:

This is an instance when there is good reason to break from color-naming convention based on the color definition. The swatch is different in all the Companion books, but it is named the same in all files of all books. By synchronizing the color in all book files to this new definition, you can change the Companion Color swatch in multiple files at one time.

5. **In the Book panel, click the empty space to the left of the Excerpts Front file to redefine the style source.**

You can change the style source at any time by clicking in this space.

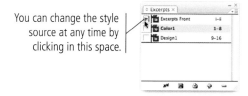

6. **Click in the empty area at the bottom of the Book panel to deselect all files.**

If nothing is selected in the Book panel, all chapter files will be synchronized. You can also synchronize specific files by selecting them in the Book panel before clicking the Synchronize button. (To select contiguous files, hold down the Shift key and click each file. To select noncontiguous files, hold down the Command/Control key while selecting the desired files.) Of course, synchronizing only certain files defeats the purpose of synchronizing, but the option is available.

7. **In the Book panel options menu, choose Synchronize Options.**

Click in this space to deselect all chapters in the book.

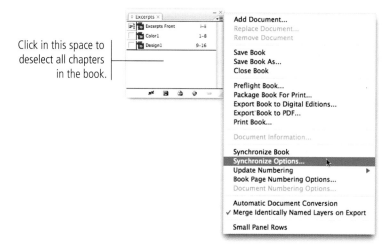

8. **In the Synchronize Options dialog box, uncheck everything except Character Styles, Paragraph Styles, and Swatches.**

In this project, your primary concern is consistency of appearance between existing files from the same series of books. The three selected options will be sufficient for your current purpose. In other cases where you combine very different files from a variety of designers, it might be useful — or, in fact, vital — to synchronize the other types of assets as well.

9. **Click OK to close the dialog box.**

10. In the Book panel, click the Synchronize button.

11. Click OK in the resulting warning.

As we mentioned, synchronizing book files can cause problems. InDesign is smart enough to recognize and warn you about one of the most common and serious problems — overset text.

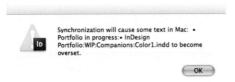

12. When the process is complete, click OK to the resulting message.

This message warns you of the potential problem we mentioned earlier — documents might have changed.

Whenever you synchronize book files — especially if you did not create the original files — you should carefully review the pages to be sure the content is still where it belongs.

13. Double-click Color1 in the Book panel to open that file.

When you synchronize files, you might have no idea what caused the problem — but you still need to fix it. You have several options:

- Edit the text to fit the overset line in the available space. Of course, this assumes you have permission to edit text, which you usually do not.

- Add text frames to the chain. This typically assumes you can add pages to a file, which you often can't.

- Change style definitions to fit text into the available space. If you synchronize again later, your changes will again be overwritten.

- Adjust local formatting of specific text in the specific file to make the layout work the way you want it to work.

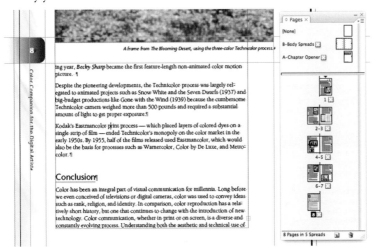

Note:

In case you were wondering, the Space Before Paragraph setting for the head 2 style was reduced in the original Color1 file to fit the text in eight pages instead of only two lines on Page 9 and a blank Page 10.

14. **Navigate to Page 7 of the file. Place the insertion point in the "In Living Color" head. Change the Space Before Paragraph setting for this paragraph only to 0.1″.**

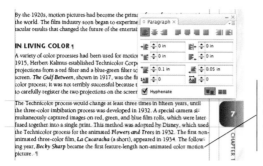

After changing the Space Before Paragraph setting for the heading, the last two lines of this paragraph again fit on Page 7.

15. **Navigate to Page 8 and review the text.**

The end-of-story character now shows, and the overset text icon is gone from the frame's out port.

Technicolor camera weighed more than 500 pounds and required a substantial amount of light to get proper exposure.¶

Kodak's Eastmancolor print process — which placed layers of colored dyes on a single strip of film — ended Technicolor's monopoly on the color market in the early 1950s. By 1955, half of the films released used Eastmancolor, which would also be the basis for processes such as Warnercolor, Color by De Luxe, and Metrocolor. ¶

Conclusion¶

Color has been an integral part of visual communication for millennia. Long before we even conceived of televisions or digital cameras, color was used to convey ideas such as rank, religion, and identity. In comparison, color reproduction has a relatively short history, but one that continues to change with the introduction of new technology. Color communication, whether in print or on screen, is a diverse and constantly evolving process. Understanding both the aesthetic and technical use of color is key to effectively communicating the messages you create as a designer. The rest of this book examines the different aspects of color that will affect your work.#

Note:

If you absolutely must adjust text in a particular file of a book, we recommend you manipulate the selected text and not the style sheet.

16. **Save the document and close it.**

17. **Save the book file and continue to the next stage of the project.**

Stage 2   Building a Table of Contents

Before desktop-publishing software automated the document design process, tables of contents and other lists (figures, tables, etc.) were created manually from page proofs — by turning each page and writing down the appropriate text and page number, and then sorting and typesetting those hard-copy lists into the final document. The process was extremely time-consuming and required precise attention to detail. If the document changed after the lists were completed, the entire piece had to be rechecked page by page.

Fortunately, InDesign includes a Table of Contents feature that automates this process, greatly improving production time and making it easier to maintain accuracy. InDesign tables of contents are based on the paragraph styles used in a layout. If you are conscientious about applying styles when you build a layout, you can easily create a thorough, accurate table of contents based on those styles.

You can define the styles that will be included in the compiled table of contents. For example, a table of contents might include Heading 1, Heading 2, and Heading 3 paragraph styles; any text set in those styles will appear in the list.

You can also determine the styles that will be used to format different elements in the compiled table of contents. Using the same example, TOC1 can be assigned to Heading 1 list items, TOC2 to Heading 2 items, and so on. When you compile the table of contents into the file, it is formatted automatically.

DEFINE A TABLE OF CONTENTS STYLE

A table of contents can be defined and applied in a single process. You can also create and save table of contents styles, which you can apply as needed in the active file, as well as import into and apply in other files. Because of the versatility allowed by styles of all types (paragraph, table, object, etc.), we recommend creating table of contents styles rather than defining a single-case table of contents.

1. **With the Excerpts book file open, double-click the Excerpts Front file in the panel to open that file.**

2. **Drag the E-Content Opener master page to the right of the Page ii icon.**

   When the new page is added, another blank page is also added because of your choices in the Book Page Numbering Options dialog box (Insert Blank Page is checked).

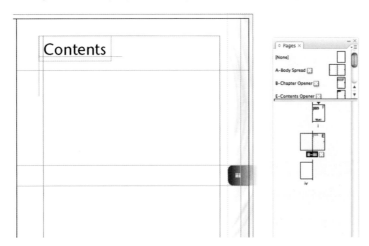

3. **Choose Layout>Table of Contents Styles.**

   If you completed Project 5, you should recognize this dialog box. It's the same one you used to manage and create text variables. You can create new styles, edit or delete existing styles, or load styles that exist in other files.

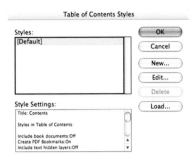

4. **Click New. In the resulting Table of Contents Style dialog box, type "Companion Contents" in the TOC Style field.**

   The TOC Style field defines the style name. This is basically the same as a paragraph style name; it is only an identifier.

5. **Delete the text from the Title field.**

   The Title field, on the other hand, is actual text that will be included at the top of the compiled table of contents. Because the "Contents" title for this layout is built into the master page, you should not include a title in the compiled table of contents.

6. **Click the More Options button on the right side of the dialog box.**

   When More Options are showing, you can control the appearance of page numbers in the table of contents.

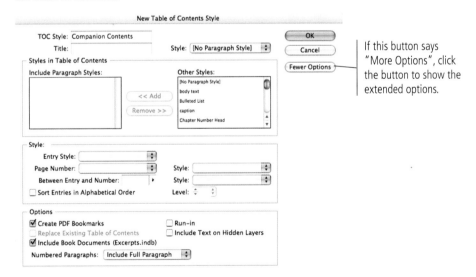

If this button says "More Options", click the button to show the extended options.

7. **Scroll though the Other Styles list, select Chapter Title, and click the Add button.**

8. **In the middle section of the dialog box, choose TOC 1 in the Entry Style menu.**

9. **Choose After Entry in the Page Number field and choose TOC Page Number in the associated Style menu. Leave all other options at their default settings.**

   You can define a number of options for each style included in a table of contents:

   - **Entry Style** defines the paragraph style that will be applied to those entries in the compiled list.

   - **Page Number** determines where the page number will be included for each entry (After Entry or Before Entry). You can also choose No Page Number to add the list entry without the associated page number.

   - **Between Entry and Number** defines the character(s) that will be placed between the list entry and the associated page number. The default option, ^t, is the special code for a tab character. The attached menu includes a number of common special characters, or you can type the code for a specific special character (see Project 6 for details).

   - You can use the Style menus in the right column to define separate character styles for the page number and the character between the entry and page number. If you don't choose a character style in one or both of these menus, that element will be formatted with the paragraph style settings defined for the list entry.

   - If the **Sort Entries in Alphabetical Order** option is checked, the compiled list entries will appear in alphabetical order rather than page-number order.

   - By default, each new style in the Include pane is added at one level lower than the previous style. You can use the Level menu to change the hierarchy of any style in the list.

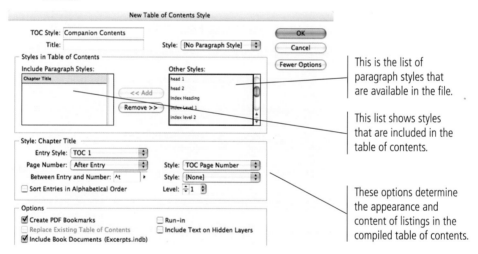

10. **In the Other Styles list, highlight head 1 and click Add. In the Style section of the dialog box, choose TOC 2 in the Entry Style menu. Choose After Entry in the Page Number field and choose TOC Page Number in the associated Style menu.**

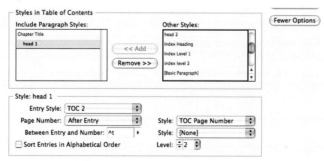

11. **In the Other Styles list, highlight head 2 and click Add. In the Style section of the dialog box, choose TOC 3 in the Entry Style menu. Choose After Entry in the Page Number field and choose TOC Page Number in the associated Style menu.**

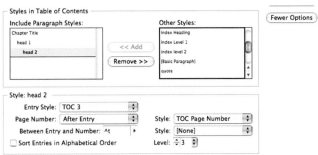

12. **Review the choices in the Options section of the dialog box.**

   • **Create PDF Bookmarks** tags the table of contents entries to appear in the Bookmarks panel of Adobe Acrobat or Adobe Reader (when the document is exported to PDF).

   • **Replace Existing Table of Contents** is only available if a table of contents has already been built in the open file. This option is more relevant when you build the table of contents than when you define a table of contents style.

   • **Include Book Documents** allows you to build a single table of contents for all files in an InDesign book file. This option is only available if the open file is part of an InDesign book.

   • **Run-in** builds a list in which all entries run into a single paragraph; individual entries are separated by a semicolon.

   • **Include Text on Hidden Layers** adds list entries even if the text is on a hidden layer. This option is unchecked by default, and should almost always remain that way — unless you have a very specific reason for listing elements that do not actually appear in the document.

   • The **Numbered Paragraphs** menu determines whether the list entry includes the full numbered paragraph (number *and* text), only the numbers, or only the text.

13. **Click OK to return to the Table of Contents Styles dialog box.**

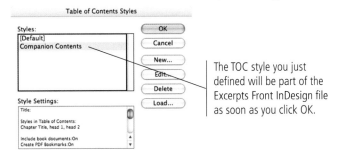

The TOC style you just defined will be part of the Excerpts Front InDesign file as soon as you click OK.

14. **Click OK to close the Table of Contents Styles dialog box and return to the document window.**

15. **Save the file and continue to the next exercise.**

Note:

Different types of projects call for different types of lists. Although called the Table of Contents utility, you can build a list of any editorial element formatted with a paragraph style. For example, some publications call for a separate table of contents listing all illustrations in the publication. If you define and apply a Figure Heading paragraph style, you can create a list of entries formatted with the Figure Heading style.

Build and Update a Table of Contents

Once a list is defined, whether for a single file or for a book, you can build it into the layout very easily. In fact, when you build a table of contents, the compiled list is loaded into the cursor; you can click to place the loaded list just as you would place any other text element.

1. **With Excerpts Front.indd open from the Excerpts Book panel, choose Layout>Table of Contents.**

    This dialog box has the same options as those available when you defined a TOC style. The only difference is that here you define a one-time table of contents list (although you can click the Save Style button to create a style based on your choices).

2. **Make sure Companion Contents is selected in the TOC Style menu.**

    Because it is the only style in the open file, it should be selected by default.

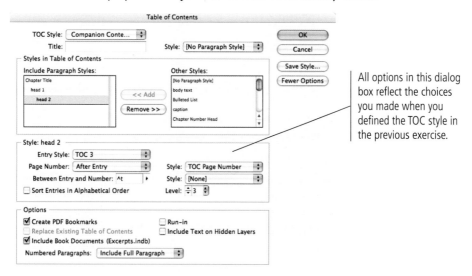

All options in this dialog box reflect the choices you made when you defined the TOC style in the previous exercise.

3. **Click OK.**

    When the list is ready, it loads into the cursor. This process might take a little while to complete, depending on the size of your book, so don't panic or try to force quit the application after a minute or two. If you're working on a very large book (such as this 400-plus-page Portfolio Series book), now is probably a good time for a coffee break.

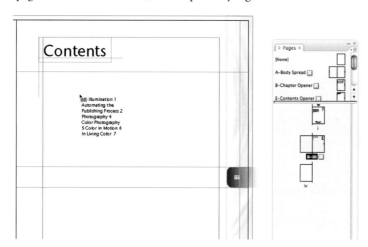

4. **Click the loaded cursor in the middle of Page iii to place the TOC into the text frame on the page.**

That's all there is to building a table of contents — whether for a single file or for multiple documents combined in an InDesign book file. After a TOC is built into a document, it is a static block of text. The applied styles can be changed as you would any other style, and you can change the text box in which a list is placed. You can change or delete items from the list without affecting the main layout.

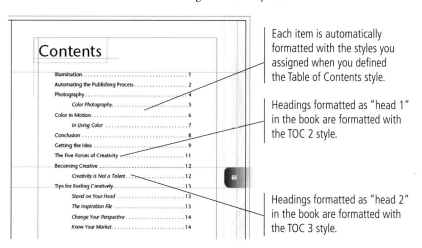

Each item is automatically formatted with the styles you assigned when you defined the Table of Contents style.

Headings formatted as "head 1" in the book are formatted with the TOC 2 style.

Headings formatted as "head 2" in the book are formatted with the TOC 3 style.

Of course, the table of contents InDesign built for this file reveals one potential problem: text that exists on the master page only (i.e., where the layout page hasn't been detached from the master) is not included in the compiled lists. The text frames for each chapter title have not been detached from the master pages, so the chapter titles do not appear in the compiled list.

5. **Double-click Color1 in the Book panel to open the file. Control/right-click the Page 1 icon in the Pages panel and choose Override All Master Page Items from the contextual menu.**

6. **Save the file and close it.**

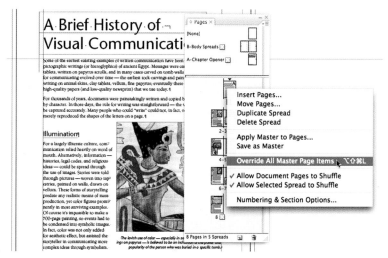

7. **Repeat Steps 5–6 to override all master page items for the first page in the Design1 file.**

8. **With Page iii of the Excerpts Front file showing, choose Layout>Update Table of Contents.**

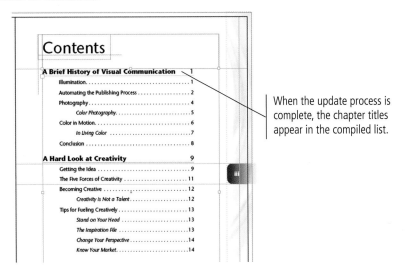

When the update process is complete, the chapter titles appear in the compiled list.

9. **Save your changes, and then close the document.**

10. **Save the book file and continue to the next stage of the project.**

Stage 3   Building an Index

An index is a map to a publication's contents, providing the reader with an easy reference to specific content. Like tables of contents and other lists, creating an index used to be an extremely time-consuming and labor-intensive process. A professional indexer was hired to read each hard-copy page of a document, write down index entries and page numbers, manually compile the final alphabetized list, and typeset that list into the document. Any changes after the index was finished meant the entire document had to be rechecked manually.

InDesign includes an Index tool that manages and automates part of the indexing process, improving the production workflow and saving considerable time when changes, inevitably, are made. It's a good idea to plan in advance when you're going to build an index. Several different elements can (and should) be defined before you build your index:

- Paragraph styles for index headings (if you decide to use them)

- Paragraph styles for up to four levels of index entries

- Character styles for the page numbers of each index entry (if you want them to be formatted differently than the index entry)

- Character styles for cross-references (if you want them to be formatted differently than the index entry)

Of these four elements, the only one that you must define in advance is the character style sheet that will be applied to the page number of individual index entries (if you decide to use this option). It is far easier to assign this style as you tag the individual entries, rather than change dozens or hundreds of entries later. The important point is that some advance planning can make your life easier. You can always change the style sheet definitions later in the process, but creating them in advance will save you time and effort in the long run.

TAG BASIC AND REVERSED INDEX TOPICS

1. **Double-click Color1 in the Excerpts Book panel to open that document.**

2. **Choose Window>Type & Tables>Index to open the Index panel.**

- Go to Selected Marker
- Update Preview
- Generate Index
- Create New Index Entry
- Delete Selected Entry

> *Note:*
>
> *Reference mode (the default) is used to add index entries in a layout. Topic mode is used to define a list of topics and review the hierarchy of included topics before compiling the index.*

3. **On Page 1 of the open document, highlight the word "hieroglyphics" in the middle of the second line of text.**

4. **Click the Create New Index Entry button at the bottom of the Index panel.**

   The New Page Reference dialog box shows the highlighted text in the first Topic Levels field.

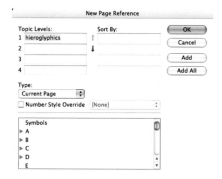

5. **Make sure the Type menu is set to Current Page and click OK.**

   You can define a number of different types of index entries; the Current Page option adds a reference to the page number where the text is currently highlighted.

   When you close the New Page Reference dialog box, you see that the highlighted text is preceded by a large caret character. This nonprinting character is an **index marker** — it indicates the location of a tagged reference, but it will not be visible in the output job.

6. **In the Index panel, click the arrow to the left of the "H", and then click the arrow to the left of the word "hieroglyphics".**

   You can see that the topic was added using the text in the Topic Levels field, and the reference was added with the Current Page number of the highlighted text.

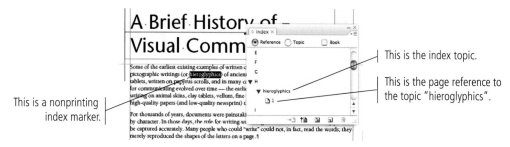

This is a nonprinting index marker.

This is the index topic.

This is the page reference to the topic "hieroglyphics".

7. **Click the arrow to collapse the "H" section of the Index panel.**

8. **Highlight the word "papyrus" in the next line and press Command-Option-Shift-[(Macintosh) or Control-Alt-Shift-[(Windows).**

   Using this key command, you can add a new Current Page reference without opening the New Page Reference dialog box.

9. **In the Index panel, expand the "P" list and the "papyrus" topic.**

Note:

If you have text highlighted, Command-Option-Shift-[(Macintosh) or Control-Alt-Shift-[(Windows) adds the highlighted text to the topic list and places an index marker for the selected text, without opening the New Page Reference dialog box.

Changing Topic Sort Order

INDESIGN FOUNDATIONS

The Sort By field allows you to change the alphabetical order of an index topic in the built index. When the index is built, the entries will appear in the list based on the Sort By text, but the entry text will still be the text defined in the Topic Levels field.

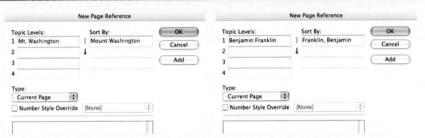

This is particularly useful for indexing abbreviations or proper names. In the examples shown here, the abbreviated text "Mt." will be alphabetized according to the full word "Mount". The name "Benjamin Franklin" will appear in the index under F instead of B, alphabetized by last name but appearing in the text in standard first name/last name order.

Reversing Index Entries

In addition to changing the sort order of a name, you can also change the actual order of the highlighted words when you add an entry to the index. When text is selected, pressing Command-Option-Shift-] (Macintosh) or Control-Alt-Shift-] (Windows) adds a reversed index entry without opening the New Page Reference dialog box. Using this key command, the highlighted text is added as an entry with the format "last word, comma all other words".

If the text "Benjamin Franklin" is highlighted, for example, using this key command will add a reference to the term "Franklin, Benjamin". In this case, the added topic will appear in the built index with the reversed text instead of simply realphabetized based on the reversed Sort By text.

If more than two words are highlighted when you add a reversed index reference, only the last highlighted word will be placed before the comma. If you add a reversed entry for the text "Martin Luther King", for example, the index topic will be "King, Martin Luther".

In a situation such as this, compound nouns that are not hyphenated can cause problems. If you highlight the text "Martin Luther King Jr." and add a reversed entry, the index topic will be "Jr., Martin Luther King". However, very few people would look for this reference in the "J" section of an index, and the point of an index is to be useable.

To prevent this type of reference, you can change the text to a nonbreaking space character between the last two words in the selection. With the nonbreaking space between "King" and "Jr.", the reversed index entry would be "King Jr., Martin Luther".

This entry was added with the text reversed in the Sort By field.

This entry was added by highlighting the text and pressing Command-Option-Shift-] (Macintosh) or Control-Alt-Shift-] (Windows).

This entry was added in reverse without changing the highlighted text.

To create this entry, we replaced the standard space between "King" and "Jr." with a nonbreaking space.

^S is the special code for a nonbreaking space. InDesign properly translates this code when it builds an index.

10. **Create new Current Page references to "rock carvings", "clay tablets", and "vellum" in the same paragraph.**

11. **On Page 2 of the document, highlight the words "Johannes Gutenberg" in the second line of the first paragraph after the "Automating..." heading.**

12. **Press Command-Option-Shift-] or Control-Alt-Shift-] to add a reversed topic reference to this name.**

13. **In the Index panel, expand the "G" list.**

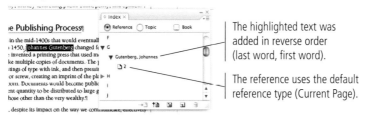

The highlighted text was added in reverse order (last word, first word).

The reference uses the default reference type (Current Page).

14. **On Page 4 of the layout, highlight the words "William Henry Fox Talbot" in the first line of the second paragraph.**

15. **Press Command-Option-Shift-] or Control-Alt-Shift-] to add a reversed topic reference to this name. Review the entry in the Index panel.**

    Only the last word of the highlighted text is placed before the comma in the index topic.

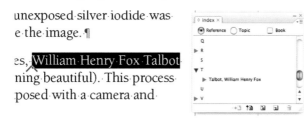

In this case, the index topic is technically correct because some people might look for the last name "Talbot" to find information about this man. Others, however, might look for his full last name "Fox Talbot", so you should add another index entry for the same text.

16. **In the text, highlight the space character between the words "Fox" and "Talbot". Choose Type>Insert White Space>Nonbreaking Space.**

17. **Highlight the entire name again and press Command-Option-Shift-] or Control-Alt-Shift-] to add a reversed topic reference to this name. Review the entry in the Index panel.**

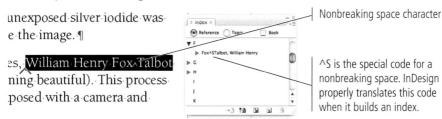

Nonbreaking space character

^S is the special code for a nonbreaking space. InDesign properly translates this code when it builds an index.

Note:

The key command for a nonbreaking space is Command-Option-X/ Control-Alt-X.

18. **Scan the text of the document and add Current Page index entries to all people mentioned in the chapter. Add all names in reverse order, using nonbreaking spaces as necessary to keep compound last names together.**

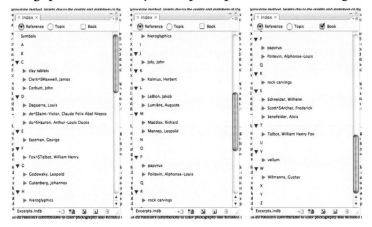

19. **Save the document and continue to the next exercise.**

 ## Add Multiple Page References

In some cases, you need to add multiple references to a specific index topic. Rather than searching through the text to find every instance of the topic, you can use the Add All button in the New Page Reference dialog box.

1. **With the Color1 file open through the Excerpts Book panel, navigate to Page 3 of the layout.**

2. **Highlight the word "Printing" in the first line of the page and click the Create New Index Entry button at the bottom of the Index panel.**

3. **In the New Page Reference dialog box, click the Add All button.**

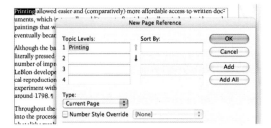

4. **Click OK to close the New Page Reference dialog box.**

5. **In the Index panel, expand the "Printing" topic in the "P" list.**

When creating an index, topics are case-sensitive. "Printing" is not the same as "printing". The word "Printing" is capitalized only once in the layout, so the Add All function added only one reference to the topic "Printing".

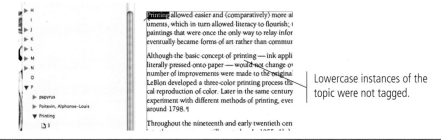

Lowercase instances of the topic were not tagged.

6. **Highlight the word "printing" in the first line of the second paragraph and click the Create New Index Entry button.**

7. **In the New Page Reference dialog box, click the Add All button and then click OK.**

8. **Review the new topic and references in the Index panel.**

   Your index now includes two references to the same term, one capitalized and one lowercase. This is not good practice, so you need to combine the two terms.

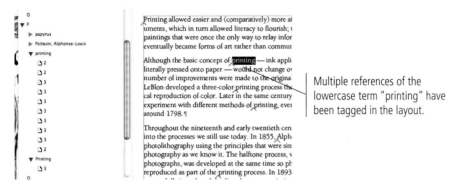

Multiple references of the lowercase term "printing" have been tagged in the layout.

9. **In the Index panel, double-click the "Printing" topic.**

   Double-clicking a term in the panel opens the Topic Options dialog box.

10. **In the pane at the bottom of the dialog box, expand the "P" list.**

    This pane shows all of the topics currently used in the document or book. In this case, you are working with an InDesign book; topics defined in the other book files (such as "Perspective") are also included in the topic list.

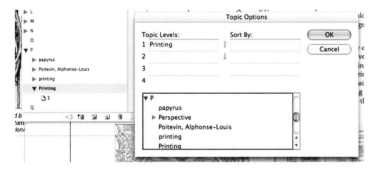

11. **Double-click the topic "printing" in the topic list.**

    Double-clicking an existing topic changes the text in the Topic Levels field.

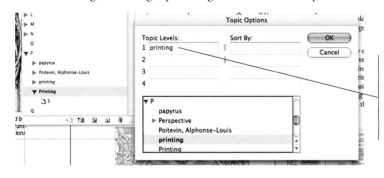

After double-clicking the lowercase "printing" in the topic list, the topic you are editing (the capitalized version) changes to reflect the topic you selected from the list.

Note:

This method of choosing an existing topic also works in the New Page Reference dialog box. When you double-click a topic in the list at the bottom of the dialog box, text in the Topic Levels field changes to reflect the topic you double-click. The index marker will be placed at the location of the highlighted text, but the reference will be added for whatever was shown in the Topic Levels field.

12. Click OK to close the dialog box, and then review the "P" list in the Index panel.

Your index now includes only a single reference to the term "printing." The page reference for the previously capitalized term has been merged into the references for the lowercase term.

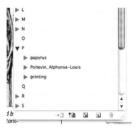

13. Save the file and continue to the next exercise.

 ADD PAGE RANGE REFERENCES

Index references are not limited to single page numbers. You can use the Type menu in the New Page Reference dialog box to define a number of reference types.

- **Current Page** gives a single-page reference for the index entry.

- **To Next Style Change** creates a page-range reference that starts at the location of the insertion point and ends at the first point where a different paragraph style has been applied in the text.

- **To Next Use of Style** creates a page-range reference that starts at the location of the insertion point and ends at the first instance in the story where a specific paragraph style has been applied in the text. When you choose this option, you can select the style that will end the range.

- **To End of Story** creates a page-range reference that starts at the location of the insertion point and ends at the last page of the current story.

- **To End of Document** creates a page-range reference that starts at the location of the insertion point and ends at the last page of the current document.

- **To End of Section** creates a page-range reference that starts at the location of the insertion point and ends at the last page of the current section.

- **For Next # of Paragraphs** creates a page-range reference that starts at the location of the insertion point and ends after the defined number of paragraphs. When you choose this option, you can define the specific number of paragraphs to include in the reference.

- **For Next # of Pages** creates a page-range reference that starts at the location of the insertion point and ends after the defined number of pages. When you choose this option, you can define the specific number of pages to include in the reference.

- **Suppress Page Range** creates a topic reference with no associated page number.

1. With the Color1 file open through the Excerpts Book panel, navigate to Page 1 of the layout.

2. Highlight the word "History" in the chapter title and click the Create New Index Entry button in the Index panel.

3. In the New Page Reference dialog box, change the capital "H" in the first Topic Levels field to lowercase.

4. Choose To End of Document in the Type menu and click the Add button.

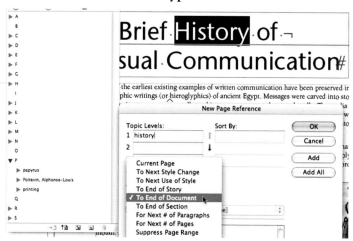

5. Click OK to close the dialog box, and then review the new topic and reference in the Index panel.

The page range reference has been added to the index. The document ends on Page 8, so the reference extends from 1–8.

6. Highlight the word "Illumination" in the heading on Page 1 and click the Create New Index Entry button.

7. In the Type menu, choose To Next Use of Style. In the related Style menu, choose head 1.

   This heading is formatted with the head 1 style. You are adding a reference that spans all text between this heading and the next "head 1" heading.

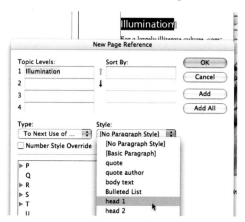

8. **Click Add, and then click OK to close the dialog box.**

9. **Review the new topic and reference in the Index panel.**

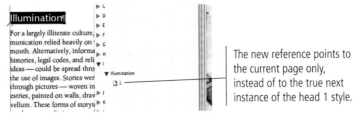

The new reference points to the current page only, instead of to the true next instance of the head 1 style.

This highlights an apparent bug in the software, or at least something that does not work intuitively. When you highlight text formatted with the same style you define in the To Next Use of Style menu, InDesign identifies the highlighted text as the next use of the style — the reference points to the location of the highlighted text only.

Solving this problem requires a workaround technique.

10. **In the Index panel, click the "1" reference to the "Illumination" topic and click the panel's Delete button.**

11. **In the resulting message, click Yes to confirm the deletion.**

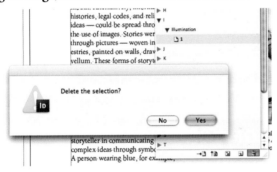

12. **In the document, highlight the word "For" at the beginning of the paragraph after the Illumination heading.**

13. **Click the Create New Index Entry button in the Index panel.**

14. **In the lower half of the dialog box, expand the "I" list of topics and double-click the word "Illumination" in the list of topics.**

As you discovered by using the Topic Options dialog box, this method changes the current text in the Topic Levels field to the topic you double-click in the list.

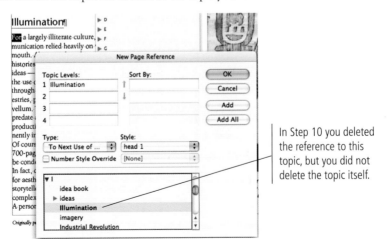

In Step 10 you deleted the reference to this topic, but you did not delete the topic itself.

Note:

If you use this workaround technique, you can simply type to replace the text in the Topic Levels field with the topic you want to reference. You can — but don't have to — select from the existing topics for this technique to work.

15. **In the Type menu, choose To Next Use of Style. In the related Style menu, choose head 1.**

16. **Click Add, and then click OK to close the dialog box.**

17. **Review the new reference in the Index panel.**

    The new reference shows the correct range between the selected text and the next instance of the head 1 paragraph style (on Page 2 of the document).

Note:

You can delete an entire topic from the index by selecting it in the panel and clicking the Delete button. If you delete a term from the index, all references to that term will also be deleted.

18. **Save the file and continue to the next exercise.**

Adding Cross-References

INDESIGN FOUNDATIONS

A cross-referenced item refers the reader to another index entry. For example, the index entry for "CIELAB" might say, "See LAB color." If you choose to create an entry as a cross-reference, you need to also define the type of notation. The Referenced field defines the topic to which a cross-reference will point; you can type in the field or drag an existing topic into the field from the list at the bottom of the dialog box.

- **See [also]** allows InDesign to choose the appropriate cross-reference method — "See" if the topic has no page references of its own, or "See also" if the topic includes page numbers.

- **See** refers the reader to another topic or topics; the entry has no page number, only text listing the cross-referenced topic. For example, if the index entry is "Dogs", the cross-reference might be "See Canine".

- **See also** directs attention to the current topic as well as other information elsewhere in the index. For example, an index item called "Dogs" may have its own list of page numbers, and then a cross-reference to "See also Pets".

- **See herein** and **See also herein** refer the reader to entries within the current index entry. For example, if the main (Level 1) index entry is "Dogs", you might want to direct the index to a subentry (Level 2 or Level 3 item) that might not be expected under this heading, such as "See herein Wolf."

- **[Custom Cross-Reference]** allows you to define the text that will be used as the cross-reference, such as "Go to" or some similar text.

ADD MULTIPLE-LEVEL REFERENCES

You might have noticed that the New Page Reference dialog box includes four fields in the Topic Levels area. These fields allow you to created multi-level or **nested index entries**. You can create up to four levels of nested index entries, depending on the complexity that a particular project requires.

1. **With the Color1 file open through the Excerpts Book panel, navigate to Page 4 of the layout.**

2. Highlight the words "daguerreotype method" in the second line of the first paragraph and click the Create New Index Entry button in the Index panel.

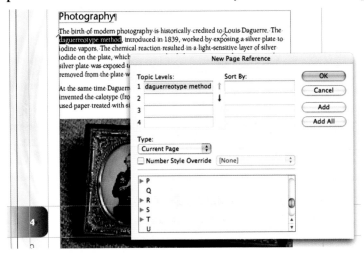

3. In the New Page Reference dialog box, click the down-arrow button in the Topic Levels area.

This button moves the selected term down one level to become a second-level index term. Of course, when you add a second-level term, you also need to define the parent term for that nested entry.

4. Click the first Topic Levels field and type "photographs".

You can select an existing topic as the first level or type a new term in the field.

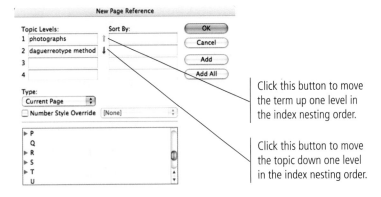

Click this button to move the term up one level in the index nesting order.

Click this button to move the topic down one level in the index nesting order.

5. Click OK to add the term and reference to the index.

6. In the Index panel, expand the "photographs" entry in the "P" list.

7. Within the "photographs" entry, expand the "daguerreotype method" entry.

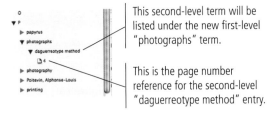

This second-level term will be listed under the new first-level "photographs" term.

This is the page number reference for the second-level "daguerreotype method" entry.

8. Save the Color1 file and close it.

9. Save the book file and continue to the next exercise.

Building an index into a document is very similar to building a table of contents. Once the index has been generated, it is loaded into the cursor so you can place it in the layout. When you are working with a book file, you can build the index into an existing chapter file, or you can add a separate back matter file to hold the index.

1. Open the file Companion.indt from the WIP>Companions folder.

2. Drag the D-Index Opener master page onto the Page 1 icon.

3. Save the file as "Excerpts Back.indd" in your WIP>Companions folder and close the file.

4. In the Excerpts Book panel, click the Add Document button. Navigate to the file Excerpts Back.indd file in your WIP>Companions folder.

5. Open the Synchronize Options dialog box from the Book panel options menu.

6. Deselect everything but the Swatches check box and click OK.

7. Make sure no files are selected in the Book panel and click the Synchronize button at the bottom of the panel.

8. Double-click the Excerpts Back file in the Book panel to open the file.

9. At the bottom of the Index panel, click the Generate Index button.

10. Delete the word Index from the Title field.

    In the Generate Index dialog box, the Title and Title Style options are the same as the related options for building a table of contents. Because the master page you're using already includes the title, you should not include a title in the built index.

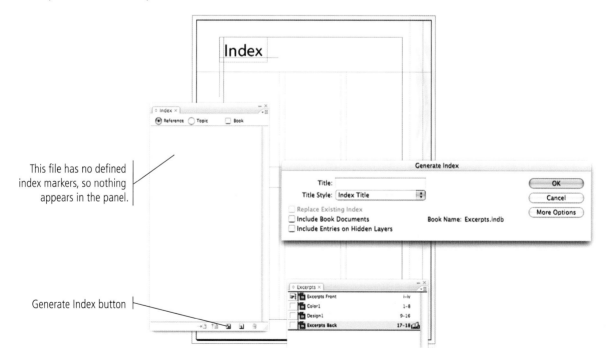

This file has no defined index markers, so nothing appears in the panel.

Generate Index button

11. **Select the Include Book Documents option.**

    Even though there are no index references in this back-matter file, it is part of the book with files that have index markers.

12. **Click the More Options button in the Generate Index dialog box.**

13. **Review the available options. Click the Following Topic menu and choose Em Space as the character that will appear between the entry text and the associated references.**

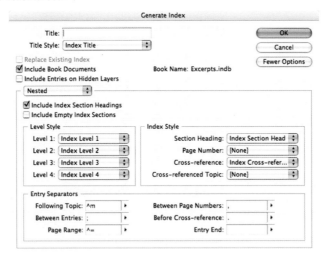

14. **Click OK to generate the index. Click the loaded cursor in the three-column text frame to place the index.**

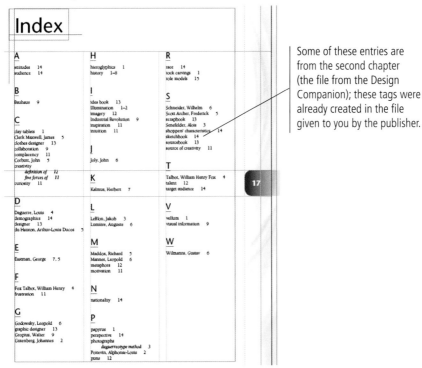

Some of these entries are from the second chapter (the file from the Design Companion); these tags were already created in the file given to you by the publisher.

14. **Save the file and close it.**

15. **Save the book file and continue to the next stage of the project.**

Options for Generating an Index

When you generate an index, you have a number of options for automatically formatting the compiled list. In many cases, the default settings will work, but you can change any or all of the following options:

- The **Nested** or **Run-in** menu (defaulting to Nested) determines how individual entries in the index will be placed. The Nested option creates each entry on its own line. The Run-In option forces all index entries to run together in the same paragraph; entries are separated by the Between Entries character.

- If the **Include Index Section Headings** option is checked, alphabetical headings (A, B, C, and so on) will be added in the compiled index.

- If the **Include Empty Index Sections** option is checked, all letter headings will be added to the built index, even if that letter has no associated terms.

- The **Level Style** menus define the paragraph styles that will be used to format the different levels of index headings. If you don't choose different styles in these menus, the default options (Index Level 1, etc.) will be created in the file and applied to the headings. (If you define your own style named "Index Level 1," your settings will be applied in the built index.)

- The **Section Headings** menu defines the paragraph styles that will be used to format the letter headings in the final index. If you don't choose a different style, the default Index Section Head will be created in the file and applied to the headings. (If you define your own style named "Index Section Head," your settings will be applied in the built index.)

- The **Page Number** menu defines the character style that will be applied to page numbers in the generated index.

- The **Cross-Reference** menu defines the character style that will be applied to the cross-references in the generated index (for example, the "See also" part of "*See also* LAB color").

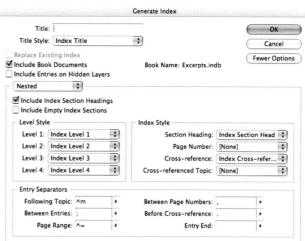

- The **Cross-Reference Topic** menu defines the character style that will be applied to the text reference of a cross-reference (for example, the "Lab color" part of "See also *Lab color*").

- The **Entry Separators** area defines the characters that will be used in specific parts of the index.

  - **Following Topic** is the character(s) between the entry text and the entry page references.

  - **Between Page Numbers** is the character(s) between individual page references.

  - **Between Entries** is the character(s) between entries in a run-in index.

  - **Before Cross-reference** is the character(s) before a cross-reference (for example, the period and space in "CIELAB. See also Lab color").

  - **Page Range** is the character(s) that separate the first and last numbers in a page range.

  - **Entry End** is the character(s) that will be added at the end of individual entries.

Stage 4 Exporting Book Files

Another advantage of combining multiple files is the ability to output those files all at once — choosing print or export settings once instead of opening each file and changing the print or export settings individually. Using the Book panel, you can output all chapter files at once, or output specific selected chapters.

 EXPORT PDF FILES FOR PRINT AND DIGITAL DISTRIBUTION

Your client asked for two separate files — one that can be printed at high quality and one that can be posted on the company's Web site and sent via email. Because the four files are combined in a single book, you can easily create these two files in a few steps.

1. **With the Excerpts Book panel open, click the empty area at the bottom of the panel to deselect all files in the book.**

2. **Choose Export Book to PDF in the panel options menu.**

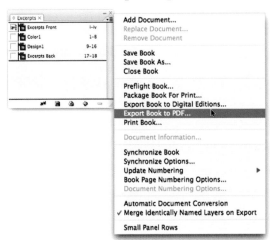

Note:

If any files are selected, the menu option changes to Export Selected Documents to PDF.

3. **Navigate to your WIP>Companions folder as the target and change the file name to "Excerpts Print.pdf".**

4. **Click Save.**

5. In the Export Adobe PDF dialog box, choose [High Quality Print] in the Adobe PDF Preset menu.

6. In the Marks and Bleeds options, check the Crop Marks option. Change the Offset field to 0.125″, and change all four Bleed fields to 0.125″.

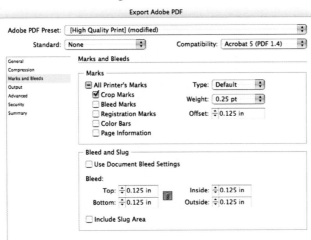

7. Click Export.

8. In the Book panel options menu, choose Export Book to PDF again.

9. Name the second file "Excerpts Digital.pdf" and click Save.

10. Choose [Smallest File Size] in the Adobe PDF Preset menu.

11. In the Compression options, change both Image Quality menus to Medium.

12. Click Export.

Using the Book utility, you now have two complete PDF files for different purposes — created in only a few easy steps.

13. Save the book file and close it.

Stage 5 Merging Data into an InDesign Layout

For the final stage of this project, you need to create a thank-you note from the publisher to previous clients. This note will be included with the printed copies of the Excerpts booklet when the sample is mailed to the clients. Your client provided a Microsoft Excel file with the client mailing addresses, as well as which book each client purchased.

Data merge is a fairly sophisticated utility in most word-processing applications; it allows you to combine text with information stored in a database (such as a Microsoft Excel file). For example, data merge allows you to write one letter, click a few buttons, and print 147 copies of the letter, each with a different mailing address. InDesign's Data Merge capabilities can be used for this type of personal letter generation, but — with a bit of advanced planning — it can also be used for more sophisticated database-driven layouts such as catalogs with graphics.

Personalized printing uses data to produce items such as catalogs that are specifically aimed at your interests. Other applications for personalized printing include newspaper inserts for a specific region. A national company might create a single weekly sale advertisement with one page that varies according to the local distribution; why, for example, would a company want to advertise snow blowers in southern California?

InDesign's Data Merge feature makes it fairly simple to create a layout incorporating variable data. Once the data source file has been established, you can create any layout you want, add the data, and create multiple versions of a finished layout in one action.

Note:

Variable database printing is currently one of the hottest topics in the graphic design and printing industries. Marketing specialists have spent millions to determine that you will open a piece of mail with your name on it far more often than one addressed to "Resident."

The Data Source File

If you have a contact manager anywhere on your computer, you are familiar with the idea of a simple database. A database is made up of **fields** that contain information. Each field has a **field name**, which is usually descriptive text that defines the contents of the field. Each listing in a database is called a **record**; each record contains every field in the database (even if a particular field contains no information for a given record).

In the following example, Name, Address, and Telephone Number are all fields. The first line of the file contains the field names "Name," "Address," and "Telephone Number". Each record appears on a separate line.

Name	Address	Telephone Number
James Smith	123 Anywhere St., Someplace, MI 99999	800-555-0000
Susan Jones	3208 Street Ct., Small Town, ID 55555	800-555-8888

InDesign's Data Merge feature does not interact directly with a database application. Data must first be exported from a database into a tab- or comma-delimited ASCII text file.

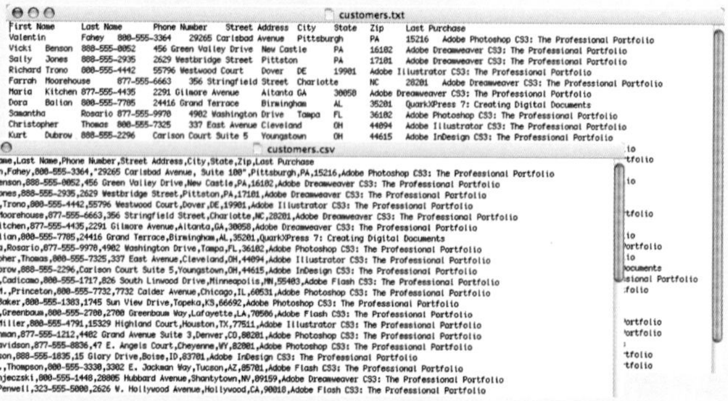

In the text file, the information in each field (called a **text string**) is separated by the delimiter (comma or tab), which tells the software that the next text string belongs in the next field. Records are separated by paragraph returns, so each record begins on a new line.

If a particular text string requires one of the delimiter characters — for example, a comma within an address — that string is surrounded by double quotation marks in the text file.

A comma contained within quotation marks is treated as a text character, not as a delimiter.

The first line of the text file should list the field names. If your database application does not export field names as the first line of the text-only file, you will need to open the file in a text editor and add the field name line at the beginning.

CREATE THE MERGE DOCUMENT AND LOAD THE SOURCE DATA

The target document for a data merge needs to include **placeholders**, or locations where the data will appear after the data merge is complete. Once you have established the data source for the InDesign file, you can easily create these placeholders anywhere in the document.

1. **Open the file letter.indd from the RF_InDesign>Companions folder.**

   Your client wrote this letter using her InDesign letterhead template. She used all capital letters to indicate where she wants the database information to be added in the letter text.

2. **Choose Window>Automation>Data Merge to open the Data Merge panel.**

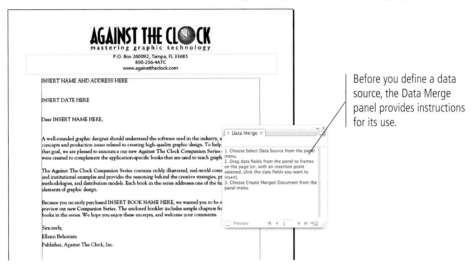

Before you define a data source, the Data Merge panel provides instructions for its use.

3. **Open the Data Merge panel options menu and choose Select Data Source.**

4. **Navigate to the file customers.txt in the RF_InDesign>Companions folder and click Open.**

When the file is processed, the available fields (defined by the first line in the data file) are listed in the Data Merge panel.

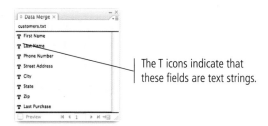

The T icons indicate that these fields are text strings.

5. **In the document, turn on hidden characters (Type>Show Hidden Characters).**

6. **Highlight the first line in the letter (excluding the paragraph return character), and then double-click the First Name item in the Data Merge panel.**

 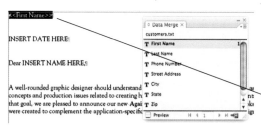

Double-clicking an item in the Data Merge panel replaces the highlighted text with a placeholder for that data field.

Cleaning Up Data

Placeholders are formatted as the field name enclosed in double brackets, such as <<Name>>, inserted anywhere in the target document.

> <<Name>>
>
> <<Address>>
>
> Dear <<Name>>,
>
> Congratulations! We are writing to inform you that your house at <<Address>> has been selected...

Once data from the source file has been merged into the document, it looks like this:

> James Smith
>
> 123 Anywhere St., Someplace, MI 99999
>
> Dear James Smith,
>
> Congratulations! We are writing to inform you that your house at 123 Anywhere St., Someplace, MI 99999 has been selected...

The same document is reproduced for every record in the text file, personalizing each copy of the letter for the intended recipient.

Notice that the address is entirely on one line of text, and that the "Dear" line includes the person's whole name — not a tremendous improvement over "Dear Occupant."

You should make sure your data includes the exact information you need. The previous example would benefit greatly from a different arrangement.

> First_Name,Last_Name,Street_Address,City,State,Zip
>
> James,Smith,"123 Anywhere St.",Someplace,MI,99999
>
> Susan,Jones,"3208 Street Ct.",Small Town,ID,55555

The target file can then appear much more personal. Placeholders can be positioned with text characters (including spaces) in between to make the document more like an actual letter:

> <<First_Name>> <<Last_Name>>
>
> <<Street Address>>
>
> <<City>, <<State>> <<Zip>>
>
> Dear <<First_Name>>,
>
> Congratulations! We are writing to inform you that your house at <<Street_Address>> has been selected for a free facelift!

Once data from the source file has been merged into this version, it looks like this:

> James Smith
> 123 Anywhere St.
> Someplace, MI 99999
>
> Dear James,
>
> Congratulations! We are writing to inform you that your house at 123 Anywhere St. has been selected...

7. Press the Right Arrow key to place the insertion point after the placeholder.

8. Press the Spacebar, and then double-click the Last Name item in the Data Merge panel.

Note:

Like a text variable, a placeholder is treated as a single character in the layout.

9. Press Return/Enter to start a new paragraph in the document, and then double-click the Street Address item in the Data Merge panel.

10. Press Return/Enter again. Add the City, State, and Zip fields on the third line, separated by the appropriate punctuation and spaces.

11. Highlight the All Caps text in the salutation line, and then replace it with the First Name data field placeholder.

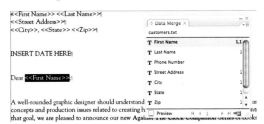

Note:

If your database file includes a salutation field, you could address the letter as "Dear <<salutation>> <<last name>>", which would result in Dear Mr. Smith instead of the less-formal Dear Jim.

12. In the third paragraph of the letter, replace the All Caps text with the Last Purchase data field placeholder.

13. With the <<Last Purchase>> placeholder selected, change the font to ATC Pine Italic.

After placeholders have been entered in the document, you can apply text and paragraph formatting as you would for any other text element.

Note:

Highlighting a few letters in any field name (in the document) automatically highlights the entire field name, including the brackets.

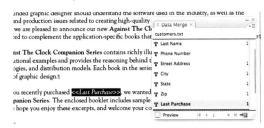

Note:

If you were going to re-use this letter, you might consider using a type variable for the date instead of simply typing.

14. Highlight the text "INSERT DATE HERE" and type today's date.

15. Save the file in your WIP>Companions folder and continue to the next exercise.

A data source file is not limited to text; you can also incorporate images in the data source file to create variable images in a layout. If you want to incorporate graphics or images in your data merge, your data source file must include a field that contains the full path to the image, beginning with the drive name where the image resides (called an **absolute path**). In the field names, the name of the image field should start with the "@" symbol (for example, "@image").

The absolute path for an image tells the Data Merge processor where to find the necessary file. On a Macintosh, the path name is separated by colons:

Hard Drive:Pictures:image.tif   Mac:Catalog Files:Pictures:sweater.tif

On a Windows computer, the path name begins with the drive letter:

C:\My Documents\Pictures\image.tif   D:\Vector files\graph.eps

The only spaces in the path name are those that exist in the name of a file or folder; no spaces should separate any of the backslash or colon characters.

Creating and Controlling Image Placeholders

When a data source includes an image field, the Data Merge panel shows a small picture icon for that field. You can attach an image placeholder to any graphics frame by selecting the frame in the layout and double-clicking the image item in the Data Merge panel.

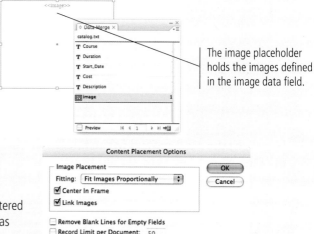

The image placeholder holds the images defined in the image data field.

When you use images from a data source file, you can choose Content Placement Options in the Data Merge panel options menu to predetermine the appearance of the image in relation to the placeholder frame.

- The **Fitting** menu includes the same options that are available for fitting placed images in a graphics frame.

- If **Center in Frame** is checked, the image will be centered within the placeholder frame after the Fitting option has been applied.

- The **Link Images** check box, active by default, links the data source images to the layout that's created when you generate the merge document. If this option is not checked, the images will be embedded in the resulting file. (Embedding images drastically increases file size; as a general rule, you should leave the Link Images box checked.)

You can preview variable images just as you preview text. If an image path is incorrect or a file is not in the path defined in the data, you will see a warning when you try to preview that record.

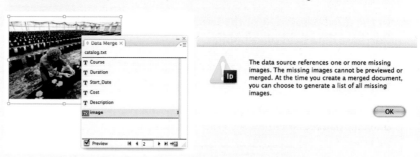

The data source references one or more missing images. The missing images cannot be previewed or merged. At the time you create a merged document, you can choose to generate a list of all missing images.

CREATE THE MERGED DOCUMENT

Once you have created your target document and formatted all of the elements, you can preview the data, and then create the merged document. InDesign uses the data source file and the target layout to create a third document — the merged file. This third file is not linked to the data source; any changes you make to the data are not applied to the merged document. If you change the data file, you have to repeat the merge of the original layout file with the changed data.

1. **With letter.indd open from your WIP>Companions folder, activate the Preview check box at the bottom of the Data Merge panel.**

   You can preview your document at any time by activating the Preview check box in the Data Merge panel. The arrows to the left and right of the record number allow you to move through each record in the merged document.

When Preview is turned on, the actual data from the source file replaces the placeholder elements.

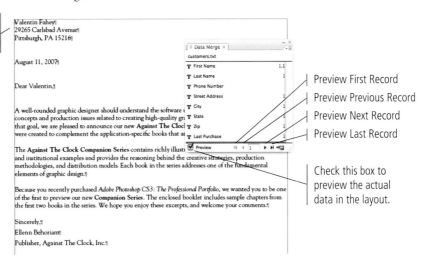

Preview First Record
Preview Previous Record
Preview Next Record
Preview Last Record

Check this box to preview the actual data in the layout.

Working with Long Text Fields

A text placeholder can be inserted anywhere in a document — on a separate paragraph line in a text block or within a text frame. Keep in mind, however, that if you attach a placeholder to a text frame, the frame must be large enough to hold the longest piece of data that exists for that field. Frames will not automatically enlarge or shrink to match the content.

When you preview the records, you can see how the formatting will apply once the data merge is complete. Even if the text for one record fits into a defined frame, not all records will necessarily fit. Make sure a text frame is large enough to fit the longest possible record field.

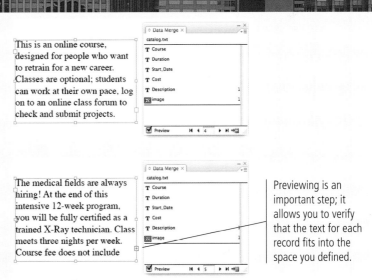

Previewing is an important step; it allows you to verify that the text for each record fits into the space you defined.

2. Choose Create Merged Document in the Data Merge panel options menu.

In the Create Merged Records dialog box, you can define specific options for your merged document. The Records tab determines which records (all, one specific record, or a specific range) will be included in the merged document.

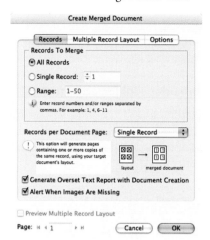

Note:

The Records per Document Page option allows you to place multiple records on a single page in the merged document. This option can be useful for creating catalog listings, multiple labels, or other projects with more than one database record on a single page.

3. Click OK to create the merged document.

Merging Multiple Records on a Single Page

INDESIGN FOUNDATIONS

You can merge more than one record onto a single page by selecting Multiple Records in the Records per Document Page menu. When this option is selected, the Multiple Record Layout tab determines how records will be placed and separated in the merged document.

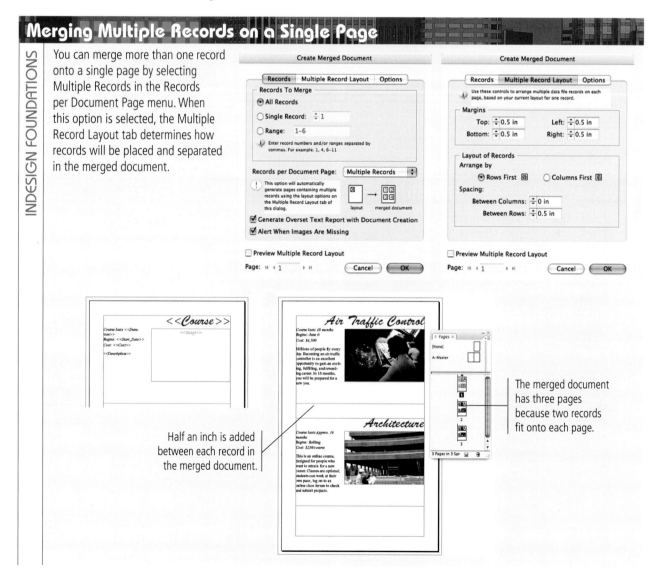

Half an inch is added between each record in the merged document.

The merged document has three pages because two records fit onto each page.

4. **When you see the message that the data did not result in overset text, click OK.**

The merged document appears on top of the original layout. Because there were 50 records in the data source, the new document has 50 pages (one page for each record).

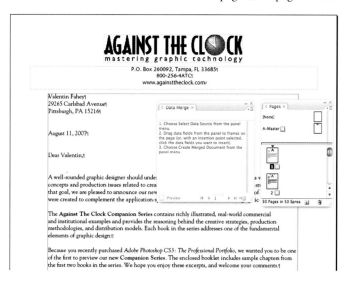

Note:

The two check boxes at the bottom of the Create Merged Document dialog box provide feedback after you create the data merge. Checked by default, these important options allow you to make sure all of your data is available and fits into the spaces you defined.

5. **Export the merged document to PDF (named "Sample Letters.pdf") using the High Quality PDF preset.**

6. **Save the merged document as "Letters Merged.indd" in your WIP>Companions folder.**

7. **Close all open files.**

Managing Empty Data Fields

INDESIGN FOUNDATIONS

When you merge data, you should be aware that one or more fields for a specific record might be empty. For example, a specific record might not include a company name. If your target document includes a company name placeholder, the merged document might end up with an empty line where that placeholder appears.

In the example shown below, the record for James Smith doesn't include a company name. In the merged document, the line is blank.

In the Options tab of the Create Merged Document dialog box, the Remove Blank Lines for Empty Fields option solves this potential problem. (The same option is available in the Content Placement Options dialog box, which you can access in the Data Merge panel options menu.) In the merged document, placeholders are ignored for fields that have no content.

Create Merged Document
Records   Multiple Record Layout   **Options**
Image Placement
Fitting: [Fit Images Proportionally]
☑ Center In Frame
☐ Link Images
☑ Remove Blank Lines for Empty Fields
☐ Page Limit per Document: 50

☐ Preview Multiple Record Layout

Page: ◄ ◄ 1 ► ►   (Cancel) (OK)

Placeholders in original document	Merged document with blank lines	Merged document without blank lines
<<First Name>> <<Last Name>> <<Company Name>> <<Street Address>> <<City>>, <<State>> <<Zip>> <<Phone Number>> Dear <<First Name>>, We are pleased to inform you that your company has been selected as one of the 25 best employers in the	Sally Jones 2629 Westbridge Street Pittston, PA 17101 Dear Sally, We are pleased to inform you that your company has been selected as one of the 25 best employers in the	Sally Jones 2629 Westbridge Street Pittston, PA 17101 Dear Sally, We are pleased to inform you that your company has been selected as one of the 25 best employers in the Eastern Pennsylvania Regional Chamber of Com- merce annual review. In recognition of your accom-

Summary

As you have seen in this project, InDesign includes tools that help with special formatting and document considerations, combining multiple files into a book, building tables of contents and indexes, and even merging variable data into a page layout.

You should now understand the importance of consistency in long-document design. By completing this project, you learned how to combine multiple chapter files into a single book, as well as how to synchronize those files so related elements remain consistent from page to page and chapter to chapter. This book-building functionality works equally well for combining single-page documents or lengthy chapters with many pages.

You also learned how to automate (as much as possible) the creation of tables of contents and indexes — two processes that used to require days of manual checking and rechecking if even a single page in the layout changed. You should understand the interaction between styles and tables of contents; effectively implementing styles throughout a long document makes it relatively easy to compile a thorough table of contents that includes every heading from Page 1 to the final page in the document.

As you have seen, there is no way for the software to identify which terms are important in a document; the process of tagging index entries is still manual. However, the ability to store index markers in a document means that compiling and recompiling the final index is far simpler than building and compiling the list by hand.

These skills are relatively rare in the graphics marketplace. Your ability to master them makes you much more marketable as a professional graphic designer.

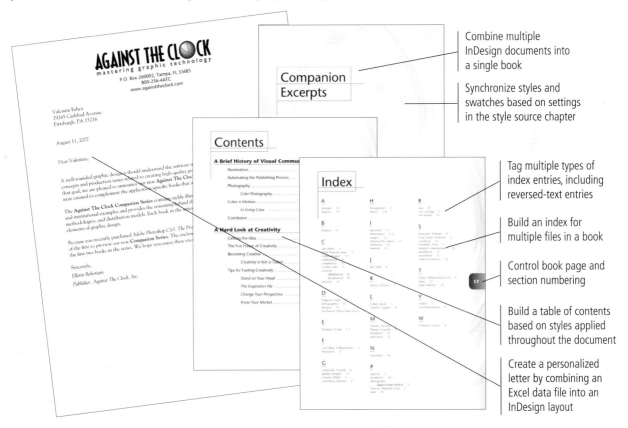

- Combine multiple InDesign documents into a single book
- Synchronize styles and swatches based on settings in the style source chapter
- Tag multiple types of index entries, including reversed-text entries
- Build an index for multiple files in a book
- Control book page and section numbering
- Build a table of contents based on styles applied throughout the document
- Create a personalized letter by combining an Excel data file into an InDesign layout

Portfolio Builder Project 8

Every professional designer needs a portfolio of their work. If you've completed the projects in this book, you should now have a number of different examples to show off your skills using InDesign CS3.

The eight projects in this book were specifically designed to include a broad range of *types* of projects; your portfolio should use the same principle.

Using the following suggestions, gather your best work and create printed and digital versions of your portfolio:

❏ Include as many different types of work as possible — one-page layouts, folding brochures, multi-page booklets, etc.

❏ Print clean copies of each finished piece that you want to include.

❏ For each example in your portfolio, write a brief (one or two paragraph) synopsis of the project. Explain the purpose of the piece, as well as your role in the creative and production process.

❏ Design a personal promotion brochure — create a layout that highlights your technical skills and reflects your personal style.

❏ Create a PDF version of your portfolio so you can send your portfolio via email, post it on job sites, and keep with you on a CD at all times — you never know when you might meet a potential employer.

Index

Index